Vocational Education in the Nordic Countries

Vocational Education in the Nordic Countries: The Historical Evolution is the first of two books that disseminate new and systematic knowledge on the strengths and weaknesses of the different models of vocational education and training (VET) in four Nordic countries. Vocational education in Europe has resisted standardisation to a higher degree than other fields of education, and during the last decade, there has been a growth in international, comparative VET research. While the Nordic countries provide an ideal case for comparative education studies, the literature in English on the Nordic VET systems is at present very limited.

This first book provides thorough examinations of VET in Sweden, Denmark, Norway and Finland over 150 years. Each section examines the historical evolution of VET at the upper secondary level in one of the four Nordic countries. Contributors also analyse how each country has tried to reform their respective VET systems, and compare the paths which each nation has taken. The book explores what can be learned from the diversity of the VET systems in the Nordic countries, which otherwise have many similarities and share a common heritage in education policy.

This volume will help strengthen the knowledge base required for transnational policy learning, and for developing vocational education internationally for the future. It will be of interest to researchers, academics and postgraduate students involved in the study of vocational education, educational studies and educational policy, education planners and teachers educators.

Svein Michelsen is Professor in Political Science at the Department of Administration and Organization Theory, University of Bergen, Norway.

Marja-Leena Stenström is Professor Emerita in Education and Working Life at the Finnish Institute for Educational Research, University of Jyväskylä, Finland.

Routledge Research in International
and Comparative Education

This is a series that offers a global platform to engage scholars in continuous academic debate on key challenges and the latest thinking on issues in the fast-growing field of International and Comparative Education.

Titles in the series include:

China's Global Rise
Higher Education, Diplomacy and Identity
Suyan Pan

Educational Choices, Aspirations and Transitions in Europe
Systemic, Institutional and Subjective Constraints
Edited by Aina Tarabini and Nicola Ingram

Cooperative Education in Asia
History, Present and Future Issues
Edited by Yasushi Tanaka

Testing and Inclusive Schooling
International Challenges and Opportunities
Edited by Bjørn Hamre, Anne Morin and Christian Ydesen

Vocational Education in the Nordic Countries
The Historical Evolution
Edited by Svein Michelsen and Marja-Leena Stenström

Vocational Education in the Nordic Countries
Learning from Diversity
Edited by Christian Helms Jørgensen, Ole Johnny Olsen and Daniel Persson Thunqvist

Higher Education and China's Global Rise
A Neo-tributary Perspective
Su-Yan Pan and Joe Tin-Yau Lo

For more information about this series, please visit: www.routledge.com/Routledge-Research-in-International-and-Comparative-Education/book-series/RRICE

Vocational Education in the Nordic Countries

The Historical Evolution

Edited by Svein Michelsen and
Marja-Leena Stenström

LONDON AND NEW YORK

First published 2018
by Routledge
2 Park Square, Milton Park, Abingdon, Oxon OX14 4RN

and by Routledge
711 Third Avenue, New York, NY 10017

Routledge is an imprint of the Taylor & Francis Group, an informa business

© 2018 selection and editorial matter, Svein Michelsen and Marja-Leena Stenström; individual chapters, the contributors

The right of the editors to be identified as the authors of the editorial material, and of the authors for their individual chapters, has been asserted in accordance with sections 77 and 78 of the Copyright, Designs and Patents Act 1988.

All rights reserved. No part of this book may be reprinted or reproduced or utilised in any form or by any electronic, mechanical, or other means, now known or hereafter invented, including photocopying and recording, or in any information storage or retrieval system, without permission in writing from the publishers.

Trademark notice: Product or corporate names may be trademarks or registered trademarks, and are used only for identification and explanation without intent to infringe.

British Library Cataloguing-in-Publication Data
A catalogue record for this book is available from the British Library

Library of Congress Cataloging-in-Publication Data
Names: Michelsen, Svein, editor. | Stenstrèom, Marja-Leena, editor.
Title: Vocational education in the Nordic countries : the historical evolution / edited by Svein Michelsen and Marja-Leena Stenstrèom.
Description: Abingdon, Oxon ; New York, NY : Routledge is an imprint of the Taylor & Francis Group, an Informa Business, [2018] | Series: Routledge research in international and comparative education | Includes bibliographical references and index. | Description based on print version record and CIP data provided by publisher; resource not viewed.
Identifiers: LCCN 2018004798 (print) | LCCN 2018016290 (ebook) | ISBN 9781315411811 (E-book) | ISBN 9781138220850 (hbk : alk. paper) | ISBN 9781315411811 (ebk)
Subjects: LCSH: Vocational education—Scandinavia—History.
Classification: LCC LC1047.S35 (ebook) | LCC LC1047.S35 V63 2018 (print) | DDC 370.1130948—dc23
LC record available at https://lccn.loc.gov/2018004798

ISBN: 978-1-138-22085-0 (hbk)
ISBN: 978-1-315-41181-1 (ebk)

Typeset in Bembo
by Apex CoVantage, LLC

Contents

List of figures vii
List of tables viii
List of contributors ix
Preface x
Acknowledgements xii

1 **The historical evolution of vocational education in the Nordic countries** 1
 SVEIN MICHELSEN

2 **The development of Finnish vocational education and training from 1850 to 1945** 24
 MARJA-LEENA STENSTRÖM AND MAARIT VIROLAINEN

3 **Sweden: the formative period for VET (1850–1945)** 46
 JONAS OLOFSSON AND DANIEL PERSSON THUNQVIST

4 **The case of Norwegian VET – origins and early development 1850–1945** 66
 SVEIN MICHELSEN AND HÅKON HØST

5 **Historical evolution of vocational education in Denmark until 1945** 84
 CHRISTIAN HELMS JØRGENSEN AND GUDMUND BØNDERGAARD

6 **The modern evolution of vocational education and training in Finland (1945–2015)** 102
 MARJA-LEENA STENSTRÖM AND MAARIT VIROLAINEN

7 **The modern evolution of VET in Sweden (1945–2015)** 124
JONAS OLOFSSON AND DANIEL PERSSON THUNQVIST

8 **Norwegian VET and the ascent and decline of social democracy 1945–2015** 146
SVEIN MICHELSEN AND HÅKON HØST

9 **The modernisation of the apprenticeship system in Denmark 1945–2015** 171
CHRISTIAN HELMS JØRGENSEN

10 **Conclusions** 191
SVEIN MICHELSEN

Index 235

Figures

6.1	Direct transition to further studies of graduates of the 9th grade of comprehensive school during 2000–2015	113
7.1	Level of highest educational attainment 20–24-year-olds, 1985–2015	135
7.2	Share of upper secondary school pupils in vocational education, 1992–2016	138
8.1	Number of students in gymnasiums and vocational schools 1935, 1955, 1960, 1965	148
8.2	Number of students in different types of vocational schools 1935, 1955, 1960, 1965	151
8.3	Percentage of youth cohorts 15–19 years old in education 1962, 1972, 1982, 1992 and 2002. From 1989 apprentices are included.	154
8.4	Students in higher education in Norway 1957–2008	158
8.5	The number of new apprenticeship contracts 1973–2017	162
9.1	Enrolment in upper secondary education 1948–2014	175

Tables

1.1	The formation of industry/craft/labour market associations and agreements	10
2.1	Occupational distribution of the population in percentages of the workforce 1880–1940	30
2.2	Vocational upper secondary education and secondary school students from 1910 to 1970	34
2.3	Apprenticeship in Finland from the 17th century to the 1920s	39
A2.1	Students in vocational education in the first year of each decade from 1820 to 1940	45
6.1	Vocational secondary education and secondary school entrants from 1940 to 1960	105
A7.1	The percentage attending upper secondary school at age 17–18 in different birth cohorts and related to sex and socio-economic group	144
A7.2	Transition rate to higher education for upper secondary school graduates within three years 1999/2000–2008/2009	144
A7.3	Distribution of upper secondary school students (year 1) by programme (general, vocational and individual programmes)	145
10.1	Nordic VET trajectories in the liberal period (1850–1945)	192
10.2	Nordic VET trajectories in the social democratic period (1945–1990)	194
10.3	Nordic VET trajectories of liberalization (1990–2015)	197
10.4	Structural characteristics of educational systems in four Nordic countries	223

Contributors

Gudmund Bøndergaard, M.A., was a previous researcher at Aarhus University, Denmark, and associated researcher in the Danish part of the Nord-VET project with a main interest in the history of apprenticeships and learning through work.

Håkon Høst is Research Professor, Nordic Institute for Studies in Innovation, Research and Education, Oslo, Norway. His research interests are vocational education and training, educational systems, skill formation systems, and the relations between the educational system and the labour market and the labour market actors.

Christian Helms Jørgensen is Professor MSO at Roskilde University in Denmark and leader of the Nord-VET project. His research covers adult education, comparative vocational education, school-to-work transitions, learning in worklife, gender and education and students' drop-out from schools.

Svein Michelsen is Professor in Political Science at the Department of Administration and Organization Theory, University of Bergen, Norway. His academic interests are focused on the study of institutional change in vocational education and higher education and their interaction.

Jonas Olofsson is a Professor at the Department of Social Work at Malmö University, Sweden. He has done a lot of research connected to the history of vocational education and training in Sweden, with a special focus on apprenticeship training.

Daniel Persson Thunqvist is an Associate Professor in Sociology at Linköping University, Department for Behavioral Science and Learning, Linköping, Sweden. His research interest includes vocational education and training, workplace learning and social interaction.

Marja-Leena Stenström is Professor Emerita in Education and Working Life at the Finnish Institute for Educational Research, University of Jyväskylä, Finland. Her research interests have focused on vocational education and training, the relations between education and working life and educational careers.

Maarit Virolainen, PhD, has been a researcher at the Finnish Institute for Educational Research (FIER), University of Jyväskylä, Finland, since 1996. Her research interests have focused on vocational and professional education, work-based and work-related learning, internships, educational careers, and transitions within education systems and from education to the world of work.

Preface

This book is the first of a two-volume series on initial vocational education and training (VET) in the Nordic countries. The first volume explores the historical development of the national systems of VET in four Nordic countries: Sweden, Finland, Norway and Denmark. The second volume examines the current situation for VET in these countries, comparing how the four VET systems have responded to a number of common challenges.

The Nordic countries often attract international interest due to their ability to combine high levels of social welfare and equality with high economic growth. They are often treated as a coherent group with a shared history and culture, and also due to their similarities regarding the universal welfare states, the consensual and well-organised labour markets and the egalitarian systems of education. The focus of these two books is not on the similarities, however, but on the differences between these countries. While they all transformed the 9/10-year, compulsory education into comprehensive school systems with mixed ability classes, their systems of upper secondary education differ considerably. Their VET systems represent very diverging models, with Sweden and Denmark as the most different systems: a statist and school-based model of comprehensive schooling (Sweden) and a dual system of collective skill formation (Denmark).

These differences make the Nordic countries a fruitful living experiment, where diverging forms of VET can be explored in quite similar societies. These two books investigate why the Nordic VET systems historically developed along diverging lines, and the implications of these differences for the current systems. The first volume includes eight chapters on the historical development of the four VET systems divided into two periods, before and after 1945. In addition, it includes two comparative chapters with a historical perspective. The second book examines the strengths and weaknesses of the four VET systems in relation to four common and interrelated challenges for VET: to simultaneously provide access to the labour market and to higher education, and to combine the inclusion of disadvantaged youth in VET with high esteem of VET among young people and employers. In addition to the comparisons of the four VET systems, the second volume includes comparisons of two multilevel case studies.

The two books are the result of a research project, Nord-VET (www.Nord-VET.dk), comprising researchers from seven research institutions from the four countries. The initial group consisted of Per-Erik Ellström, Linköping University in Sweden, Marja-Leena Stenström, University of Jyväskylä in Finland, Ole Johnny Olsen, University of Bergen in Norway and Christian Helms Jørgensen, Roskilde University in Denmark as project leader. In addition, the project has included the following researchers: from Finland Maarit Virolainen, University of Jyväskylä; from Sweden Daniel Persson Thunqvist and Anders Hallqvist, Linköping University, and Jonas Olofsson, Malmö University; from Denmark Lene Larsen and Gudmund Bøndergaard, Roskilde University; from Norway Svein Michelsen, University of Bergen, Håkon Høst, the Nordic Institute for Studies in Innovation, NIFU, and Anna Hagen Tønder, the Institute for Labour and Social Research, Fafo.

The formation of the research group grew out of previous Nordic collaboration on VET, school-to-work transitions, students' drop-out and learning in working life. This explains why the fifth Nordic country, Iceland, is not included in the project. The group is grateful for the funding obtained from NordForsk for the period 2013–2017 as part of the research programme Education for Tomorrow. Since very little comparative research in the Nordic VET systems had been done previously, the Nord-VET project spent the first two years producing 12 country reports, four for each VET system, based on the examination of common research questions. The reports focussed on (1) the historical evolution of the VET systems, (2) the current situation for these systems, (3) recent reforms and innovations in VET and (4) multilevel case studies in the health sector and the construction sector. These reports have been very valuable for the subsequent comparison across the countries. Our reports and these two books draw extensively on existing national research on VET. This has presented challenges to making systematic comparisons, since the existing research has proved to be very diverse and uneven. In addition, the project covers a very broad field of research and represents the first attempt to compare the Nordic VET systems. Therefore, our research has an explorative character to some degree, and some questions are only given preliminary answers. The broad scope of the project has invited an interdisciplinary approach, which has matched well with the broad disciplinary background of the members of the research group, covering sociology, political science, history, youth studies and education studies. Consequently, the research has been driven more by an empirical and problem-oriented approach, than by a specific conceptual framework.

Inspired by the fruitful collaboration in the group, the ambitions of the project expanded and the project plan was extended, even beyond the initial funding. It is only thanks to the strong engagement of the participants in the project and the support of their research institutions that we have succeeded in completing these two volumes. I want to thank all the participating researchers and their institutions for their great contribution to the project.

Christian Helms Jørgensen
Roskilde, January 2018

Acknowledgements

This book is the result of a research project, Nord-VET, covering Sweden, Finland, Norway and Denmark funded by the NordForsk research programme Education for Tomorrow. NordForsk is an organisation under the Nordic Council of Ministers that provides funding for and facilitates Nordic cooperation on research. We want to thank NordForsk for the financial support and for facilitating fruitful collaboration with other projects in the programme.

We also want to thank the members of the international advisory group to the project, Professor Alison Fuller, University College London, and Dr. Lorenz Lassnigg, Institute for Higher Studies in Vienna, for feedback and support for the project. In addition, we are grateful for productive discussions with European colleagues at international conferences, where we have presented preliminary results of the project.

1 The historical evolution of vocational education in the Nordic countries

Svein Michelsen

Introduction: explorations into the origins of Nordic VET

The Nordic countries represent a challenge to the study of vocational education and training (VET) and VET systems. The Nordic region denotes a geographical denomination consisting of a cluster of countries, which, measured by numerous approaches, are considered as similar. They share a number of commonalities, which makes them meaningful and interesting to study jointly. What they have in common outweighs the differences. The concept of a Nordic model is broad, vague and ambiguous, but in many fields of research, it has often served as a helpful reference for observers of *varieties* among nation states and commonalities among Nordic states. Nordic VET systems are for the most part characterized as strong systems, and attract a considerable part of the youth population (Iversen, 2005). However, in the comparative literature on VET systems, the *differences* are normally emphasized rather than the similarities. For the most part attention has been focused on Sweden and Denmark as archetypal exemplars of different VET systems. In the literature on collective skill formation systems, Denmark has evolved into a role model system with a strong and well-functioning VET system based on apprenticeship and enterprise-based learning (Busemeyer and Trampusch, 2012). Sweden, on the other hand, has often been treated as the primary example of a statist, egalitarian social-democratic school model, where upper secondary VET is embedded in a publicly funded and comprehensively organized school (Dobbins and Busemeyer, 2014). The Norwegian and Finnish VET systems have received less international attention. For the most part they are represented as school-based, statist systems, similar to Sweden, but still somewhat different (Allmendinger, 1989). In conventional typologies of VET, Nordic systems have had no clear place. Measured by such yardsticks, what Nordic VET systems have in common is that they are different, and that the differences are significant and persistent.

However, a closer look also reveals emerging commonalities. Whereas school-based VET was regarded as a superior form of training in the golden period of social democracy, the enterprise has been rehabilitated under neo-liberalism as a place of learning. Also in Nordic school-based systems, apprenticeship has (re-)emerged as a highly relevant template for organizing VET (Nilsson, 2007). Through policy transfer, where policy instruments, mechanisms and structures have been borrowed from well-performing neighbours, the various national VET systems often comprise very different and even contradictory elements. The old distinction between school-based and apprentice-based systems have become increasingly blurred, and conceptions of 'mixed systems' have gained ground in comparative VET research. This also applies as far as characterizations of the Nordic countries are concerned. The Danish apprentice system is often considered as more 'blurred' than the Austrian, German and Swiss dual systems (Graf, 2013), and perhaps a bit similar to the mixed Dutch system (Anderson and Nijhuis, 2012; see also Iversen, 2005, p. 55). This resonates somewhat with newer conceptualizations of the Norwegian VET system, which in spite of its strong school-based character, has developed an apprentice-based system combining training in school and in the firm. Also in Finland, a more practice-oriented system is in the making, involving employers in new ways and in Sweden apprenticeship is being tried out. Furthermore, new forms of articulation with the educational system have been attempted in order to promote the status and esteem of VET tracks as well as the attractiveness of apprenticeship schemes. In this process older boundaries between vocational and general education, between secondary and higher education (HE) have been challenged. Seemingly, the Nordic countries are developing towards a common, extended repertoire of VET reforms in order to create better conditions for social inclusion and labour market access, more diversity in educational choices, attempting new gateways to higher education as well as securing and safeguarding transitions into working life during the life cycle.

Rather than emphasizing structural differences in the organization of VET, its size should also be accounted for and analyzed. It has been maintained that the Nordic countries represent a distinct approach to education, training and skill formation (Pontusson, 2005). They devote more of their resources to education than the continental countries like Germany and Austria or liberal countries like the USA. Vocational education has accounted for a smaller share of upper secondary education in the Nordic social market economies than in the continental countries. They place more emphasis on general education and public funding, and rely more on schools rather than firms to provide vocational training. (Denmark is seen as a hybrid case). In contrast to the liberal countries, there are higher standards at the lower end of the skill hierarchy. High public spending on education (general, vocational as well as higher education) and a low private share have been related to the strong egalitarian tradition in the Nordic countries, as well as the persistent high economic performance of the Nordic countries. In the 1990s they were singled out among the world's most competitive nations, measured by World Economic Forum rankings. In February 2013 the Nordic model was lauded by *The Economist* as the next 'supermodel'.

Nordic skill formation has been associated with a new type of policies, the idea of the enabling state and the social investment agenda (Gingrich and Ansell, 2015; Morel, Palier and Palme, 2015). High levels of investment in education are still significant, but there is a growing interest in the supply side, in flexibilization and in firm-based forms of skill formation. According to Morel,

Palier and Palme (2015) the key to success seems to be the fact that the Nordic countries have not pursued a simple re-orientation strategy with their welfare systems towards more activation, but have instead combined strong protection with heavy social investment in skill formation.

Education has traditionally not been regarded as part of welfare (Wilensky, 1975). But relations between welfare and capitalism have emerged as a fruitful research agenda. Of particular relevance to the investigation of Nordic VET is the comparative work of Gøsta Esping-Andersen (1991). His 'three worlds of welfare capitalism' approach emphasize the similarities of the Nordic countries and the significance of universalist welfare insurance or 'decommodification', that is 'the degree to which they permit people to make their living standards independent on pure market forces. It is in this sense that social rights diminish citizen's status as commodities' (Esping-Andersen, 1991, p. 23). This perspective also provides an interesting link to the formation of the social democratic comprehensive school. Such arrangements were believed to be conducive to greater social equality, and similar ideas were harboured by the social democratic parties in all four countries in the post-war period, where the school system were regarded as a strategic part of a future encompassing welfare state. A stream of authors argue that a specific Nordic or social democratic model has evolved with equity, participation and welfare as the major goals and the publicly funded comprehensive school system as the major institutional form (Lundahl, 2016; Wiborg, 2009; Arnesen and Lundahl, 2006; Antikainen, 2006, Telhaug, Mediås and Aasen, 2006). The establishment and growth of the comprehensive or unitary school principle in the Scandinavian and Nordic countries has been described as a progressive development, as part of the process towards a more equal society, and as an important precondition for the development towards the greater equality for all children, irrespective of social background. Through these processes the old diversity of post-obligatory parallel school types were first broken down and eliminated, and a lower, comprehensive secondary educational level constructed. The prospects of organizational integration and amalgamation between general education and vocational education and training became a central concern in the Nordic countries during the 1970s. We maintain that this feature is crucial for understanding the specific development of Nordic VET. All the four Nordic countries developed comprehensive lower secondary schools, but they diverged as far as the issue of upper secondary comprehensive school was concerned.

Welfare arrangements structure social relations, which in turn have important implications for the structuring of power in society as well as relations between employers and employees (Kangas and Palme, 1998). But Nordic VET researchers have so far not showed much interest in the dynamics of the welfare state as important drivers for the re-formation of VET and their implications. The main focus for Nordic VET research has been on traditional areas like industry and crafts, while welfare state research has focused processes of decommodification. The linkages between VET and the welfare state and how they have been formed historically in the Nordic countries are so far a quarry that remains to be mined systematically. There is also a divide between the historical literature on VET and the literature on the formation of the comprehensive school (Wiborg, 2009; Schriewer et al., 2000; Leschinsky and Mayer, 1999). VET is hardly mentioned in the literature on the comprehensive school, while comprehensivization has not been treated much in the VET literature. The general theme in the (scarce) contributions has for the most part been the academization of VET and its consequences (Heikkinen, 2004). Going against the statics of established academic boundaries, the book attempts a more systematic exploration of the historical formation of relations between VET and welfare and the comprehensive school in the Nordic countries. The various chapters reveal long-term trajectories, continuities and ruptures in the articulation between the evolving educational system, the comprehensive school and VET in Finland, Sweden, Denmark and Norway.

From these various points of view, it seems worthwhile to investigate the experience of the Nordic countries and the institutional development of their VET systems as they have emerged historically. How do they combine social and economic goals in VET? How do they combine high educational levels and a mass higher education system with vocational education and training? How do they combine labour market participation and social inclusion with educational mobility? However, systematic cross-national comparative studies of the historical formation of VET institutions and policies in the Nordic countries have not been carried out, and for some of these countries available materials on historical developments in VET are patchy and not easily accessible. Therefore we ask: What is the character of these VET systems? What are the differences? What are the similarities? What set them apart from other systems? How did they come about? How could similarities and variations in trajectories and outcomes be explained?

Making sense of the evolution of Nordic VET

Much of VET research takes its point of departure in case studies or cross-national comparative studies of reform trajectories in a selection of countries. The most interesting of these rely on a mixture of historical institutionalism, partisan politics and varieties of capitalism. Others depart from perspectives emanating from the welfare state or human capital formation. We acknowledge the significance of the theoretical approaches, which recently have enriched the field of skill formation, the cross-national comparisons of different skill regimes, which has emerged, as well as the fruitfulness of historical diachronic analysis. The book is not strictly historical, but also relies on a plurality of theoretical perspectives and approaches. These approaches comes from a number of different disciplines; from pedagogics, political science and political economy, sociology and organization theory and public administration, each emphasizing different aspects of the emergence of Nordic VET. We rely on a mixture of approaches: historical institutionalism in its various forms, (partisan) politics and political regimes, varieties of capitalism, worlds of welfare capitalism/human capital as well as contributions emanating from the sociology of educational systems, organization theory and pedagogics. The different perspective can be regarded as competing or as additive; that is, they combined contribute to the analysis of the topic, emphasizing different aspects of the research topic. We argue that there is a need for a multiplicity of theories rather than a single approach, where existing approaches and bodies of knowledge could be integrated into a combination that illuminates Nordic VET in different ways and from different angles. This makes the book theoretically complex and eclectic, but it allows a more nuanced interpretation of trajectories and drivers.

Such an approach has implications for the definition of VET. VET is an elusive concept. VET can be regarded as a standardized policy area, a policy sector or as a broad social and organizational field. In comparative terms, VET has traditionally been defined in opposition to general education, as practical education, as education and training for manual labour, or as training for the hand and not the mind. Comparative practice has almost exclusively been defined in relation to industry and the crafts, that is; working life in a traditional sense. We have not followed this convention. Instead we have sought to enhance our understanding of the specificities in the historical formation of VET in the Nordic countries by expanding the object of enquiry. Many important changes in the development of vocational training have happened outside core industrial and craft areas. In order to capture these changes we have investigated reforms in the broader institutional framework of the educational system as well as welfare service undergirding education and labour market training. The boundaries of VET are intrinsically unclear and varied in time and space. The investigation of the historical evolution of VET systems requires a processual and pragmatic approach, which allows the discovering of dynamic interrelations between domains as well as processes of differentiation and integration of policy areas in which vocational education and training is embedded. This implies that institutional change over time has to be accounted for. It also implies that institutional domains and policy areas that conventionally are considered as separate can be viewed as interrelated, dynamic and volatile.

Theoretical perspectives

In order to provide an adequate analysis of the evolution of Nordic VET systems, we have to equip ourselves with the necessary conceptual toolkit. The international comparative literature on vocational education and training systems and their developments has been multiplying fast the last 30 years. The thematic range, the disciplines and research domains contributing to it, and the modes of inquiry have become broader and more multifaceted. There is no general agreement on the value of typologies in VET, and a variety of models, typologies and ideal types are in use. Economic approaches focus on the requirements of the economy. Other approaches focus on political dynamics, partisan politics, electoral systems or political explanations in general when making sense of the formation of VET systems and trajectories. Some approaches, like political economy, combine these elements (Martin and Swank, 2012), while others depart from a functionalist perspective (Hall and Soskice, 2001). Furthermore, VET is increasingly not treated in isolation, but as embedded in broader societal configurations, and a series of studies have emerged, linking VET to a variety of other fields of research (Busemeyer, 2014; Thelen, 2014; Iversen and Stephens, 2008; Iversen and Soskice, 2006).

First, there is the issue of diachronic analysis and the significance of the past. Do we really need to understand the historical dynamics of VET institutions in order to understand the workings of contemporary VET systems? The claim is that attention to historical structure of institutions and power dynamics matter for contemporary VET reforms. A variety of approaches examining the production and reproduction of skill formation regimes have yielded results that seem to indicate that the historical regime differences and legacies are still valid today, and remain crucial for understanding how different countries experience new structural problems and their capacity to act and react on them (Busemeyer and Trampusch, 2012a; Thelen, 2004). The classical historical institutionalist analysis of path dependency emphasizes the resilience of institutions and practices. VET systems are difficult to construct and reconstruct. They also foster resilience, hence the significance of path dependency. Path dependency refers to processes of self-reinforcing processes that exhibit increasing returns (Pierson, 2004). Once a path is formed, the probability of further steps along the same path increases, with each move along that path. In its more restrictive versions, fundamental changes happen through critical junctures or unsettled times, setting the path for a new course (Collier and Collier, 2002). A number of different trajectories might be suggested ranging from path stabilization, path departure and path switch, depending on the type of institutional change which is unfolded over time and observed in the various national development paths. In this type of modelling, periods of stasis and short, formative, critical junctures could be identified.

However, the neat picture of critical junctures and long periods of stasis and short periods of radical change has its problems. Historical institutionalist theory has developed significantly with vocational education and training as one of the most interesting areas.

Newer versions emphasize that this is an oversimplification. Change might be gradual but none the less transformative. A large variety of different types of such gradual changes could be identified (Hacker et al., 2015; Mahoney and Thelen, 2010; Streeck and Thelen, 2005; Thelen, 2004). These include *displacement*, where more recent structures gradually gain on older ones; *layering*, where newer structures infuse older ones rather than replace them, changing them in the process; *conversion*, where older institutions are reinterpreted and re-functionalized; *drift*. where older institutions are starved out and neglected, or *survival and return*, where older dormant institutions can be reactivated and return. VET institutions might be undermined through processes of drift or conversion, the very opposite of the classical reproduction elements associated with path dependency. Thus, investigating gradual change processes in periods conceived as static, becomes a priority in each of the cases studied – in this case the development of vocational training in a period where older guild forms were liberalized and replaced by new school-based and formalized firm-based apprenticeship arrangements under organized capitalism and social democracy. The slow and gradual growth of vocational schooling can be contrasted with other forms of gradual institutional change, which have been more prevalent in apprenticeship, where processes of displacement, conversion, and survival and return might be observed. Multiple interests might also produce a more *oscillatory* trajectory (Campbell, 2004). This type of reasoning portrays institutions as composites. Successful coalitions that produce reforms might generate reactions from other actors, where competing interests are mobilized and alternative policy solutions advocated. At some point composites might evolve into compounds or new amalgamations. Mixed VET systems provide interesting environments for the study of such processes, where reforms in one part of the system might trigger reform in others through combinations of drift and conversion. Furthermore, institutional design as a product of political master planning or political compromise is one thing; their enactment by rule-takers is quite different (Rothstein, 2010; Streeck, 2009). Social democracy carried the promise of the comprehensive school as an egalitarian institution, but the actual realization of these ideas is a different story. Actors might comply with new institutionalized rules and regulations, while others might resist or undermine them, depending on prior socialization and dispositions. These actor constellations might also change over time, producing possibilities for creeping change from below (Mahoney and Thelen, 2010).

Historical institutionalist analysis of VET and VET trajectories favours long-term case studies where the significance of distant causation, antecedents and origins are emphasized (Pierson, 2004). In line with this approach we take a long-term view on the evolution of vocational education and training in Finland, Norway, Denmark and Sweden, focusing the period 1850–2015. Analyzing the formation of VET systems in four different countries over such a long period is a truly daunting task. In general terms, this period could be represented in terms of three consecutive reform waves, which have affected the educational landscape (Iversen and Stephens, 2008). In the first period, the institutionalization of vocational schooling was conditioned by two general trends: the general expansion of compulsory and post-compulsory schooling, and the formalization and incorporation of particularistic vocational courses and/or apprenticeship arrangements into public schools and programmes (Benavot, 1983, p. 65). While only a small percentage of youth age cohorts went through post-obligatory education at the turn of the 19th century, the second wave marked the universalization of secondary education. The remarkable post-war growth of vocational education and training made VET into an institution of considerable political and economic significance. However, as general education expanded at equally fast or faster rate during the 1970s, it has been suggested that the percentage of secondary students enrolled in VET programmes was consistently reduced in Western Europe in this period (Benavot, 1983).

The rise of post-war VET could thus be related to its subsequent decline. The third phase marked the massification of higher education (HE). HE has swiftly become a major provider of (highly educated) labour in the new and advanced research-based knowledge society. While the educational expansion took place under the golden age of strong and continuous economic growth, the third phase was characterized by declining growth rates and recessions as well as problems of labour market inclusion. Because of its manual qualities, VET was often considered as particularly suitable for youth with practical orientations and 'weak learners'. This development left policy makers with ongoing worries about the social esteem of VET and to which extent VET was organized properly in order to fulfil its various missions. Also relations between VET and higher education have evolved into a contested area. This type of long-term process provides a valuable baseline for insights in the development of vocational schooling.

In line with the three phases and their drivers we have identified three distinct periods in VET formation. The first dates back to the interaction of democratization and industrialization, the demise of the guilds and the formation of VET systems. The second is related to the ascent of social democracy, the development of a new universalist welfare state and the formation of a comprehensive educational system into which VET became embedded. The third is related to the ascent of new neoliberal policies, the reconstruction of VET systems and the expansion of HE. This type of approach allows periodized contextualized generalizations on the formation of VET across the four countries as well as the identification of VET routes and continuities across these periods. Furthermore, the periodization adheres to conventions across a number of theoretical approaches relevant to the study of VET, allowing extensions and combinations in the analysis of the various routes taken.

Measured by comparative methodological literature, our cross-national study of the evolution of VET systems in the four nation states could be regarded as a structured and focused comparative cross-national study of four distinct cases (Bennett and Georg, 2005). However, our approach is also informed by the older concept of area studies. Area studies point to peculiarities shared by a cluster of cases belonging to a specific area or region, in this case the Nordic region. The four nation states all form important parts of each other's international environment, as well as in the construction of each other's specificity. They have a shared but intertwined history, full of tensions, of which much has centred between the two early consolidated regimes and imperial powers, that of Sweden and Denmark. Norway remained a part of the twin kingdom Denmark-Norway and the Danish-Norwegian realm until 1814. Norway was then separated from Denmark, formed its own constitution and declared itself as a sovereign state and thereafter assented to Swedish rule, an arrangement which lasted until 1905. These legacies have produced a political pattern of ambivalence, where the identification and definition of appropriate solutions in VET has gravitated in different directions, towards 'Danish' and 'Swedish' solutions. Finland's history is much more bound up with Sweden, which during the

17th century was a European multi-ethnic empire reaching far into the Baltics. In 1809, Sweden was forced to surrender Finland to Russia. Finland gained independence in 1917, when the Russian empire collapsed. Various forms for collaboration have also emerged in the form of the Nordic association and the Nordic Council, which was established in 1952 as a forum for Nordic collaboration and coordination in various areas. A passport union and a common labour market agreement was established during the 1950s. Actually, the Nordic region has been called 'The other European community' and has remained the least integrated part of Western Europe (Bergman and Strøm, 2011). Whether or not a Nordic identity actually exists, is disputed (Stråth and Sørensen, 1998). There are clear differences as far as the national realizations are concerned. Still, Kettunen claims that significant historical facts have to be discarded if the term Nordic is rejected. It refers to a Nordic context in which national identities and institutions have been shaped (Kettunen, 2006, p. 53).

Trajectories and drivers

In the book we use historical institutionalism as a heuristic device in order to analyze processes over time. But it requires additional theoretical substance and grounding in empirical contexts. An important source of inspiration for investigating varieties of VET comes from the variety of capitalism (VoC) literature, which argues that the diversity of various national types of capitalism can be captured through the distinction between coordinated (CME) and liberal (LME) forms of market economies. The fundamental opposition is related to the structure of coordination of the firm (Hall and Soskice, 2001). LMEs dominated by market-based forms of coordination are associated with highly stratified systems of education as well as the production of general skills. In CMEs, where economic actors are coordinated through non-market means, it has been possible to develop collectively organized apprenticeship schemes.

This kind of approach has also sparked off historical institutionalist studies on the political and historial origins of skill formation systems, which have been very helpful in explaining pervasive and persistent differences between Anglo-Saxon and Continental countries in VET system formation (Thelen, 2004). Strongly simplified, this literature suggests two development routes, *the continental* and *the liberal* route. In the *liberal* route, where guilds were weak or abolished, the artisan sector was not able to monopolize the production of skills. Because employers were poorly organized, employers aimed at deregulation of markets in order to reduce the influence of trade unions. The *continental* route was significantly different. In this case, a strong artisan training system was an important precondition for the production of skilled labour in sufficient numbers. Therefore, unions tended to develop a common interest with industrial employers in building a cooperative vocational training system based on the competencies and identity of the skilled worker. As a result, a cooperative framework of industrial relations gradually evolved in these nation states. This literature has also illustrated problems with policy learning based on 'best practices' from coordinated countries to liberal countries. The explanation has been attributed to institutional complementarities between VET and types of capitalism (Hall and Soskice, 2001), which limits possibilities for change as well as learning from other types of systems.

Denmark, Finland, Norway and Sweden are often viewed as examples of 'corporatist' industrial relations systems with high capacity for coordination, where union density has been high, and where collective bargaining is institutionalized and relatively centralized (Moene and Wallerstein, 2001). Patterns of employer/trade union organization and central agreements developed relatively parallel in Norway, Denmark and Sweden, Finland somewhat later (see Table 1.1).

After the initial confrontations between the employers and the unions, a pattern gradually emerged, where central agreements and tariff building gradually emerged as conducive to both employer and worker interests. Furthermore, there is a strong tradition for cooperation between employers, unions and the state (Katzenstein, 1985). However, the capacity for coordinated involvement among employers has not been utilized in VET in the construction of apprentice systems in all four cases. This alerts us to the fact that actual employer cooperation and commitment in VET does not necessarily follow from a capacity of coordination. Coordination is also a question of politics, not necessarily institutions (Thelen, 2014).

Starting from a peripheral position compared to the centres of industrialization in Germany and England, the Nordic countries have been catching up (Iversen and Thue, 2008). Senghaas (1985) finds that the Nordic model of economic development is special because these economies, unlike most other peripheral countries, were able to combine economic growth with welfare. A closer comparative analysis of the four Nordic countries, however, requires a more nuanced view. Nordic economic historians have identified two distinct Nordic patterns, that of an East Nordic model (Sweden-Finland) and a West Nordic model (Norway-Denmark) and two distinct development paths. The east path was based on the formation of large-scale manufacturers and cartels with mining/forestry as core industries (Fellman, 2008), while the west descended from smaller entrepreneurs and agricultural capitalism in Denmark

Table 1.1 The formation of industry/craft/labour market associations and agreements

	Denmark	Finland	Norway	Sweden
Joint Representations of Crafts and Industry	1879[1]		1886[1]	
National Confederations of Trade Unions	1898	1907[2]	1899	1898
National Federation of Employers	1896	1907	1900	1902
First Central Agreement	1899	1944	1935[3]	1938

[1] *The joint representation of crafts and industry* in Denmark was formed in 1879, The Norwegian organization in 1886.
[2] The first confederation of unions in Finland was founded in 1907, but dissolved in 1930. The same year a new organization was founded.
[3] For Norway and Sweden this refers to the central agreements *Hovedavtalen* (1935) and *Saltsjöbadenavtalet* (1938).

(Trampusch and Spies, 2014) and the maritime sector/fish industry in Norway (Iversen and Thue, 2008). These routes have produced different conditions for the formation of VET structures, gravitating in different directions. However, in economic history and in historical studies on the formation of Nordic capitalism and business systems, VET is not much focused, with some notable exceptions. The different chapters will provide added information about the nexus between the formation of VET and economic routes.

The primacy of politics represents a different approach (Berman, 2006). Here different streams of research can be mobilized to the study of the formation of VET and Nordic VET systems. In a broad sense this includes the significance of the formation of political systems, electoral systems and party systems as well as partisan politics/consensualist politics. The Nordic countries have been associated with a culture of consensus and compromise, and policy styles characterized by legalism, consulting and consensual solutions (Katzenstein, 1985). Compromises were struck during the interwar years between the labour party on the one hand and the right on the other hand, between industrial and agricultural interests in Denmark, Norway and Sweden (Arter, 2008). They are also associated with multiparty political systems. The social democratic parties and the coalitions of which they were a significant part, laid the foundations for the social democratic welfare states as we presently know them. These coalitions held during the post-war period and were strongly important for educational reforms in general and welfare reforms. Measured by these lenses, the formation of educational policies and VET structures in the Nordic countries could be represented as outcomes of encompassing coalitions and compromises, facilitated by a specific 'legalistic' policy style based on corporatism, extensive consultation and the practice of broad government commissions.

Partisan politics on the other hand attribute central importance to the ideological differences between groups within society and the parties that represent these groups. Partisan politics is often depicted as power struggles between the left and the right parties, suggesting significant differences in policy output between left and right wing governments as far as redistribution is concerned. As access to VET historically has been skewed towards the less wealthy part of the population, it could be expected that the left would be in favour of VET spending, while the right would oppose it (Ansell, 2013). However, the character of educational systems might change this assessment. During the first wave in the provision of public VET, when enrolment was low and the large majority of youth went directly into the labour market after completing obligatory primary education, the small number of available VET schools primarily benefitted the middle classes. Only when enrolment increased significantly did the left find increased public investments in vocational secondary education beneficial. Under conditions of massification in secondary education, however, the right and their parties might also be willing to support increased spending in VET in order to protect against the pressure on general education. When it comes to higher education, it has been suggested that the situation will be reversed (Ansell, 2013). Increased public, higher education spending will be favoured by the right in restrictive or elitist higher education systems, as it shields their electorate. Under conditions of strong expansion and massification, parties on the left will also be more willing to support higher education, while the right will tend to be more restrictive.

The social democratic parties were historically anchored in the labour classes, and linked to the labour movement and to socialism. Eventually they all opted for a reformist course (Berman, 2006), the Norwegian path somewhat belated compared to the others (Sejersted, 2011). The social democrats have been the largest party for most of the period in all four countries, and they achieved this position without necessarily being majority parties. Social democratic dominance could therefore be related to the prevalence of policies for redistribution in education, and the expansion of VET. Still they differ somewhat as far as strength and duration is concerned. In Denmark, the social democrats reached a peak in the 1930s. In Norway, this was the case between 1945 and 1969. The Swedish Social Democratic Party was by far the strongest and the most durable. It was the dominant party in Sweden from the 1930s up to the 1980s. In Finland and Denmark, the social democratic parties were weaker and the need for compromise with other parties more urgent. Differences in social democratic VET policies could also be related to variations in social democratic strength in the four Nordic countries, the political systems into which they were embedded, as well as the strategies that they developed.

But partisan politics dynamics might vary over time, depending on characteristics of the educational system. The social democrats have usually been related to the comprehensive school and late tracking as the preferred organizational form. The right has been represented as in favour of more segmented structures and early tracking. Segmented tracks or streaming protects the rich from meritocracy; consequently, political parties supporting rich groups can support public provision for VET tracks under such conditions. When there was no streaming, the upper classes seemed to turn against educational spending (Ansell, 2013). Ansell holds that the provision of VET has distinct partisan effects and that the financing of education in general has been highly dependent on partisan politics, depending on levels of enrolment and forms of organization. These propositions provide a useful baseline for the analysis of the political dynamics in VET in the Nordic countries in the massification and universalization of secondary education, where the comprehensive school assumed considerable importance.

Collective skill formation systems

Rather than relying on politics or VoC, we have seen a number of studies combining the two. This type of studies has challenged and enriched the study of VET significantly. Among the most important/interesting contributions is the Busemeyer/Trampusch (TB) volume from 2012 on collective skill formation systems, that is, systems that are collectively organized, because firms, intermediate associations and the state cooperate in the process of skill formation in vocational education and training. The evolution of VET systems is not just considered as the direct result of government policies but as inextricably related to a country's broader economic and institutional environment and its capacity for coordination. This perspective poses four central questions: Who provides the training? Who pays? Who controls? What are the relations between VET and the general educational system? The typology offered provides a grid along two binary divisions, that of the degree of public commitment to vocational training and the extent to which firms are directly involved in the training. The combination of the two dimensions produces four categories: statist regimes, liberal skill formation regime, collective skill formation regimes and segmentalist skill formation regimes.

In statist systems, the state is highly involved in VET, while employer interest and influence remains subordinate. In collective skill formation systems, conflicts between state intervention and firm autonomy are solved in specific ways. First, the firm is more involved in the production and financing of training than in systems considered as statist or liberal. But preserving as much autonomy for the firm as possible does not contribute to the active participation of the firm in collective training arrangements. However, if the autonomy of the firm is constrained too much by external regulations, firm participation in apprentice training is no longer viable. Second, there is the central role of intermediate associations and trade unions in the administration and reform of VET. The difference to liberal skill formation is that the willingness of firms to participate in VET is much higher, and a considerable percentage of youth enter internal labour markets for training.

The literature on collective skill formation offers an exciting conceptualization of the combined effects of state commitment and employer involvement to the formation of VET. It represents a move from one factor analysis like the economic or the political formation of VET in favour of the structuring power of historically shaped constellations of factors, where the state and the employers/ unions all play important but different roles. Inspired by this perspective, we explore the different paths taken in the Nordic countries. We ask how the tensions between the employers and the state have evolved. We ask: who provided the training, who paid and who controlled. We have also tried to investigate relations between VET and the general educational system.

Earlier studies have depicted Denmark as an example of a collective skill formation system, in contrast to Sweden, which traditionally has been regarded as a prime example of a statist skill formation system embedded in the state upper secondary comprehensive school (Dobbins and Busemeyer, 2014). Adding the Finnish and the Norwegian trajectories to the comparative analysis of Nordic skill formation systems might provide a more adequate basis for more nuanced interpretations. The strength and structure of the social democratic state provide central conditions for state intervention in VET, state financing and the character of policy reform. The Nordic countries are all normally considered as highly collectivist and coordinated, but employer preferences have gravitated in different directions, towards school-based VET rather than firm-based apprentice training, the reverse or both, for a number of reasons. A significant event in point is the construction of the comprehensive school. The results from comparative studies of VET in Denmark and Sweden suggest that the development of the comprehensive school seems to be negatively related to the position of the employers and the firm (Dobbins and Busemeyer, 2014). At some point the state-led rise of the comprehensive school in Sweden meant that firm-based apprentice skill formation was threatened and eradicated. Swedish employers were coordinated and strong, but not strong enough (Dobbins and Busemeyer, 2014).

Measured by this type of analysis, the formation and implementation of the upper secondary comprehensive school model can perhaps be considered as a pretty good proxy for measuring power relations between the employers and the state. Activating the employers in work-related training could count as a distinct advantage, but would not be sufficient in order to re-construct statist systems into collective skill formation systems. The Norwegian path, which combined apprenticeship and the comprehensive school, suggests that the employers found space for autonomy and firm-based training within such a structure, and apprenticeship has been growing steadily since the formation of the upper secondary comprehensive school. In Finland, the employers have consistently advocated preferences for school-based VET as the main option. There was simply no basis for the collective organization of skills in industry. Furthermore, the integration of VET and general education was rejected in favour of a statist, preparatory school-based VET system with few connections to general education, while apprenticeship has been developed and maintained as an auxiliary mechanism for the skilling of adults and outsiders.

VET and Nordic welfare capitalism

In welfare research the Nordic model has become a standard concept (Christiansen and Markkola, 2006). Of particular relevance is the work of Gøsta Esping-Andersen (1991), which attributes a number of distinct qualities to the Nordic welfare regimes. In the world of welfare, three worlds of welfare regimes have been identified, that of liberal, Christen Democratic and Social Democratic regimes (Esping-Andersen, 1991). They offer different social rights to workers, and shape labour markets as well as social stratification. Esping-Andersen (1991) argues that these types of states are distinct, and they use resources on different types of policies. Two different factors are considered important: stratification and decommodification. Decommodification occurs when a service is given in the form of an individual right, and when an individual can maintain a livelihood independent of the market. Stratification turns on the extent to which social rights upholds the social structure. Together they form a two-dimensional space for identification of three welfare regimes. The Social Democratic welfare regimes are related to the Nordic countries, the liberal states associated with the Anglo-Saxon countries and the Corporatist regime with the continental, Catholic nation states. The three regime types are seen as characterized by their own separate logic, owing their origins to different historical forces following different trajectories.

Furthermore, these welfare arrangements are expensive, and require participation in the labour market, a high level of taxation as well as willingness to pay (Esping-Andersen, 1991). A central element in the Nordic welfare model is the universality of benefits and comprehensive services. Universalism is a cornerstone of public service delivery, and use has been linked to the needs of the individual, rather than their positions or contributions. The historical welfare state literature points towards the significance of the Social Democratic class compromise and the emerging post-war social-democratic order (Christiansen and Markkola, 2006). At the core were the labour movement and the social democratic parties' ability to build and sustain broad alliances behind social policy reform, often together with agrarian interests. Other contributions emphasize the longer historical roots and a common consensus tradition (Baldwin, 1989) and the contributions of the employers (Swenson, 2002). Kettunen (2006) holds that two ideas facilitated these compromises. First, strong trade unions were intended to extend democracy as popular movements and as one of the two parties making agreements on the labour market. Thus, trade unions were seen as carriers of democracy in two senses, as *a popular movement* and as *a labour-market party* (Kettunen, 2006). Second, virtuous circles between efficiency, solidarity and equality could be achieved through the forging of compromises between the different collective interests within society, capitalists, worker and farmers. Kettunen (2001) holds that the confidence in the virtuous circle between efficiency, solidarity and equality could be seen as embedded in three ideological elements; the spirit of capitalism, the utopa of socialism and the idealized heritage of the free independent farmer.

The golden age of social democratic welfare after the second world was structured by virtuous circles of uninterrupted growth and welfare development, supported by a wave of industrialization. The Social Democrats pursued a welfare state that would promote universalism and equality. The ambition was to fit all social policy elements into an encompassing and coherent framework, that of the welfare state and the construction of extensive public services (Kettunen, 2006). These services defined and met the needs of health, care as well as education. Social democratic welfare policies have placed great emphasis on the protection of the individual from risk under various phases of the life cycle, where youth were defined as a particularly vulnerable group. These particular features sketch out the importance of 'decommodification', providing the basis for demand-led VET expansion and the role of VET in Universalist welfare policies and setups for social inclusion.

But this is only part of the story. The formation of the Nordic welfare states also provided new conditions for 'commodification' (Kettunen, 2006). Through social democracy, the Universalist ideal of social rights based on citizenship became linked to the normalcy of wage work. These two features were reinforced though the construction of extensive public services (Kettunen, 2006). The build-up of the modern welfare state secured a swift widening of female employment and the reconstruction of the male-breadwinner family into the modern two-income family. The early entry of women into the labour market (compared to the rest of OECD) fuelled demand for services to support participation, which in turn provided the basis for a growing public sector. As new labour markets emerged in public welfare, conditions for the organization and profile of employer and employee interests changed. These new interests were organized equally well or even better than the manufacturing sector, modifying tendencies towards disorganization induced by the private service sector. As a result, new and more encompassing coalitions were formed around the welfare state and an expansive and inclusive educational system. These policies could also build on a tradition of active labour market policies (ALMP). In much welfare research, ALMP policies have been represented as a break with social democratic values and older practices of decommodification (Merkel and Petring, 2007; Huo, 2006). However, older post-war welfare policies were not entirely an era of passive income protection (Bonoli, 2014). Active policies were introduced quite early, for the most part though vocational training of various types for unemployed, with Sweden in front. Such policies adhered to older Protestant values of regarding work as a social duty as well as social democratic values of keeping as much of the population as possible in income-related and taxpaying activities (Kettunen, 2001). While older post war Nordic ALMP grew out of labour shortages, the new version developed on the basis of high and long-term unemployment (Green-Pedersen et al., 2002, p. 316). In a period characterized by the coevolution of norms of universalization of secondary education for youth and continuing youth unemployment, new policy instruments and measures like the development of state guarantees for youth employment and/or education and training were developed and refined. The flip side of this development has been increasing normative pressure for unemployed youth or other target groups to participate in activation/upskilling measures or taking on jobs.

The incorporation of VET into the policy agenda of expansive, redistributive welfare states had a number of implications, producing multiple omegas, goals and orientations, e.g. towards decommodification, redistribution and inclusion, as well as commodification, parity of esteem, educational efficiency and labour market integration. Achieving a productive balance between these diverse goals in VET has obviously not been easy. This situation faced state policymakers and employers with a number of difficult issues. How could welfare be related to economic efficiency? How could strong state steering of VET be combined with employer influence or autonomy in skill formation? How could inclusion be reconciled with VET esteem? How could labour market inclusion be related to access to higher education? These goals might be considered as contradictory, as trade-offs or dilemmas, where policy makers face a choice between different suboptimal alternatives, as mutually compatible or perhaps as wicked problems – problems that are complex, open ended, or intractable. In turn these omegas, trade-offs, balancing acts and how they have been handled had considerable implications for the provision and structuring of vocational training in its various forms.

The three worlds of skill formation

Contributions emanating from the variety of capitalism literature (VoC) also emphasize the mutual interaction between VET systems and welfare production regimes and the significance of political and institutional conditions for investments in human capital (Iversen, 2005). This type of contributions has emphasized the linkages between investments in human capital, international product market strategies, electoral politics and social protection (Iversen, 2005, p. 5). They are also to some extent compatible with historical institutionalist approaches. As previously mentioned, early VoC contributions isolated two different types of economies. When VoC literature engaged with issues of relations between welfare, capitalism and democracy, important contributions have adopted an equivalent of the three worlds of welfare categorization, producing a very interesting analysis of the three worlds of human capital formation; each with their specific configuration of traits, drivers and historical trajectories. One continental or Christian Democratic regime characterized by vocational training in firm-specific and industry-specific skills but less spending on public education; as well as the separation between welfare arrangements/social policies and education. One liberal regime characterized by heavy private investment in general skills but modest spending on public education and redistribution. And last but not least: one social democratic regime, characterized by redistribution and heavy investment in public education where education is recognized as a part of the welfare state (Busemeyer, 2014; Iversen and Stephens, 2008). The 'three world' baseline is also clearly visible in Martin and Swanks treatise on the origin of employer coordination (Martin and Swank, 2012) as well as Thelen's analysis of liberalization (Thelen, 2014). The ongoing relevance of the three-group structure is interesting when analyzing Nordic skill formation paths. As pointed out by Gingrich (2015), the three worlds of welfare capitalism, the three worlds of skill formation, as well as the three worlds of economic coordination look remarkably alike, measured by the group of countries depicted. Over time these three worlds have certainly changed, but the configurations of institutions in which skill formation and VET is embedded seemingly continues to structure reform trajectories and reform outcomes.

The structural position of VET in these 'worlds' varies significantly, as previously argued. Unlike the liberal countries, capacities for coordination and political preference formation have been sustained in the collective bargaining system, and integrated participation from employers remains an important feature of Nordic social democratic governance systems. New mechanisms for employer influence in skill formation at the central and local levels have also been constructed in order to secure labour market relevance and legitimacy.

The liberal countries (Anglo-Saxon countries) have developed a skill formation regime with a strong bias towards academic higher education, like the US system with its characteristic focus on college education. In this type of skill regime VET is generally seen as an inferior and unpopular track for disadvantaged youth who did not succeed in entering higher education (Thelen, 2014).

The result has been a continuous development towards higher applications rates as well as enrolments in higher education (Thelen, 2014). The continental route has provided conditions for a more restricted higher education system (Powell and Solga, 2011, p. 50). In these systems the popularity of the apprentice system has been substantial, and in Germany the scale and scope of HE remains below average for OECD countries in terms of enrolment and funding. Still, it has proven difficult to transcend the great HE-VET divide (Baetghe, 2006). Yet, there are concerns that HE expansion might impair the German dual system, that apprenticeship is confined to the manufacturing sector, while the service sector is exposed to liberalization and the market. Based on Anglo-Saxon/continental comparisons, it has been suggested that strong systems of vocational training may inhibit the overexpansion of HE and 'master disease' (Busemeyer, 2014). The nexus between VET and HE in the Nordic countries has unfortunately not been much researched. All the Nordic countries have fairly similar higher education systems in the sense that they belong to what Ansell (2013, p. 165) calls the Mass Public Model, characterized by high enrolment rates, by being almost entirely public and supported by high funding levels in higher education. In all the Nordic countries new forms of articulation between a Universalist upper secondary education level with strong VET elements and a mass higher education system have developed. Model logic in line with the 'the three worlds of welfare' would suggest the presence of a specific social democratic expansive or redistributive pattern which structures relations between VET and HE. Still, model logic has a tendency of ignoring the complementary and competitive relations between educational levels. The various country chapters explore the relations between VET and higher education in the four countries.

Summing up

The aim of the book is to develop and disseminate new and systematic knowledge on the origins and evolution of Nordic VET systems. These systems have many similarities and share a common heritage in education policy and welfare policies as well as social organization. We claim that Nordic VET requires more attention in VET research. These systems stand out due to their egalitarian, comprehensive and inclusive traditions. What they have in common is that VET has emerged in state-led educational systems with a strong welfare orientation, coordinated market economies as well as similar state, political and administrative cultures and traditions. Still, they look very different measured by conventional typologies of VET. The literature in English on the Nordic VET systems is at present limited. In the last few years a number of contributions have given us a better understanding of Nordic VET systems. But they are scattered, and there is a lack of comparative and historical studies. Thus, we have attempted to provide systematic, comparative studies of the historical formation of VET institutions and policies in four Nordic countries. The different chapters offer studies of the four VET system´s historical developments. They have evolved into different shapes but they seem to follow similar trajectories. The theoretical baseline is grounded in a combination of current typologies of VET/skill formation systems, historical institutionalism and welfare capitalism. We also offer a focus towards the dynamics of the educational system and the position of VET in relation to the formation of the comprehensive school and mass higher education systems.

The book offers a total of ten chapters divided into three parts. The introductory chapter sets the stage for the empirical cases presented. The first part deals with the period 1860–1945, is structured by case studies of the origins of Norwegian, Finnish, Danish and Swedish VET. The second part is organized along similar principles exploring developments during the social democratic period 1945–2010 as well as the new policies of re-liberalization at the end of this period. The last and final part provides an extended cross-national and diachronic analysis of trajectories and drivers for the four countries, emphasizing both similarities and differences in development routes.

References

Allmendinger, J. (1989) 'Educational systems and labor market outcomes', *European Sociological Review*, vol. 5, no. 3, pp. 231–249.

Anderson, K. M. and Nijhuis, D. O. (2012) 'The long road to collective skill formation in the Netherlands', in Busemeyer, M. B. and Trampusch, C. (eds.) *The Political Economy of Collective Skill Formation*, Oxford, Oxford University Press, pp. 101–126.

Ansell, B. W. (2013) *From the Ballot to the Blackboard: The Redistributive Political Economy of Education*, Cambridge, Cambridge University Press.

Antikainen, A. (2006) 'In search of the Nordic model in education', *Scandinavian Journal of Educational Research*, vol. 50, no. 3, pp. 229–243.

Arnesen, A. L. and Lundahl, L. (2006) 'Still social and democratic? Inclusive education policies in the Nordic welfare states', *Scandinavian Journal of Educational Research*, vol. 50, no. 3, pp. 285–300.

Arter, D. (2008) *Scandinavian Politics Today*, Manchester, Manchester University Press.

Baetghe, M. (2006) 'Das Deutsche Bildungs-Schisma. Herausforderungen für die Berufsausbildunsgforschung', in Eckert, E. and Zöller, A. (eds.) *Welche Probleme eine vorindustrielles Bildungssystem in einer nachindustriellen Gesellschaft hat*, SOFI-mitteilungen, no. 34, Soziologisches Forschungsinstitut and der Universität, Göttingen, pp. 13–27.

Baldwin, P. (1989) 'The Scandinavian origins of the social interpretation of the welfare state', *Comparative Studies in Society and History*, vol. 31, pp. 3–24.

Benavot, A. (1983) 'The rise and decline of vocational education', *Sociology of Education*, vol. 56, no. 2, pp. 63–76.

Bennett, A. and Georg, A. (2005) *Case Studies and Theory Development in the Social Sciences*, Cambridge, MIT Press.

Bergman, T. and Strøm, K. (2011) 'Nordic Europe in a comparative perspective', in Bergman, T. and Strøm, K. (eds.) *The Madisonian Turn. Political Parties and Parliamentary Democracy in Nordic Europe*, Ann Arbour, University of Michigan Press, pp. 36–66.

Berman, S. (2006) *The Primacy of Politics: Social Democracy and the Making of Europe's Twentieth Century*, New York, Cambridge University Press.

Bjørnson, Ø. (2001) 'The social democrats and the Norwegian welfare state: Some perspectives', *Scandinavian Journal of History*, vol. 26, no. 3, pp. 197–223.

Bonoli, G. (2014) 'Active labour market policies and social investment', in Morel, N., Palier, B. and Palme, J. (eds.) *Towards a Social Investment Welfare State? Ideas, Policies and Challenges*, Bristol, Policy Press, pp. 181–205.

Busemeyer, M. R. (2014) *Skills and Inequality: Partisan Politics and the Political Economy of Education Reforms in Western Welfare States*, Cambridge, Cambridge University Press.

Busemeyer, M. R. and Trampusch, C. (2012a) 'The comparative of political economy of collective skill formation', in Busemeyer, M. R. and Trampusch, C. (eds.) *The Political Economy of Collective Skill Formation*, Oxford, Oxford University Press, pp. 3–40.

Busemeyer, M. R. and Trampusch, C. (eds.) (2012b) *The Political Economy of Collective Skill Formation*, Oxford, Oxford University Press.

Campbell, J. L. (2004) *Institutional Change and Globalization*, Princeton, Princeton University Press.

Christiansen, N. F and Markkola, S. (2006) 'Introduction', in Christiansen, N. F., Petersen, K., Edling, N. and Haave, P. (eds.) *The Nordic Model of Welfare: A Historical Reappraisal*, University of Copenhagen, Museum Tusculanum Press, pp. 9–31.

Christiansen, N. F. and Petersen, K. (2001) 'The dynamics of social solidarity: The Danish welfare state, 1900–2000', *Scandinavian Journal of History*, vol. 26, no. 3, pp. 177–196.

Collier, R. B. and Collier, D. (2002) *Shaping the Political Arena: Critical Junctures, the Labor Movement, and Regime Dynamics in Latin America*, Notre Dame, University of Notre Dame Press.

Crouch, C., Sako, M. and Finegold, D. (2001) *Are Skills the Answer? The Political Economy of Skill Creation in Advanced Industrial Countries*, Oxford, Oxford University Press.

Demker, M. and Svåsand, L. (2005) 'Den nordiska fempartimodellen: En tilfällighet eller et fundament?', in Demker, M. and Svåsand, L. (eds.) *Partiernas århundre. Fempartimodellens uppgång och fall i Norge och Sverige*, Stockholm, Santerus Forlag, pp. 9–38.

Dobbins, M. and Busemeyer, M. L. (2014) 'Socioeconomic institutions, organized interests and partisan politics: The development of vocational education in Denmark and Sweden,' *Socio-Economic Review*, vol. 13, no. 2, pp. 259–284.

Esping-Andersen, G. (1991) *The Three Worlds of Welfare Capitalism*, Princeton, NJ, Princeton University Press.

Fellman, S. (2008) 'Growth and investment: Finnish capitalism, 1850–2005,' in Fellman, S., Iversen, M. J., Sjøgren, H. and Thue, L. (eds.) *Creating Nordic Capitalism: The Business History of a Competitive Periphery*, Basingstoke, Palgrave Macmillan, pp. 139–218.

Fellman, S., Iversen, M. J., Sjøgren, H. and Thue, L. (eds.) (2008) *Creating Nordic Capitalism: The Business History of a Competitive Periphery*, Basingstoke, Palgrave Macmillan.

Gingrich, J. (2015) 'Coalitions, policies and distribution: Esping-Andersen's three worlds of welfare capitalism', in Mahoney, J. and Thelen, K. (eds.) *Advances in Comparative-Historical Analysis*, Cambridge, Cambridge University Press.

Gingrich, J. and Ansell, B. (2015) 'The dynamics of social investment: Human capital, activation and care', in Beramendi, P., Haüsermann, S., Kitschelt, H. and Kriesi, H. J. (eds.) *The Politics of Advanced Capitalism*, Cambridge, Cambridge University Press, pp. 282–304.

Graf, L. (2013) *The Hybridization of Vocational Training and Higher Education in Austria, Germany and Switzerland*, Berlin and Toronto, Budrich UniPress Ltd, Opladen.

Green, A. (2004) *Education and State Formation: The Rise of Education Systems in England, France and the USA*, Beijing, Educational Science Publishing House.

Green-Pedersen, C. (2002) 'New public management reforms of the Danish and Swedish welfare states: The role of different social democratic responses', *Governance*, vol. 15, no. 2, pp. 271–294.

Hacker, J. S., Pierson, P. and Thelen, K. (2015) 'Drift and conversion: Hidden faces of institutional change', in Mahoney, J. and Thelen, K. (eds.) *Advances in Comparative-Historical Analysis*, Cambridge, Cambridge University Press.

Hall, P. H. and Soskice, D. (2001) *Varieties of Capitalism. The Institutional Foundations of Comparative Advantage*, Oxford, Oxford University Press.

Hansen, H. F. (2011) 'NPM in Scandinavia', in Christensen, T. and Lægreid, P. (eds.) *Ashgate Research Companion to New Public Management*, Aldershot, Ashgate, pp. 113–129.

Heikkinen, A. (2004) 'Models, paradigms or cultures of vocational education', *European Journal of Vocational Training*, 32, no. 2, pp. 32–44.

Huo, J. (2006) *Third Way Reforms: A Comparative Study of Social Democratic Welfare State Reforms After the Golden Age*, Dissertation, Chapel Hill, University of North Carolina.

Iversen, M. J and Andersen, S. (2008) 'Co-operative liberalism: Denmark from 1857 to 2007', in Fellman, S., Iversen, M. J., Sjøgren, H. and Thue, L. (eds.) *Creating Nordic Capitalism: The Business History of a Competitive Periphery*, Basingstoke, Palgrave Macmillan, pp. 265–335.

Iversen, M. J. and Thue, L. (2008) 'Creating Nordic capitalism – the business history of a competitive periphery', in Fellman, S., Iversen, M. J., Sjøgren, H. and Thue, L. (eds.) *Creating Nordic Capitalism: The Business History of a Competitive Periphery*, Basingstoke, Palgrave Macmillan, pp. 1–19.

Iversen, T. (2005) *Capitalism, Democracy and Welfare*, Cambridge, Cambridge University Press.

Iversen, T. and Soskice, D. (2006) 'Electoral institutions and the politics of coalitions: Why some democracies redistribute more than others', *American Political Science*, vol. 100, no. 2, pp. 165–181.

Iversen, T. and Stephens, J. D. (2008) 'Partisan politics, the welfare state and the three worlds of human capital formation', *Comparative Political Studies*, vol. 41, no. 4–5, pp. 600–637.

Kangas, O. and Palme, J. (2005) 'Coming late – catching up: The formation of a "Nordic model"', in Kangas O. and Palme, J. (eds.) *Social Policy and Economic Development in the Nordic Countries*, Basingstoke, Palgrave Macmillan, pp. 17–53.

Katzenstein, P. J. (1985) *Small States in World Markets: Industrial Policy in Europe*. Ithaca and London, Cornell University Press.

Kettunen, P. (2001) 'The Nordic welfare state in Finland', *Scandinavian Journal of History*, vol. 26, no. 3, pp. 225–247.

Kettunen, P. (2006) 'The power of international comparison – A perspective on the making and challenging of the Nordic Welfare State', in Christiansen, N. F., Petersen, K., Edling, N. and Haave, P. (eds.) *The Nordic Model of Welfare. A Historical Reappraisal*, Copenhagen, Museum Tuscalanum Press, pp. 31–67.

Korsnes, O. (1996) *Industri og samfunn. Framlegg til program for studiet av norsk arbeidsliv*, Bergen, Doktoravhandling Sosiologisk Institutt., University of Bergen.

Kristensen, P. and Lilja, K. (2011) *Nordic Capitalism and Globalization: New Forms of Economic Governance and Welfare Institutions*, Oxford, Oxford University Press.

Leschinsky, A. and Mayer, K. U. (1999) *The Comprehensive School Experiment Revisited: Evidence from Western Europe*, Frankfurt am Main, Peter Lang.

Lundahl, L. (1997) 'A common denominator? Swedish employers, trade unions and vocational training', *International Journal of Training and Development*, vol. 1, no. 2, pp. 91–103.

Lundahl, L. (2016) 'Equality, inclusion and marketization of Nordic education: Introductory notes', *Comparative & International Education*, vol. 11, no. 1, pp. 1–10.

Lundahl, L., Erixon Arreman, I., Lundström, U. and Rönneberg, L. (2010) 'Setting things right? Swedish upper secondary school reform in a 40 year perspective', *European Journal of Education*, vol. 45, no. 1, pp. 46–59.

Mahoney, J. and Thelen, K. (2010) 'A theory of gradual institutional change', in Mahoney, J. and Thelen, K, (eds.) *Explaining Institutional Change. Ambiguity, Agency and Power*, Cambridge, Cambridge University Press, pp. 1–37.

Martin, C. J and Swank, D. (2012) *The Political Construction of Business Interests: Coordination, Growth and Equality*, Cambridge, Cambridge University Press.

Merkel, W. and Petring, A. (2007) 'Social democracy in power: Explaining the capacity to reform', *Zeitschrift für Vergleichende Politikwissenschaft*, vol. 1, no. 1, pp. 125–145.

Moene, K. and Wallerstein, M. (2001) 'Inequality, social insurance, and redistribution', *The American Political Science Review*, vol. 95, no. 4, pp. 859–874.

Morel, N., Palier, B., Palme, J. (eds.) (2015) *Towards a Social Investment Welfare State? Ideas, Policies and Challenges*, Bristol, Policy Press.

Nelson, M. (2012) 'Continued collectivism: The role of trade self-management and the social-democratic party in Danish vocational education and training', in Busemeyer, M. R. and Trampusch, C. (eds.) *The Political Economy of Skill Formation*, Oxford, Oxford University Press, pp. 179–204.

Nilsson, A. (2007) 'Current national strategies in vocational education and training: Convergence or divergence?' *European Journal of Vocational Training*, no. 41, pp. 150–162.

Pierson, P. (2004) *Politics in Time: History, Institutions, and Social Analysis*, Princeton and Oxford, Princeton University Press.

Pontusson, J. (2005) *Inequality and Prosperity: Social Europe Versus Liberal America*, Ithaca and London, Cornell University Press.

Powell, J. J. W. and Solga, H. (2011) 'Why are higher education participation rates in Germany so low? Institutional barriers to higher education expansion', *Journal of Education and Work*, vol. 24, no. 1–2, pp. 49–68.

Rothstein, B. (2010) *The Social Democratic State: Swedish Model and the Bureaucratic Problem*, Pittsburgh, University of Pittsburgh Press.

Schriewer, J., Orivel, F., Sherman Swing, E. (2000) 'European educational systems: The framework of tradition, systemic expansion, and challenges for restructuring', in Swing, E. S., Schriewer, J. and Orivel, F. (eds.) *Problems and Prospects in European Education*, Westport, Preager Publishers, pp. 1–20.

Sejersted, F. (2011) *The Age of Social Democracy: Norway and Sweden in the Twentieth Century*, Princeton and Oxford, Princeton University Press.

Senghaas, D. (1985) *The European Experience: A Historical Critique of Development Theory*, New Hampshire, Berg Publishers.

Sørensen, Ø. and Stråth, B. (1997) *The Cultural Construction of Norden*, Oslo, Universitetsforlaget.

Streeck, W. (2009) *Re-Forming Capitalism: Institutional Change in the German Political Economy*, Oxford, Oxford University Press.

Streeck, W. and Thelen, K. (2005) *Beyond Continuity: Institutional change in Advanced Political Economies*, Oxford, Oxford University Press.

Swenson, P. A. (2002) *Capitalists Against Markets: The Making of Labour Markets and Welfare States in the United States and Sweden*, New York, Oxford University Press.

Telhaug, A. O., Mediås, O. A. and Aasen, P. (2006) 'The Nordic model in education: Education as part of the political system in the past 50 years', *Scandinavian Journal of Educational Research*, vol. 50, no. 3, pp. 245–283.

Thelen, K. (2004) *How Institutions Evolve: The Political Economy of Skills in Germany, Britain, The United States, and Japan*, Cambridge, Cambridge University Press.

Thelen, K. (2014) *Varieties of Liberalization and the New Politics of Social Solidarity*, Cambridge, Cambridge University Press.

Thelen, K. and Busemeyer, M. L. (2012) 'Institutional change in German vocational training: From collectivism toward segmentalism', in Busemeyer, M. R. and Trampusch, C. (eds.) *The Political Economy of Skill Formation*, Oxford, Oxford University Press, pp. 3–40.

Thue, L. (2008) 'Norway: A resource based and democratic capitalism', in Fellman, S., Iversen, M. J., Sjøgren, H. and Thue, L. (eds.) *Creating Nordic Capitalism: The Business History of a Competitive Periphery*, Basingstoke, Palgrave Macmillan, pp. 394–494.

Trampusch, C. and Spies, D. C. (2014) 'Agricultural interests and the origins of capitalism: A parallel comparative history of Germany, Denmark, New Zealand, and the USA', *New Political Economy*, vol. 19, no. 6, pp. 918–942.

Wiborg, S. (2009) *Education and Social Integration: Comprehensive Schooling in Europe. Secondary Education in a Changing World*, New York, Palgrave Macmillan.

Wilensky, H. (1975) *The Welfare State and Equality*, Berkeley, University of California Press.

2 The development of Finnish vocational education and training from 1850 to 1945

Marja-Leena Stenström and Maarit Virolainen

Introduction

The history of Finnish vocational education and training (VET) in the 1800s and 1900s can be seen as a history of solutions that actors have created in response to the need for building an education system that suits a modern nation-state society (Kettunen, 2013). Finland was part of the Swedish Kingdom for about 500 years leading up to 1809, when Finland became part of the Russian Empire as a Grand Duchy. Economically, Finland has been a static, agrarian country with a social structure based on estates (Laukia, 2013a; Klemelä, 1999). During the period as the autonomous Grand Duchy of Finland, Finnish society began undergoing rapid social and economic change and new structures of economy, education and governance were developed. The period under the rule of the Russian Empire has been seen as decisive for the development of indigenous production, education and social policy (Heikkinen, 2001).

Since 1809, different social groups have gained more possibilities to articulate their political and cultural interests (Heikkinen, 2001). Even though the laws passed under the rule of Sweden were retained, ideological and industrial restructuring was starting to take place in the society (Gluschkoff, 2008; Manninen, 2003; Hirvonen, 2002). The Fennoman nationalist movement and ideology was built during that time, in the 19th century. It stated the need for schools, including vocational schools, and contributed to the development of the Finnish language and literature. The movement raised the Finnish language significance to that of Swedish, which was the language of the dominant, high-prestige minority in their common history.

Emerging pressure for the development of political and economic structures was reflected in the statements of an early proponent of the Fennoman movement, the journalist and historian Adolf Ivar Arwidsson. In the 1820s, he started to propagate the need to find a shared understanding for the formation of the Finnish nation (Heikkinen, 2001). Increasing nationalism required the mobilisation of the common people and abandonment of elitism among the Swedish-speaking upper class, which managed to retain much of its power due to existing family networks and continued to form the core of the industrial and administrative elite (Gluschkoff, 2008; Hirvonen, 2002; Heikkinen, 2001). Since the 1840s, the rise of nationalistic ideas meant the development of education, which was seen to play a central role in uniting the nation (Manninen, 2003; Klemelä, 1999). Finally, vocational education started to take shape more effectively after Finland's independence in 1917. The industrialisation had begun to expand slowly and the Finnish economy grew favourably at the end of the 1920s (Laukia, 2013b, p. 104). At the beginning, the export industry had no connections to former guilds and their craft traditions (Sakslind, 1998). Domestic import emerged, and especially those industries (e.g. metal and textile industries) that had previously been orientated toward the Russian market turned to cater to the Finnish domestic market (Rainio-Niemi, 2004, p. 155).

The development of education and its policy in Finland has been periodised by several authors placing emphasis on different characteristic factors of these decades. For example, authors like Tuomisto (1986), Kyöstiö (1955) and Heikkinen (1995) vary in how they emphasise elementary education and the establishment of VET schools, whose programmes were previously based on elementary education. The official phases of Finnish history have been outlined as three periods: 1) the phase under Sweden until 1809; 2) the phase under the Russian Empire as a Grand Duchy 1809–1916; and 3) the phase of Finnish independence since 1917 (see, e.g. Lehtisalo and Raivola, 1999). To portray the early development of VET in Finland, we utilised the periodisation of Kyöstiö's (1955) division as a starting point, but combined it with Tuomisto's (1986) views pointing to the period of general education as the establishment of the folk school system (i.e. elementary education) which has provided an important foundation for vocational education. Also, both Kyöstiö (1955) and Heikkinen (1995) agree on the 1840s and 1880s as decades marking decisive historical turning points in broad terms. Kyöstiö (1955) investigated the early stages of VET. He divided the development of early VET into three periods: 1) the prephase and time of guild systems until the year 1842; 2) the exploratory stage leading to VET 1843–1885; and 3) the foundation stage of VET from 1885, although the country-wide network of vocational schools (*ammattikoulut*, in Finnish) was created only in the 1960s.

As this chapter elaborates the historical evolution of the Finnish vocational education and training (VET) system mainly at the level of secondary education, we focus on the period ranging from the 1850s to the 1940s, adopting the classification just mentioned. The historical turning points examined in this chapter are divided into three periods: 1) the early roots of Finnish VET; 2) the phase of Finnish general education (referred to as the development of the folk or elementary school system); and 3) the foundation phase of the institutionalised VET.

The early roots of the Finnish VET: guild systems and Sunday schools

Guild systems

The early roots of the present Finnish vocational education system are found in the growth of medieval craft guilds. In 1720, a decree concerning the guild system was legislated in Sweden and Finland (see also Olofsson and Persson Thunqvist, 2018). It stated that those who wanted to work as a craftsman should undergo four years as an apprentice and journeyman. The route from apprentice to master was neither easy nor short, since it took at least six years and in practice often even ten years. Between one quarter and one third left their apprenticeship without the journeyman certificate (Koskela, 2003; Kyöstiö, 1955). The guilds had a monopoly for studying craftsmanship in towns. The largest groups of artisans were tailors, shoemakers, blacksmiths and carpenters. The aims of the guilds emphasised a wide-ranging educational perspective and a class-conscious socialisation process. The ruling time of guilds was from the 1740s to 1860s, although the development of the guilds stagnated when Finland became an autonomous Duchy of the Russian Empire and new forms of production started to emerge and change their position (Paloheimo and Uotila, 2015; Heikkinen, 2000). The Finnish guilds never reached a position as strong as the guilds in Denmark.

As the demands of society changed, the vocational education provided by the guilds was criticised. The university student leader and national romantic writer Adolf Ivar Arwidsson saw that the old guild system took too long (six to eight years, on average) and that it was too inflexible to be able to meet the challenges of the economy (Laukia, 2013a). Also, the famous Finnish statesman Johan Wilhelm Snellman criticised the traditional vocational education organised by the guilds and considered the quality of the resulting products too poor (Laukia, 2013a). The guilds operated mainly in towns and differences between rural communities and towns were considerable until the gradual liberalisation of trade and industry (Heikkinen, 2004). In 1868, the obligatory guild system was repealed, most of the former mercantilistic restrictions concerning trade were abolished and the timber industry was liberalised (Rainio-Niemi, 2004). Finland experienced a smooth transition from the old society of privilege to the deliberated class society (Rainio-Niemi, 2004). An important change occurred in 1879, when the workforce gained the freedom to choose their living and work places as a result of new legislation, the 'Liberation of Occupations Act' (*elinkeinovapauslaki*, in Finnish) (Paloheimo and Uotila, 2015; Laukia, 2013a). The Act abolished the privileges of the guild system. Furthermore, the legislation concerning the statutory protection of the workforce ended (Laukia, 2013b, p. 44). In 1883, employers' rights concerning their employees were redefined when employers' duty of custody and authority over employees, as well as the right of having them in service for the duration of their contract, was abolished (Rainio-Niemi, 2004). This process launched a modernisation of societal life. Especially, people who did not own any land started to move from the countryside to towns in their search for work.

Sunday and preparatory schools

Already since the late 1820s, Finnish Sunday schools had been established by municipalities and private bodies following Nordic examples. A 'Decree on

Sunday Schools' set out in 1842 required organising the teaching of reading, writing, numeracy and Christian doctrine. As such, Sunday schools provided a general education rather than specific vocational training (Klemelä, 1999, p. 35). The decree ordered that Sunday schools were to be established in each town. Later on, these schools came to be seen as the first actual vocational schools and predecessors for the later expansion of vocational school-based education as they were intended to fulfil the aim of educating apprentices (Klemelä, 1999, p. 34; Tuomisto, 1986, p. 71). In 1858, a decree was established to reform Sunday schools into a school of two grades, followed by a two-grade evening school. After the reform, Sunday school was intended for apprentices and the evening school for journeymen. Sunday school graduates were not qualified craftsmen until acquiring professional competence through the apprentice-journeyman-master system (Heikkinen, 1995, p. 163). The language of most of the Sunday schools was Swedish (Heikkinen, 1995). Although the tie with Sweden had broken at the beginning of the 1800s, the tradition of Sunday schools had been well-established by the Western influences. The model of the Danish Sunday schools came to Finland via Sweden (Somerkivi, 1950).

The lifespan of the Sunday school system as a leading education provider lasted around half a century. At the outset, Sunday schools provided a general education for cities' craftsmen, resembling the existing, more religious Sunday schools arranged by Lutheran priests. They were organised by initiative-taking individuals, bourgeoisie or craftmen in cities such as Turku, Porvoo, Helsinki, Uusikaupunki, Oulu, Tammisaari, Naantali, Kajaani, Vaasa and Viipuri (Somerkivi, 1950). In the beginning, they focused on general education, but later they were redefined to be more professionally oriented by Acts of Senate in 1847 and 1858. They started to lose their importance in 1868, when the guild system was overruled and were then cancelled by an Act passed in 1885 and thereafter reformed as craft schools (i.e. *käsityöläiskoulut*, in Finnish) (Heikkilä, 2003, p. 15; Somerkivi, 1950, p. 16). One reason why the Sunday school system deteriorated was that the folk school system (*kansakoulu*, in Finnish) replaced the general elementary vocational school system. A 'Decree on Folk Education' was given in 1866 (Jalava, 2011). It was preceded by the reorganisation of communities' governance in the countryside (Puranen, 2011). The reorganisation gave the right for local decision making to groups holding community meetings or authorities empowered by the community. It was in their power to decide on the provision and organisation of basic folk education, regionally. At times, the communities were reluctant to fund folk education and considered the literacy education provided by the Lutheran church sufficient. Similar reforms of local governance took place in cities in 1873 (Puranen, 2011). Folk schools were created to provide a basic education in literacy, mathematics and crafts for children.

Later on, Sunday schools and evening schools were further reformed and developed. According to the 'Decree on Craft Schools' passed in 1885, Sunday schools and evening schools were to be developed gradually into craft schools, whose purpose was to teach skills and knowledge considered necessary for craftsmen (Klemelä, 1999, p. 38). The craft schools followed the tradition of the Sunday schools, where students worked at a workplace during the day and studied in the evenings (Koskela, 2003). The regulations for craft schools were updated by another decree issued in 1900. Besides craft schools operating evenings, this new decree also mentioned so-called 'preparatory vocational schools', which operated in the daytime and were intended for folk school graduates (Klemelä, 1999, p. 39).

Preparatory vocational schools were established because students typically finished folk school at the age of 13 or 14. The 'Decree on Working Conditions' in 1889 required that the daily working hours of children under the age of 12–15 years does not exceed a maximum of seven hours (Klemelä, 1999, p. 40). The work day of those under 15 years of age was considered too short by employers who thus did not like to hire them. Therefore, there was a need for a preparatory school to fill the gap between folk school and employment. The preparatory school lasted two years. Since the 1920s, the instruction given at vocational preparatory schools developed into the largest and most significant form of VET for crafts and industry (Klemelä, 1999, p. 50).

The need for wider education in crafts and industry was most often argued for with respect to technological developments. Technological development was seen to be raising the demands for professional competence, the work accordingly requiring school based vocational education. On the other hand, arguments for the necessity of Sunday schools, craft schools and preparatory vocational schools were based on these schools' function as a means of social control (Klemelä, 1999, p. 194).

The phase of general education: building the folk school

The period from the 19th century to the 1960s can be characterised as a time of building the folk school system as the establishment and introduction of elementary education for the whole of the population was a radical novelty and change for the society. The historical shift from elementary education promoted by church policies to state-led school policies and municipalities followed the general Nordic pattern. The idea of the folk school was based on the idea that each child should get a similar basic education regardless of social class, gender or domicile (Leino-Kaukiainen and Heikkinen, 2011). The folk school education was more versatile than the education provided by the church. The decree on the four-year folk school for rural pupils and the six-year folk school for urban pupils was given in 1866. The Act defined the duty of organising elementary school education for the municipalities and the duty of elementary instruction (e.g. literacy) for the church and home. In practice, the first folk schools were private, financially supported by the state (Leino-Kaukiainen and Heikkinen, 2011). Often the employers of large-scale industry (e.g. Finnish forestry industry companies such as Yhtyneet Paperitehtaat) established folk schools for their employees, because they considered workers required being taught proper manners and attitudes.

The establishment of folk schools by the decree given in 1866 was an outcome of a wider Fennoman programme of folk enlightenment (Laukia, 2013a; Rinne, 2013; Heikkinen, 2004). As a result of the Fennoman movement, some larger towns started organising more systematic teaching of general subjects, home economics and handicraft in continuation classes. In addition, the 'Liberation of Occupations Act' in 1879 in practice abolished the guilds and offered the freedom of choosing one's place of residence to all citizens, thus enabling free movement within the country, and it obliged employers to release employees under the age of 15 to attend preparatory school for learning (Laukia, 2013b; Heikkinen, 2004). In practice, for those under 15 years of age this meant either attending continuation classes in a folk school or at a school for crafts and industry. Initially, the establishment of the folk school system progressed slowly because many municipalities resisted the schools due to their novelty and efforts demanded from local communities (Puranen, 2011; Heikkinen, 2004). In 1890, over three quarters of the urban children and a fifth of the rural children went to school. The folk school did not become a reality as fast as its founders had hoped. Folk school had been a school for farmers and was becoming a school for workers (Koskela, 2003).

In Finland, the 'Compulsory Education Act' came into force in 1921. According to this law, each Finn had a duty to participate in compulsory education from the age of seven until 12. Mikael Soininen (former Johnsson) in particular, as an active Fennoman, promoted the Finnish cooperative movement and the development of the folk school system. He was both the head of the Teacher Seminar and the inspector and head of the Board of Education (Heikkinen, 2004). Under his influence, handicraft was included in the curriculum of the folk school system (Laukia, 2013a).

The continuation of studies after completing the compulsory education was further discussed in, for example, a committee nominated for this purpose [Jatko-Opetuskomitea] (Laukia, 2013b). In the following decades, between the 1920s and 1940s, there were repeated initiatives by the Ministry and Board of Education as well as Teacher Seminars to develop the continuation school system into a practically oriented general vocational system of education (Heikkinen, 2004). In particular, advocates of the comprehensive continuation school system defended it for the majority of the age group (except for grammar school students) and as citizenship education. The original mission of the continuation school system was to provide education for citizenship. Secondarily, it was expected to offer occupational guidance, and thirdly to provide practical and occupation-oriented education (Kailanpää, 1962; and see also Heikkinen, 2004). In 1943, continuation school became obligatory for applicants to other schools such as vocational schools. Although the aim of the folk school was to educate good citizens rather than skilled workers, the competition between the students of the folk school system and those of the vocational school system lasted until the end of the 1950s (Laukia, 2013a; Jauhiainen, 2002; Halila, 1963). The administration of the general education was managed by the Ministry of Education, which developed the folk and continuation school systems, whereas the Ministry of Trade and Industry was the proponent of the distinctive VET programme (Heikkinen, 2004).

The foundation phase of institutionalised VET

The rapid population growth and beginning of industrialisation set their own demands for the organisation of education. During the period of 1850–1940 the population of Finland grew by more than 2 million inhabitants. While there were about 1.6 million inhabitants in the Grand Duchy of Finland in 1859, the population of Finland was nearly 4 million by 1940. The population growth slowed down in rural municipalities, whereas population centres like cities and towns were growing as a result of migration. In 1940, 52% of the population earned their living from primary production (see Table 2.1). Agriculture dominated as the major occupation of the population at the beginning of Finnish independence (since 1917), although industry had started to emerge and diversify since the 1800s. The pressures for educational reforms increased due to the growth of the economy and industry, but, above all, they were enhanced by societal trends such as the labour movement, the women's movement, the temperance movement and the growth of nationalism (Koskela, 2003).

Vocational education and educated people were needed when new technologies, such as machines, railroads and electricity, were launched. In addition, there was great demand for vocational education and vocational skills because the existing formal education system concentrated only on the education of civil servants and educated citizens. Also, people with an academic education would study technology for additional practical skills. The need to change and reorganise vocational education became recognised (Laukia, 2013a).

The Finnish VET started to diversify in the late 19th century. The first institutions of vocational and professional education and training were created at the beginning of the 19th century, but acquiring occupational skills at an

Table 2.1 Occupational distribution of the population in percentages of the workforce 1880–1940 (adopted from Laukia, 2013b, p. 324)

Year	Agriculture %	Industry and crafts %	Transportation %	Commerce %	Public services and independent professions %	General worker, labourer, etc. %	No occupation or unspecified %	Total %
1880	77.1	6.5	2.1	1.0	2.7	4.2	6.4	100
1890	74.7	8.0	2.1	1.2	2.9	4.4	6.7	100
1900	58.0	10.6	2.8	2.0	2.8	15.8	8.0	100
1910	66.3	12.2	2.9	2.2	2.6	6.0	7.8	100
1920	65.1	14.8	3.3	3.4	3.3	3.9	6.2	100
1930	59.6	16.9	3.8	4.3	4.1	5.3	6.0	100
1940	51.5	21.0	4.6	5.1	6.1	5.3	6.4	100

Note: The significant change in the figures for the agricultural workforce and general workers is due to a change in the approach to statistical categorisation as of the year 1900.

educational institution was still uncommon. In several sectors of production the vocational education and training were initiated by organising the training for foremen. As a result, educational institutions became differentiated in that the training of management-level professionals was provided at vocational colleges and the training of workers at vocational schools (Klemelä, 1999). For example, schooling for seafaring started in 1813, and schooling for health care and midwifery in 1816 (Tiilikkala, 2011; Klemelä, 1999). The first business school was established in 1839 in Turku (Klemelä, 1999, p. 188). Also, the roots of technical education go back to the 1840s when so-called technical ´real schools´ were established. The first school of agriculture was established in 1840, and the first forestry college in 1861 (Laukia, 2013a; Tiilikkala, 2011; Klemelä, 1999, p. 189).

Furthermore, the first schools for crafts and industry were established by the Board of Manufacture on the basis of the 'Training of Craftsmen and Manufacturers Act' for the country passed in 1842, and the 'Technical Real Schools Act' (a base for engineering programmes) passed in 1847 (Heikkinen, 2004). In the capital, Helsinki, the first vocational school was established in 1899. During 1900–1916, several vocational schools were established also in the other coastal cities besides Helsinki, including population centres such as Pori, Porvoo, Kotka and Viipuri. The first inland vocational schools were established in 1912 and 1917 in Tampere and Kuopio. The vocational school system was influenced by higher technical education and craft schools, folk schools and Sunday schools. In addition, ideas for organising vocational education were sought from abroad, mainly from Germany (by reformistic pedagogical movements, especially the one developed by Georg Kerschensteiner), Austria, Switzerland and the Netherlands (Laukia, 2013a, 2013b). In different VET fields, schools developed different administration and control systems, and they received separate decrees of their own (Klemelä, 1999, p. 194).

In 1920, the lower preparatory vocational school system was abolished and the upper preparatory vocational school system was shaped into a 'general' vocational school system (Nurmi, 1983). The curriculum required of these general vocational schools included the syllabus of the folk school and continuation school systems and they offered both theoretical and practical subjects. In parallel, apprenticeship training and school-based VET started to clearly diverge after 1920, but vocational schools were not established to replace apprenticeship training (Koskela, 2003).

In Finland, between the First and Second World Wars, there were many workplaces where having a vocational education was not required. During 1920–1940, the majority of the folk school graduates did not continue their studies at any educational institutions (Laukia, 2013b, p. 106). On the other hand, there were also places of vocational education that provided advanced-level certificates for certain occupations. On the whole, the vocational education of that time varied greatly regarding extent, level and administration.

Parallel to establishing VET schools, discussions on organising continuation schools progressed. For example, Jalmari Kekkonen, the pioneer and inspector of VET in crafts and industry, suggested that attending a continuation school should serve as the preparation for apprenticeship school to thus replace the declining evening/part-time schools (Heikkinen, 1995). Many farmers also saw continuation school as an alternative to VET in rural communities because of the difficulties in providing full-time education after the initial compulsory grades and organising vocational schools for rural people. The proponents of VET for crafts and industry, on the contrary, defended the need for organising VET as an entity with purposes of its own against the general citizenship education ('School for Citizenship' in 1958) and academic education, and they emphasised VET's link to industry (Heikkinen, 2004). In urban municipalities, VET schools were favoured as a substitute for continuation schools until the 1940s.

The first proponents for organising VET came from the field of administration or were leaders from different industries. The issue of VET was not a separate project for them and was seen to be related to the development of the nation-building project (Heikkinen, 2004). Finnish societal development in the 1920s was particularly affected by the civil war and the societal reforms that followed it. The civil war that Finland went through from 1917 until 1918 represented a stark contrast to the more peaceful consolidation of group interests in other Nordic countries. After the civil war, reforms in land ownership enabled landless farmers to buy their own land and to become independent farmers. Also, new farms were established (Rainio-Niemi, 2004, p. 158; Kettunen, 1986, p. 106). As a result of the land reform, the amount of small-scale, independent farms increased considerably, that is, by around 100,000 farms (Kettunen, 1986, p. 106). Accordingly, the agricultural policy of independent Finland targeted raising a new class of autonomous, small-scale farmers. Eventually, the emergence of this class of small-scale farmers raised the socio-political question of their poor livelihood; they owned too little land and forestry to provide for their family's livelihood. The dissatisfaction with their livelihood led to the demand for other occupations and training, as well as to migration. The government wished to create better conditions for these farmers by providing educational opportunities for them. However, the students of the agricultural schools were mostly boys from large farms (Klemelä, 1999, p. 189).

After Finland's independence in 1917, the number of vocational schools and students increased gradually (see Table A2.1, Appendix), although towns were not very interested in establishing new vocational schools as these operated with limited financial support from the state (Laukia, 2013a). The first 'Vocational Institutions Act' (*Laki ammattioppilaitoksista*) was issued in 1939, but it came into effect only in 1942 because of the Second World War. In the 1940s, the curriculum of vocational schools included also general subjects, such as the mother tongue (Finnish language), arithmetic, physics and citizenship education. In those days, however, cooperation with industry and commerce was limited to visiting firms.

Due to both ideological reasons and the lack of vocational schools, Finnish employers started to express more interest in organising vocational training, but only from the early 20th century onward, when private industries like Wärtsilä,

Kymi and Yhtyneet Paperitehtaat started to set up schools of their own (Laukia, 2013b, p. 116; Kivinen and Peltomäki, 1999). In the Finnish industry of the 1920s, the production of pulp, newsprint and plywood as well as metal and textiles was increasing rapidly and there was acute demand for an educated labour force (Rainio-Niemi, 2004, pp. 154–155). These schools, so-called private industrial schools (*Yksityisteollisuuden ammattikoulut*, in Finnish) operated under the Department of Trade and Industry. Administratively, these private industrial schools operated like municipal schools and followed the Ministry's guidelines. The private industrial schools focused more on working life than did the regular vocational schools. Later on, many of these schools changed into institutes providing specialisation and further training (Laukia, 2013b, p. 116). The former education demanded from the students admitted to these schools changed due to changes in the education system and society, particularly in reaction to increasing urbanisation and industrialisation. During 1939–1959, students were recruited for industrial vocational schools on the basis of their folk school education, as was the case for public vocational schools (Laukia, 2013b, p. 249).

On a national level, the Institute for Occupational Advancement (*Ammattienedistämislaitos*, in Finnish) was founded as a result of the educational project of artisans and small-scale manufacturers in 1922 (Kettunen, 2013). The institute was owned by a private foundation but financially supported by the government. It started to arrange lectures on non-technical topics for foremen in the manufacturing industry (Kettunen, 2013). Despite the organisation, Finland's crafts remained marginal compared to the export (metal and wood-processing) industry, rural industries and rural agricultural production. At the end of the 1920s, on the administrative state level, the systematisation and centralisation of vocational education and training was planned for the first time (Klemelä, 1999). The Vocational Education Department was established to the Ministry of Trade and Industry in 1942. Prior to its establishment, the administration of VET was diffuse (Heikkinen, 1995, p. 351).

VET and social inclusion

In the early stages, discussions about organising post-compulsory education and the vocational education track alongside the general upper secondary education took place with concern over the increasing number of general upper secondary school graduates. During 1930–1935, their annual number was around 2,000–2,500. The State Council appointed a committee to restrict the flood of upper secondary school graduates (Laukia, 2013b, p. 161; Kiuasmaa, 1982, p. 227). According to this committee, the annual graduation rates were excessive. The problem stemmed from the fact that besides youths from the traditional Swedish-speaking intelligentsia, the general upper secondary schools also attracted students from the working class and farming families, and women's schooling increased as well. The emergence of a Finnish-speaking intelligentsia was seen as suspicious by some of the existing elites.

According to the committee's report, the provision of VET was to be increased so that working-class Finnish-speakers and youths from farming families could seek education and training for practical occupations (Laukia, 2013b, p. 162). The committee's recommendations thus supported the prevailing class and gender division. By increasing the number of places for VET, the places for the upper secondary education would be secured for the offspring of the intelligentsia (Laukia, 2013b, p. 162).

At the beginning of the 1900s, the number of vocational school students was quite modest in comparison to that of the secondary and general upper secondary school students (see Table 2.2). In 1910, there were 10,600 students in vocational schools and their number had increased to 20,400 students by 1940. Correspondingly, the enrolment figures for secondary schools were around 24,300 students in 1910, and circa 59,300 students in 1940 (Laukia, 2013b). While the number of VET students increased, the size of the youth cohort also increased. Therefore, the share of educated citizens did not increase in the same proportion as the overall number of students.

VET was expected to prevent poverty and protect the youth from marginalisation. Education policy, social policy and professional skill requirements were intertwined (Kaarninen, 1995, p. 69). In the period from 1900 to 1940, most VET students came from working-class families in towns where schools had been established to prevent social problems and marginalisation (Heikkilä, 2003). In smaller towns, students' background varied more. There were few vocational school students from farming families as these schools were located in towns or other larger population centres (Laukia, 2013b, p. 142). VET was also gender specific (Klemelä, 1999). Crafts education was aimed at boys. Separate preparatory schools were established, those for boys and those for girls. Originally, the most important VET field for women was home economics, since most women working outside their home were employed to work in the homes of more affluent families.

The decree issued in 1920 stated that vocational schools were meant both for boys and girls. In practice, vocational schools were established separately for boys and girls for different fields. Girls' and boys' vocational schools also differed in terms of their aims (Jauhiainen, 2002). The aim of girls' education was to prepare them to become housewives and servants. Boys were trained for employment outside their home and to become supporters of their families. The views about the different aims of VET for boys and girls were related to perceptions

Table 2.2 Vocational upper secondary education and secondary school students from 1910 to 1970 (Laukia, 2013b, p. 328, p. 334)

Year	VET students	Secondary school students
1910	10,639	24,354
1920	14,009	32,448
1930	18,013	49,589
1940	20,380	59,302

about women's role in the labour market in general. Women's work outside their home was questioned, but their learning practical tasks in connection with either home-based or paid work was accepted (Lähteenmäki, 1995). The gender issue was also seen in vocational teacher education. Vocational teacher education for so-called male branches was provided in Hämeenlinna, and correspondingly for so-called female branches in Jyväskylä (Laukia, 2013b, p. 214).

The demand for VET for the young did not arise from economic development only; people were also concerned about the youths' development, use of time and societal inclusion. At school, working-class youths could be controlled and raised for citizenship by teachers and under the Ministry's supervision (Kivirauma, 1992).

Emerging employer and employee organisations and their relations

Finnish employees started to organise themselves into employer and business organisations at the beginning of the 1900s. The primary reason employers began organising themselves as a group was their urge to build a counterforce to the emerging labour unions and to unite against workers' strikes (Nieminen, 2000). Another reason was that employers wanted to express their interests to the state with more weight. The aim of the organisations was to 'conduct studies and give a voice to opinions on the demands of the confederation and its members regarding legislative, administrative, technical and economic issues' (Nieminen, 2000; Mansner, 1981, p. 35).

The General Confederation of Employers in Finland (*Suomen Yleinen Työnantajaliitto,* in Finnish) started to operate in 1907, but the first national branch-level organisations had already been established during 1899–1900 by tailors, bakeries and the printing industry (Nieminen, 2000). At the beginning of the 1900s, the newly organised employer organisations took a cautiously positive attitude toward collective agreements at first, but after a dispute over the terms of the collective agreements as well as strikes and lockouts in the metal industries during 1908–1909, they started to fight against collective branch-level agreements (Nieminen, 2000).

In 1918, the employers reorganised the General Confederation of Employers in answer to the labour market's growing demands and renamed it to the Finnish Employers' Confederation (*Suomen Työnantajain Keskusliitto*, STK, in Finnish). Employers united their forces to keep the rising labour movement divided by fighting against collective agreements (Nieminen, 2000). Many employer organisations decided not to negotiate with trade unions, therefore collective agreements were rare until after the Second World War (Nieminen, 2000). For example, in the 1920s, the General Confederation of Employers forbade the employers' organisations or individual employers to negotiate with organised labour. The main aim was to keep the relationship between employers and employees firmly bilateral (Rainio-Niemi, 2004, p. 174). With respect to VET, this meant that there was neither any agreement nor negotiations between the interest groups concerning the development of vocational education nationally.

As the international labour movement started to emerge, interest in city workers' positions started to emerge in Finland in the 1880s, and a workers' association was established in Helsinki in 1883. Especially the cane manufacturer Viktor Julius von Wright wanted to improve the workers' circumstances and consolidate relations between employers and employees. He had acquainted himself with the 'social questions' and social democratic movement during his studies and visits abroad, such as in Germany (Pinomaa, 1931). The aim of the Wrightist workers' movement was to improve the workers' economic and cultural position, such as by developing the folk school system as a basis for further studies (Laukia, 2013b, p. 46). The craftsmen and professional workers of the towns joined the Wrightist associations. Although the movement aimed at improving relationships between employers and employees as well as to foster vocational education, no vocational education and training system based on the relationships between employers and employees arose (Heikkinen, 2011). At the beginning of the twentieth century, the political workers' movement replaced the Wrightist workers' movement (Laukia, 2013b, p. 46).

The Association of Finnish Trade Unions (*Suomen Ammattijärjestö*, SAJ, in Finnish), later called the Central Organisation of Finnish Trade Unions (SAK), was established in 1907. It aimed to promote union coverage, to accumulate information, to publish activities, to consult member organisations and to foster international cooperation (Rainio-Niemi, 2004, p. 129). The adopted principle of equality between political and corporate functional branches of the labour movement and the strategy for addressing the class struggle went hand in hand with the aims of the Social Democratic Party (Rainio-Niemi, 2004, p. 129).

At the beginning, the trade unions were not yet interested in vocational education, and as late as in 1930 they had no demands for vocational education (Heikkinen, 1995, p. 194). The workers resisted participation in apprenticeship training because of its low salary. Until the 1940s, it was characteristic that the workers were organised through political parties, and the trade union was built on its connections with these (Heikkinen, 1995, p. 194; Kettunen, 1986). Accordingly, the trade unions were not independent from the parties. The current position of the trade unions arose only in 1940, when the employers' union (STK) accepted the Central Organisation of Finnish Trade Unions (SAK) as the workers' representative and as a negotiation party.

The demand of the labour movement for power and equity in industrial relations was largely based on the living conditions of rural workers, crofters and landless people (Waris, 1932; Heikkinen, 2004). The industrial relations after Finland's independence and civil war (1917–1918) pushed the negotiations toward a corporatist regulation of work conditions. The state moderated consensual negotiations between employers and employees at the local and national level (Heikkinen, 2004). Still, collective bargaining was not particularly well-developed in Finnish industries in the 1920s and 1930s. Its effectiveness depended on the industrial field, showed seasonal variation, and was characterised by locality (Kettunen, 1986). A coordinated labour market system emerged in Finland only after the Second World War (Rainio-Niemi, 2004, p. 171).

In 1917, the Finnish Senate nominated the Vocational Training Council (Ammattikasvatusneuvosto) to assist the Board of Industry with issues concerning vocational education. The Council consisted of one representative of the Council (state administration), three teachers of VET, three representatives of employers and three representatives of employees (Laukia, 2013b, p. 93). The status of the Council was regularised in 1926, and in 1942 became part of the Ministry of Trade and Industry. The regulation defined the composition of the employers' representatives as follows: one member from large-scale industry, one member from small-scale industry and one member from agriculture. The composition of the employees' representatives was also regulated: three members should represent different occupations and fields of industry. The representation of employers, employees and teachers in the Council initiated a basis for multi-actor cooperation, negotiation and defining of educational goals as well as cooperation for VET in Finland. It enhanced the centralised approach and official bodies' role of organising VET, consolidating educational interests over party interests.

Formation of apprenticeship training as youngsters' minor route to the labour market

In Finland, apprenticeship training became considerably weaker when traditional guilds were abolished in 1868. Even when the traditional guilds ceased to exist, their duties were reorganised when the law by parliament ordered societies for merchants and handicrafts to be established in towns (Kettunen, 2001). These societies earned the right to acknowledge masters and journeymen (Heikkilä, 2003; Laine-Juva and Änkö, 1968; Somerkivi, 1950). Membership in these societies was an obligation to masters of occupations. The dominant crafts of the time included professions such as shoemaker, tailor, painter, carpenter, bricklayer, tanner, clockmaker and blacksmith (Heikkilä, 2003). These societies acted locally and did not become particularly strong due to the low level of agreement between competing members (Heikkilä, 2003). Their duty was to control the training of novices. During the rule of guilds, it had only been possible to gain a position as an acknowledged craftsman via an apprenticeship and further studies as a journeyman. The role of traditional occupations changed when industrial production of goods increased and replaced manufacturing step by step. While in the early 19th century apprenticeship had been seen as the road to the status of a skilled master for many rural children and a lawful way to earn a livelihood (Kivinen and Peltomäki, 1999), the situation changed further in 1879 due to the freedom of trade and freedom of occupation.

In towns, the low status of handicrafts and poor economic situation of landless citizens drove apprentices to become employees as unskilled factory workers, while the masters gradually became entrepreneurs and employers (Kivinen and Peltomäki, 1999; Särkikoski, 1993). Apprentices and journeymen were paid like other employees, and the apprenticeship tradition became part of the system of wage-paid employment but without the former opportunities to advance in a career to the skilled position of a master (Kivinen and Peltomäki, 1999). Small entrepreneurship remained in a relatively weak position in the sparsely populated countryside, and apprenticeship training seemed to wither. In Finland, the increased social effects of industrial wage work resulted in the promotion of vocational education, which was seen as a way to normalise wage work and regulate the lives of working life families in towns (Kettunen, 2013). The developing Sunday schools and crafts education replaced the educational duties of the former guild system in towns (Heikkilä, 2003).

At that time, employers' interests in developing VET were diverse and depended on the field of production. On the one hand, the factory owners had little interest in instructing apprentices. Since the skill requirements for many duties were low, a skilled labour force could be hired from abroad and investment in training was not considered profitable (Kivinen and Peltomäki, 1999). The Taylorist principles of management and dividing tasks into smaller entities which demanded less skills were seen as a way to support small-scale industries in competition (Kettunen, 2013; Heikkilä, 2003). Accordingly, it was considered possible to learn the necessary skills through experience at work in the factories, therefore theoretical knowledge was not needed. Some societies responsible for supervising training in towns considered specialist vocational schools better than traditional apprentice training (Heikkilä, 2003, p. 17). On one hand, the employer organisation (Finnish Employers' Confederation, EK) supported apprenticeship in addition to school-based VET (Laukia, 2013b, p. 222) as these emphasised the training of skilled workers. Yet, the employee organisations (Central Organisation of Finnish Trade Unions, SAK) were against this as they viewed apprenticeship as a narrow vocational qualification with limited future options and without general education subjects. Also, the trade union considered it a better solution to increase the number of vocational schools (Kivinen and Peltomäki, 1999). It suspected that apprenticeship training would provide employers with a cheap labour force (Kivirauma, 1992).

When the apprenticeship training did not recover through initiatives taken of increasing industrial life, the Finnish state tried to get municipalities and industrial enterprises to take responsibility for training (Heikkinen, 2000). Accordingly, the Apprenticeship Act was issued in 1923.

Apprenticeship training was meant to prepare for acquiring a craft or industrial occupation that required at least two years of learning. Apprentices were 15–18-year-olds. In the 1920s, the number of apprenticeships was increasing, but in the 1930s the popularity of this option decreased due to economic recession and the attraction of vocational schools (Laukia, 2013b, p. 105). The employers were not enthusiastic about the law issued on apprenticeships in 1923 as it meant more regulation, and subsequently it was soon declared a failure (Kivinen and Peltomäki, 1999; Helvelahti, 1949). Employers also wanted to have compensation for the education they provided. The government paid employers a small sum for taking on a poor apprentice, but they were not satisfied with the compensation for training apprentices at the workplace (Kivinen and Peltomäki, 1999). In general, they refused to negotiate with organised workers (Rainio-Niemi, 2004). Apprentices' wages were considered to be too high and the wages of qualified workers did not differ very much from those of unskilled workers. Altogether, the reasons for employers' dissatisfaction with the new Apprenticeship Act were numerous. It was seen to create too many obligations for employers; it was difficult to terminate apprenticeship relations; the young apprentices were unwilling to commit themselves to long-term apprenticeship relations; there was no motivation to teach apprentices; authorities did not supervise apprenticeships; and arranging the theoretical instruction as part of an apprenticeship was problematic. These difficulties remained quite the same until the 1990s (Kivinen and Peltomäki, 1999). The gradual development of the legislation for apprenticeship training before the Second World War is presented in Table 2.3.

The apprenticeship system declined in Finland for several reasons. First, the traditional guild system was abolished in 1868 and the societies that were to supposed take their position in supervising apprenticeship training did not succeed in forming a new, acknowledged and appreciated system. In parallel, industrialisation changed the forms of production, and the freedom of occupation gained in 1879 increased citizens' opportunities for choosing their career. Also in parallel, vocational schools, preparatory schools and special vocational schools, including schools founded by industrial enterprises themselves, began to attract students (Heikkilä, 2003; Kivinen and Peltomäki, 1999). In addition, several consecutive parliaments made decisions that promoted equal educational opportunities and the institutionalisation and centralisation of schooling in the public sector. Furthermore, the Federation of Finnish Employers was in favour of school-based VET. The systematisation and centralisation of vocational education and training was planned for the first time at the end of the 1920s (Klemelä, 1999). The administration of vocational education and training

Table 2.3 Apprenticeship in Finland from the 17th century to the 1920s (adopted from Kivinen and Peltomäki, 1999, p. 81)

Period	Legislation	Description
Early industrialisation, 18th to late 19th century	Ordinance on halls (1739)	• increasing competition • increasing number of apprenticeships • division of labour
First industrial age, late 19th and early 20th century	Freedom of trade (1879) Lower-level trade schools (1885)	• apprentices become wage earners • handicrafts become small-scale industries • general education
Issue of vocational education	Apprenticeship Act (1923)	• general vocational schools (1920) • fostering craft and industry occupations

was dispersed under several ministries and central administrative boards until the 1960s.

Conclusion

The years 1850–1945 can be seen as a period of building the basis for the Finnish nation-state society and VET system. During this period, Finland emerged from being an autonomous Grand Duchy of the Russian Empire to become an independent state as of 1917. The Fennoman nationalist movement had started to promote a shared understanding of the formation of the Finnish nation already in the 1820s (Heikkinen, 2001). The rise of nationalistic ideas meant making the development of education a priority in the society as education was seen to play a central role in uniting the nation (Klemelä, 1999).

The first institutions of vocational and professional education and training were created at the beginning of the 19th century. In the first place, training was initiated to promote the adoption of new technologies, industries and knowledge, and to educate supervisors. Employers' interest lay in keeping the control of supervisory qualifications in their own hands (Kettunen, 2013). Vocational education started to develop more effectively after Finland's independence in 1917, when the number of vocational schools and students gradually increased. In the 1920s and 1930s, the large-scale industry and its employers were the main drivers of the employers establishing their own vocational schools. The lack of employer coordination and worker orientation toward state-led vocational schools influenced employers to invest mainly in their own vocational schools, also due to patriotic nationalism, while the trade unions had no organised demands for vocational education in the 1930s (Heikkinen, 1995, p. 194).

In addition, towns (municipalities) were key drivers of organising VET, even though their interest in establishing new vocational schools was limited due to the lack of financial support even with normative incentives from the state. In parallel, municipalities also had to take charge of organising continuation classes in folk school, and subsequently the municipalities were not eager to uphold two parallel systems (continuation folk school classes and VET) (Laukia, 2013b, p. 290). The first 'Vocational Institutions Act' was launched in 1939, but came into effect only in 1942 because of the Second World War. The Act confirmed the position of vocational schools and the position of the state as the main drivers of VET (Laukia, 2013b, p. 291)

An Apprenticeship Act was passed, aiming at extending the apprenticeship system to the existing industry already in 1923, but it was later declared a failure (Kivinen and Peltomäki, 1999). The number of apprentices increased in the 1920s, but decreased again in the 1930s because of the economic repression and the emerging attractiveness of vocational schools.

The period of Finnish VET from the 1840s to the 1940s featured a trend of increasing school-based education and decreasing apprenticeship training, although the development of a school-based form of VET into the dominant model of initial vocational education and training only began after the Second World War. Several traits of the societal development contributed to the enhancement of school-based education and the decline of the apprenticeship system, as follows.

First, the introduction of a school-based vocational education was connected with the rising nation state and increasing state control over organising education and society more generally. The central role of the state and the municipalities had been emphasised in the planning of the Finnish VET since the late 19th century (Kettunen, 2001).

Second, school was a seemingly neutral forum for social mobility, which served the interests of the Fennoman movement that promoted the concept of Finland as an autonomous nation during the time when Finland was still a Grand Duchy under Russian rule. The Finnish nationalist movement and its interest in establishing and unifying Finnish-speaking people as one nation gained momentum through the establishment of the Finnish folk education system. The building of the school-based VET system was accelerated by the relatively late but rapid industrialisation and its demands to adjust to the technological changes of the times. The shift from an agricultural toward an industrialised society started to take place and created new groups of industrial workers in towns (Waris, 1932).

Third, school was a relatively autonomous area for learning and discipline, reconciling class interests that had clashed in the Civil War in 1918. Instructional aims and teaching arrangements could be defined independently at the school level.

Fourth, schools were differentiated as various types – folk school (elementary), continuation school, vocational school, apprenticeship training – that emphasised their particular function and special character (Heikkinen, 1995, p. 390).

Relating to different occupational fields, schools further developed specific administration and control systems, and also received separate decrees of their own (Klemelä, 1999, p. 194). Diversifying and growing industries replaced agriculture and estate-based production as the dominant forms of production, and the demand for skills in specialised occupational fields changed rapidly. This intensified the juxtaposition of general versus vocational education as the main forms of post-compulsory education. This juxtaposition of general upper secondary education and vocational upper secondary education later increasingly became the topic of policy discussions. Demands to reorganise their relation in order to provide equal opportunities along either path later inspired several reforms and pilots, such as the compulsory school reform, upper secondary reform and youth education pilot projects.

References

Gluschkoff, J. (2008) *Murtuva säätyvalta, kestävä eliitti: Senaattori Lennart Gripenbergin sukupiiri ja sääty-yhteiskunnan muodonmuutos*, Helsinki, Suomalaisen Kirjallisuuden Seura.

Halila, A. (1963) *Jyväskylän seminaarin historia*, Porvoo, WSOY.

Heikkilä, D. (2003) 'Käsityön ammatillinen opetus Suomessa 1700-luvulta nykypäiviin', in Anttila, P., Heikkilä, D. and Ylönen, I. (eds.) *Suomalaisen käsityökoulutuksen vaiheita 1700-luvulta 2000-luvulle, Jyväskylä, Suomen käsityön museon julkaisuja 22*, pp. 7–48 [Online]. Available at www.craftmuseum.fi/kassaatko/julkaisut.htm (Accessed 27 September 2017).

Heikkinen, A. (1995) *Lähtökohtia ammattikasvatuksen kulttuuriseen tarkasteluun: Esimerkkinä suomalaisen ammattikasvatuksen muotoutuminen käsityön ja teollisuuden alalla 1840–1940*, PhD thesis, Tampere, University of Tampere.

Heikkinen, A. (2000) 'Suomalaisen ammattikasvatuksen alkuvaiheita', in Rajaniemi, A. (ed.) *Suomalaisen ammattikasvatuksen historia*, Helsinki, Opetus-, kasvatus- ja koulutusalojen säätiö, pp. 10–25.

Heikkinen, A. (2001) 'The transforming peripheries of vocational education: Reflections from the case of Finland', *Journal of Education and Work*, vol. 14, no. 2, pp. 227–250.

Heikkinen, A. (2004) 'Models, paradigms or cultures of vocational education', *European Journal of Vocational Training*, no. 32, pp. 32–44.

Heikkinen, A. (2011) 'Elatus, oppi, ja kumppanuus', in Heikkinen, A. and Leino-Kaukiainen, P. (eds.) *Valistus ja koulunpenkki: Kasvatus ja koulutus Suomessa 1860-luvulta 1960-luvulle*, Helsinki, Suomalaisen Kirjallisuuden Seura, pp. 37–73.

Helvelahti, H. J. (1949) 'Oppisopimuslaki ja sen uudistaminen', *Käsityö ja Teollisuus*, vol. 45, no. 2, pp. 26–27.

Hirvonen, P. (2002) 'Saarnatuolista sisäpiiriin: Alfred Kihlman ja liikemiesverkostojen muotoutuminen 1850–1860-luvun Suomessa', *Historiallinen aikakauskirja*, vol. 100, no. 4, pp. 364–374.

Jalava, M. (2011) 'Kansanopetuksen suuri murros ja 1860-luvun väittely kansakoulusta', in Heikkinen, A. and Leino-Kaukiainen, P. (eds.) *Valistus ja koulunpenkki*, Helsinki, Suomen Kirjallisuuden Seura, pp. 74–94.

Jauhiainen, A. (2002) *Työväen lasten koulutie ja nuorisokasvatuksen yhteiskunnalliset merkitykset: Kansakoulun jatko-opetuskysymys 1800-luvun lopulta 1970-luvulle*, PhD thesis, Turku, University of Turku.

Kaarninen, M. (1995) *Nykyajan tytöt: Koulutus, luokka ja sukupuoli 1920- ja 1930-luvun Suomessa*, Helsinki, Suomen Historiallinen Seura.

Kailanpää, A. (1962) *Kansalaiskoulu*, Porvoo, WSOY.

Kettunen, P. (1986) *Poliittinen liike ja sosiaalinen kollektiivisuus: Tutkimus sosialidemokratiasta ja ammattiyhdistysliikkeestä Suomessa 1918–1930*, PhD thesis, Helsinki, Suomen Historiallinen Seura.

Kettunen, P. (2001) 'Millaisiin kysymyksiin ammatillisella koulutuksella on vastattu?', in Anttila, A.-H. and Suoranta, A. (eds.) *Ammattia oppimassa*, Tampere, Työväen historian ja perinteen tutkimuksen seura, pp. 52–91.

Kettunen, P. (2013) 'Vocational education and the tensions of modernity in a Nordic periphery', in Buchardt, M., Markkola, P. and Valtonen, H. (eds.) *Education, State and Citizenship*, Helsinki, Nordic Centre of Excellence NordWel, pp. 31–55.

Kiuasmaa, K. (1982) *Oppikoulu 1880–1980: Oppikoulu ja sen opettajat koulujärjestyksestä peruskouluun*, Oulu, Pohjoinen.

Kivinen, O. and Peltomäki, M. (1999) 'On the job or in the classroom? The apprenticeship in Finland from the 17th century to the 1990s', *Journal of Education and Work*, vol. 12, no. 1, pp. 75–93.

Kivirauma, J. (1992) *Työvoimatarpeesta koko ikäluokan kouluttamiseen: Ammatillisen koulutuksen suunnitteluperiaatteiden tarkastelua 1900-luvun alusta 1980-luvulle*, Publication Series A: Research 160. Turku, University of Turku.

Klemelä, K. (1999) *Ammattikunnista ammatillisiin oppilaitoksiin: Ammatillisen koulutuksen muotoutuminen Suomessa 1800-luvun alusta 1990-luvulle*, PhD thesis, Turku, University of Turku.

Koskela, H. (2003) *Opiskelijoiden haasteellisuudesta ammattiopintoihin sitoutumisen substanssiteoriaan: Grounded theory -menetelmän soveltaminen ammattioppilaitoksen opettajien kuvauksiin opetettavistaan*, PhD thesis, Joensuu, University of Joensuu.

Kyöstiö, O. K. (1955) *Suomen ammattikasvatuksen kehitys käsityön ja teollisuuden aloilla: 1, Ammattikasvatuksen esivaihe vuoteen 1842: Die Vorstufe der Berufserziehung bis 1842*, PhD thesis, Jyväskylä, Jyväskylän kasvatusopillinen korkeakoulu.

Lähteenmäki, M. (1995) *Mahdollisuuksien aika: Työläisnaiset ja yhteiskunnan muutos 1910–30-luvun Suomessa*, PhD thesis, Helsinki, Suomen Historiallinen Seura.

Laine-Juva, Y. and Änkö, M. (1968) *Käsityön ja pienteollisuuden parissa: Helsingin Käsityö- ja Teollisuusyhdistys 1868–1968*, Helsinki, Helsingin Käsityö- ja Teollisuusyhdistys.

Laukia, J. (2013a) 'Education of skilled workers and citizens: Vocational education in Finland', in Aaltonen, K., Isacsson, A., Laukia, J. and Vanhanen-Nuutinen, L. (eds.) *Practical Skills, Education and Development: Vocational Education and Training in Finland*, Helsinki, Haaga-Helia University of Applied Sciences, pp. 9–19.

Laukia, J. (2013b) *Tavoitteena sivistynyt kansalainen ja työntekijä: Ammattikoulu Suomessa 1899–1987*, PhD thesis, Helsinki, University of Helsinki.

Lehtisalo, L. and Raivola, R. (1999) *Koulutus ja koulutuspolitiikka 2000-luvulle*, Porvoo, WSOY.

Leino-Kaukiainen, P. and Heikkinen, A. (2011) 'Yhteiskunta ja koulutus', in Heikkinen, A. and Leino-Kaukiainen, P. (eds.) *Valistus ja koulunpenkki: Kasvatus ja koulutus Suomessa 1860-luvulta 1960-luvulle*, Helsinki, Suomalaisen Kirjallisuuden Seura, pp. 16–36.

Manninen, J. (2003) 'Valoa valtion yössä: Modernin valtion oppi Suomessa 1830–1831', *Historiallinen Aikakauskirja*, vol. 101, no. 2, pp. 228–247.

Mansner, M. (1981) *Suomalaista yhteiskuntaa rakentamassa: Suomen Työnantajain Keskusliitto 1907–1940*, Helsinki, Teollisuuden kustannus.

Nieminen A. (2000) 'Finnish employer confederations: Streamlining inner organization and regulating national capitalism', in Jensen, C. S. (ed.) *Arbejdsgivere i Norden: En sociologisk analyse af arbejdsgiverorganisering i Norge, Sverige, Finland og Danmark*, København, Nordisk Ministerråd, pp. 287–371.

Nurmi, V. (1983) *Kasvatuksen traditio*, Porvoo, WSOY.

Olofsson, J. and Persson Thunqvist, D. (2018) 'Sweden: The formative period for VET (1850–1945)', in Michelsen, S. and Stenström, M.-L. (eds.) *Vocational Education in the Nordic Countries: The Historical Evolution*, 1st ed., London, Routledge, pp. 46–65.

Paloheimo, M. and Uotila, M. (2015) 'Elinkeinoluvat ja talouselämän monipuolistuminen 1800-luvun alun Suomessa', *Ennen ja nyt: Historian tietosanomat*, no. 3 [Online]. Available at http://www.ennenjanyt.net/2015/09/elinkeinoluvat-ja-talouselaman-monipuolistuminen-1800-luvun-alun-suomessa/ (Accessed 28 September 2017).

Pinomaa, V. (1931) *Viktor Julius von Wright: Käsityöläisveteraanin muistelmia*, Helsinki, K. F. Puromiehen kirjapaino.

Puranen, J. (2011) *Eripuraa kansakouluista: Kansakouluriidat Kuopion kihlakunnassa 1876–1904*, Pro Gradu thesis, Joensuu, University of Eastern Finland.

Rainio-Niemi, J. (2004) 'Paths in the Austrian and Finnish history: Finland', in Konrad, H., Pletersek, M., Rainio-Niemi, J., Stenius, H. and Strutz, A. (eds.) *Smallcons Project: A Framework for Socio-Economic Development in Europe? The Consensual Political Cultures of the Small West European States in Comparative and Historical Perspective* [Online]. Available at https://static.uni-graz.at/fileadmin/_Persoenliche_Webseite/strutz_andrea/Results_WP10.pdf (Accessed 27 September 2017).

Rinne, R. (2013) 'Koulutuksen muotoutuminen ja sen selitykset', in Antikainen, A., Rinne, R. and Koski, L. (eds.) *Kasvatussosiologia*, 5th rev. ed., Jyväskylä, PS-kustannus, pp. 49–99.

Sakslind, R. (1998) *Danning og yrkesutdanning: Utdanningssystem of nasjonale moderniseringsprosjekter*, Oslo, Norges forskningsråd, no. 103.

Särkikoski, T. (1993) 'Teorian ja käytännön välissä: Tekniikan professionaalistuminen Suomessa', in Konttinen, E. (ed.) *Ammattikunnat, yhteiskunta ja valtio: Suomalaisten professioiden kehityskuvia*, Jyväskylä, University of Jyväskylä, 55, pp. 78–105.

Somerkivi, U. (1950) *Sunnuntaikoulujen perustamisesta, Erip.: Suomen kouluhistoriallisen seuran vuosikirja Koulu ja menneisyys VIII*, Turku, Suomen Kouluhistoriallinen Seura.

Tiilikkala, L. (2011) 'Ammatillinen opettajuus ja opettajankoulutus', in Heikkinen, A. and Leino-Kaukiainen, P. (eds.) *Valistus ja koulunpenkki: Kasvatus ja koulutus Suomessa 1860-luvulta 1960-luvulle*, Helsinki, Suomalaisen Kirjallisuuden Seura, pp. 312–324.

Tuomisto, J. (1986) *Teollisuuden koulutustehtävien kehittyminen: Tutkimus teollisuustyönantajien koulutustoiminnan ja kvalifikaatiointressien historiallisesta kehityksestä Suomessa*, PhD thesis, Tampere, University of Tampere.

Waris, H. (1932) *Työläisyhteiskunnan syntyminen Helsingin Pitkänsillan pohjoispuolelle*, Helsinki, Into (this edition 2016).

Appendix

Table A2.1 Students in vocational education in the first year of each decade from 1820 to 1940 (adopted from Klemelä, 1999, p. 420)

	1820	1830	1840	1850	1860	1870	1880	1890	1900	1910	1920	1930	1940
Seafaring institutions	11	48	110	128	127	173	209	156	245	218	107	255	353
Business colleges			38	7	24	47	67	443	754	1,975	3,160	3,199	3,352
Agricultural schools								539	1,053	1,783	1,910	3,997	3,130
Forestry schools									14	157	167	172	315
Institutes of technology								223	449	552	503	1,574	2,068
Vocational schools								1,650	2,605	2,993	3,438	4,657	5,893
Handicraft schools									3,173	2,065	3,502	1,934	2,540
Domestic services									35	843	1,183	2,062	2,519
Nursing and health education									64	53	39	163	525
Total	11	48	148	135	151	220	276	3,011	8,392	10,639	14,009	18,013	20,695

The number of students in agricultural schools includes students in gardening institutions.
The number of students in institutes of technology in 1900 does not include students of the Pori industrial school.
The number of students in domestic education in 1900 does not include the number of students in specific housewife education institutions.
Differing from other fields of education, the number of students in nursing education refers to the number of graduates from 1910 to 1940, according to Statistics Finland.
The names of handicraft education institutions also changed throughout 1980 and 1990.

3 Sweden

The formative period for VET (1850–1945)

Jonas Olofsson and Daniel Persson Thunqvist

Introduction

Is there any such thing as a Swedish model of vocational education? The answer is 'yes' there probably is. Development of the Swedish model of vocational education during the past 100 years has entailed a less prominent role for apprenticeship as compared to school-based education. In Sweden, the involvement and operative responsibility of trade and industry in relation to education came to be less evident than in countries with strong apprenticeship systems (Nilsson, 2013; Olofsson, 2005).

This chapter examines the period for vocational and training (VET) in Sweden that stretches from the dissolution of the guilds by the passing of the Free Trade Act in 1864 until 1945. We will analyse structural conditions, political stakeholders and ideas behind the development of VET. First, VET is contextualised in relation to broader political and social developments in the education system. Based on Swedish education history studies, various lines of development are identified that have been driven by different competing societal motives and challenges for VET. The overview reveals a shift in educational debates over time from articulating predominantly social-political motives to societal motives emphasising VET as a vital factor for social development and economic growth.

Second, the dissolution of the old classical apprenticeship system is analysed against the backdrop of economic change and fast industrialisation during the last decades of the 19th century and the beginning of 20th century. The breakthrough of modern industry in Sweden led to a strong demand for a different and school-based vocational education. The constitution of practical vocational schools in 1918 can be interpreted as the foundation of the distinguished Swedish school-based VET system. The shift from an apprenticeship system to a school-based model of VET was not a straightforward process, however. The third section focus on the reforms during the interwar period, demonstrating how different forms of VET, balancing on the border between the logic of school and the logic of work, unfolded in a tension-laden interplay between different stakeholders.

The Swedish VET system was further developed through the main agreement by the two head organisations at labour market in 1938. The trade union organisation and employer organisation agreed that school-based and publicly organised vocational education should be strengthened and that the apprenticeships should function as a complement, not as a main road for vocational learning. Finally, the implications of the historical analysis are further discussed in terms of the institutional conditions and dynamics for an expansion of VET and apprenticeship based on voluntary agreements between the labour market partners.

The position of VET in the education system until mid 1900

The following section distinguishes some lines of development of compulsory education in Sweden that are important for understanding the position and significance of vocational education and training in the broad societal discussion during the first half of the 1800s until the 1940s.

A school for citizens

The French Revolution and new liberal ideas in the wake of the Age of Enlightenment initially influenced the discussion about a national education for citizens in Sweden during the first decades of the 1800s. This was especially apparent after the political revolution in 1809, the dissolution of absolute monarchy, and the reform initiatives launched in a number of areas. New thoughts were expressed, regarding a utilitarian school for citizens that would encompass all children across the traditional class boundaries, and were discussed in Parliament (Richardson, 1990).

But it was not until 1842 that Parliament ruled on the establishment of elementary school (folkskolan). However, the actual design of elementary school took on a different character than what many of those who had originally taken the initiative had intended. To a great degree, elementary school came to be a tool through which adaptation and subservience to an established, distinctly hierarchical social order were driven into citizens' consciousness. The importance of the provision of practically useful knowledge and skills was subordinate to drilling students in the catechism. Elementary school thus came to serve as an important instrument for strengthening the position of the state Lutheran Church in the face of threatening dissolution tendencies. It is also important to note that elementary school was not an obligatory school for citizens; in practice, we then had a parallel school system. Elementary school came to be a school for poor people, while the wealthy educated their children privately or sent them to grammar school, thus carefully avoiding all contact with elementary school.

Basic school

The most central issue in education policy from the latter half of the 1800s until the mid-1900s, and the decision on the so-called comprehensive school in 1950, involved the principle of a common basic school for all children (bottenskola) (Isling, 1973). At its core, the issue entailed the position and status of elementary school in relation to other education and school forms. Above all, it entailed the relationship between elementary school and grammar school. As time went on, a number of education forms with a more or less clear connection to elementary school were also developed. The supply of education at the end of the 1800s and the beginning of the 1900s can be compared to a buffet: along with girls' schools and junior secondary schools (from 1905), it eventually came to include e.g. business schools (from 1913), technical upper secondary schools and training schools, municipal vocational schools, and continuation schools after 1918 (Marklund, 1980). This increased educational supply can be interpreted as an expression of the growing needs for both more advanced and differentiated education. At the same time, it was precisely the situation that elementary school was not a self-evident merit for continued studies at grammar school that brought about the establishment of education forms that could serve as a bridge between education at a lower and a higher level.

Gradually, however, there was an intensification of attempts to link elementary school and grammar school in accordance with the basic school ideal. A number of liberal and social democratic governments appointed committees to examine the possibilities to establish a basic school. In 1894, it was determined that the first three grades in the then six-year elementary school could serve to qualify a student for entry into grammar school. This entailed that the first three elementary school years were now obligatory, since one could complete a corresponding education as a private person.

Then, in the 1918 School Commission appointed by Minister of Education and Religion and leading social democratic education politician Värner Rydén, the issue of an obligatory basic school and a uniform educational system was given a central position. The Commission's report (presented in 1922) suggested a type of comprehensive school system. All children would attend elementary school for six years. All public financial support for alternative schools on the elementary level would be phased out. All higher education would be based on the sixth year of elementary school. However, the Commission's suggestions were not heeded. After a long political mangling, in 1927 Parliament decided on a so-called double affiliation between elementary and grammar school. This entailed that it was possible to leave elementary school for junior secondary studies already after the fourth grade. In practice, the idea of a common basic school for all children was not fulfiled until after the final decision on the establishment of the comprehensive elementary school in 1962.

A civic curriculum code

An essential question, then, is what the driving force was behind the liberal and social democratic politicians' arguments for an obligatory basic school at the end of the 1800s and the first decades of the 1900s. The perspective on this has shifted among education historians (Boli, 1990). The fundamental aspect was intentions of socialisation and ideas of a civic integration. Englund (1981) speaks of a specific civic curriculum code that was chiselled out in debates and commissions – perhaps the most clearly within the framework of the 1918 School Commission – at the beginning of the previous century, and that came to characterise much of the thought and reform work in school policy for a long time. This code comprised a number of ingredients. One was the liberal concept of all people's equality. Through greater equality in the area of education, social mobility – or as it was called at the time, 'class circulation' – could be facilitated. In turn, this was important for all individuals to be able to come into their own, without social or economic barriers keeping them from developing their full potential. By extension, this was also motivated from a national economic perspective: it would enable a more effective use of resources and a more effective division of labour. Furthermore, the code would lead to a stronger feeling of belonging, reduce social conflicts, and result in a more friction-free national identity. The ambitions to develop the idea of basic school in the form of a comprehensive school common to everyone was thus guided by, according to Englund, a striving for stronger social belonging, fewer class conflicts, and increased social mobility. The ultimate effect was that a more civic-oriented education, an education for one's future adult life was advocated without necessarily accepting a more direct link to working life; on the contrary, the risks involved with such a link at an all too early stage were stressed.

An important motive behind the successive extension of the school system (Katz, 1995) concerns the importance of education in 'improving' the individual in various ways, especially those from a poor background. More education would stimulate qualities like virtue and responsibility, as well as discourage an immoral lifestyle, waste, abuse, and the dissolution of families. Social wrongs would be alleviated through diligence.

The limited importance of vocational education

In discussions on the school reforms of the first decades of the 1900s, issues involving vocational education played a limited role. The perspective on vocational education was mainly socio-political as a means to leading working-class youths onto constructive paths, and to working against social and political instability. A more advanced vocational education had indeed been established through the business schools and technical upper secondary schools discussed earlier, but these were programmes for a highly limited group. The need for regulation of the basic vocational education was voiced in various arenas, among other things in connection with the discussions on reform during and just after the First World War. Meanwhile, the municipal apprenticeship and vocational schools, established in 1918 and supplemented with municipal training schools in 1921, had a highly limited reach. The municipal vocational schools mainly offered education on a part-time basis for those who were already employed. Full-time courses were relatively short, and seldom lasted more than five months. As late as the 1940s, a total of only around 10,000 students a year took part in the programmes offered by the vocational schools. The traditional education, offered by companies themselves in apprentice-like forms, had also been substantially weakened, which became even more obvious after the economic crisis and high unemployment of the 1930s. A special commission – the first of its kind – was appointed at the beginning of the 1930s. Now more vocational education was recommended, not least for unemployed youths (SOU, 1934:11). Among other things, the commission recommended that youths aged 16–20 receive a vocational education within industry with a state-financed salary. While the recommendation of state-financed apprenticeships was defeated due to opposition from the labour market organisations, the commission did result in a temporary effort to offer vocational education for unemployed youths in the schools.

The parties took the initiative to promote a voluntary, collective labour agreement-regulated apprenticeship programme, which resulted in the establishment of a labour market trade council (*Arbetsmarknadens yrkesråd*) in 1944. The council served as a consultation authority for questions involving vocational education between the main actors on the labour market. As will be discussed later, however, the parties contributed to blocking all initiatives for legislation of apprenticeship, which could have led to its assuming the organisation of a dual education system, like that in Denmark and Germany, in which vocational education is to a great degree the responsibility of companies and labour organisations. Instead, however, Sweden ended up with a mainly school-based vocational education. The general subordinate position of VET up to the 1940s can be illustrated in the fact that the concept of vocational schools was largely absent from all school policy discussions until the 1940s (Marklund, 1980).

The apprenticeship system in the late pre-industrial period

This section discusses the development of the classical apprenticeship system in Sweden during the structural shift to a 'modern' industrialised society, with altered conflict patterns on the labour market. Until 1847, there was a law that regulated education of apprentices and journeymen, and determined the status of mastery (Edgren, 1987). The conditions for craftsmanship in the cities were determined by the general guild order of 1720. Market conditions were strictly regulated, and the social power and status order was anchored in judicial legal framework. It was not until the ordinance on expanded free trade in 1864 (SFS, 1864:41) that the regulation of the apprenticeship system through legislation ceased. There was no longer a requirement of mastery for craftsmen and those running factories. Craftsmanship societies were now voluntary, and served no public or legal function. Issues of the education of apprentices and journeymen were left completely out of legislation.

The free trade reforms from the mid-1800s and the regress of the older craftsmanship also entailed that education in this area lost ground. The structure of the labour market changed radically during the time after the 1890s

(Schön, 2010). A number of larger export companies had begun competing through their production with those in other countries (Lindell, 1992). A powerful growth began within a number of industry branches, above all the paper and pulp industry, ore export and the growth industry, strongly focussed on the export market. As opposed to Denmark, where the apprenticeship system was strongly linked to smaller and medium-sized businesses and craftsmanship, to a certain degree the growing Swedish 'big industry' overshadowed small businesses, which partly created different conditions for the existing apprenticeship system in Sweden (Busemeyer, 2015).

The changes in working life entailed demands for changes to the existing educational system, as well as increased cooperation between the business world and the state, the latter of which was expected to play a more active and supportive role. When the need for basic vocational education began to be voiced again at the end of the 1800s and the early years of the 1900s, it was the needs of industry that lay behind the decision to establish special vocational schools. However, just like in the past, vocational education still had social political motives. Socially rootless workers in the cities should be trained to be industrious, morally virtuous citizens who could contribute to society. Immoral living should be discouraged and morality encouraged. The increased interest in a lower technical education resulted among other things in the establishment of Sunday schools and evening schools, often by private actors, to which the state in the 1880s began issuing a limited amount of money in order to partially finance them. If one can speak of a political breakthrough for publicly organised vocational education, this came with the 1918 parliamentary decision on practical schools for youths (Olofsson, 2005; Nilsson, 1981).

The interwar period: an unregulated model of vocational education

The 1918 Practical Youth School reform can be seen as a turning point as the state took a stronger interest in initial VET both as a means to govern societal growth and social control. The reform introduced Apprenticeship school and Vocational school, and, in 1921, the Workshop school. The first modern laws on vocational education and training were passed in 1918 and 1921 (SFS, 1918:771; SFS, 1918:1002; SFS, 1921:705–707; Prop., 1921:1). On those occasions, the government appropriated state subsidies for municipalities that established so-called vocational youth schools. These were apprenticeship and vocational schools focussing on industry, handcrafts, commerce and domestic work as well as workshop schools concentrated more specifically on handcraft and industry. The apprenticeship schools were meant to offer elementary theoretical training related to various occupations, whereas the vocational schools were to provide a more advanced supplementary education. The prerequisite for admittance was, in both cases, that the student be employed. The training was to take place during the students' spare time, on evenings and Sundays, and was considered complementary to the actual workplace-based training.

The workshop schools which were introduced a couple of years after the apprentice and vocational schools, added something very important. First, employment was not a prerequisite for admission to the programmes – being 13 years of age and having completed elementary school sufficed. Second, the workshop schools were to offer a full-time education. These prerequisites were of great principal importance. They resulted in a form of vocational training that was completely separate from gainful employment and apprenticeship and that was given in a separate environment not connected to a workplace. Vocational education was, thus, transformed from a spare-time into a full-time occupation.

It is of some interest to note the justification for the workshop school reform. Behind the proposition, which had been drafted by the Swedish National Board of Education, loomed a distrust of the efficiency and developmental potential of apprenticeship. It was emphasised that apprentices were often taken advantage of as cheap labour, and that qualified supervision was often lacking (Prop., 1921:1). It was also stressed that the existence of public or municipal responsibility for the schools could be interpreted as a guarantee for a qualitatively satisfactory education. It was pointed out, among other things, that training within individual firms could "invite greater utilization of apprentices' labour than could be considered compatible with the educational mission" (our translation).

Afterwards, we can infer that the indirect criticism of the apprenticeship and vocational school reforms reflected in the workshop school decision can likely be explained by the deteriorated situation on the labour market. The end of the First World War was followed by a severe crisis involving a tremendous increase in youth unemployment. Vocational education appeared to be an important means of counteracting unemployment. At the same time, the crisis revealed a fundamental weakness of apprenticeship as the training places decreased in connection with trade recessions.

How, then, did the above-mentioned reforms affect the possible future development of vocational training in general and apprenticeship in particular? It should be pointed out, as mentioned before, that the numbers of students in these types of schools were very small. Thus, their practical and economic importance should not be exaggerated. Nonetheless, the reforms were important in principle. Intense political discussions about vocational education followed during the 1920s and 1930s, i.e. two decades struck by massive unemployment (Olofsson, 2005; Schröder, 1991). The employer and labour organisations also became more and more engaged in these discussions. In particular, the following four elements of the legislation on vocational youth schools and workshops schools passed in 1918 and 1921 turned out to be of long-term importance:

- The question of compulsory attendance at schools for apprentices and unemployed youth was avoided. On the other hand, compulsory school attendance came to be an important instrument for developing apprenticeship training in a number of countries where such training has a strong position today.

- With few exceptions, only school-based vocational education – particularly under public, but also under private management – could be offered government subsidies. The exceptions concerned very limited grants to master craftsmen who accepted apprentices. Such grants were introduced in 1917 and still remained into the 1980s.
- Nothing was said about the possibility to induce businesses to assume collective responsibility for vocational training through special education fees. In other countries, the redistribution of costs for education between large and small firms became a decisive part of the regulation and financing of apprenticeship.
- The question of apprentices' educational and contractual terms was not mentioned but was taken to be the firms' responsibility. The entire reform package was based on an unregulated model of vocational training (Olofsson, 2005).

Workshop schools and apprenticeship through collective agreement (c. 1938–1945)

The difficult economic situation during all of the interwar period and the Second World War caused businesses' interest in recruiting apprentices to be very weak. In general, vocational education was very limited in scope. The employer and labour organisations had a difficult time agreeing on the terms of apprenticeship training. This was a matter of apprentices' wages and work conditions as well as of guaranteeing the quality of their education. In several public enquiries, such as the Enquiry on Workshop Schools in 1938, it was emphasised that the number of apprentices fell very short of the actual needs (SOU, 1938:26). It was estimated that approximately 5 per cent of industry workers had experience of any type of organised vocational training.

However, the high rate of unemployment – not least the worries about youth unemployment – in combination with a lack of qualified manpower in some areas resulted in increased public interest in vocational education (SOU, 1934:11). As part of the economic policy, parliamentary decisions were taken on vocational courses and appropriations to vocational schools. Demands were made for legal regulation of apprenticeship, i.e. for businesses to be required by law to employ apprentices, but these proposals from handicrafts organisations were rejected. Instead, in connection with the Saltsjöbaden negotiations in the 1930s, the then principal organisations on the labour market – the Swedish Employers' Confederation (SAF) and the Swedish Trade Union Confederation (LO) – agreed that vocational training should be regulated by voluntary collective agreements within each trade association without governmental interference.

Public enquiry on the need for a new vocational education programme

The Enquiry on Workshop Schools from 1938 carried out a survey of the educational activities of individual companies (SOU, 1938:26). The results of the enquiry indicated that the standard of vocational training was acceptable in only a few major companies. In most cases, the training was quite unsystematic and narrow in content. Theoretical elements were included only in exceptional cases. In addition, the enquiry report stressed that an increasingly forced working pace in combination with a system of payment by results made it more and more difficult to find space and supervisors for apprentices in companies. For this reason, it was recommended that vocational education be organised in such a way that less strain would be placed on businesses. Workshop schools should be established in different parts of the country. The intention was not to completely relieve trade and industry of responsibility for vocational training; rather, it was to achieve a more efficient allocation of responsibility between stakeholders in working life, on the one hand, and the state, the counties, and the municipalities, on the other.

According to the report, greater importance should be attached to the employer and labour organisations' interest in school-based vocational education and training. First, responsibility for public vocational education should be separated from the National Board of Education and transferred to a new authority, the Royal Board of Vocational Education (Kungliga överstyrelsen för yrkesutbildning – KÖY), through which the labour market organisations would have direct access to executive functions. Second, the concerned actors in the different trades should organise special apprentice boards. Such boards (later referred to as trade boards) were established after a few years, but then based on agreement rather than governmental pressure. The intention was that these boards would enforce the collective agreements' provisions on apprenticeship within each individual trade. In 1944, the Royal Board of Vocational Education (i.e., KÖY) was established in order to increase and co-ordinate public commitment to vocational education, while giving the employer and labour organisations clearer insight into the workings of the government's educational authority. These stakeholders turned out to have a dominating position on the KÖY board. However, there was no talk of the authority intervening to encourage apprenticeship education and training. The regulation on which the Royal Board of Vocational Education was established stipulated that it should "supply information and advice, suggestions for organisational schemes, courses of study, etc." (SFS, 1943:963). The explanation for this cautious attitude on the part of the government was that apprenticeship was primarily seen as a concern for individual businesses and employer and labour organisations; it did not constitute part of the regular educational system.

Initiatives of the employer and labour organisations after the Saltsjöbaden agreement

The criticism of the existing vocational education system voiced in the Enquiry on Workshop Schools was repeated in a report presented in 1944, via the labour market organisations' committee on vocational education, by the LO and SAF: *Report including Proposed Measures for the Promotion of*

Apprenticeship (Arbetsmarknadsorganisationernas yrkesutbildningskommitté, 1944). The Committee on Vocational Education had been appointed for the distinct purpose of resolving disagreements between the concerned organisations regarding their views on vocational education and, in addition, making a clear delineation between the state and trade and industry as regards responsibility for such education. The background was the demand for apprenticeship legislation discussed above. In addition, the trade-union side was concerned that the apprentices might be exploited as cheap labour without being offered qualified training. The employers, on their part, took the view that clearer regulation was needed to abate individual businesses' uncertainty concerning investments in workplace training.

By and large, the report was a self-critical account of the educational efforts made by trade and industry. Quantitatively, the training was considered entirely inadequate. In addition, apprenticeship was carried out more or less aimlessly and depended on the goodwill of foremen and experienced workers (Arbetsmarknadsorganisationernas yrkesutbildningskommitté, 1944). Moreover, the Committee on Vocational Education admitted that the apprentices were often exploited as cheap labour. Against this background, the committee was not particularly surprised at the fact that dropping out of the training programmes was common. A vicious circle had been created. The dropout rate reduced businesses' willingness to employ apprentices and to allocate resources to improving the training. Moreover, individual employers' fear that their investments in apprenticeship would finally favour competing firms (e.g. when a 'fully trained' apprentice is employed at another company) was a significant obstacle to the possible expansion of apprenticeship. Thus, to encourage firms to invest more in apprenticeship, businesses' and apprentices' mutual commitments had to be clarified and regulated. In addition, co-operation between firms should increase.

Even if the report of the Committee on Vocational Education paid a great deal of attention to the shortcomings of apprenticeship, it should be emphasised that the school-based education organised by the municipalities was subjected to even more severe criticism. Compared to the Enquiry on Workshop Schools, there was the considerable difference that criticism of the vocational schools had principle and political overtones. School-based education should be regarded as complementary to the 'actual' vocational training taking place in the companies, and the number of students in vocational and workshop schools should only be allowed to increase during economic downturns when the number of apprenticeship places in the firms decreased. In general, workplace-based vocational training was to be preferred over school-based education, partly because it could more easily be adapted to current needs, and partly because it put less strain on the state's economic resources.

To handle the problems of education, the Committee on Vocational Education took the view that both employers and trade unions must assume greater responsibility for managing, financing, and determining the content of the training programmes. All proposals that apprenticeship should be regulated by law were rejected. Instead, apprenticeship and apprentices' legal labour status should be based on voluntary settlements between employer and labour organisations in the form of collective agreements. To render the efforts of these stakeholders more efficient, a new labour market agency, the Swedish Trade Council, should be established. The purpose of the new council would be to co-ordinate the work of the employer and labour organisations, both in relation to the governmental educational authorities and vis-à-vis the apprentice boards of the various trades. The primary objective of the apprentice boards was, exactly as proposed by the Enquiry on Workshop Schools, to develop the content and forms of apprenticeship in the various trades.

The ideas behind the VET reform of 1918 were revived such that vocational education and training should be organised as a firm-based apprenticeship supplemented with theoretical instruction in the evenings and at weekends. The Committee on Vocational Education rather regretted that the organisation of training had shown a tendency to develop in the quite the opposite direction. Decisions to invest more in schools were regarded with distrust. Vocational training that was school-based and completely separate from working life would lead in the wrong direction, away from the real production setting, the "workshop air" and the technical innovation work constantly going on in the companies (Arbetsmarknadsorganisationernas yrkesutbildningskommitté, 1944, p. 56). A more efficient and comprehensive apprenticeship would, thus, provide the basis for future vocational training, whereas school-based education would be complementary. The main task of the employer and labour organisations was to create good conditions for apprenticeship. This would be done through agreements in each trade between the employer and labour organisations.

Expansion of VET based on voluntary initiatives

In this final section, we expound on the consequences of the historical analysis and further develop the discussion of the institutional conditions for the budding education model during the first half of the 1900s. The first vocational education reforms in 1918 may represent the starting point for an education model that would, internationally, later be primarily associated with the 'progressive social democratic' school-based VET-model that developed after the Second World War (e.g. Busemeyer, 2015; Aasen, 2003). At the same time, it is important to stress that during the first half of the 1900s this model assumed that the labour market partners would take an active responsibility for VET. Apprenticeship was central here, and was to be supplemented with training at municipal vocational schools.

First, we discuss the various processes and circumstances that contributed to Sweden's not developing legislation for an apprenticeship system of the type developed in, for instance, Germany and Denmark. Next, we look at the conditions for a possible expansion of initial VET within the framework of a voluntary model, based on an active influence from and responsibility-taking by parties on the labour market and private companies. Finally, we discuss the background to the increased interest in publicly organised initial VET during the 1930s.

Why not apprenticeship legislation?

Two questions discussed in connection with the 1918 parliamentary decision on practical schools for youths would resurface repeatedly in the decades that followed. These concerned, first, the question of special apprenticeship legislation; that is, whether companies should be forced to offer vocational training to newly recruited youths. Also discussed in this context was the possibility to extend the compulsory school attendance for young people. In practice, the 1918 decision on practical schools for youths assumed some form of legislated regulation of vocational education, which had also been suggested in the preparatory work for the proposition.

The original intention had been for the apprenticeship and vocational schools to offer training to youths employed at industrial companies (Berge, 1962). However, the opposition to compulsory legislation was too strong, primarily from the employers' organisations, which asserted that the training requirement would be too economically cumbersome. The resistance from employers was also grounded in the fact that they were not completely satisfied with the changes to the apprenticeship schools' education, which was seen as all too general in nature. The unions, on the other hand, were not unequivocal opponents to legislation on the apprenticeship programme. At various times, LO had made positive statements concerning suggestions for legislation, but at the same time stressed the importance that the salary terms for apprentices must not drastically diverge from the salary provisions for younger manpower in the collective labour agreements. There was also a fear that apprenticeship legislation could be used to implement salary reductions, and that the employment conditions for older, unskilled manpower would be threatened.

The possibilities to realise apprenticeship legislation were definitively closed in connection with the presentation by LO and SAF of their ideas for the future vocational education in the report from the 1944 labour market committee on vocational education (Arbetsmarknadsorganisationernas yrkesutbildningskommitté, 1944). Here, it was stressed that apprenticeship should be regulated through a contract between the union organisations rather than through legislation. The organisations stressed that the companies' apprenticeship should be supplemented with vocational theory education at vocational schools, but that the main part of the vocational education should be based on apprenticeship. It was only in cases in which the union organisations were unsuccessful in impelling companies to develop apprenticeship – in both quality and volume – that there was reason for the state and the municipalities to set aside additional budget amounts to support the publicly organised vocational education. In practice, however, apprenticeship would continue to be poorly developed; and the union organisations' interest, communicated through the labour market trade council, came to be increasingly oriented toward a publicly organised vocational education provided within the schools.

Why, then, did apprenticeship never attain any greater reach within the framework of initial VET during the decades after the first vocational school reforms? There are actually a number of explanations for this, though the one that is reasonably most apparent is that no compulsory apprenticeship legislation, like in Germany or Denmark, was ever enacted in Sweden. The opposition from both employer and employee interests may have played a role in this. Until the 1940s and the establishment of the labour market trade council, the parties were in deep disagreement as to how VET should be arranged. On the one hand, employers were eager to increase the number of apprentices in the companies to meet the need for qualified manpower. On the other hand, there was a desire to decrease the importance of the municipal schools – partly because they were not regarded as meeting a sufficiently high standard, and partly in order to decrease the amount of state support. The unions, however, made a demand for fewer apprentices. They asserted that apprentices were all too often abused as cheap manpower (SAF, 1939). Some unions instead advocated for a more regulated education, in which the vocational schools would play a decisive role. The unregulated apprenticeship model was seen as a threat as it weakened the control over the supply of manpower, which indirectly reduced the possibilities to influence salary formation (Arbetsmarknadskommittén, 1939). To achieve this, apprenticeship regulations were advocated, to direct the stream of educated workers to the appropriate trade groups. The opposition between the parties had a paralytic effect, and prevented any and all efforts to further develop the apprenticeship programme on a voluntary basis, which was central in the 1918 decision.

The prevalence of collective labour agreements can be an explanation for why the apprenticeship model, alongside the public school system, had such a limited reach. The apprenticeship agreements that were established – the first of which was within the automobile industry in 1938 – led to higher salaries for apprentices, which in turn reduced companies' (particularly the small and medium-sized ones) interest in hiring apprentices (Vahlberg, 1938). Theoretically, a lower salary during an apprenticeship can also be motivated by the idea that this reflects the apprentice sharing the cost of the investment in education with the other two financers, the employer and the state. In exchange, the education results in more secure employment conditions and a higher salary. While the union organisations asserted that higher apprentice salaries facilitated recruitment to apprenticeship programmes, employers stressed that, on the contrary, it was essential to have lower apprentice and entry-level salaries – and a significant gap between the salaries of qualified workers and unskilled manpower – in order to increase young workers' interest in educating themselves. The differences between the union organisations in their views on apprentices' terms and benefits, among other things regarding salaries and leave arrangements, remained even after the agreement between LO and SAF on the apprenticeship programme in connection with the establishment of the labour market trade council in 1944 (Arbetsmarknadskommitténs Förhandlingar, 1950).

The other matter of dispute that arose in connection with the 1918 parliamentary decision, which would resurface again in the future, involved the central management of VET. Those who regarded vocational education as part of industrial policy, rather than education policy, asserted that the responsibility for it should be placed with a separate authority, set apart from other education and preferably within a department responsible for industrial matters (SOU, 1938:54). Those who, on the other hand, argued that VET should be administrated in close connection to other education programmes instead called for a common authority for all education. In the preparatory work for the 1918 legislation on practical schools for youths, there had been a suggestion for a separate state authority for vocational education. In the proposition Värner Rydén, the social democratic Minister of Education and Religion, also supported the idea that while vocational education should certainly still be sorted under the Ministry of Education and Religion, a special board for vocational education should be established alongside the National Board of Education. However, Parliament ruled that issues concerning vocational education would be handled within the Board of Education. This did not put the matter to rest, however; demands for a special authority for vocational education would resurface. The union organisations were a strong driving factor in this. More precisely, the discussion concerned how the cooperation between schools and working life should be organised – and here, the possibilities for the labour market partners in the management of vocational education at all levels were seen as guaranteeing a stronger link to working life. Corporate-assembled authority and board organisations were not a new phenomenon in Swedish administrative policy (Rothstein and Bergström, 1999). As regards vocational education, the first step was taken in the parliamentary decision of 1918. According to Parliament, a majority of the local boards for apprenticeship and vocational schools should be comprised of representatives of employer and employee organisations.

Driving forces for an increased political interest in VET

An important condition for the VET trajectory before the Second World War, discussed earlier, involves the dominant socio-political perspective on VET for young people. Detailed analyses of the political discussion on VET during the time between the wars (Olofsson, 2005) clearly show that politically responsible social democrats in government still had far to go to reach the ideas that would later be central in the reformation of the educational system in connection with the labour movement's after-war programme. In light of the central role that has internationally been ascribed to the social democratic-driven reformation of the educational system (e.g. Busemeyer, 2015), it is therefore interesting to look at the political driving forces for change to vocational education that existed before the Second World War, and that preceded the later development.

During the 1930s, the political interest in VET grew. An expression of this can be seen in the efforts within the framework of unemployment policy, among other things through special courses for the unemployed at municipal vocational schools as well as training schools for unemployed youths. A rough estimate shows that just over a third of the positions in the public vocational education were held by unemployed youths in the middle of the decade. The high unemployment among young people at the time is naturally an important explanation for why education issues drew increasingly greater attention.

Another explanation for the political attention was the difficulties companies reported having in recruiting qualified manpower, despite the high unemployment. In the most difficult years of crisis during the first half of the 1930s, the number of people participating in vocational education had decreased. Experience had shown that, during times with a weak economy, companies had difficulties supporting apprenticeships to any sufficient degree, which served to motivate increased public contributions (Nationalekonomiska föreningens förhandlingar, 1936).

The 1938 Committee on Training Schools and the 1939 Committee on Rationalisation were appointed in order to examine various problems within vocational education. Among other things, the Committees analysed the qualification requirements, which were considered to follow the technical developments of the time, and the need for special courses for unemployed youths. The social democratic youth association played an important role in this, supporting demands for both courses in the municipal vocational education and special jobs reserved for young people (Schröder, 1991).

The increased interest in vocational education issues was reflected in Parliament. A motion presented by representatives of the Liberal Party in Parliament in 1938 is especially worth mention in this context – partly because it contains ideas and suggestions that were only realized many years later, and partly because it indirectly says a great deal about how the attitudes regarding vocational education among responsible politicians would change in the years to follow (1938 års riksdag. Motioner i Första kammaren, Nr 145).

The authors of the motion noted that there was an imbalance between the various education forms. Although vocational education was much more important for the majority of people in society, it comprised far fewer students than grammar school. Only just over 7 per cent of the total number of people aged 14–20 years had some form of vocational education. Furthermore, most courses were offered only part-time, with a small number of teaching hours each week, with the intention that this would be combined with work. The courses were also too short. Therefore, the authors asserted that the courses could hardly be regarded as meeting the requirement of a 'basic vocational education'. Such an education was not to be overly specialised and narrow, but should provide knowledge and skills that crossed over occupation boundaries. The motion called for a broader educational content to offer students the possibility to orient themselves between various occupations. A broader education would also offer better protection against unemployment during periods of low demand for manpower.

The costs of vocational education could be seen as a 'capital investment' whose dividends were found in a future growing economy, which among other things would contribute to alleviating the burden of an increasing demographically conditional need for support (1938 års riksdag. Motioner i Första kammaren, Nr 145, p. 8). In order to improve the conditions for VET within industry, the authors of the motion indicate that they would be open to an apprenticeship law. As for vocational education in schools, it was assumed that improved standards and increased student volumes could only be realised through increased state subvention. The first step would be to appoint a committee in order to create the conditions for a vocational education in a form that was ordered and 'according to plan'.

The motion anticipates many of the ideas within the area of vocational education that were brought up after the Second World War. The view of VET as an investment would resurface during the decades after the war in the wake of increased insight into the economic significance of education for both the individual and society. It is also interesting to note that the idea that industry should be able to singlehandedly organise a satisfactory education from a national economic perspective was in principle rejected. Even though it was stressed that many of the practical elements of the education were most effectively organised within companies, the weight should be placed on education in the schools. This final point was by no means an uncontroversial view at the end of the 1930s. A more common opinion, in accordance with the vocational school charter at the time, was that vocational education in the schools should be seen as a supplement to the apprenticeship programmes offered by companies.

In practice, the motion questioned the voluntary model (assumed a heavy engagement by industry) of VET in Sweden at the time. In the light of the aforementioned conflicts of interest between the labour market partners, the state's passivity was increasingly viewed as unsatisfactory.

No intentions for changes during the 1930s

The motion was denied by Parliament. However, it is interesting to look at a number of points from the discussion that followed. Above all, the discussion shows that the responsible actors in the government, the social democrats, were still far from the ideas that would be suggested a number of years into the 1940s when the political guidelines for the time after the war were being worked through. Arthur Engberg, a cabinet minister with responsibility for education issues – who was also regarded as one of the social democrats' leading ideological politicians – questioned the need for a 'basic vocational education' on several grounds (1938 års riksdag. Första kammarens protokoll, Nr 23, p. 57): an all-round education did not have a place in vocational training, which should rather be focussed on practical skills. It was the companies themselves who should primarily provide for the education of their new employees. It should be a matter of an apprenticeship directly linked "to the daily experience" (1938 års riksdag. Första kammarens protokoll, Nr 23, p. 59). To facilitate this, trade organisations and companies should conduct thorough observations in order to determine in detail the various elements of the apprenticeship programme. This was a completely different direction than the authors of the motion had had in mind.

While the interest in VET increased at the end of the 1930s, both within and outside Parliament, at the level of the leading government there was virtually no desire to reform the system. The decisions by Parliament in 1918 and 1921 on limited state support for municipal vocational education, which was intended as a supplement to the apprenticeship programme within companies, would continue to be applied. Parliament did add a decision on special vocational courses, but with a socio-political background within the framework of unemployment policy.

A sign of the relative backwardness of the parliamentary treatment at the end of the 1930s is the relatively positive attention given to thoughts on obligatory courses in household work for girls over and beyond the education provided in elementary school and the so-called continuation school. Many suggestions in this vein were presented. In a motion by the Right wing, it was suggested that women did not only have a need for vocational courses in order to perform a job, they should also be taught household economics and how to care for the home (1938 års riksdag. Motioner i Första kammaren, Nr 124, p. 7). Society, according to the authors of the motion, placed special demands on women. They had the main responsibility for the home and their children, and thereby also indirectly for the economic standing of the family. For girls from poor families, an education in household work and home care was especially important. A significant minority of the members of the upper and lower chambers supported the suggestion, but the motion was ultimately denied (1938 års riksdag. Andra kammarens protokoll, Nr 36, p. 45). Generally – and despite a relatively high participation in education by women – VET was seen as a matter for men, especially in relation to industry. Women were to be mainly diverted to domestic training. This view began changing at the end of the 1940s, however, against the background of an increasing lack of manpower.

Another expression of the passive stance of those who were politically responsible regarding vocational education issues at the end of the 1930s was the treatment of a resolution from the International Labour Organisation (ILO) on matters of education. The resolution cited the need for ordered conditions and an increased government responsibility for vocational education. In January 1940, the social democratic Minister of Social Affairs Gustav Möller noted that Sweden had traditionally had no greater comprehensive state interventions in the area of vocational education. Furthermore, the parties on the labour market had just taken the initiative to establish committees and agreements on apprenticeship through the Labour Market Committee (1940 års riksdag. Kungl. Maj:ts proposition, Nr 19, p. 6). There was therefore no reason for Parliament to make any decisions in response to the ILO's resolution. Instead, suggestions from the parties on the labour market should be awaited. Parliament followed Möller's recommendation without debate.

Conclusions

The legislation on apprenticeship within the field of craftsmanship was overturned in Sweden in connection with the trade freedom reforms in the mid-1800s. This must be seen against the background of industrialisation and the striving for more market-like conditions for production and trade. Meanwhile, the need for ordered forms of vocational education became increasingly clear at the end of the 1800s and the beginning of the 1900s, now against the background of the industrial companies' need for competent manpower in parallel with a political desire to socially include workers in the cities.

In connection with the vocational education reforms around 1920, an education model began to take form that at its core was built on a combination of instruction in the workplace and education in school. The education model assumed a voluntary engagement on the part of companies. However, we have been able to note that there were substantial institutional barriers to the development of a vocational education in Sweden based on voluntary initiative and significant employer responsibility. Furthermore, it is apparent that the opposition between the union organisations acted as a barrier to realising the intentions behind the reforms of 1918.

Consequently, no institutional conditions were ever created for an expansion of VET, which was thus dependent on the voluntary initiative of private companies. It was only after the 1940s that any such conditions were created, but these were placed mainly within the schools. Apprenticeship was marginalised as an education model, and the public responsibility for skills supply was increasingly stressed.

References

1938 års riksdag. Andra kammarens protokoll (Parliament Protocol), Nr 36, Stockholm, Parliament Protocol.

1938 års riksdag. Första kammarens protokoll (Parliament Protocol), Nr 23, Stockholm, Parliament Protocol.

1938 års riksdag. Motioner i Första kammaren (Parliament Motions), Nr 124, *Av herr Domö m.fl. om beredande åt den kvinnliga ungdomen av ökad utbildning i hemvård och därmed närbesläktade samhälleliga uppgifter*, Stockholm, Parliament Motions.

1938 års riksdag. Motioner i Första kammaren (Parliament Motions), Nr 145 *Av herr Larsson, Sam, m.fl., om allmän översyn av vårt folkbildningsväsen*, Stockholm, Parliament Motions.

Aasen, P. (2003) 'What happened to Social-Democratic Progressivism in Scandinavia? Restructuring education in Sweden and Norway in the 1990s', in Apple, M.W. (ed.) *The State and the Politics of Knowledge*, NewYork, Routledge, pp. 109–147.

Arbetsmarknadskommittén (1939) *PM angående åtgärder för främjande av lärlingsutbildningen.* Bilaga till Arbetsmarknadskommitténs protokoll 20–21/9 1939, Stockholm, Arbetarrörelsens arkiv.

Arbetsmarknadskommitténs Förhandlingar IV (22 februari 1943–15 mars 1950) *Minnesanteckningar från sammanträde med regeringen den 2 mars 1950 kl. 14.15*, Stockholm, Arbetarrörelsens arkiv.

Arbetsmarknadsorganisationernas yrkesutbildningskommitté (1944) *Betänkande med förslag till lärlingsutbildningens främjande.* Stockholm, LO and SAF.

Berge, T. (1962) 'Vår yrkesutbildning', *Tidskrift för praktiska ungdomsskolor. Organ för svenska yrkesskolföreningen*, vol. 43.

Boli, J. (1990) 'Medborgarskapet, samhällsomdaningen och uppkomsten av det svenska folkskoleväsendet', in Englund, T. (ed.) *Politik och socialisation. Nyare strömningar i pedagogisk forskning*, Uppsala, Pedagogiska institutionen, pp. 25–58.

Busemeyer, M. (2015) *Skills and Inequality: Partisan Politics and the Political Economy of Education Reforms in Western Welfare State*, Cambridge, Cambridge University Press.

Edgren, L. (1987) *Lärling-gesäll-mästare. Hantverk och hantverkare i Malmö 1750–1847*, Lund, Dialogos.

Englund, T. (1981) *Perspektiv på svensk skolutveckling under 1900-talet utifrån skolreformerna 1918/19: skolan som ideologisk statsapparat i det borgerliga samhället*, Göteborg, Pedagogiska institutionen.

Islings, Å. (1973) *Samhällsutveckling och bildningsideal*, Stockholm, Svenska lärarförbundet.

Katz, M. B. (1995) *Improving Poor People: The Welfare State, The "Underclass," and Urban Schools as History*, Princeton, Princeton University Press.

Lindell, I. (1992) *Disciplinering och Yrkesutbildning. Reformarbetet bakom 1918 års praktiska ungdomsskolereform*, Uppsala, Föreningen för svensk utbildningshistoria.

Marklund, S. (1980) *Skolsverige 1950–1975. Del 1. 1950 års reformbeslut*, Stockholm, Liber.

Nationalekonomiska föreningens förhandlingar (1936) *Arbetslöshetspolitik under högkonjunktur*, Stockholm, Nationalekonomiska föreningen.

Nilsson, A. (2013) 'Lärlingsutbildning – ett alternativ i yrkesutbildningen 1940–1970', in Håkansson, P. and Nilsson, A. (eds.) *Yrkesutbildningens formering i Sverige 1940–1970*, Lund, Nordic Academic Press, pp. 25–58.

Nilsson, L. (1981) *Yrkesutbildning i nutidshistoriskt perspektiv. Yrkesutbildningens utveckling från skråväsendets upphörande 1846 till 1980-talet samt tankar om framtida inriktning*, Göteborg, Göteborgs universitet.

Olofsson, J. (2005) *Svensk yrkesutbildning. Vägval i internationell belysning*, Stockholm, SNS Förlag.

Prop. (1921:1) (Government Bill) *Statsverkspropositionen. Åttonde huvudtiteln: Yrkesundervisningen*, Stockholm, Government Bill.

Prop. (1940:19) (Government Bill) *Kungl. Maj:ts proposition till riksdagen med anhållan om riksdagens yttrande angående de av den internationella arbetsorganisationens konferens år 1939 vid dess tjugofemte sammanträde fattade beslut; given Stockholms slott den 19 januari 1940*, Stockholm, Government Bill.

Richardson, G. (1990) *Svensk utbildningshistoria*, Lund, Studentlitteratur.

Rothstein, B. and Bergström, J. (1999) *Korporativismens fall och den svenska modellens kris*, Stockholm, SNS Förlag.

SAF (1939) *PM angående organisationen av den lägre yrkesundervisningen för hantverk och industri*, Svenska Arbetsgivarföreningen september 1939, Föreningen Stockholms Företagsminnen.

Schön, L. (2010) *Sweden's Road to Modernity: An Economic History*, Stockholm, SNS Förlag.

Schröder, L. (1991) *Från springpojke till fullgod arbetare. Om bakgrunden till 1930-talets ungdomsreservarbete*, Uppsala Papers in Economic History, Research Report, 27.

SFS (The Swedish Code of Statutes) (1864:41) *Kongl. Maj:ts Nådiga Förordning, angående utvidgad näringsfrihet; Gifwen Stockholms Slott den 18 Juni 1864*, Stockholm, SFS.

SFS (The Swedish Code of Statutes) (1918:1002) *Kungl. Maj:ts Nådiga Stadga för den kommunala yrkesundervisningen*, Stockholm, SFS.

SFS (The Swedish Code of Statutes) (1918:771) *Kungl. Maj:ts Nådiga Kungörelse angående statsunderstöd åt skolor för den lägre yrkesunder*, Stockholm, SFS.

SFS (The Swedish Code of Statutes) (1921:705) *Kungl. Maj:ts Nådiga Kungörelse angående statsunderstöd till kommunala och enskilda anstalter för yrkesutbildning*, Stockholm, SFS.

SFS (The Swedish Code of Statutes) (1921:706) *Kungl. Maj:ts Nådiga Stadga för den kommunala yrkesundervisningen*, Stockholm, SFS.

SFS (The Swedish Code of Statutes) (1921:707) *Kungl. Maj:ts Nådiga Kungörelse med bestämmelser angående statsunderstödda enskilda anstalter för yrkesutbildning*, Stockholm, SFS.

SFS (The Swedish Code of Statutes) (1943:963) *Kungl. Maj:ts Instruktion för överstyrelsen för yrkesutbildning*, Stockholm, SFS.

SOU (Swedish Government Official Reports) (1934:11) *Utredning angående åtgärder för bekämpande av ungdomsarbetslösheten. Avgiven den 29 mars 1934 av 1934 års sakkunniga rörande ungdomsarbetslösheten*, Stockholm, SFS.

SOU (Swedish Government Official Reports) (1938:26) *Betänkande och förslag angående centrala verkstadsskolor m.m.*, Stockholm, SOU.

SOU (Swedish Government Official Reports) (1938:54) *Betänkande med utredning och förslag angående överstyrelse för yrkesutbildning. Avgivet av verkstadsskoleutredningen*, Stockholm, SOU.

Vahlberg, G. (1938) 'Fackföreningsrörelsen och yrkesutbildningen', *Ungdomens yrkesutbildning under debatt*, Stenografiskt protokoll från Sveriges socialdemokratiska ungdomsförbunds yrkesutbildningskonferens i Stockholm den 28–29 September 1938, Stockholm, SSU.

4 The case of Norwegian VET – origins and early development 1850–1945

Svein Michelsen and Håkon Høst

Introduction

This chapter traces the origins of Norwegian vocational education and training (VET) for industry and crafts in the period 1850–1945. We investigate the formation of vocational schools, the breakdown of the guilds and formation of new collective actors in skill formation; the employers, the organizations they formed and their relations to the workers' organizations in skill formation. But skill formation cannot fruitfully be explained by socio-economic institutions alone. We also emphasize the significance of democratic institutions and political systems, and the role of political parties and social movements in the formation of the Norwegian national VET system and structures. In the chapter, we try to integrate these different streams of thought, focusing the significance of the interaction of democratization and industrialization in the formation of VET. As democratization preceded industrialization, the realization of industrial development and VET schooling in Norway was mediated by an evolving democratic nation state. Employers and workers in crafts and industry gradually formed strong organizations, but were internally divided in training questions. The state could not be used to overcome these collective action problems in order to make employers agree on VET policies. While a new regulatory system for the crafts was built after a period of lawless conditions, training in the industrial firm remained legally unregulated.

The formation of vocational education and training in 19th century Norway

The development of various type of vocational or practical education was a social question of considerable significance during the most part of the 19th century. It had implications at almost every level of the education structure and was extremely complex. Some Norwegian peculiarities can be identified, but the development also reflected general ongoing modernization processes in the Nordic countries as well as everywhere else in Europe. A central element was the breakdown of the guilds and the emerging industrialization. The development of more practical or vocational forms of education and training was initially based on private initiatives and local actors (Grove and Michelsen, 2005). The breakthrough for state financing of practical education and training came in the 1840s, when provision of resources was made to local agricultural schools as well as navigation and sailor schools. The municipalities also had to do their part. Little by little, different school-like institutions were formed. Practical or technical work can be seen as a common denominator for these schools. However, these schools were not only intended to serve practical purposes. They were also regarded as educational in a broad sense. A variety of reform projects and school types were formed, advocating different combinations of general and vocational education, spanning from industry and crafts, commerce, handicrafts and home economics, to more general practical schools or work schools. The boundaries between them were blurred, and were continuously subjected to definition and redefinition processes by social actor groups like employers, educationalists, artisans, intellectuals, philanthropists, civil servants and politicians.

The basic level in the emerging VET system for industry and crafts was the technical evening schools, which descended from older school forms like the Sunday schools and the drawing schools. After 1848, these schools experienced an upward turn, and a wave of school foundations followed. The municipalities, local financing and local actor constellations were decisive elements, but school plans and curriculum had to be approved by the Ministry of Education. Teaching in these schools varied considerably in their degree of specialization, regulations had to be sufficiently flexible in order to accommodate these peculiarities. Also relations between general primary education and the technical evening schools were an endemic problem. The Ministry of Education held firm that general education was not a task to which these schools should dedicate resources. They should concentrate on the primary subject matter for these schools, schooling for work. The technical evening schools were considered useful by contemporary observers, but also as insufficient surrogates for a proper craftsman's training. Standards were far too low, applications for school places were random and there were severe problems in keeping these schools afloat over time. Furthermore, it was maintained that this type of school was incapable of meeting new and more ambitious policy goals, as teaching took place in the evening. Students attending school after work were often tired, and suffered from lack of concentration and lack of progress. Dropout rates were considerable (Kjeldstadli, 1989). Instead, day schooling was launched as an important pedagogical and social policy improvement. Soon demands surfaced from industry for the formation of short, practically oriented workshop schools preceding apprenticeship and work. The first pre-apprenticeship school formed in 1910. The aim of this school type was to provide the students with basic practical skills and/or prepare them for apprenticeship. Machinery in industrial firms was often costly, and operation required considerable skills. Allocating this type of work to inexperienced apprentices was not a very good idea. Instead, a reform of basic vocational training for industry was needed in the form of practical craft and industry schools preparing for working life. This produced ongoing tensions between two different ways of organizing basic VET, vocational schools preceding apprenticeship, and technical evening schools providing education during apprentice training or supplementing work. Relations to general education were unclear, providing conditions for a plethora of different schools and school types with negligible central coordination and governance structures. As the guilds were weak and industrialization late, technical education in general was not much developed. The state catered for the elite and the university, and the municipalities took care of primary, obligatory education for all children. Vocational education and training was located somewhat uneasily in between. Filling this regulatory gap became a central concern for policymakers and actors in VET.

The democratic and bureaucratic origins of Norwegian VET

Several factors were important for the formation of VET institutions and structures. Having developed as an integral part of the Danish-Norwegian realm for 600 years, there was no centralized Norwegian state, and the Norwegian territories were governed as an assemblage of regions from Copenhagen, the capital of the twin kingdom (Maliks and Bull, 2014). Through these processes, a dualistic social structure had emerged. The peasantry was dispersed and tied to subsistence agriculture, while the small urban population depended on exports and foreign trade (Senghaas, 1985). In 1814, Norway was separated from Denmark, and declared itself as a sovereign state with a separate democratic constitution. Thereafter Norway reluctantly assented to Swedish rule after a short and bloodless war. In the new regime, the civil servants enjoyed a strong position. The merchant elites had been decimated during the Napoleonic wars, and there were no competing elites like the nobility. Thus, industrialization and skill formation policies were governed by an emerging bureaucratic state (Rokkan, 1987). Gradually the farmers acquired more influence in Parliament and after 1860 a majority. As Parliament was not bicameral, like in Denmark and Sweden, there was no institutional check as well as no basis on which to build such a second chamber (Sejersted, 2011). Business interests therefore became more dependent on democratic processes and state intervention than in Sweden, where big business interests were stronger as well as more autonomous (Sejersted, 2011). The rise of parliamentary rule compounded this development. In general, the political elites were preoccupied with state- and nation-building, not industrialization and skill formation for the middle classes. Rural districts were protected by the constitution and guaranteed a solid majority in Parliament. Urbanization processes gradually diluted the position of the rural areas vis-a-vis the towns, which in 1814 was 9 to 1 measured by population size. The constitution's §57, adopted in 1859, secured the rural areas at least 60% representation, irrespective of population size. For a long time, rural interests supported austerity policies, effectively curtailing state financing of technical and vocational education. The middle classes did not possess the necessary political capital in order to extract state commitment to technical education (Sakslind, 1998; Hanisch and Lange, 1985). Cultural and political issues were more important than economic modernization in the dominant discourse of the day.

The industrialization process was slow and sluggish, and did not speed up before 1900–1920 (Venneslan, 2007; Hodne and Honningdal Grytten, 2000). In 1840 industry contained only 10% of the gross national product. A total of 90% of the exports were tied to timber, fish and iron products. Small firms dominated the industrial structure. In 1896, 65% of registered factories employed less than 20 workers, and only 12 factories employed more than 400 workers (Venneslan, 2007). In 1890, the number of industrial workers constituted just about 7% of the total workforce. Even if we include artisan trades, industry was the smallest sector in the economy at the end of the 19th century, and industry's share of the gross national product (GNP) had only reached 15% in 1896. The Norwegian economy became really industrialized when electricity and electrical motors emerged (Venneslan, 2007). The average size of the firms is also significant. Some 65% of registered factories employed less than 20 workers. Only 12 factories employed more than 400 workers (Venneslan, 2007). The Norwegian businesses also developed fewer links for cross-sectoral and inter-firm coordination than any other Nordic country (Moen, 2011). Available capital was scarce, and most firms were family owned. Farm ownership could not be subjected to market transactions due to the prevalence of allodial legal traditions. An important part of the industrialization was related to the abundantly available hydraulic power, which supplied the basis for electrochemical and electrometallurgical industry. To a considerable extent, these industries represented enclaves of a larger European market, where a few foreign companies invested heavily (Senghaas, 1985). For the most part, Norwegian industry was embedded in older structures related to the primary industries that had developed in the first part of the 19th century. During the recession at the turn of the century, smaller and medium-sized firms expanded while big industry ground to a halt, reproducing older industrial structures and interests dominated by smaller entities and local markets (Halvorsen, 1993). For long, there was simply no need for an advanced technical college. The Norwegian College of Advanced Technology was formed in 1910, considerably later than its Nordic equivalents. The remaining technical schools were downgraded as part of the process (Halvorsen, 1993).

The weak position of the guilds

The dominant economic doctrine of the twin kingdom for Denmark and Norway had been mercantilism. It was based on the notion that processing of commodities was to be organized through internal production chains before they were exported as well as the practice of high tariffs. This had made the furthering of crafts and guild privileges into an important policy area. In 1662 the towns had acquired a monopoly on commerce and trade. Apprentice training was organized according to the classical guild principles, embedded in a contract, which specified the number of years which the apprentice was to serve, as well as obligations and rights. Norwegian guilds were not that much developed (Huchinson, 2014). In the 1840s, a total of 46 guilds were registered in the country, distributed by 15 different trades (Pryser, 1999).

After 1814 the new civil servant state adhered to 'laissez faire' polices and freedom of trade, which had been written into the constitution. It has been asserted that Norway probably was more laissez faire than any other of the Nordic states in this period (Grieg, 1958). The reason for this was not ideology 'as such', but the need to pacify and restrict the growing influence from Parliament (Seip, 1959). This peculiar practice of bureaucratic liberalism persisted throughout the civil servant regime. The struggle on guild privileges and regulations commenced from the very beginning of the new regime (Dokk, 1958). The Constitution's §101 stated that new and durable restrictions on freedom of enterprise should not be accepted (Hodne and Honningdal Grytten, 2000). In 1816, a separate commission recommended that old established ways for the training of journeymen and masters were to be abolished. A law based on this proposal was passed by Parliament in 1827, but the king refused approbation due to protests from master craftsmen. Finally, in 1839 the law was approbated. The formation of new guilds was prohibited, and older guilds were to be made obsolete when all recognized master artisans (per 1840) had deceased. Regulations specifying the number of years to be endured in the trade before certification were abolished. In trades not structured by guilds, a journeyman's test was not required, and a public letter from two trusted men skilled in the trade sufficed as a proxy for a masters' certificate. In rural areas, the principle of freedom of trade only applied for a limited number of trades, and some could only be practiced with royal permission. Still, rural handicrafts could not be imported into the towns or exported overseas. By the law of 1839, all crafts were liberated both in rural areas and in the towns. Any man older than 21 years could now engage in any form of craft. In principle, the law eradicated the older categories of master, journeyman and apprentice as well as established relations between them. There was no longer any moral duty on behalf of the masters to provide work to journeyman and apprentices. Any man older than 21 years could now engage in any form of craft. In the abolition of the guild regulations, the civil servants and the farmer's representatives in Parliament stood firm against artisan interests (Kaartvedt, 1984), and in the towns both merchants and paupers supported the law (Pryser, 1999).

Also, commerce was gradually freed from older regulations, but in this area the path was somewhat more erratic. In 1816, the government instigated requirements for a citizen's charter in all types of commerce. In order to acquire such a charter, the applicant should be older than 25 years, and provide proof for four years of apprenticeship as a commerce journeyman. There is much to suggest that the new regulations were due to popular outcry about the low morale and unfair practices among tradesmen. These regulations were controversial; they excluded the rural population, as obtaining a citizens' charter was limited to the towns. On the other hand, registered ship-owners in rural areas were granted the right to settle where the requirements of the district permitted it, and where the location was more than three Norwegian miles at a distance from the nearest town. The range of products allowed for trade was rather limited, and imports/exports remained reserved for the towns. Gradually the required distance to the towns was reduced, and more products allowed as well. This type of liberalization process also met protests, now from the privileged merchants in the towns, but the state did not budge.

The artisans felt, with good reason, that the laissez faire policies would reduce the significance of the guilds and curtail their power. Coordination of craft interests became an important issue, and a number of local associations formed in the towns. *Christiania Craft Association* formed in 1838 as an association for master craftsmen in the capital. In 1871, the Christiania Association was consolidated by a merger with *Christiania Technical Association* and *The Norwegian Association of Crafts and Industry in Christiania*. The formation of the association was the result of an alliance between university professors and prominent representatives from the master artisans. Its aim was the gathering of men from all social classes for the furthering of inventions and technical progress. The civil servant regime was deeply embedded in a system of consultancy with a variety of common weal associations. As a poly-technical society, the craft and industry association was considered as a common weal association rather than an interest organization (Hoel, 1914). The coalition between the artisans and the professors did not last for long. Only craftsmen and businessmen remained in the association, reconstructing it in the direction of an interest association.

The ascent of the new liberal state

As Parliament asserted itself more and more forcefully, a variety of social movements were mobilized and evolved through that very process. The farmers and the labourers organized themselves and became distinct political forces. Political parties were formed, first the liberal party (Venstre) and then the right party or the conservatives (Høire). Eventually a grand liberal coalition emerged which assumed power in 1884 and parliamentary rule was gradually established. After 1884 and the peaceful breakup between Norway and Sweden in 1905, the election system was fashioned into a majoritarian 'winner takes all' system (Sejersted, 2011). However, cleavages in early 20th century Norwegian politics did not coalesce into one axis. Instead a multi-party system emerged, where the socialist-oriented Labour Party (*Arbeiderpartiet*) as well as a number of other parties emerged (Rokkan, 1987). The former 'catch all' liberal party gradually split in several warring wings. Various constellations between parties failed. Instead the liberal party was consolidated, with clear fronts against both the radical socialists and the conservatives. The consolidated liberal party combined liberalist thinking with new notions of state intervention. The state was perceived as an institution that could be fruitfully used for social policy modernization purposes. Still, the liberals held their distance to the left flank of the labour party and its persistent Marxist ideology. However, policies were often radical, in the sense that central social policy issues in the form of labour protection and insurance as well as the 8-hour working day were high on the political agenda (Bjørnson, 2001). There was not much power that resided in the economic sphere. Rather than accepting the autonomy of the employer and the firm, new social policies and legislation produced the basis for increasing state intervention and union codetermination in the shaping of working conditions, the alleviation of social risk and the acceptance of the 8-hour working day. Norway very early, in 1906, granted money to the trade union's voluntary unemployment fund. It was basically defined as help to self-help, and the public contribution was quite low. The radicalized Labour Party watched the development from the outside the parliamentary arena (Bjørnson, 2001, p. 151), but the party was able to conduct more radical socialist policies from its local strongholds in the townships. The year 1935 was a game-changer. It marked the de-radicalization of the Labour Party into a more revisionist stance. As the Labour Party ascended to power, new compromises were forged with farmer interests and the labour market actors, producing conditions for regime change and the ascent of the social democratic state.

The formation of collective institutions and actors and the re-form of the crafts

When confronted with the consequences of the withering of guild regulations, the crafts institutions mobilized and reorganized, and craft associations were formed in all towns. A new central level association was formed that attempted to bridge craft and industrial interests: *The Joint Norwegian Representation of Crafts and Industry* (NFHI), was formed in 1886 by 25 local associations in crafts and industry. It was based on a Danish ideal: *The Joint Representation of Danish Industry and Craftsmen*, established in 1879 (Brochman, 1936). The general idea behind the new association was that the crafts had to seek cooperation with industry rather than confrontation. The focus was on issues of mutual interest to industry and crafts, and not political issues as such. The association soon became influential in public debate, and the state provided resources for the production and distribution of its periodical. Although interest articulation elements became more pronounced, the association retained much of its public weal recognition. A number of reform proposals were launched by the association for the reconstruction of more adequate craft regulations, for the formation of technical schools and for the development of an apprentice act. The Association was instrumental in revoking the previous laissez faire policy framework in the crafts, and eventually succeeded in closing the 'lawless interregnum' (Løken, 1985). In 1894 a new law for the crafts was passed by Parliament. It was no longer possible to obtain a craftsman's certificate without a journeyman's test. In 1907 the business Act was passed, where a citizen's letter was made into an obligatory precondition for enterprise formation. A citizen's letter required at least three years of practice in the trade; documented book-keeping skills from a school accepted by the Ministry of Trade, Seafaring and Industry; or a letter of recommendation from trustworthy men with at least five years of experience in the business. Persons who possessed a citizen's charter were allowed to work in the crafts, but they had to hire a certified journeyman. In practice this opened up for the industrialization and capitalization of the crafts, and shipping capital entered this area.

The Norwegian Federation of Employers (NAF) formed in 1900 (Petersen, 1950). It grew out of the NFHI. The purpose was the furthering of viable and durable relations between employers and workers, relations between employers, as well as the handling of social questions of interest to employer members. Capacity for employer coordination grew quite fast. In 1920, the number of members had reached 2 000 enterprises employing approximately 395 000 workers (Petersen, 1950). What sparked off the formation of the employers' association was the establishment of The Norwegian Federation of Labour (AFL) in 1899. Also, the Labour Federation grew fast, and in 1920 union density was on a par with Sweden (Christiansen et al., 2006). The labour movement came to integrate a variety of different groups with different ideologies and strategies, both towards each other, and towards the employers (Bjørnhaug et al., 2000). Some organized on the basis of the skilled worker or craft-based principles, others on the basis of semi- or unskilled interests or the unity of the workplace. Also, employees from the public sector and the municipalities were unionized relatively early. They differed on many accounts, and some central commentators regarded the AFL as the equivalent of a Donau Monarchy as far as interest structure was concerned (Ousland, 1974). The different groups gradually identified with each other in ideological terms. Within the AFL peak organization, the various unions and associations were brought together in an alliance and subjected to systematization processes (Bjørnson, 2003). However, a common approach to training and remuneration based on the strong position and identity of the skilled worker did not materialize. Differences reflected local-, firm- and industry-specific training practices and traditions.

The strategy of the Federation of Employers remained defensive in orientation (Petersen, 1950). Unlike the AFL, the employer organization did not form through organization of local associations. It was constructed from above, assisted by the NHIF. Admittedly, local employer organizations and branch organizations existed prior to its formation, but also these organizations had evolved as defensive measures taken by local employers within the various sectors and regions. As power concentration was a sensitive issue at the time of its inception, the employer federation started out with a quite decentralized structure (Petersen, 1950), but soon it developed elements reminiscent of a more centralized combat organization in order to handle issues of contention and conflicts (Petersen, 1950). As relations to the association of crafts and industry loosened, the domain of the Association of Employers expanded, in order to include questions of social reform. In 1920 also a separate employer organization for the crafts formed.

After the initial confrontations between the employers and the unions, a pattern gradually emerged, where the employers did not attempt to crush neither worker unionization nor tariff building (Bjørnson, 2003). Union formation and collective agreements were gradually viewed as producers of stability, conducive to both employer and worker interests (Bjørnson, 2003). The first national collective agreement was formed in 1909 in the iron industry. A new working day, and a new regulated type of working life was in the making. This development culminated in the Basic Agreement in 1935, where the right to unionization, worker representation, wage negotiations and principles for layoffs became institutionalized. Workers accepted the need for productivity development and rationalization, while the employers accepted workers' right to unionization. Central wage negotiations on the basis of older wage categories like the skilled-, semiskilled- and unskilled workers secured possibilities for coordination across firms, industries and between industries.

Even so, space for the firm was secured through local wage negotiations and firm autonomy in the placing of workers in the various wage categories.

Tensions between crafts and industry

From its inception, the Association of Crafts and Industry was dominated by the crafts (Hald, 1969). The emerging industries were weak and unorganized. After a while, it was felt among industrialists that there was a need for a separate organization for industry. In 1901 two separate chapters of the NHIF were formed, one for industry and one for the crafts. But this was not enough. In several areas, the interest of the export industries did not sit well with the domestic industry and the interests of the crafts. The diversity of interests was contained in the association through the formation of a third chapter for the export industries in addition to crafts and domestic industry. Still unrest persisted. Among the various sources of contention were skill formation and craft regulations. In the views of big industry, craft regulations impeded industrialization. In particular, the export industries promoted strong laissez faire policies and freedom of enterprise. The boundaries of craft law were regarded as arbitrary and outdated, as technological change and standardization processes constantly intervened in a number of contested work areas. Some branches relied entirely on on-the-job training, while in others informal versions of apprenticeship modelled on older craft traditions continued to exist (Kjeldstadli, 1989). As much of big industry was situated next to natural resources in 'company towns' outside the boundaries of the townships, craft regulations and restrictions often did not apply. Nor did it apply to the belt of small craft businesses and shops that evolved around these core companies in rural areas, which were not allowed to train and certify journeymen. The result was heterogeneity within and between industries and crafts. Local adaptation processes and flexibility counted more than industry- and branch-specific standardization. It was impossible to agree on a common legal framework for VET, within industry or between industry and the crafts.

For a long time, interest articulation and collaboration between industry and crafts persisted within one organization. However, the export industries worked for a separate organization of industry, and eventually they succeeded.

The Norwegian Association of Crafts (NHF) and The Norwegian Association of Industry (NI) were established as separate organisations in 1919. The Norwegian Association of Industry (NI) organised industrial firms and their interests in question of industrial policy and regulations as well as taxation, while The Norwegian Association of Crafts organized craft employers, domestic industries not included. NI organized according to a pattern developed by the Swedish Association of Industry (Hald, 1969). It was a 'first order association' with firms as members (van Waarden, 1995) but also a peak organization, organizing sector associations or branch associations. The association grew slowly but steadily, and the number of peak branch organizations affiliated to the association increased from 11 in 1919 to 19 in 1938. NI was, like its predecessor, quite cautious in its policies, and would only engage in matters where full agreement had been secured among members. NI became heavily engaged in the fight over craft regulations. If constraints were attempted to be imposed on free trade and freedom of enterprise in industry, NI resisted. If specific branches of industry wanted constraints in trades within their domain, such regulations were actively resisted only in so far as they represented impediments for other branches of industry. These issues put a constant strain on the relations with the craft association and their members (Hald, 1969). At first relations between the two associations was stable, but subsequently competition evolved between them in the area of domestic industries, and there is much to suggest that workable agreement on demarcations between the two was not found.

Appropriate state commitment and employer interest in VET

In spite of the tensions regarding craft regulations, the search for common ground in vocational education and training for industry and the crafts continued. A joint committee for vocational training as well as a joint office for vocational schooling were formed. They were located in the secretariat of the association for the crafts, allegedly due to 'practical' reasons (Hald, 1969). In most respects, this arrangement constituted a continuation of older policies and practices of common interests in the field of vocational schooling, and it lasted until 1933. A number of reform proposals were discussed in this forum, which for the most part focused on the construction of a separate apprentice act, with public registration and control of apprentice contracts. However, these propositions failed to gain the necessary internal support among industrial employers and master artisans, and were voted down in in the Craft and Industry Associations. In 1921, another type of reform proposal was worked out, based on the Swedish law on vocational schools of 1918, which suggested that the technical evening schools would be organized under the purview of the municipal school boards. Also, this proposal was highly controversial, and failed to make an impression. A possible institutionalization of apprentice training organized by working life without the state was discussed in the aftermath of the Danish apprentice act of 1921, but did not produce the necessary support in industry or in the crafts associations. Interest in apprentice regulation faded out as the downward business cycle kicked in.

Since the inception of the employer organizations, one of the most important strategies for the elevation of craft and industry was a more adequate representation of these interests in Parliament and in local government councils. In two-party systems, conservative parties are normally 'catch all' parties, while in multiparty systems they are smaller, catering for a smaller constituency in general and business in particular. In multiparty systems, it is normally assumed that the formation of employer organizations could be analyzed as part of the conservative right party's strategy in order to cater for an important part of their constituency (Martin and Swank, 2012). As the conservative party Høire evolved, it accumulated similarities with political parties usually found in two-party systems as well as those of multiparty systems (Seip, 1980). Høire emerged out of the resistance to the extension and universalization of parliamentary democracy. When the battle was lost, the party regrouped, centralized, and liberalism in its economic form was adopted (Seip, 1980). But relations between the employer organization and the emerging party system were complicated. In general, industrialists were disappointed with the state. They wanted more political influence and better conditions, and they wanted representation in Parliament. Data on political representation among industrialists show increasing participation in Parliament from the 1880s and up to the 1920s (Enerstvedt, 1967). The majority, 60 percent, represented the conservatives, while 40percent represented the liberal parties. After 1910, the tendency consistently shifted towards the conservatives. In order to counteract what was seen as rising socialism, proportional representation to Parliament had been adopted in 1921 (Kaartvedt, 1984). By that time, this threat outweighed earlier misgivings among both the liberals and the conservatives on this issue. By 1930, the leading industrialists had consolidated their position in the conservative party, Høire, which now emerged as 'their' party. However, the voice of the employers remained weak in Parliament (Enerstvedt, 1967). As the various branches of industry were split in questions of trade protection, tariffs and training, Høire could not do much in one direction without disappointing other interests in the industrial community.

The profile of the new association of industry emphasized principles and values like freedom of enterprise, equal treatment and the common interest of industry. The association was clearly 'voluntarist' in the sense that it was not invested with any delegated authority binding members to the policies of the organization, in contrast to peak employer and worker organizations which often wielded considerable powers and developed quite different organizational structures and procedures. It also held limited financial resources. From the very beginning, the association asserted that there were no strings attached to membership beyond the membership fee, and the association did not have the authority to impose policies on member firms. It was not a strong association, in the sense that it was not designed to overcome collective action problems by means of discipline, duties, procedures and ability to control individual member behaviour. It still retained features similar to that of a common weal organization focusing on information and the social value for industry as the provider of national wealth.

The most common perception among industrialists was that industrial training was a matter for industry, and not the state to decide. Internal differences in strategies on skill formation were admittedly there, but the state should decidedly not be used in order to overcome internal differences in industry, the NI warned. In spite of its liberalist orientation, the NI gradually developed auxiliary and pragmatic ways of engaging with the state bureaucracy. NHIF, the mother organization of the association of industry, had been heavily involved in a number of public commissions (Hald, 1969). NI continued this tradition. The liberal regime had delegated a considerable lot of authority from Parliament to the government. A number of professional organizations as well as employer and employee organizations in crafts and industry had been formed, and they were incorporated into the new liberal state apparatus though a variety of commissions. It was the Eldorado of organized minorities (Seip, 1963). New rules structuring relations between politics and administration were introduced (Jacobsen, 1964). Bureaucracy was reformed, laissez faire ideology abandoned and notions of state-led reform strengthened. A supplement branch of the bureaucracy grew up based on technical expertise rather than law, and means-end rationality rather than legal norms. The consequence was that bureaucracy opened up to social groups and movements. Shielded by state regulations, such groups were able to develop influence and even state-sanctioned authority from within the state bureaucracy. Thus, state capacity and the state administrative traditions came to include considerably more than the classical traits of Weberian bureaucracy and rule of law.

To what extent does this general picture hold as far as VET is concerned? Participation in public administration, committees and councils had its attractions for the employers. Participation carried a promise of influence and autonomy. But such arenas had to be created through state intervention. Already in 1914, the Association of Industry and Crafts had proposed the construction of a state council for vocational schools for industry and crafts. The proposal was taken up by the Ministry of Education, but was voted down in Parliament. The Association therefore found it necessary to establish a private committee for the promotion of training and education in industry and crafts. Applications for state funding were routinely sent to the Ministry of Education, and routinely declined. A ministry with a heart for the business community was not to be found anywhere (Tønneson, 1965). Industry was 'the ugly duckling' (Hald, 1969). In 1933 the state finally agreed to being represented in a reorganized Council of Vocational Training, modelled on Denmark. The Norwegian Federation of Labour was also represented, together with NI and NHF, while the Association of Employers was not.

The 'inferior' position of industry and crafts in the state bureaucracy and the difficulties in developing VET policies and structures illustrates the contradictions and tensions in state-employer relations during the late liberal regime in

Norway. Compared to agricultural interests, industry really had a hard time. It could also be contrasted with the position of handicrafts and domestic science. In handicrafts as well as domestic science, supportive local societies and huge national peak organizations had been formed, which wielded considerable influence, like The Norwegian Handicraft Association, The National Society of Women, the influential Royal Norwegian Society for Development, as well as a host of local associations and organizations (Melby, 1995; Mohr, 1985). In both areas separate state councils as well as permanent positions for stewards in the Ministries of Education (1921) and Agriculture (1916) were formed. In this way, these actor groups could achieve representation and influence on policy formation, rulemaking, rule interpretation and implementation. Few countries had a better and more thorough system for state support and financing of the home economics school system than the Norwegians (Fuglerud, 1980). Industry lacked such a home. Educational policies were more attuned to nation-building and general education than vocational training for industry. As agricultural interests were not separately organized until the 1920s in the form of a farmer's party, they had become part of the great liberal reform coalition, focusing on social reform and smallholder democracy (Rokkan, 1987). The liberals were totally dependent on the farmer vote, and considerable concessions had to be conceded to rural interests. These interests also came to hold a firm grip on all parties when the great liberal alliance evaporated, as compromises always had to be negotiated. The position of handicrafts is also a case in point. Handicraft had traditionally been related to 'folk' art and national motives (Kloster, 1958). Norwegian sociologist Eilert Sundt defined it in broad terms as general skills in rural areas (Sundt,1867). Handicraft was all kinds of rural production for practical and aesthetical use. The broadness of handicraft made it intrinsically different from crafts, according to Sundt, as crafts were specialized. During the 1860s a number of schools for handicrafts were formed both in the towns and in rural areas. These schools aimed at developing prowess in hand work and self-sustainability (Fleischer, 1914), and the total number of pupils and courses exceeded that of any other type of vocational or practical school type at the time. This type of modernization project was able to integrate rural and urban interest as well as the mobilization of state protection and state resources. The institutionalization of regulation for vocational schools, on the other hand, activated these cleavages, creating very difficult conditions for political compromise and state commitment.

The state, the school and the employers

The development of vocational schooling was also heavily influenced by other school modernization concepts. Perhaps the most significant was that of the comprehensive school. In Norwegian society, the comprehensive school signalled nation building and the formation of a school for all, independent of class and geography. School policies had been an all-important lever in the rise of the liberal party to power, and through a series of events conditions for a new and more unitary school system for basic education was established (Telhaug and Mediaas, 2003). In 1896 a five-year comprehensive school system was formed and in 1920 a seven-year template was established, bringing all children up to the age of 14 into the range of a comprehensive primary school system. As more ambitious goals for the expansion of the comprehensive school was formed by the liberals, policies threatened to affect organized interests in working life and the autonomy of their schools.

Alternative reform concepts emphasized the desirability of the parallel school concept, the worth of practical schooling and the salience of a separate technical educational system for the working class. One particular school modernization project attracted interest from a variety of political actors, the idea of a more practical continuation school for working-class children, inspired from Kerschensteiner (Gonon, 1992). The target group was youth who had absolved obligatory primary education and who had entered the labour market at the age of 14. Transitions from school to work marked the beginning of a life phase where there was great need for distinct forms of pedagogical intervention. Such a school had to be practical, it was argued, but the children of the labour classes also needed character formation and support. Such a school would form a bridge between the primary school and life. If such a school should reach its purpose, it had to be obligatory for both sexes.

When such a scheme was introduced to Parliament in 1918, there was considerable sympathy from the liberals, the conservatives as well as the left radicals (Fredriksen, 1980). Streaming a considerable percentage of youth cohorts into such a practical-general school would significantly alleviate the problems in the overburdened lower secondary grammar school which served the upper and the middle classes. It also provided possible benefits for industry and craft interests through the provision of new legal foundations of VET schooling and the prospect of increased state financing. Also, the radical socialists nourished conceptions of a separate school system for and of the working classes (Sejersted, 2011). The price that had to be paid was the integration of VET schooling into a legal framework structured by the practical continuation school and the state. Furthermore, in Parliament compromises had to be negotiated with rural interests. It was unthinkable to devise and implement such a reform only for the towns. As long as rural interest commanded an absolute majority in Parliament, this political lock-in structured practical party policy outlooks. The practical continuation school was a policy solution generated to solve urban youth problems of social integration and socialization. It required new and more robust forms of organizing education and training for all, while rural interests demanded flexibility and possibilities for local adaptation. Political interests in forcing the issue faded, due to a number of factors. There were major problems in accommodating rural requirements. Furthermore, the employers were unable to muster the necessary internal agreement in support of the plan. General education was for the primary school, they argued. The segment of industrialists in favour of the scheme was defeated. The business cycle had turned downwards, and the state suffered considerable financial problems. The liberals lost their comfortable majority in Parliament in 1918, which paved the way for a less stable political situation and alterations in government between the liberals and the conservatives during the 1920s (Demker and Svåsand, 2005). The complexity of the issue defied the construction of a compromise, based on an encompassing reform coalition. The result was problem reduction in complexity and scope. Industrial training was taken out of the policy puzzle. Industrial training remained the business of industry. The tradition of voluntarism persevered, like in England (Sheldrake and Vickerstaff, 1987). The vocational schools were drawn out of the general discussion on a compulsory lower secondary education, and remained unprotected by law. The short-term consequences were disastrous for the technical evening schools, which during the recession were not able to hide behind public regulations. Instead these schools went through the heaviest cuts in Norwegian school history (Tønnesen, 1965).

Conclusion

The interaction between democratization and industrialization, partisan politics and the character of economic coordination constituted important drivers in the formation of the VET systems in European countries. As democratization preceded industrialization, the realization of industrial development and VET schooling in Norway was mediated by an evolving democratic nation state. During the first phase of industrialization, Norway was dominated by a civil servant state with a strong laissez faire orientation. The principle of freedom of enterprise was not only a doctrine enshrined in the constitution, but also a political practice used by the civil servants in order to pacify Parliament. These principles and practices were also applied against the weak guild system, which was abolished. Industrialization was slow and characterized by small firms, and capacity for coordination was low. In this period Norway's political and economic institutions bear most of the hallmarks of a liberal political structure and a liberal production system, producing significant legacies for vocational education and training.

After the turn of the century, conditions changed considerably in the political system as well as in the production system. A centralized multisector employer organization (NAF) was formed as well as well as an encompassing national peak association of worker unions (AFL). Together with the state, a new framework was formed for the negotiating of industrial peace, centralized bargaining and labour protection. A coordinated space for industrial relations was emerging. The organization of employer interest was characterized by the segmentation of industrial action and wage negotiation on the one hand, and skill formation on the other. Skill formation jurisdiction remained in the hand of another and older employer organization, that of the NHIF. Even though crafts and small-sized industrial interests had managed to build an encompassing association at the national level on skill formation, it was a loose federation organized as an 'apolitical' public interest association with limited ability to bind individual member firms. As the organization fragmented into several groups with different opinions and different training strategies, a common template for VET could not be developed. Also, the workers' unions were strongly divided on these issues, and the symmetrical organization of unions and employers amplified divisions between different areas of working life. The unions managed to develop a common interest with the industrial employers in building a cooperative industrial relations system, based on collective and centralized wage negotiating and social protection arrangements. In some industries, this collaboration depended on the skilled workers' competences and identities, while in others skill formation was based on the job-training or a mix of these. The divisions between rural and urban areas and regulations added to the fragmentation of employer interests in training. The loose connection between work skills, training and wages provided important conditions for the construction of collective wage categories in the industrial relations system.

The craft system reorganized and recovered after the 'lawless interregnum', and a new regulatory system for the crafts was built. New encompassing organizations for skill formation connecting industry and crafts emerged, but significant continuities from the guilds to industry, based on the strong position of the skilled worker, did not emerge in skill formation. Employers were divided, and the liberal state could not be used to overcome these collective action problems in order to make employers agree on VET policies. Training in the industrial firm remained legally unregulated. Also, relations between general education and vocational schooling remained loosely coupled in this period. In Norwegian society, the comprehensive school signalled nation building and the formation of a school for all, independent of class and geography. Also, schools for handicrafts and home economics were able to integrate rural and urban interest as well as the mobilization of state protection and state resources. The traditional core of VET, technical schools and apprenticeships, were not. In a sense, vocational education and training remained a double periphery, subjected to marginalization processes both from the industrial relations system and from the educational system. The result was a loosely organized assemblage of VET institutions in industry serving local employers, unprotected by law.

References

Bjørnhaug, I., Bjørnson, Ø., Halvorsen, T. and Ågotnes H.-J. (eds.) (2000) *I rettferdighetens navn. LO 100 år: Historiske blikk på fagbevegelsens meningsbrytninger og veivalg*, Oslo, Akribe.

Bjørnson, Ø. (2001) 'The social democrats and the Norwegian welfare state: Some Perspectives', *Scandinavian Journal of History*, vol. 26, no 3, pp. 197–223.

Bjørnson, Ø. (2003) 'Kamp og krise. Framveksten av et organisert arbeidsliv i privat og statlig sektor 1900–1940', in Heiret, J., Korsnes, O., Venneslan, K. and Bjørnson, Ø. (eds.) *Arbeidsliv, historie samfunn. Norske arbeidslivsrelasjoner i historisk, sosiologisk og arbeidsrettslig perspektiv*, Bergen, Fagbokforlaget, pp. 45–108.

Brochmann, J. H. H. (1936) *Hans Jacob Luihn, 1824–1909: en norsk haandverker i det nittende aarhundrede*, Norges Håndverker forbund, Oslo, Grøndahl & sønn.

Christiansen, N. F., Petersen, K., Edling, N. and Haave, P. (2006) *The Nordic Model of Welfare: A Historical Reappraisal*, Copenhagen, Museum Tuscalanum Press.

Demker, M. and Svåsand, L. (2005) 'Den nordiska fempartimodellen: En tilfällighet eller et fundament?', in Demker, M. and Svåsand, L. (eds.) *Partiernas århundre. Fempartimodellens uppgång och fall i Norge och Sverige*, Stockholm, Santerus Forlag, pp. 9–38.

Dokk, T. (1958) 'Håndverkernes sosiale og økonomiske stilling gjennom tidene', in *Håndverksliv. Et verk om håndverk og husflid. Ved Norges Håndverkerforbunds 75 års jubileum*', Bind 1, Oslo, A. S. Norsk Faglitteratur G. Reinert, pp. 59–82.

Enerstvedt, R. T. (1967) 'Toppskiktet i næringslivet. Politisk deltakelse og partipreferanse 1890–1940', *Tidsskrift for Samfunnsforskning*, no. 8, pp. 269–291.

Fleischer, H. H. (1914) 'Om arbeidet for husflid og haandgjerningsundervisning i Norge 1814–1914', in *Kirke og undervisningsdepartementets jubileumsskrifter 1914*, Oslo, J. M. Stenersens Forlag. Kap. 9.

Fredriksen, P. (1980) *Kunnskap og makt gjennom 100 år. Linjer i arbeiderbevegelsens skolepolitikk fram til 1940*, Oslo, Hovedoppgave i Historie, Universitetet i Oslo.

Fuglerud, G. (1980) *Husstellsskolenes historie i Norge*, Oslo, Grøndahl & Sønn Forlag A.S.

Gonon, P. (1992) *Arbeitsschule und Qualifikation. Arbeit und Schule im 19. Jahrhundert, Kerschensteiner und die heutigen Debatten zur beruflichen Qualifikation*, Bern, Peter Lang.

Grieg, S. (1958) 'Laugsoppløsningen i Norge i europeisk lys', in *Håndverksliv. Et verk om håndverk og husflid*, Ved Norges Håndverkerforbunds 75 års jubileum Bind 1, Oslo, A. S. Norsk Faglitteratur G. Reinert, pp. 50–82.

Grove, K. and Michelsen, S. (2005) *Lærarforbundets historie*, Bergen, Vigmostad og Bjørke.

Hald, K. (1969) *Norges Industriforbund 1919–21 januar1969*, Oslo, Norges Industriforbund.

Halvorsen, T. (1993) *Profesjonalisering og profesjonspolitikk. Den sosiale konstruksjon av tekniske yrker*. Department of Administration and Organization Theory, Bergen, University of Bergen.

Hanisch, T. J. and Lange, E. (1985) *Vitenskap for industrien. NTH – En høyskole i utvikling gjennom 75 år*, Oslo, Universitetsforlaget.

Hodne, F. and Honningdal Grytten, O. (2000) *Norsk økonomi i det 19. århundret*, Bergen, Fagbokforlaget.

Hoel, A. (1914) 'Norges Tekniske Undervisningsvæsen 1814–1914', in *Kirke og Undervisningsdepartementets Jubileumsskrifter 1914*, Oslo, J. M. Stenersens Forlag, Kap 3.

Huchinson, R. (2014) 'Christianias fremvekst og Bergens relative stagnering – i lys av hendelsene i 1814', in Bull, I. and Maliks, J. (eds.) *Riket og regionene. Grunnlovens regionale forutsetninger og konsekvenser*, Oslo, Akademisk Forlag, pp. 203–227.

Jacobsen, K. D. (1964) *Teknisk hjelp og politisk struktur: en studie av norsk landbruksforvaltning 1874–1899*, Oslo, Universitetsforlaget.

Kaartvedt, A. (1984) *Drømmen om borgerlig samling. Høyres historie 1884–1918*, Oslo, Cappelen.

Kjeldstadli, K. (1989) *Jerntid. Fabrikksystem og arbeidere ved Christiania Spigerverk og Kværner Brug fra om lag 1890 til 1940*, Oslo, Pax Forlag.

Kloster, R. (1958) 'Den gamle folkekunsten, husflid og håndverk', in *Håndverksliv. Et verk om håndverk og husflid. Ved Norges Håndverkerforbunds 75 års Jubileum*, Bind 1, Oslo, A. S. Norsk Faglitteratur G. Reinert, pp. 83–99.

Løken, J. C. (1985) 'Håndverk og utdanning', in Halle, E., Wasberg, G. C. and Opstad, S. (eds.) *Historiens mesterprøve. Norges Håndverker forbund 1886–1996*, Bind 2, Oslo, A. S. Norsk Faglitteratur G. Reinert, pp. 87–130.

Maliks, J. and Bull, I. (2014) 'Med regionen som utgangspunkt', in Bull, I. and Maliks, J. (eds.) *Riket og Regionene. Grunnloven og regionale forutsetninger og konsekvenser*, Oslo, Akademisk Forlag, pp. 9–39.

Martin, C. J. and Swank, D. (2012) *The Political Construction of Business Interests: Coordination, Growth and Equality*, Cambridge, Cambridge University Press.

Melby, K. (1995) *Kvinnelighetens strategier: Norges husmorforbund 1915–1940 og Norges lærerinneforbund 1912–1940*, Universitetet i Trondheim, Den allmennvitenskapelige høgskolen, Det historisk-filosofiske fakultet.

Moen, E. (2011) 'Norway: Raw material refinement and innovative companies in global dynamics', in Kristensen, P. H. and Lilja, K. (eds.) *Nordic Capitalism and Globalization*, Oxford, Oxford University Press, pp. 141–182.

Mohr, V. A. (1985) *Arbeidet til husflidens fremme 1890–1930. En undersøkelse av husflidbevegelsens undervisningsarbeide*, Oslo, Universitetet i Oslo.

Ousland, G. (1974) *Fagorganisasjonen i Norge*, Oslo, Tiden.

Petersen, E. (1950) *Norsk Arbeidsgiverforening 1900–1950*, Oslo, Grøndahl og sønns boktrykkeri.

Pryser, T. (1999) *Norsk historie 1814–1860*, Oslo, Det norske Samlaget.

Rokkan, S. (1987) *Stat, nasjon, klasse. Essays i politisk sosiologi*, Oslo, Universitetsforlaget.

Sakslind, R. (1998) *Danning og Yrkesdanning. Utdanningssystem og nasjonale moderniseringsprosjekter*, Oslo, NFR KULTs skriftserie no. 103.

Seip, J. A. (1959) 'Det norske system i den økonomiske liberalismens klassiske tid' (1850–1870)', *Historisk Tidsskrift*, no. 39, pp. 1–58.

Seip, J. A. (1963) *Fra ettpartistat til embedsmannsstat og andre essays*, Oslo, Universitetsforlaget.

Seip, J. A. (1980) *Dyd og Nødvendighet. Høires historie gjennom hundre år 1880–1980*, Oslo, Gyldendal.

Sejersted, F. (2011) *The Age of Social Democracy: Norway, Sweden in the Twentieth Century*, Princeton and Oxford, Oxford University Press.

Senghaas, D. (1985) *The European Experience: A Historical Critique of Development Theory*, New Hampshire, Berg Publishers.

Sheldrake, J. and Vickerstaff, S. (1987) *The History of Industrial Training in Britain*, Aldershot, Avebury.

Sundt, E. (1867) *Om husfliden i Norge*, Kristiania, Abelsted Bogtrykkeri.

Telhaug, A. O. and Mediås. O. A. (2003) *Grunnskolen som nasjonsbygger: fra statspietisme til nyliberalisme*, Oslo, Abstrakt forlag.

Tønneson, K. D. (1965) 'Et departement med det rette hjertelag for næringslivets vel', in *Historisk Tidsskrift bind 44, hefte 1*, 1–16, Idunn.

van Waarden, F. (1995) 'Employers and employer's associations', in Ruysseveldt, J., Huiskamp, R. and van Hoof, J. (eds.) *Comparative Industrial & Employment Relations*, London, Sage Publications, pp. 68–108.

Venneslan, K. (2007) 'Eventyrlig industrivekst.' in Bore, R. R. and Skoglund, T. (eds.) *Fra håndkraft til høyteknologi – norsk industri siden 1829*, Oslo, Statistisk Sentralbyrå, pp. 45–66.

5 Historical evolution of vocational education in Denmark until 1945

Christian Helms Jørgensen and Gudmund Bøndergaard

In comparison with the other Nordic countries, the current Danish system of upper secondary vocational education (VET system) represents the purest form of apprenticeship model. It has more similarities with the dual systems in the German-speaking countries, than with its Nordic neighbours. Like these neighbours, elementary education in Denmark has been transformed into a unified, public, comprehensive school for all. While the other Nordic countries have taken steps to integrate the upper secondary level, Denmark has maintained a separate system of apprenticeships. The question is why this traditional form of VET in Denmark has survived the shift from a feudal, agrarian society to a modern, industrial and later a knowledge-based society. Earlier studies (Thelen, 2004; Archer, 1979) have highlighted the importance of the transition period from a feudal to a capitalist economy for the subsequent trajectory of the national VET system. The dissolution of the guilds raised the question of what new institutions were established and which coalitions were formed between the key stakeholders in the process of developing new regulations of skill formation. What form of collaboration could the state and the labour market organisations agree on to ensure a high quality of skills? In addition, what role would the state take on in the field of VET in connection with the expansion of state-regulated and state-financed general education at all levels? Would the state organise school-based vocational education, or try to integrate VET into the overall educational system? What was the position of the Social Democratic Party, which had a decisive role in the development of the comprehensive public education system? These key challenges were decided upon in the period of transition after the adoption of the principles of liberalism with the Free Trades Act of 1857 until the late 1930s, when a new Apprenticeship Act recognised the self-governance of the labour market organisations in the field of VET.

This chapter explores this transition process with a problem-based approach that seeks to identify the key challenges for the stakeholders of the Danish VET system, and examines how these challenges were managed in a process of struggles, negotiations and compromises. A major challenge for VET during this period was to establish new forms of regulation to maintain the quality of vocational training after the guilds lost their control of the apprenticeship system. The outcome of this process depended on the contentious interactions between the organisations of the artisans and the new industries, between the organisations of skilled and unskilled labour and not least, the interests and the role of the state. It is argued that in the Danish case, like in Germany (Thelen, 2004), strong forms of path dependency and continuity can be identified with regard to the institutional architecture of the VET system.

The historical analysis in this chapter draws on historical institutionalism (Steinmo, 2008; Thelen, 2004) and comparative historical analysis (Mahoney and Thelen, 2010). As described in Chapter 1, this entails a case-based, empirical exploration of the complex social and political interactions of stakeholders in a temporal perspective. Outcomes of such processes, like the current Danish VET system, are seen as the aggregate result of multiple events and interactions that combine the micro and the macro level in a specific context. The analysis is conflict-oriented and explores the diverging strategies and resources of multiple stakeholders in order to identify causal configurations. The intention is to do this without reducing the process to simple power play or zero-sum games, but with openness to the dynamic and context-bound articulation of stakeholder interests, and to trade-offs, inconsistencies and dilemmas in political processes. In order to explain the coherence and continuity of the Danish VET system, it also tries to identify processes of institutionalisation, where alliances of stakeholders make compromises and agreements that stabilise interest coalitions over time.

The following analysis is based on a combination of systematic research in earlier historical studies in the Danish VET system, among them the historical studies published by Nord-VET project (Bøndergaard, 2014; Jørgensen, 2014). The analysis includes studies of original policy documents, government proposals and official reports relating to the key stakeholders in VET. In addition, the examination of the effects of reforms and of the impact of external shifts builds on a large variety of primary and secondary data.

The chapter begins by tracing the roots of the modern VET system in the medieval apprenticeship system, and examines how the common standards of occupational training were maintained by the guilds. Next, it investigates the transition period from the abolition of the rights of the guilds until the passing of the first Apprenticeship Act in 1889. The emphasis is on how the main stakeholders dealt with the challenge of a declining quality of training after the demise of the binding regulation by the guilds. Subsequently, the chapter examines how the demand for school-based training was managed and how the emerging vocational schools connected to traditional apprenticeships. Finally, the chapter examines the gradual institutionalisation of the system of occupational self-governance that reinstated a system of collective skill-formation based on reforms of apprenticeships.

The guild-based regulation of apprenticeships until 1858

The current VET system in Denmark is based on an apprenticeship model, which is rooted in the pre-capitalist apprenticeships regulated by the guilds. Both represented collective forms of skill formation (Martin, 2012; Nelson,

2012) that obliged the individual master or company to organise the training of young people in accordance with common occupational standards. The guilds enforced these standards through the mandatory apprenticeship contracts, tests for completed apprenticeship (journeyman tests) and the master craftsman's qualifying examination. In addition, the guilds exercised a variety of social and cultural practices that supported the members' sense of belonging to an occupational community (Epstein, 2008).

The medieval guilds in Denmark were semi-autonomous institutions that were recognised by the king and town municipalities, but the artisans were not assigned the same civil rights and status as the merchants. The secondary status of the artisans contributed to making them adopt the rules of the German guilds, which were known for craft traditions with a high standard of technical skills and respect for the practical work (Madsen, 1905). Inspired by their German examples, the guilds defined in detail how the training should be organised, what vocational disciplines the apprentices should learn, and the mutual obligations that applied between the apprentice, the journeyman and the master. Failure of the master to comply with those agreements could result in expulsion from the association, receiving no work and losing their collegial support. Specific provisions for training were included in the statutes of the guilds, and the enforcement of the quality of training was ensured through the collegial supervision of the guild's members (Eriksen, 1984; Riismøller, 1940). The regulation of the work of the artisans by the guilds ensured the professional quality of their products, and at the same time ensured a monopoly for the guild. On several occasions (in 1526, 1616 and 1681), the king intervened and tried to abolish the guilds with the claim that they misused their monopoly to fix prices and deliver inferior quality (Knie-Andersen, 2009; Nyrop and Sølver, 1929). The attempts to reduce the role of the guilds were also based on the interests of the nobles and other social groups to have their own craftsmen employed, without regard to the regulation of the guilds. The introduction of absolutism in the 1660s was supported by the clergy and the incipient urban bourgeoisie, and reduced the position of the landed nobility (Zerlang, 1976). This shift heralded a new period for the guilds' apprenticeship regime and a consolidation of the guilds' control of the professional quality (Kløcker-Larsen, 1964). The requirements that the master had completed an apprenticeship and the master craftsman's qualifying examination were now enshrined in law. This represented recognition by the state of the collective regulation through the guilds of skill formation in pre-modern apprenticeships.

The guilds included masters, journeymen and apprentices in one organisation, but quite early the journeymen began to organise separately from the masters. In 1648, the skilled carpenters formed a distinct organisation of the journeymen as part of the guild, and it was recognised by the public authorities (Ravn, 1982). An indication of the strength of this early organisation was the 'great carpenter strike' in 1794, where 400 carpenters went on strike to defend the rights of German carpenters working in Denmark (Sørensen et al., 1992). The separate organisation of the journeymen inside the guilds was a first step to advance their autonomy. This was taken a decisive step further with the formation of independent trade unions in the 1870s, which controlled their own strike fund. The strength of the unions, their high organisational density in some industries and the deep-rooted demarcations between the different occupations was the result of long historical traditions of the craftsmen's organisations. In parallel to the separate organisation of employers and employees, the two parties maintained a consensual cooperation on the modernisation of apprenticeships.

Skill formation in the guild system

A key element of the guilds' apprenticeships was the training provisions, which required the masters to train the apprentice to a level where he could carry out a practical and theoretical test for completed apprenticeship. The pre-modern form of apprenticeships was a combination of work and training, as is the case for modern apprenticeships. During the era of the guilds, completing an apprenticeship also entailed a strong element of upbringing and of being socialised to a particular social role and a particular position as a citizen in society. The apprentices lived, ate and worked in the master's home and workshop, and the master thus took over the father's place by taking responsibility for the upbringing of the apprentice from childhood (Sørensen, 1984). It was the master's responsibility to ensure that the apprentice could pass the test, which worked as a quality control. The masters had an interest in ensuring that the apprentice could pass the apprenticeship test in the best possible way, because this was not only an assessment of the apprentice's skills, but also a judgement of the master's own professional qualifications (Nyrop, 1893). In many trades, the master was required to pay a fine to the poor of the town or a compensation to the apprentice, if he had not prepared the apprentice properly for the test for completed apprenticeship (Hansen et al., 1994; Betænkning 504, 1968).

At the time of the guilds, the apprenticeship system in Denmark was closely connected to the German guild culture. Until the loss of the German-speaking duchies Schleswig and Holstein in 1864, Denmark was part of the German-speaking cultural area in northern and central Europe, which had a significant impact on the development of the apprenticeship system in Denmark (Juul, 2013). The precondition for becoming a master was extensive work experience in the profession, and the journeyman was only considered fully trained when he had been abroad on his journeyman years. While the requirement for craftsmen to travel abroad was formally lifted in 1794, the tradition did not disappear (Petersen-Studnitz, 1882). The journeymen travelled mostly to Germany, Switzerland and the Netherlands, where they could depend on extensive support from the guilds in foreign cities. During these working trips, experiences were exchanged and the journeymen brought new knowledge about the latest technology back to the Danish artisans (Andresen and Agersnap, 1989). For the youths engaged in the commercial sector, the lack of adequate language skills before leaving was a greater barrier than it was for the craftsmen. However, it was common up to the First World War for large trading firms to arrange for young aspiring employees (skilled workers) to work at foreign companies for a period of six months or a full year (Hansen, 1998).

The regulation of apprentices' training by the guilds developed through processes of struggles and compromises with the state, the nobles, the clergy and the merchants. As a result of these struggles, the guilds gained considerable organisational strength and autonomy in relation to the state and the dominant classes. Over many centuries, the Danish apprenticeship system evolved under influence from the German-speaking part of Europe and the cultural interchanges made during the journeymen's years, and through German craftsmen working in Denmark. The apprenticeship system imposed binding quality requirements on the training provided by the individual employers, especially through the journeyman's and master's examinations and stipulations for the content of training. This specific historical heritage is one of the preconditions for the gradual reinstatement of the collective regulation of apprenticeships by the labour market partners after the dissolution of the guilds. This helps explain why the current Danish VET system has more similarities with the German dual system than with the VET systems in the other Nordic countries. However, in the period after 1945, the Danish VET system developed towards the other Nordic countries in a process of institutional layering (see Chapter 10).

The Free Trade Act and the demise of the guilds

The social and political situation in Denmark shifted from the end of the 18th century, as profound land reforms split up the large estates and changed a class of low-productive serfs into a class of independent farmers. The land reforms and the continuation of absolutism until 1848 entailed a substantial weakening of the position of the Church and the nobility. The reforms created the basis for a new agricultural capitalism, which from the 1880s developed into an export-oriented economy based on the processing of livestock products like ham, bacon and butter for export (Zerlang, 1976). The rapid construction of dairies and slaughterhouses was driven by cooperatives controlled by the farmers. The strong cooperative movement represented a parallel to the guilds as independent organisations of collective social and economic interest. This organisation meant that wealth was channelled back into the modernisation of agriculture. In addition, this economic model held back the development of an autonomous class of industrial capitalists. The backwards industrialisation from agriculture stimulated the growth of local craft-based production for the mechanisation of agriculture, for the food-processing industry and for import substitution of consumer goods (Senghaas, 1985). Industrialisation was slow and late and did not allow for a high concentration of industrial capital. The agro-industrial complex opted early for specialisation and diversification, and standardised mass production only developed on a larger scale after 1945. These particular conditions can explain why the skilled craft workers have been dominant in the Danish labour movement from the founding of the trade union movement until today.

The guild system was abolished in France after the French Revolution, and the ideas of political freedom, parliamentary democracy and a free market spread around Europe. In Denmark, the mercantilist belief in state control was replaced by the faith of liberalism in free trade. For a longer period, the Danish guilds had been under attack for being antiquated and unable to catch up with the technological renewal accompanying the industrial revolution. The detailed regulation of the crafts by the guilds met increasing critique by merchants, civil servants and the emerging industrialists from around 1840 (Juul, 2013). It was claimed that the regulation mostly served the goal of maintaining the monopoly of the masters, and that the qualifications of the craftsmen were inadequate. As a result, the Trades Act of 1857 established freedom of trade and deprived the guilds of virtually all their rights and privileges. The key measures to control the quality of apprenticeships, the journeyman's test and the Master craftsman's examination, were abolished.

After the guilds lost their influence, the efforts of the crafts and industries to establish new organisations to represent their interests met with many obstacles in the new climate of liberalism and competition among employers. The artisans and manufacturing industry had diverging interests concerning the regulation of apprenticeship. In Sweden, divergences blocked the collaboration of these groups of employers to instate a collective regulation of training. In spite of these differences also existing in Denmark, a large group of Danish craft and industrial associations founded a 'Joint Representation' ('*Fællesrepræsentation for Dansk Industri og Haandværk*') in 1879 to represent the interests of both small and large employers. Although this alliance did not hold for many decades, it proved to be fruitful for all parties (Hassø, 1940). Earlier, the guilds had represented each craft individually, while in the Joint Representation they could act with more unified strength and were thus able to cooperate for the common interest of safeguarding the vocational training (Rasmussen, 1969; Nyrop and Sølver, 1929). In the commercial sector, the merchants had lost their monopoly on trading, as agriculture and industry found their own marketing avenues outside of the merchants' houses, and in 1890, the Danish Chambers of Commerce was established as a joint national organisation (Hansen, 1995).

During the 1890s, the labour movement's political and industrial organisations achieved a geographical spread and popular support. Following widespread struggles with employers, the local trade unions merged into nationwide trade federations, which in 1898 joined forces in the Danish Confederation of Trade Unions (LO). In a parallel process in the late 1800s, the employers formed employers' organisations, which were later gathered into the Confederation of Danish Employers (DA) (Madsen, 1988). This process of centralisation was driven by labour conflicts between employees and employers, which culminated in 1899 in the most wide-ranging labour dispute ever in Denmark. The conflict resulted in the so-called 'September Agreement', which was based on the mutual recognition of each party's right to organise. The agreement refers decisions on contentious issues for negotiation and mediation, i.a. due to the interests of the employers to take these issues out of the parliamentary field. To support the functioning of this centralised bargaining system, over the following decades the state established a number of centralised mediating institutions by law (Due et al., 1993). The September Agreement laid the foundation for an institutionalised central agreement system supported by legislation. This later became a model for a cross-class coalition on the regulation of apprenticeships through national and local trade committees (Swenson, 1991). These bodies and the central Apprenticeship Council were recognised by the state and in 1937 were granted the legal right to supervise apprenticeships (Juul and Jørgensen, 2011).

Decline and revival of apprenticeships

In the decades following the implementation of the Trade Act, the labour market organisations recognised that the deregulation had led to a gradual deterioration of the training of apprentices (Hansen, 1995). Without regulation, employers who were not trained in an occupation took young people into an apprenticeship, and this had a profound impact on their training. The professional interest that had previously characterised the master, was replaced by a financial interest, namely the desire to earn as much as possible from the apprentice. While the master had previously considered the apprentice a guild brother, the industrial employer now regarded the apprentice more as an employee (Larsen, 1962).

After the abolition of the mandatory contract, it became common for apprentices to leave after a year or two to take higher paid employment as semi-skilled workers in specialised workshop production. Thus, the employers who had invested in the training of apprentices could no longer be sure to reap the rewards when the apprentices, during their final years, could perform almost a full journeyman's work at apprentice pay levels. Some employers sought to remain competitive by basing their production on having many apprentices without providing qualified training. After the dissolution of the guild system, the employers increasingly began to exploit the apprentices, lowering the quality of their education and thus undermining the apprenticeship system (Betænkning 145, 1956).

The employer organisations expressed deep concern over the decreasing quality of the craft workers' qualifications and demanded that the state intervene. A Labour Commission was appointed with representatives from both crafts and industry (Petersen-Studnitz, 1882). It confirmed the critical state of the training of the apprentices, because the financial interest of the individual master had replaced his obligation to provide a broad and qualified training (Arbeiderkommissionen, 1878). As a result, the government passed an Apprenticeship Act in 1889 with the support of the crafts as well as the manufacturing industry. The Apprenticeship Act was the first step in a process that gradually reinstated the quality procedures that had earlier been in the hands of the guilds. The first step was to restore the compulsory training contract and require that the masters made their apprentices attend vocational evening schools. The binding contract was important for the employers' inclination to invest in the training of apprentices. Later reforms in 1921 and 1937 re-imposed in a new form the former measures of quality control from the guild system. These included the introduction of a mandatory journeyman's test controlled by the trade committees, the requirement that the master and trainer should have passed a journeyman's test and the introduction of compulsory, supplementary, school-based training in all occupations (Bøndergaard, 2014).

The role of the state in vocational training

The Apprenticeship Act was important for the revival of apprenticeships in Denmark during this period of industrialisation and liberalisation. A relevant question is why the state intervened earlier and more extensively in the field of VET in Denmark than in the other Nordic countries. State regulation was not an obvious option considering the strong liberalist tradition in Danish politics and the relative weakness of the state. The land reforms had created a new strong class of independent farmers that asserted itself through the Liberal Party, the cooperative movement, the establishment of folk high schools and a nationalist movement for state building from below ('Grundtvigianism') (Korsgaard, 1997). The ideas of this movement supported freedom of trade and were anti-state and anti-academic, and it opposed the development of a strong central state and a centralised education system (Campbell and Hall, 2006). As the position of the nobility had been reduced and the urban, industrial bourgeoisie was weak, the state had room to manoeuvre in order to mediate between the emerging new social classes, the free peasants and the working class. In 1901, an alliance between the Liberals and the Social Democratic Party forced the king, as representative of the state, to fully recognise the principle of parliamentary majority. This 'red-green' political alliance between the peasants and the workers' parties was reinforced in the 1930s in a large social reform, where social benefits for the unemployed were exchanged for financial support for the farmers. This was an important step towards the realisation of the social democratic welfare state after the war. The main building blocks of the universal welfare state were laid by the end of the 19th century by the Liberals in a struggle with the Conservatives, and subsequent social reforms were based on a social alliance between the class of freeholding peasants and the working class (Baldwin, 1990).

Denmark was at the European forefront in developing an elementary school system and promoting literacy in the population. The state was the main driver of the project of building a unified, national education system during the 19th century (Wiborg, 2009). This project gave priority to Christianity, reading, writing and arithmetic to form good citizens to serve the nation, and did not include vocational training (Larsen et al., 2013). Vocational training remained an integrated part of the trades and was firmly under the control of the guilds until 1858. When the state deprived the guilds of their rights, it did not take any initiatives to control the apprentices' training. General education for apprentices was offered by private charitable organisations and the business associations in Sunday and evening schools.

The state's involvement in vocational training through the Apprenticeship Act was not linked to the building of a unified education system. It was mainly a response to the demand from a broad coalition of artisans and industrialists, who were concerned over the decline in the quality of training (Petersen-Studnitz, 1882). This broad coalition can explain why the Apprenticeship Act had a general coverage across sectors and regions. The uniform regulation promoted the formation of a coherent and independent VET system that developed separately from general education in the Latin Schools, which a reform in 1903 transformed into 3-year gymnasiums. It is somewhat paradoxical that the effect of state intervention was to strengthen the autonomy of the self-regulation of the labour market organisations. The consensus among employers in Denmark to allow the state a regulatory role can be explained by the characteristics of the Danish production regime (Pettersson, 2006). Craft-based production was dominant and large-scale industry was weak, especially compared to Sweden.

Another explanation for the broad acceptance of state intervention in VET is that it corresponded to the state's regulation of the labour market. The September Agreement of 1899 laid the foundations for long-lived consensual labour relations that also came to characterise the collaboration in the field of vocational training. To support the September Agreement, the state followed up by passing legislation on the establishment of a Labour Court and an arbitration institution ('Forligsinstitutionen') that gave the voluntary agreements a wider and more binding role. In a similar process, state intervention in VET aimed at supporting the voluntary regulation, on which the labour market organisations in the core sectors of industry had previously agreed.

In addition, the acceptance of state regulation can be explained by a particular type of policy process from below, which was initiated by the labour market organisations. The process was started by organisations in the core sector of the economy, which made agreements to improve the quality of apprenticeships among their members. Subsequently, the state extended this regulation through laws that generalised the quality requirements to the entire labour market. Moreover, the legal requirements (for example for school attendance) were introduced gradually. The first Apprenticeship Act in 1889 was prepared in a commission in 1875 and the bill was proposed, rejected and renegotiated three times before it was passed in a modified version (Juul, 2013). In the first place, it was left to the partners in each occupation to decide on the implementation of the reforms, before the requirements were later made universally binding. The supervision of the quality of the training in the individual companies was first organised jointly on a voluntary basis by the workers and the employers' organisations in some occupations in the 1920s. Later, in 1937, the occupational self-governance was written into the apprenticeship legislation. Thus, the training committees acquired the legal authority to deny companies the right to train apprentices, if they did not fulfil the quality standards set by the committees (Juul, 2009; Rasmussen, 1954).

The governments did not intervene unilaterally in the apprenticeship system, but tried to gain support for reforms among the major stakeholders. State regulation of VET was not part of the building of a unified national education system, but a response to demands from the main stakeholders in VET. Moreover, legislation in the field of VET served to strengthen the autonomy of the VET system in relation to the state. Consensus was achieved by preparing new laws in commissions composed of representatives of all the key interest groups. In this way, the apprenticeship system was maintained with broad support from the major stakeholders across sectors based on occupational self-governance and supported by state regulation. The main principles of this form of governance have been maintained until today. The key role of the labour market organisations has ensured that the qualifications conveyed in VET, mainly through work-based learning, are in accordance with the requirements of the labour market. This is why the transition from VET to employment generally has been, and still is, very smooth for young people completing a VET programme.

The expansion of vocational schools

The establishment of the first vocational schools took place concurrently with the building of a national education system and a nation state in Denmark and in the 19th century, with both internal and external drivers. The introduction of public compulsory schooling in Denmark by law was connected to the land reforms which, from the early 19th century, reduced the position of the landed nobility and created a strong class of freeholding peasants. The formation of a state education system was part of a nation-building project that intensified after a series of military defeats. This included the defeat to England in 1807, the loss of Norway in 1814 and of the German-speaking duchies in 1864, which reduced Denmark to a minor peripheral European state.

Compulsory school attendance for all children from the age of seven until their confirmation at age 14 was introduced by law in 1814. Separate private schools preparing for the Learned School (Latin School) existed for the upper classes, and the public schools in rural and in urban areas were regulated by two separate decrees. However, the common public school was intended for all children. One reason why this succeeded was the absence of confessionary divisions in the Danish population at a time when religious orientation still played a central role in the school system (Korsgaard, 1997). The building of a national school system did not involve the vocational training of apprentices, which took place after completion of the compulsory school. However, the wide coverage and high consistency of the elementary school provided a strong basis for an efficient VET system. The medieval apprenticeship was based exclusively on learning through work, but during the 19th century, various initiatives emerged to form vocational schools. The history of the school component of apprenticeship training is closely interwoven with the history of the inadequate teaching in the primary schools. One educational initiative came from the Folk High Schools that offered courses for apprentices. Another initiative was the free Sunday schools that were established for craftsmen by philanthropists in the early 1800s to compensate for the failure of the primary schools to teach children reading, writing and arithmetic (Nyrop and Sølver, 1929). The Sunday schools only provided education in general subjects and attracted craft and commercial apprentices, as well as journeymen and masters (Petersen-Studnitz, 1882). Yet another initiative to raise the educational standards of the apprentices came from the absolutist state, which was concerned with the low quality of training (Juul, 2013). At the beginning of the 19th century, apprentices and craftsmen were allowed to attend courses at the Academy of Fine Arts, but their participation interfered with the education of young people from higher social strata and generated much resentment (Wagner, 1999).

In the same period, the trades associations established vocational schools with evening classes to supplement the apprentices' training in the workplace due to the growing requirement in some occupations for drawing skills. The Technical Society (*Det Tekniske Selskab*) was established in 1843 by members of various guilds, with the objective of promoting technical and theoretical knowledge among craftsmen. Before 1850, more than ten vocational schools had been established (Juul, 2013). In the second half of the 19th century, broad vocational schools that covered both crafts and industrial requirements were formed, and commerce schools were established as an integral part of the apprenticeship system (Hansen, 1995; Lampe, 1969). It was a common feature of the first colleges for commerce, trades and industry that they originated in the trades' forms of organisation, i.e. first the guilds and later the chambers of commerce or craft and industry federations.

In the second half of the 19th century, schools for apprentices developed both as educational institutions separate from apprenticeships, and as a supplementary vocational education for apprentices. A decisive factor for the subsequent evolution of the vocational schools was the early passing of an Apprenticeship Act in 1889. The law included a requirement for apprentices to attend school-based learning as part of an apprenticeship. The masters were required to provide the necessary time for apprentices to attend technical or commercial schools. The Apprenticeship Act in 1921 made attending evening schools mandatory for all occupations, and the master was obliged to pay the fee. These stipulations resulted in a significant strengthening of the school-based part of apprenticeships, and affected not only the crafts, but also the commercial schools (Hansen, 1995). These legal requirements promoted the growth of vocational schools as part of the apprenticeship system. The schools were initiated and managed as private institutions by the trade organisations, but were later turned into public vocational schools. The vocational schools had no links to the academic upper secondary schools (Latin schools) that gave access to the university.

A reform in 1903 removed the parallel double structure of education by reforming the Latin School and introducing the middle school. This was an important step towards creating a 'ladder system' of education, which connected the elementary school to the upper secondary school (Wiborg, 2009). The Latin School was changed so that it started with a 4-year middle school, preceding 3 years of gymnasium (Skovgaard-Petersen, 1967). The middle school established a bridge from the elementary school to the Gymnasium and opened a vertical ladder that in principle made it possible for all young people to climb up to the highest levels. However, it was not until the 1960s that any significant number of youths from outside of the social elite could take advantage of this opportunity. In addition, at the post-compulsory level, a three-tier system prevailed. After completion of apprenticeships, vertical progression was only possible through a few post-secondary programmes (like the 3-year Teknikum engineer) located in the vocational schools.

The Social Democratic Party and VET

The Social Democratic Party was the driving force behind the realisation of comprehensive schooling in Denmark – and in the other Nordic countries (Wiborg, 2009). The position of the Social Democratic Party and the trade union movement was also essential for the development of VET. In their first political programme (1876), the Danish Social Democratic Party demanded *"common, equal and compulsory schooling"* organised by the state (Det socialdemokratiske Arbejderparti, 1876), and later *"public technical and vocational education"* (Socialdemokratiet i Danmark, 1913). The demand of the Social Democrats, when they first entered the government in 1916, was that the private school system should be taken over by the state, and all young people should be ensured compulsory public education until the age of 18 years. A full-time continuation school for the 14–18 year olds had been proposed by social reformers in Parliament several times from 1872. However, the proposals were turned down by the Liberals and Grundtvigians, who insisted that labour was more appropriate than education for the formation of young people after leaving compulsory school (Ehlers, 1983). In addition, youth labour was indispensable for agricultural production. In 1919, the Social Democratic Party proposed a full-time youth school in Parliament, which was to be a compulsory continuation school for the 14–18 year olds. The protagonist for this proposal was inspired by Kerchensteiner's idea of a work school (Nørgaard, 1978). However, the main objective of this proposal was not to replace apprenticeships with school-based training, but to protect young people under the age of 18 from being exploited by capitalist industry. In the 1920s, municipal attempts to build youth schools only succeeded in enrolling insignificant numbers of young people. When the Social Democratic Party took over government in the 1930s, the youth school was realised, but not as compulsory and full-time day school. Even though vocational subjects could be included in the curriculum, they were not related to the VET system. Municipal youth schools never became a competitor to the vocational schools for apprentices. These conditions made apprenticeships the only real opportunity for education and training for young people outside the narrow social elite until the late 1950s. Apprenticeships enrolled around

15% of a youth cohort and the gymnasiums recruited less than 2% in the mid-1930s. The share of young people enrolling in apprenticeships increased to 30% in the 1950s and over 40% in the 1960s (Albæk, 2004).

The strong cross-class alliance behind apprenticeships did not imply agreement in Parliament over reforms of the Apprenticeship Act. Prior to the reform of 1921, the Social Democrats had proposed a number of improvements for apprentices, among them municipal supervision of the treatment and training of apprentices. As these proposals were not included in the reform, the Social Democratic Party opposed the law, which was passed in 1921 by a government of the Liberal Party. In the 1930s, the Social Democratic Party almost gained a majority in Parliament with 46% of the vote. Furthermore, in 1936 the Social Democrats, together with the left-wing liberals (the Radicals), gained a majority in both chambers. They could pass the Apprenticeship Act of 1937 against opposition from the Liberal Party, who claimed it was an expression of socialism and state bureaucracy (Juul, 2009).

The state gained more control of the vocational schools as public funding increased, but the schools remained separate from the public elementary school and general education. This was mainly the result of the strong position of the craft unions, which opposed the integration of the general and vocational schools (Christensen, 1985). In the interwar period, the Social Democratic Party wanted to make day classes in vocational school mandatory. Due to opposition from employers, it was left to the trade committees to decide whether they would implement it. As a result of the Apprentice Acts of 1921 and 1937, and higher government subsidies, the vocational schools expanded strongly in the interwar period (Hornby, 1966). However, and in contrast to the earlier Social Democratic claims, the vocational schools developed separately from general education.

The Social Democratic Party's policy on VET reflected a conflict between the fundamental political demand that "*society takes over the vocational education of youth*" (Christiansen, 1918, p. 9) and the interests of the craft unions in retaining their control of VET, which was crucial for their existence. To become a member of a craft union, the applicant had to present a journeyman's certificate. In addition, the collective agreements applied to what was defined as 'craft work'. Consequently, VET was vital for the position of the craft unions in a period, when industry reorganised work and tried to replace skilled workers with unskilled and semiskilled workers. An important factor for the outcome of this conflict was the organisation of skilled and unskilled workers in separate unions and the dominant role of the craft unions in the trade union confederation, LO (Galenson, 1955). This situation influenced not only the LO, but also the policy of the Social Democratic Party on the question of training (Christensen, 1985). For this party, social policy and the protection of apprentices from exploitation was just as much a concern as appropriate training. The first Apprenticeship Act included stipulations to protect the apprentices from mistreatment, underpayment, long working days (over 12 hours) and care during sickness. This reinforced the relations between the craft unions and the Social Democratic

Party around policies to resolve the conflict between the economy and social welfare through reforms of the apprenticeship system. In the interwar period, the Social Democratic Party gave up the demand to substitute apprenticeships with school-based training. The party turned revisionist quite early as it came in government and shifted from being a working-class party to become a 'people's party' (Bryld, 1979). Another important factor for the pragmatic policy of the Social Democratic Party after taking over the government was that the party never acquired a parliamentary majority of its own, as it did in Norway and Sweden. Accordingly, the policy of the Social Democrats was based on compromises with the liberal parties in Parliament.

Conclusion: apprenticeships from the guilds to occupational self-governance

The Danish development trajectory in the period before 1945 has many similarities with the other Nordic countries in what Senghaas (1985) calls a 'Scandinavian development path' (that includes Finland). They developed small, open and export-orientated economies, consensual and well-organised labour markets, emerging universal welfare states and a dominant role for the Social Democratic Party. However, we also find some special characteristics in the Danish development, which help to explain the divergence of the Nordic VET systems that became especially pronounced from the 1960s onwards.

Historically, the Danish VET system developed strong connections to the guild and apprenticeship system in the German-speaking countries. Through the guilds, the medieval artisans in Denmark managed to maintain a semi-autonomous position vis-à-vis the state and the other social classes. The guilds developed a complex set of procedures to maintain control over the production of skills and to secure the quality of apprenticeships by obliging the masters to follow common standards for training. These procedures provided the masters with a shared pool of journeymen with certified skills and a monopoly on the work of the occupation. A growing critique of the guilds and the quality of apprenticeships in the first half of the 19th century culminated in the removal of the guilds' right to control apprenticeships. As the lack of collective regulation quickly led to deterioration in the quality of training, the VET system faced the challenge of developing new forms of regulation after the demise of the guilds.

The response to this challenge from the stakeholders in the Danish VET system was to agree on the common regulation of apprenticeships across the crafts and industry, and to make the common standards generally binding through legislation. An inter-class coalition of artisans, industrialists and skilled workers' unions supported the gradual reintroduction of the former quality measures for apprenticeships through the Apprenticeship Acts of 1889, 1921 and 1937. The trades committees hereby acquired the right to supervise companies that were not members of an employer organisation. For the employers, the advantage of state intervention in training was that it imposed equal standards and obligations on all employers and in this way reduced the problem of 'free riders'. The trade committees had the authority to exclude employers from the right to train apprentices if the training was deficient. With this collective form of governance, the labour market organisations maintained control of apprenticeships and also acquired state support to extend the exercise of their authority. This institutional architecture promoted the development of occupational labour markets with strong certification and protection of skills through the trade committees.

Another reason for the centralised and standardised regulation of apprenticeships was that it was in accordance with the general framework for cooperation between the labour market organisations. The grounds for a centralised, corporatist regulation of the labour market were established in 1899. A major conflict that year ended with a general, central agreement between the main organisations, which paved the way for a variety of institutions and procedures for conflict regulation of labour market disputes. The regulation of training was embedded in this overall institutional framework for the negotiation and management of the common interests of the organisations.

The specific historical trajectory of the Danish VET system can also be explained by the Danish social and economic structure in this period. The class of large industrial capitalists was relatively weak, due to the predominance of craft-based, small and medium-sized companies and the strength of the cooperatives in the processing of agricultural products (Dobbins and Busemeyer 2014; Pettersson 2006). The influential class of independent farmers opposed centralised state governance. The Danish Social Democratic Party shifted at an early stage from being a party for the working class to become a 'people's party' (Bryld, 1979). It never won a parliamentary majority on its own, and it had to share the rule of government with smaller centre parties. This parliamentary situation mirrors the Danish class structure, where the urban and agrarian middle classes and the craft workers have played a dominant role. It was a political configuration that required governments to form alliances and seek consensus from a broad range of stakeholders in the policy-making process (Due et al., 1993).

Due to the relative weakness of the state and the strong coalition behind the apprenticeship system, vocational education was not drawn into the governments' nation-building project along with the general school system, but left in the hands of the labour market organisations. The key role of the labour market organisations and the early inclusion of mandatory school-based training in the Apprenticeship Act restricted the opportunities of the municipalities to establish school-based training as an alternative to the apprenticeship system for social policy reasons, as happened in Norway and Sweden. This strong position of apprenticeships was reinforced by the standardised organisation of apprenticeship, due to the uniform and universal legal regulation across sectors, including the commercial/business sector. The position of apprenticeship training and the specific institutional architecture around apprenticeships in Denmark laid the foundation for the continued vitality of apprenticeships in the post-war period and right up to the present day.

References

Albæk, K. (2004) *Om lærepladsspørgsmålet*, Memo no. 212, Blå Memoserie, Copenhagen, University of Copenhagen.

Andresen, C. E. and Agersnap, F. (1989) *Dansk erhvervshistorie 1880 til vore dage*, Copenhagen, Nyt fra Samfundsvidenskaberne.

Arbeiderkommissionen (1878) *Betænkning afgiven af den ifølge kgl. Resolution af 20de September 1875 til Undersøgelse af Arbeiderforholdene i Danmark nedsatte Kommission*, Copenhagen, Schultz.

Archer, M. S. (1979) *Social Origins of Educational Systems*, London, Sage Publications.

Baldwin, P. (1990) *The Politics of Social Solidarity*, Cambridge, Cambridge University Press.

Betænkning 145 (1956) *Betænkning afgivet af den af Arbejds- og Socialministeriet den 21. Oktober 1952 nedsatte Lærlingekommission*, Copenhagen, Statens Trykningskontor.

Betænkning 504 (1968) *Betænkning vedrørende Kvinders Uddannelsesproblemer*, Copenhagen, Undervisningsministeriet.

Bøndergaard, G. (2014) *The Historical Emergence of the Key Challenges for the Future of VET in Denmark*, Nord-VET, Roskilde, Roskilde University [Online]. Available at http://nordvet.dk/ (Accessed 15 January 2018).

Bryld, C. (1979). *Det danske socialdemokrati og revisionismen*, Copenhagen, Selskabet til Forskning i Arbejderbevægelsens Historie.

Campbell, J. L. and Hall, J. A. (2006) 'Introduction: The state of Denmark', in Campbell, J. L., Hall, J. L. and Pedersen, O. K. (eds.) *National Identity and the Varieties of Capitalism – The Danish Experience*, Copenhagen, DJØF Publishing, pp. 3–50.

Christensen, E. (1985) *Konflikter mellem faglærte og ufaglærte arbejdere*, Aalborg, Aalborg Universitetsforlag.

Christiansen, C. (1918) *Lærlingespørgsmaalet, Krav til Lærlingelovens Revision*, Aarhus, Lærlingenes Landsforbund i Danmark.

Det socialdemokratiske Arbejderparti (1876) *Program og Love*, Copenhagen, Hovedbestyrelsens Forlag.

Dobbins, M., & Busemeyer, M. R. 2014. Socio-economic institutions, organized interests and partisan politics: the development of vocational education in Denmark and Sweden. *Socio-Economic Review*, vol. 13, no. 2, pp. 259-284.

Due, J., Madsen, J. S., and Jensen, C. S. (1993) *Den danske model*. Copenhagen, Jurist-og Økonomforbundets Forlag.

Ehlers, S. (1983) 'Ungdomsskolens oprindelse', *Uddannelseshistorie, Årbog 1983*, pp. 7–44.

Epstein, S. R. (2008) 'Craft guilds in the pre-modern economy: A discussion', *The Economic History Review*, vol. 61, no. 1, pp. 155–174.

Eriksen, J. M. (1984) *Håndværkerlavene i Danmark 1400–1600*, Copenhagen, University of Copenhagen.

Galenson, W. (1955) *Arbejder og arbejdsgiver i Danmark*, Copenhagen, Danske Forlag.

Hansen, F. L. (1995) *Fra laug til lov: Handelskolernes opståen*, Frederiksberg, Danmarks Handelsskoleforening.

Hansen, F. L. (1998) *I lovens navn: Handelskolernes udvikling 1920–1965*, Frederiksberg, Danmarks Handelsskoleforening.

Hansen, F. L., Olsen, N. L. and Haugstrup, H. (1994) *Horsens Handelskole 125 år 1869–1994*, Horsens, Horsens Handelskole.

Hassø, A. G. (1940) *Et Bidrag til Københavns Haandværks Historie i det sidste hundred Aar*, Copenhagen, Chr, Erichsens Forlag.

Hornby, H. (1966) *Bidrag til Dansk Håndværkerundervisnings historie*, Copenhagen, Teknisk Skoleforening.

Jørgensen, C. H. (2014) *The Current State of the Challenges for VET in Denmark*, Nord-VET, Roskilde University [Online]. Available at http://nord-vet.dk/ (Accessed 15 January 2018).

Juul, I. (2009) 'Fra lavsvæsen til fagligt selvstyre: Arbejdsgivernes indflydelse på erhvervsuddannelserne i perioden 1857–1937', *Oekonomi og Politik*, vol. 82, no. 3, pp. 3–14.

Juul, I. (2013) 'De danske håndværkeruddannelse i krydsfeltet mellem det europæiske og det nationale', *Uddannelseshistorie 2013*, pp. 60–80.

Juul, I. and Jørgensen, C. H. (2011) 'Challenges for the dual system and occupational self-governance in Denmark', *Journal of Vocational Education & Training*, vol. 63, no. 3, pp. 289–303.

Kløcker-Larsen, F. (1964) *Lærlingeuddannelsen i Danmark. En redegørelse for de af lærlingeloven af 1956 omfattende uddannelse*, Copenhagen, Einar Harcks Forlag.

Knie-Andersen, B. (2009) *Guldsmede og guldsmedelaug i Danmark 1429–1900*, Copenhagen, National Museum of Denmark.

Korsgaard, O. (1997) *Kampen om lyset: dansk voksenoplysning gennem 500 år*, Copenhagen, Gyldendal.

Lampe, J. (1969) 'Træk af handelsskolernes historie', in *Årbog for Dansk Skolehistorie 1970*, Copenhagen, Selskabet for Dansk Skolehistorie, pp. 7–21.

Larsen, C., Nørr, E. and Sonne, P. (2013) 'Da skolen tog form', *Dansk skolehistorie*, Bd. 2, Aarhus, Aarhus Universitetsforlag.

Larsen, K. F. (1962) *Lærlingeuddannelsen i Danmark*, Copenhagen, Institut for Organisation og Arbejdssociologi.

Madsen, J. (1905) *Danmarks Industri og Haandværk*, Copenhagen, A. Christiansens Forlag.

Madsen, K. J. (1988) 'Erhvervsuddannels ernes udvikling i en samfundsmæssig sammenhæng', in *Uddannelse*, vol. 21, no. 3, pp. 173–183.

Mahoney, J., and Thelen, K. (eds.) (2010) 'A theory of gradual institutional change', in Mahoney, J., and Thelen, K. (eds.) *Explaining Institutional Change: Ambiguity, Agency, and Power*, Cambridge, Cambridge University Press, pp. 1–37.

Martin, C. J. (2012) 'Political institutions and the origins of collective skill formation systems', in Busemeyer, M. R., and Trampusch, C. (eds.) *The Political Economy of Collective Skill Formation*, Oxford, Oxford University Press, pp. 41–67.

Nelson, M. (2012) 'Continued collectivism: The role of trade self-management and the Social Democratic Party in Danish vocational education and training', in Busemeyer, M. R. and Trampusch, C. (eds.) *The Political Economy of Collective Skill Formation*, Oxford, Oxford University Press, pp. 179–202.

Nørgaard, E. (1978) 'Ungdomsskolen og K.M. Klausen', *Uddannelseshistorie Aarbog 1978*, pp. 103–115.

Nyrop, C. (1893) *Bidrag til dansk haandværkerundervisnings historie*, Copenhagen, Nielsen and Lidiche.

Nyrop, C. and Sølver, A. (1929) *Fællesrepræsentationen for Dansk Industri og Haandværk 1879–1929*, Copenhagen, Nielsen & Lydiche.

Petersen-Studnitz, A. (1882) 'Hvad danske industridrivende forlanger af Staten, En oversigt'. *Nationaløkonomisk Tidsskrift*, Bind Første række, vol. 20, pp. 81–206.

Pettersson, L. (2006) *Är Danmark bättre än Sverige? Om dansk och svensk yrkesutbildning sedan industrialiseringen*, Malmø, ØI Forlag.

Rasmussen, S. (1954) *1929–10. december 1954*, Jubilæumsskrift, Copenhagen, Metalindustriens Lærlingeudvalg.

Rasmussen, V. (1969) 'De tekniske skolers historie', *Årbog for Dansk Skolehistorier 1969*, pp. 7–41.

Ravn, T. B. (April 1982) 'Fra svendelav til fagforening, Brud eller kontinuitet?' *Arbejderhistorie*, pp. 3–16.
Riismøller, P. (1940) *Fra svendekro og lavshus*, Copenhagen, Det Schønbergske Forlag.
Senghaas, D. (1985) *The European Experience: A Historical Critique of Development Theory*, Berg, Leamington Spa.
Skovgaard-Petersen, J. (1967) 'Den politiske drøftelse af forbindelsen mellom almueskolen og den lærde skole', *Årbog for Dansk Skolehistorie 1967*, pp. 85–110.
Socialdemokratiet i Danmark (1913) *Program og Love*, Vedtaget af Kongressen 1913, Aarhus, Arbejderpartiets Bogtrykkeri.
Sørensen, J. H. (1984) 'Lærlingeuddannelsernes historie – fra erhvervsindføring til ungdomsuddannelse', in Jakobsen, A. (ed.) *Erhvervsuddannelse – krise og fornyelse*, Copenhagen, Erhvervsskolernes Forlag, pp. 252–267.
Sørensen, P., Grelle, H. and Nielsen, V. O. (1992) *Under herrer og mestre. Om arbejdsvilkår og Danmarks første storkonflikt i 1794*, Copenhagen, SFAH.
Steinmo, S. (2008) 'Historical institutionalism', in Keating, M. and Della Porta, D. (eds.) *Approaches and Methodologies in the Social Sciences, a Pluralist perspective*, Cambridge, Cambridge University Press, pp. 118–138.
Swenson, P. (1991) 'Bringing capital back in, or social democracy reconsidered: Employer power, cross-class alliances, and centralization of industrial relations in Denmark and Sweden', *World Politics*, vol. 43, no. 04, pp. 513–544.
Thelen, K. (2004) *How Institutions Evolve: The Political Economy of Skills in Germany, Britain, the United States, and Japan*, Cambridge, Cambridge University Press.
Wagner, M. F. (1999) *Det polytekniske gennembrud. Romantikkens teknologiske konstruktion 1780–1850*, Aarhus, Aarhus Universitetsforlag.
Wiborg, S. (2009) *Education and Social Integration: Comprehensive Schooling in Europe*, New York, Palgrave Macmillan.
Zerlang, M. (1976) *Bøndernes klassekamp i Danmark*, Copenhagen, Medusa.

6 The modern evolution of vocational education and training in Finland (1945–2015)

Marja-Leena Stenström and Maarit Virolainen

Introduction

In Finland, 1945–2015 was the period during which the welfare state became the main player in organising vocational education and training (VET). Accordingly educational institutions have expanded to respond to challenges arising from the emergence of the welfare state, especially the social division of labour and the development of production technologies (see e.g. Henriksson et al., 2006). Finland was mostly an agrarian society and structured by small local communities during the beginning of the period 1945–2015. Before the Second World War, the need for establishing traditions for vocationally oriented education was limited because most citizens learned their occupations in the context of everyday routines at work and in daily life (Antikainen, 1993, p. 103). Finland started to catch up with other Nordic countries and modernised as industrialisation started to become effective. Industrial culture created new kinds of occupational needs; craftsman-like skills lost the central value that they had possessed in the agrarian society, where many goods for households had been produced by families themselves or bought from local craftsmen. The VET system constructed after World War II played an important role in modernising the Finnish nation state. The VET model linked school-based with work-based learning and connected education with the labour market in a specific, Finnish way (see, e.g. Dobbins and Busemeyer, 2015).

The aim of this chapter is to elaborate the historical evolution of the Finnish vocational education and training (VET) system as it unfolded from 1945 to 2015. The focus of our research was on the development of VET as an institutionalised education at the upper secondary level (initial vocational education and training). To begin with, we made an analysis of its development in relation to that of the Finnish state because the state has been a central player in redefining and reorganising VET in Finland. Our findings show how the organising of Finnish upper secondary VET is linked to the construction of Finland as a welfare state, and we present what kinds of gradual, neo-liberal deregulations have influenced the VET development since the 1990s. The emphasis of our analyses was on the recognition of major turning points, in part since there has been only scarce historical research on the role of the different players as co-determinants of Finnish VET, also taking into account the policies of the different employer and employee organisations and individual policymakers with respect to VET.

The historical turning points described in this chapter are divided into three periods: 1) the emergence of VET and the welfare state from 1940 to 1960; 2) the time of rapid growth and consolidation of the welfare state in the 1970s and 1980s; and 3) the time of the challenges of Europeanisation and globalisation since the 1990s. The analyses presented in this chapter are partly based on previous VET research, statistics and policy papers.

Emergence of VET and the welfare state from 1940 to 1960

Post-war development of Finnish VET

In Finland, school-based vocational education and training emerged on a large scale only during the societal reconstruction after the Second World War, when Finnish educational policy was intertwined with the project of the welfare state (Stenström and Virolainen, 2014a). Finland shifted from a socially supported small-scale farming society to a welfare state of social security and paid work (Laukia, 2013b, p. 172; Kettunen, 2001, 2013).

After the Second World War, the economic structure started to diversify and became less dominated by agriculture. The industry, trade and public services were strengthened and there were demands for rural life to be modernised (Laukia, 2013a, 2013b, p. 172). The task of the Finnish industry was to produce the goods necessary to pay for the substantial war reparations demanded from Finland (Kivinen and Peltomäki, 1999). Heavy industry dominated, and new methods of mass production in the textile, clothing, leather, shoe and food industries emerged. At the same time, small-scale farming decreased dramatically.

The change in the dominant forms of production was more rapid in Finland than in the other Nordic and European countries (Haapala, 2006). However, it took until the 1960s for the share of the Finnish working population involved in agriculture to decrease to the level (36%) already seen in other Nordic countries by 1930 (Christiansen et al., 2006). The settlement of the population evacuated from the Karelian part of Finland during the Second World War and the number of returning war veterans increased the numbers of the agricultural population as they maintained an agrarian culture after the Second World War. Furthermore, agricultural production was slow to modernise as crofters did not consider the new technology to be cost-effective (Itälä, 2000). When the amount of industry, trade and public services increased, urbanisation started as people moved from the countryside to the cities. Urbanisation was also late in transforming Finnish society compared to its transformation of other Nordic countries (Christiansen et al., 2006, p. 356). Industrialisation, the expansion of the economy and new ways of living created new occupations for which vocational education and training was needed. In addition, after the Second World

War, there was a great demand for skilled workers in the labour market since only 5% of industrial workers had gained training for their job before entering to the labour market (Tuomisto, 1986).

The demand for organising VET for the young did not arise from economic development only. Policymakers were also concerned about youths' development, use of time and societal inclusion during a time of societal change toward industrialisation and increasing migration. VET was expected to protect youth from poverty and marginalisation. Vocational school was perceived as workers' school. There were few vocational school students from farming families in the VET schools as these schools were located in towns and other population centres (Laukia, 2013b, p. 142).

The new law (Finland. *Laki ammattioppilaitoksista* 184/1958) concerning vocational education meant that all municipalities consisting of more than 20,000 inhabitants had to have a vocational school and smaller municipalities had to reserve study places for their youngsters at these schools (Laukia, 2013a). The law initiated Finnish VET's expansion and further differentiation in the 1960s and 1970s (Klemelä, 1999). It established school-based VET as the dominant model of VET in Finland, although Sunday schools can be seen as the first actual vocational schools and predecessors of the later expansion of vocational school-based education (Klemelä, 1999, p. 34; Tuomisto, 1986, p. 71). The vocational schools operated under the Ministry of Trade and Industry; more specifically, in the fields of industry, construction, handicraft, home economics and traffic (Laukia, 2013b, p. 228). This field-specific division of Finnish VET established itself long-term, yet separate gender-specific vocational schools were to change into vocational schools for both girls and boys (Laukia, 2013b, p. 229).

During the period from the 1950s to the 1960s, new types of education and training institutions for industry, technology and business were constructed in particular (Klemelä, 1999). In parallel, agricultural institutions suffered from a lack of students and increasing financial difficulties, but their maintenance was defended with the intention to prevent young people from moving away from rural areas. VET was also set a regional task: it was committed to getting young people to stay in their place of residence in order to slow down the concentration of people in towns (Laukia, 2013b, p. 231). The expansion of VET at the time was not only an outcome of established new vocational institutions; the number of students increased due to the baby boom that followed the Second World War and resulted in larger age cohorts among the young. This meant that the increase of the number of VET students was particularly strong during the period of 1950–1960 (Klemelä, 1999). In 1950, less than 30,000 persons studied at vocational institutions, whereas by 1960 their number had almost doubled (see Table 6.1). In parallel, the number of youths who completed the matriculation examination of the general upper secondary schools also increased; more specifically, from less than 5,000 annual graduates to over 20,000 in the 1970s (Kaarninen, 2011).

The expansion of VET was coordinated by the state administration, which was centralised in the 1960s. Until the 1960s, the administration of vocational education and training was shared by several ministries and central administrative boards.

Table 6.1 Vocational secondary education and secondary school entrants from 1940 to 1960 (Laukia, 2013b, p. 328, p. 334; Kaarninen, 2011, p. 409)

Year	VET students[1]	Secondary school entrants[3]	Share of secondary school entrants among 11-year-olds[4]	Live births related to cohorts of secondary school entrants (birth year)[5]
1945	20,380[2]	15,580	25%	67,713 (1934)
1950	29,098	18,956	27%	78,164 (1939)
1960	56,733	37,089	38%	103,515 (1949)

1   The number of VET students adopted from Laukia, 2013b, p. 328. The figure refers to students of all grades (1–3, depending on the field) in VET schools and is thus not comparable with the number of secondary school entrants.
2   The number of VET students in the year 1940, whereas the numbers in the other columns relate to year 1945.
3, 4   Numbers adopted from Kaarninen, 2011, p. 409.
5   Data on live births adopted from Statistics Finland population figures.

In 1966, the Finnish National Board of Vocational Education was established as part of the Ministry of Trade and Industry, and in 1968 the Board was transferred to the Ministry of Education. Finally, in 1991, the general (Finnish National Board of General Education) and vocational (Vocational Board of Education) boards were merged to form the current Finnish National Board of Education (FNBE) (Cedefop ReferNet Finland, 2011, p. 30). Since then, the cooperation between vocational and general upper secondary education institutions has increased; for example, the youth education pilot project started in 1992.

Employer and employee organisations' emerging interest in participating in defining VET

Following the Second World War, apprenticeship training continued to hold a central status as a form of initial vocational education and training (VET) in many countries (e.g. in Germany, Austria, Denmark). In Finland, on the contrary, apprenticeship training was reformed into a minor route (Olofsson and Wadensjö, 2006). In Finland, at their outset, the export industries had no connections to former guilds and their craft traditions (Sakslind, 1998). Some factory owners who were oriented toward mass production (e.g. steel and paper mills) had established vocational schools of their own to train a specialised, skilled workforce. The number of these industries' vocational schools increased between the 1960s and 1980s (Tuomisto, 1986, p. 306; Laukia, 2013a). Industries which had no particular interest in taking on the responsibility for youth training by developing apprenticeships left this task up to the state and municipalities. The new Apprenticeship Act of 1968 did not change the situation because both employers and employee organisations saw apprenticeships as complementary to school-based forms of vocational education. Apprenticeship played only a marginal role in certain specialised fields of industry (Kivinen and Peltomäki, 1999).

After the Second World War, VET increasingly became a topic of both industrial policy and education policy discussions. The political parties highlighted different aspects of VET. The labour movement emphasised the role of general subject matter in VET. The non-Socialist political parties and employers stressed direct task training at workshops. The Agrarian League advocated the expansion of the vocational and secondary school networks in rural areas (Itälä, 2000).

In Finland, the class compromise between capitalists and labourers was built through agreements between the government, the Finnish Employers' Confederation (STK) and the Central Organisation of Finnish Trade Unions (Suomen Ammattijärjestöjen Keskusliitto, SAK) after the Second World War, when employers were forced to accept collective negotiations with organised labour (Nieminen, 2000). The parity-based forms of collective labour relations were constructed in the manufacturing industries through a process that spread from the national central level to the national sectoral level and finally to the local and workplace levels (Kettunen, 2001). The autonomy of collective agreements was still limited though, due to governmental regulation of wages and prices until the middle of the 1950s, and the disagreements in the relations culminated in the General Strike of 1956 (Kettunen, 2001). In the 1960s, the negotiations between the labour market organisations improved once the trade union movement was gradually reunified between 1964 and 1969 (Bergholm, 2016, p. 59). From the end of the 1960s, the 'income' policy began (Bergholm, 2016). A new type of intertwining of labour market agreements with social and economic policies was introduced (Kettunen, 2001). In parallel, the consensus enabling the development of the welfare state was built on the basis of income policy agreements, in which the parties represented the central interest organisations of blue- and white-collar workers, private and public sector employers, agricultural producers and the government (Kettunen, 2001).

The employers' organisation wanted to drive its privileges in VET policy issues and established an educational department within the Finnish Employers' Confederation (STK) in 1952 (Tuomisto, 1986, pp. 199–200). It acknowledged the purpose of school-based VET and identified its duties, including research on educational demand, making long-term educational forecasts, and consulting and organising educational bodies to support the planning of education. In parallel, trade unions had no independent line concerning vocational education in the 1950s, but their representatives participated in working with the Vocational Training Council (Ammattikasvatusneuvosto) and the planning of VET curricula (Heikkinen, 1995, p. 200).

The interest of employer organisations in educational policy continued to increase only in the 1970s with the establishing of the comprehensive school system and the reforming of upper secondary vocational education (Purhonen, 2000). In the 1970s, the Finnish Employers' Confederation (STK) considered collaborative relations with the trade union movement to be necessary in order to guarantee industrial peace and social stability (Bergholm, 2016, p. 70). However, the employers' and employees' attitudes differed from each other with respect to reforming upper secondary education. The employers emphasised occupational skills as a central task of VET, whereas the employees' organisations stressed that general components should comprise VET (Koskela, 2003, p. 44).

The cooperation between employers, employees and teachers continued in the 1980s. Their organisations participated in the curriculum planning for upper secondary vocational education. The activities of the Vocational Training Council (Ammattikasvatusneuvosto) ended in 1987 and its work was delegated to field-specific Training Committees in 1988 (Laukia, 2013b, p. 93). Different vocational fields had their own Training Committees that consisted of representatives from employer, employee, teacher and educational administrations (Suursalmi, 2003, p. 12). The purpose of these committees was to develop VET in cooperation between employers and educators. Both the employer and employee representatives agreed for the forming of the vocational training to be led by the state and municipalities (Kivinen and Peltomäki, 1999).

The period of rapid growth and consolidation of the welfare state from 1970 to 1980

Strengthening school-based VET – the reform of vocational upper secondary education

The period from the 1960s to 1980s was a period when the issue of enhancing universal general education and equality dominated educational policy, while the stratified development of the education system lost ground (cf., Heikkinen and Henriksson, 2001). In the 1960s, Finland looked to Sweden for educational reform models since it was seen as one of the pioneers of the modern Nordic welfare state (Aho et al., 2006, p. 33). The Finnish Parliament decided to introduce the reform of the common basic education. The reform was implemented during the years 1972–1977 and established a unified comprehensive school system (*peruskoulu,* in Finnish) (Laukia, 2013a; Salminen, 1999). The left-wing government led by the Social Democratic Party made educational reform its primary goal and emphasised the importance of social and economic equality (Aho et al., 2006). The reform divided opinions among politicians, despite its main objective of offering the same quality education in the form of 9 years of compulsory comprehensive schooling to all children regardless of their socioeconomic background, domicile, gender or mother tongue.

After the compulsory school reform, which integrated former primary and stratified lower secondary education to cover grades 1–9 (for those aged 7–16 years), it was felt that the reform of the non-compulsory upper secondary education system was also necessary. The reason for reorganising the existing upper secondary education was to improve educational planning and the control of the number of study places, as well as to provide a study place for every compulsory school graduate in either general upper secondary education or vocational upper secondary education (Virolainen and Stenström, 2015; Salminen, 1999).

The 1971 Committee for Education prepared the upper secondary education reform and the government confirmed its direction in 1974. According to the government's decision, vocational education and training should in principle be developed as an educational pathway to higher education studies, and it should be compatible with the upper secondary school system (Klemelä, 1999); however, the reforms of the upper secondary schools and vocational schools were implemented separately. The reform aimed at educational equality, the rationalisation of education, the unification of diffuse VET, a decrease in consecutive qualifications taken by individuals and the removal of dead ends in the educational structure, while it increased the number of study places in order to meet the number of compulsory school graduates (Salminen, 1999).

The Finnish upper secondary vocational education reform was carried out field by field in the period from 1982 until 1988. In contrast to Sweden, the idea of comprehensive upper secondary education was rejected in Finland, because there was no consensus within political parties to make a decision about a unified upper secondary education (Meriläinen and Varjo, 2008). The reform period of 1982–1988 unified vocational curricula into a smaller number of programmes, resulting in a system with 25 basic programmes and 250 lines of specialisation at school and college levels (Stenström and Virolainen, 2016).

The general education component introduced in the vocational upper secondary and post-secondary education curricula was meant to orient students toward trades and corresponding occupations. The aim of the general education component was to enable young people to develop a more general perspective on the field of production (Ekola, 1991). The national policy of vocational education was to broaden the scope of the VET provision, to raise national standards, and to prepare students to be able to meet the demands of working life. In practice, the teaching of occupational skills and knowledge was reorganised by educational institutions to form part of practica (Klemelä, 1999). Replacing workplace learning with practically oriented studies at VET schools reflected the notion of school-based VET. Along with the reform of the 1980s, there were demands for raising the status of school-based vocational education and training to be on par with the general education (Borgman and Henriksson, 2000). The reform failed to materialise some of the expectations with which it had been loaded. The new system did not fully succeed in promoting equality and removing the influence that students' social background held in education (Stenström, 1997). Nevertheless, the vocational upper secondary reform was important in that it was the first time that post-compulsory education was planned as a whole in Finland.

Access to higher education in the 1980s

In general, there were no direct routes from vocational education to higher education before the upper secondary education reform took place in the 1980s (Numminen, 2000). Some exceptions to this general rule existed though, since some regional higher education institutes in the fields of technology and commerce accepted students who had completed post-secondary vocational programmes (*opistoaste*, in Finnish). They were able to gain eligibility for higher education, such as on the basis of recommendations or if they completed some additional studies (Kaarninen, 2013, p. 29). In the 1980s, the Ministry of Education designed the Development Plan for Education, in which many revisions were planned to make vocational education more competitive with the general education (Aho et al., 2006, p. 80). A decree (Finland. Asetus 275/1984) was issued to give vocational college (*opisto*, in Finnish) graduates limited eligibility to progress in the same educational fields as the students at universities. Despite this, stratified compulsory education was abolished, but the routes within post-compulsory vocational education still remained disparate and stratified in aiming at differing groups of entrants.

The vocational upper secondary education reform that took place from 1982 until 1988 initiated a route to higher education through the post-secondary vocational programmes. The Vocational Education Act (Finland. Laki ammatillisista oppilaitoksista 487/1987) opened a channel from VET to university studies and other higher education (Laukia, 2013b, p. 285). The 3-year VET programmes provided general eligibility for higher education, while 2-year programmes gave eligibility for further studies within the same field. This was the first time that an Act integrated VET consistently and as part of the overall Finnish education system. The VET route's binary position with respect to general upper secondary education was not abolished though (Lasonen and Young, 1998).

Challenges of Europeanisation and globalisation since the 1990s

A need to reform upper secondary and higher education

Since the 1990s, Finland can be seen as an emerging liberalistic EU state. In 1995, Finland joined the European Union. Furthermore, at the beginning of the 1990s, the concurrent rapid collapse of the banking system and the fall of Soviet trade swiftly changed the social and economic situation (Heikkinen, 2001). The need to reform Finnish upper secondary and higher education had been recognised already before the economic change toward recession, though. In order to find solutions for the development of the education system, two experimental projects were started in parallel: the youth education pilot project and the polytechnics experiment (polytechnics would later be renamed universities of applied sciences, UAS). The experimental reforms were informed by social scientific ideas concerning the development of the welfare state in late modernity, such as the concepts of individualisation and reflexivity (see e.g. Atkinson, 2010; Beck, 1992; Giddens, 1990). The post-Second World War reorganisation of welfare services and civic rights by the state had intervened in the continuation of the existing social class structure and familial bonds, thus reorganising society itself.

The central idea of the youth education pilot project in the 1990s was to investigate opportunities for the development of upper secondary education. The experiment was a compromise of educational policy, resulting from left-wing social democratic interest in following the Swedish model of a unified upper secondary education system having been rejected (Meriläinen and Varjo, 2008). However, the experiment's legislative framework allowed general and vocational upper secondary institutions to collaborate regionally. The pilot approach did not become a model practised in the whole of the country; yet some interest has remained, particularly in double qualifications.

Contrary to the youth education experiment, the parallel polytechnics experiment received a permanent position later on, in the 1990s. The Finnish polytechnics were developed from former vocational colleges and higher vocational education institutions. The principles underlying polytechnic education derived from the need for a highly trained expert workforce. The polytechnic reform created a binary system of higher education in Finland and established a systematic route for students to extend their studies from VET to higher education. In an international context, the Finnish acronym 'AMK' (*ammattikorkeakoulu*, in Finnish, literally means 'vocational higher education institution') has also been used to differentiate AMKs from British polytechnics (e.g. Ahola, 2006). Both Finnish traditional science universities and polytechnics were governed by the Ministry of Education (Stenström and Virolainen, 2014b).

Alongside the youth education experiment and establishing AMKs, the upper secondary VET system was reorganised into study programmes based on occupational sectors and fields. Until 1995, students were offered three levels of vocational qualifications: school level (2–3 years), college level (2–4.5 years), and higher vocational level (3–4.5 years). After the curriculum reform in 1995, the number of Finnish upper secondary VET qualifications was reduced considerably and subsequently 77 basic vocational qualifications were provided with each taking 2–3 years to complete (Stenström and Virolainen, 2016).

A need to enhance the links between VET and working life

In the 1990s, the influence of employers' interests in educational policy increased since a severe economic recession and increasing unemployment weakened labour's negotiating power. The market-oriented ideology of the 1990s supported the demands of employers, who succeeded in their labour market and economic policy objectives (Nieminen, 2000). The recession sped up the state's need to enhance the links between school and working life. In particular, the growth of the unemployment rate to 20% led to an increasing demand to develop apprenticeship training, but apart from the school-based VET (Kivinen and Peltomäki, 1999). A new Apprenticeship Act was launched in 1992 (Finland. Laki oppisopimuskoulutuksesta, 1605/1992). Its aim was to improve the status of apprenticeship training as a work-oriented form of training in an otherwise mainly school-based vocational education system during the time of recession (Poutanen, 2008). Furthermore, it was hoped that the apprenticeship training would interest unemployed, unskilled young people at risk of marginalisation as a means of gaining a job to earn their livelihood (Kivinen and Peltomäki, 1999). Unfortunately, the attractiveness of the apprenticeship route was hampered by its status as a secondary option, and it consequently remained a minor route of youth education and a less significant part of active labour market schemes for youth.

The international trends in education policy started to have more of an effect on the developing VET in Finland during the 1990s. Accordingly, the issue of lifelong learning became a more prominent theme of educational policymaking as did the development of Finnish adult education in the 1990s. Following the OECD report's considerations regarding the importance of a knowledge-based economy and combined with the demise of Taylorism, the demand for the continuous updating of skills was generally acknowledged (OECD, 2007). Growing priority was given to the recognition of informal and non-formal learning in European education and training systems. In Finland, competence-based qualifications for adults came into force with the implementation of the Vocational Qualifications Act in 1994 (Finland. Ammattitutkintolaki 306/1994), and these were also included in the Vocational Adult Education Act. The Finnish National Board of Education created a framework in close cooperation with the leading labour market organisations representing employers and employees and with teachers: so-called qualification committees were organised as the quality of competence in test performances was to be assured on a tripartite basis between the separate representatives of employers, employees and teachers (Finnish National Board of Education, 2010).

Since 2001, the structure and curricula of initial vocational education and training have been renewed in response to the lack of cooperation between Finnish VET and the working world (Klemelä, 1999). The number of vocational qualifications was reduced to 52 and study programmes to 113. All initial vocational qualifications were extended to consist of 3 years of full-time study (Stenström and Virolainen, 2014a; Finland. *Laki ammatillisesta peruskoulutuksesta* 630/1998). In addition, on-the-job learning (work-related learning) was simultaneously incorporated into the curriculum, lasting at least 6 months. This has been one of the most central Finnish VET reforms undertaken since the year 2000.

Further efforts to achieve closer cooperation between VET and the workplace also included the adoption of a new form of assessment, that is, vocational skills demonstrations (Stenström et al., 2006). In contrast to adult competence test performances administered by the Qualification Committees, young students were asked to demonstrate their practical skills during their initial VET. It was preferred for students to demonstrate their skills in practical work situations or in practical assignments. The skill assessments were arranged in collaboration with representatives of the school, employers and employees aiming toward formative assessment, differing thus from the adults' summative competence-based qualifications (Räkköläinen, 2011). These enhancements of school-based VET with on-the-job learning and skills demonstrations became distinctive characteristics of Finnish VET in contrast to the Swedish school-based model of organising VET. In Sweden, the links from VET to the working world were increased later, in the 2010s (Virolainen and Persson Thunqvist, 2017).

The curriculum of the Finnish VET system was reformed again as part of a wider VET reform that started in 2015 and is set to continue until 2018. The reform concerns funding, administration, regulation, legislation, qualification structure, models for organising education and providers of education (Opetus- ja kulttuuriministeriö, 2016). Since VET in Finland is mostly funded by the state, thorough multi-level changes can be expected (see Stenström and Virolainen, 2014a; Rauhala, 2013). The newly reformed model of VET should be in place by 2018. The new curriculum reform reflects the need to harmonise the Finnish VET system with the European Qualification Framework (EQF) and European Credit System for VET (ECVET) (Virolainen and Stenström, 2015; Cedefop, 2008). By defining the initial VET curricula in terms of the competence-based approach and competence points, the national qualification framework seems to continue to follow the prevailing national model. The dominant VET model is school-based even though the curriculum is equivalent to competence-based qualifications targeting adults and is thus somewhat closer to the outcome-based approach. The competence points can be gained through skills demonstrations, which should promote individual pace of progression. As such, the national curriculum framework is still committed to providing equal educational opportunities and access to higher education. Parallel economic cut-backs in the funding for VET institutions are related to the recession in Finland that started in 2008, and concerns have been raised about the sufficiency of collaborations between VET schools and employers as well as regarding educational supplies.

The role of outcome-based approaches has been given increased attention in European discussions ever since the European Commission's 2009 recommendation to its partner countries to organise a transfer system for study credits (Kärki, 2014; Bjørnåvold and Pevec Grm, 2013; Cedefop, 2008). The European Credit System for Vocational Education and Training (ECVET) is expected to facilitate the recognition of prior learning and existing competences.

Improving the standing of VET in the 2000s

At present, in Finland almost all young people finishing compulsory comprehensive school have access to either general upper secondary education or upper secondary vocational education and training (Cedefop Refernet Finland, 2011, p. 38). According to the annual statistics for post-compulsory education in Finland, nearly all comprehensive school graduates apply for further studies, and a total of 94% go on to further studies aiming at a qualification or degree (Figure 6.1) (Statistics Finland, 2017).

The VET reforms introduced after the Second World War have changed the position of vocational education in the Finnish school system. The popularity and status of vocational education and training has increased, particularly since

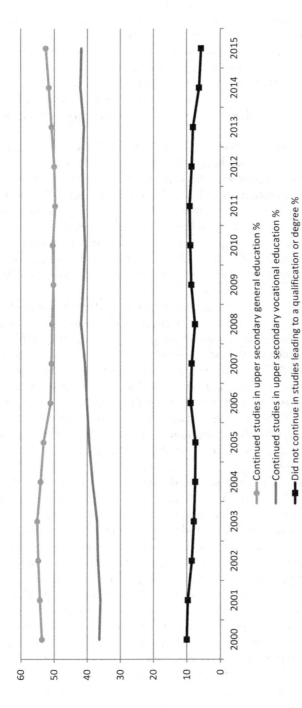

Figure 6.1 Direct transition to further studies of graduates of the 9th grade of comprehensive school during 2000–2015 (Statistics Finland, 2017)

the early 2000s (see Figure 6.1) when work-related learning (on-the-job learning) began to be implemented in the VET curriculum. The increase in Finnish VET's success has coincided with the combination of VET students' eligibility for higher education and the enhancement of educational institutions' connections to the working world, both at the institutional and the regional levels of pedagogy and curriculum planning. Furthermore, international exchange programmes and graduates' opportunities to participate in World Skills competitions have improved the image of VET (Virolainen and Stenström, 2014; Ruohotie et al., 2008).

In the period from 2000 until 2015, the interest in VET had increased; after completing their compulsory basic education, more than half of the students continued in general upper secondary education (52%) compared to 42% in initial vocational education and training (Statistics Finland, 2017). Regarding gender segregation, the shares of men and women among the new students were almost equal (women 51%, and men 49%). However, most fields are gender-segregated, reflecting the gendered division of work in the labour market. For example, in the field of health, welfare and sports, the share of women was 82%, while in the field of technology and transport it was only 20% (Statistics Finland, 2016b; Kuusi et al., 2009).

In contrast, only 32% of the general upper secondary school graduates in 2015, upon passing the matriculation examination, immediately continued their studies leading to a qualification or degree from: a university (16%), a university of applied sciences (former 'polytechnic', 11%), or a VET institute (5%) (Statistics Finland, 2017). In the 10 years from 2005 to 2015, the share of general upper secondary school graduates who did not immediately continue with further studies in the autumn upon passing their matriculation examination grew from 58% to 68% (Statistics Finland, 2017). On the whole, the number of higher education applicants has also remained at a relatively high level in relation to youth unemployment since the 1990s (Alatalo et al., 2017; Virolainen and Stenström, 2014).

Despite its success and the increased participation rate in VET, there still remain some challenges for Finnish VET and its future development. For instance, the attrition rate of dropouts is a challenge. During the academic year 2013–2014, a total of 7% of students attending a qualification or degree programme discontinued their studies and did not resume them in any other education leading to a qualification or degree (Statistics Finland, 2016a).

Also, the increased popularity of VET along with changing work and competence requirements has created new demands regarding VET (Laukia, 2013a). There is a need to develop the VET system so as to be more responsive to the heterogeneous student population in order to meet both the needs of those aiming to participate in Skills Competitions (Ruohotie et al., 2008) and those under the threat of dropping out (e.g. Kuronen, 2010). For those young people who do not get employed directly after completing the VET and those who want to continue their studies, the opportunities for further and higher education are important.

The prevention of dropping out has included promotion of inclusive policies. Since 1996, youth under 24 years of age have been obliged to participate in education or an apprenticeship training programme in the sense that unless they apply for vocational training or participate in labour market policy programmes, they will lose their unemployment benefits. Since 2013, the Finnish youth guarantee has demanded that communities offer everyone under the age of 25 years, as well as those who have recently graduated and are under 30 years of age, either a job, on-the-job training, a study place or rehabilitation (Ministry of Education and Culture, 2017).

In future, VET providers' role and responsibilities in achieving the goals of both the youth guarantee and ambitious, high-achieving students have to be combined with the latest reform of the Finnish VET system adopted since 2015. In addition to the new curricular changes, the decrease in governmental funding (VET budget) is an obstacle to be overcome in trying to achieve Finland's educational and policy goals. Since education providers' funding by the state has been cut and a considerable number of VET teachers have been made redundant, the completion of the personal study plans targeted by the curriculum reform may be compromised. Even though the sizes of the youth cohorts in VET have decreased, the new trend of decreased funding and increased redundancies has raised concern as there are less human resources to support students' individual plans and to organise regional collaborations with the working world. Furthermore, changes in the provision of general, common studies may have an effect on VET graduates' participation in higher education in the future.

Transitions from VET to the labour market and higher education (HE) in the 2000s

The transition from VET to the labour market or higher education is a critical period for VET graduates. Statistics relating to this transitional phase have often been used as assessment criteria for the effectiveness of VET in many countries, and this has also been the special focus of the Nord-VET project. Since 2008, the Finnish economy has been suffering from recession, which is reflected in the employment levels of VET graduates. As an outcome of the recession, Finland's employment rate of IVET (initial vocational education and training) graduates aged 20 to 34 years in 2016 was lower (75.5%) than in Denmark (87.4%) and Sweden (88.7%) (Cedefop, 2017). Furthermore, the Finnish employment rate for 20- to 64-year-olds in 2016 was lower (72.9%) than in other Nordic countries (Denmark 76.5%, Sweden 80.5%, Norway 79.1%), yet higher than in the EU (70%) (Cedefop, 2017).

As the descriptions and analyses in the previous sections show, Finnish education policy has paid a lot of attention to the transitions between different educational levels. Since the VET reform has been completed in the 2000s, there are no longer any dead ends between the different levels of education. The eligibility of VET graduates for higher education was developed in several stages alongside the development of the universities of applied sciences (UAS, formerly 'polytechnics') and in relation to the curricular reforms of upper secondary VET in 1995 and the 2000s. The statistics indicate that around one quarter (26%) of the new UAS students in 2013 had a VET qualification prior (Hintsanen et al., 2016). The number of those who undertook a direct transition from initial VET to a UAS was smaller; about 14% to 19% of graduates with a VET qualification at the upper secondary level moved on to higher education (HE) at a UAS within 3 years of their VET graduation (Kilpi-Jakonen et al., 2016; Stenström and Valkonen, 2012). Even though the number of students with a VET background entering HE was not extensive, VET students have emphasised the option of eligibility for HE as having been a motivating factor in their choosing VET in the first place.

On the societal level, the expansion of the HE system through the introduction of the UAS system has been justified by demands for innovation to promote the knowledge society and its economy. The establishment of the UAS system enhanced the professional projects and status of some gender-specific welfare state professions that it addressed in its curriculum, such as giving more educational support to nurses and midwives. In the 2000s, such professions have weakened due to marketisation and managerial ethos influencing the organising of health and social services as part of the changes introduced in the welfare state (Henriksson et al., 2006). Recently, in 2016, some universities of applied sciences introduced qualification-specific entrance examinations for applicants from VET schools. This change may have an effect on VET students' participation in UAS studies in the future.

Conclusion

After the Second World War, Finland shifted from being a socially supported small-scale farming society to becoming a welfare state of social security and paid work (Kettunen, 2001). The modern welfare state was established gradually and its formation played a crucial role in the defining of its education policy (Järvelä, 1991, p. 35). The formation of Finland's VET was also linked to the development of its industrial culture. The structure of the Finnish occupational culture changed from one of agriculture to that of industry later than had occurred elsewhere in Europe, but at a rapid pace following the Second World War due to the increased demand for skilled workers in the labour market as the Finnish industry had to produce the goods necessary to pay the substantial war reparations demanded from Finland.

Taylorist industrial culture assumed there to be a distinction between intellectual and manual labour. The emerging VET followed this distinction by making supervisory education and initial VET separate forms of education (Väärälä, 1995, p. 118). Also, technological developments and a more detailed division of the labour market created an increasing need for VET. The aspirations to increase the cooperation between different vocational sectors strengthened during the 1950s. The drivers for the strengthening of the cooperation were the industries and trades of the network (Heikkinen and Henriksson, 2001). Later, the state and municipalities acted as drivers of the Finnish initial vocational education and training. The law of 1958 initiated Finnish VETs' expansion and further differentiation in the 1960s and 1970s, and promoted the state-led form of school-based VET as the dominant model of VET in Finland (Klemelä, 1999).

In the 1970s and 1980s, the general education policy also included increasing educational and regional equality. The set target of the education policy was to educate the whole age group in compulsory education and in the post-compulsory education. The function of the VET system was to guarantee social mobility and the possibility of getting a job (Väärälä, 1995). Full employment was the goal of the society, but in the 1990s the stable labour market became unstable mainly due to the economic depression and simultaneous globalisation. The changed labour market situation demanded different kinds of skills and necessitated reforming the VET system. For VET, this meant placing increased emphasis on individuality, employability and entrepreneurship.

In addition, the 1980s and 1990s were decades in which Finnish VET was struggling to gain esteem in comparison to the general upper secondary education. As a result, VET's general content and curriculum were developed to meet the changing demands of the working world. In the 1990s, the adoption of lifelong learning policies promoted the abolishment of dead ends in Finland's educational structure and implemented opportunities for transitioning from VET to higher education were developed. Further on, VET's developments in the 2000s emphasised building firmer connections with the working world.

It is typical of the Finnish VET system that the degree of cooperation between employers, employees, education administrators and teachers has varied between the different VET reforms, depending on their main focus, but such cooperation has been a continual part of VET since it was introduced in 1917 by the Vocational Training Council. In the Finnish school-based model of VET, the role of ministry-led committees and negotiations between employers and employees as well as with various other interest groups has been significant in defining its curriculum and programme structure (see, e.g. Salminen, 1999; Ekola, 1991). The development of the Finnish VET system has seen the interests of employers and trade union actors, as well as of other interest groups like teachers and communities, mediated and coordinated via state bureaucracy in several consecutive reforms during the 1980s, 1990s and 2000s (see also Busemeyer, 2015, p. 39).

Since the Second World War, both Finnish vocational upper secondary and post-secondary education expanded, and successive reforms reconstructed VET into its current, improved form (Virolainen and Stenström, 2015). Participation in VET increased in the 2000s, and the attraction to the Finnish school-based system of vocational education and training has been steadily growing until recently. The latest reform phase started in 2015 and is set to continue until 2018. The improvements to the initial VET's status were mostly the outcome of the reforms of its curriculum and qualification structure, as well as having opened the way for VET graduates' eligibility for higher education.

In particular, three developmental trends have had a crucial impact on the current status of VET. First of all, the general education component within VET was developed along with its continuous pedagogical renewal. From the early stages of the Finnish VET system, the curriculum of vocational education has included both practical and theoretical studies. This has created a basis for participation in higher and further education as well as for lifelong learning.

Secondly, higher and further education opportunities have been created to provide the option of continued learning beyond VET. The Finnish universities of applied sciences were developed from former vocational colleges and higher vocational education institutions in the 1990s, and the removal of dead ends in the education system has increased the prestige of VET.

Thirdly, practical studies (work-based learning) have been an important component of vocational training education, although they have not been dominant in Finnish VET since the time of the craft guilds in the 19th century. And since the introduction of a legislative framework in 1958 and the implementation of a financial basis via the welfare state, VET has been institutionalised and developed into a school-based system. Compared to other Nordic countries, it is notable that Finnish VET emerged on a large scale only after the Second World War as the apprenticeship model typical to Denmark and Norway was not particularly strong in Finland prior to the war. Also, the later apprenticeship training has played only a marginal role in educating comprehensive school graduates in VET.

The reforms of the Finnish VET system have reorganised its relationship to the working world on several occasions. In the 1960s, the cooperation between education and the working world was increased, marking a partial shift from school-based learning to learning at the workplace. The upper secondary education reform in the 1980s, on the contrary, aimed at enhancing school-based vocational education independent from business life and replaced work training with practically oriented studies. Until the turn of the millennium, initial vocational education was mainly organised by vocational schools with few links to the working world. Since the turn of the millennium, a number of new initiatives have been taken with the aim of strengthening the relation between vocational education and working life. These include, in particular, the adoption of on-the-job learning periods in the curriculum and related vocational skills demonstrations. The main outcome of these latest reforms has been increased participation in VET (see also Stenström and Virolainen, 2014b, p. 48; Virolainen and Stenström, 2014).

The latest curriculum reform, which adopts a more competence-based approach, continues to enhance the connections between educational institutions and the working world. The increasingly more competence-based approach reflects the adoption of European trends in Finnish education policy. This adoption of a strongly competence-based approach has raised concerns about a possible shift toward narrowly defined outcome-based qualifications as seen elsewhere in Europe, such as in the United Kingdom (Wolf, 2011).

Steering toward such an outcome-based approach has been criticised as some see it as a threat to understanding the meaning of the general skills and theoretical knowledge learned in vocational education (Young and Allais, 2009).

References

Aho, E., Pitkänen, K. and Sahlberg, P. (2006) *Policy Development and Reform Principles of Basic and Secondary Education in Finland Since 1968*, Washington, DC, The World Bank, 2.

Ahola, S. (2006) 'From "different but equal" to "equal but different": Finnish AMKs in the Bologna Process', *Higher Education Policy*, vol. 19, no. 2, pp. 173–186.

Alatalo, J., Mähönen, E. and Räisänen, H. (2017) *Nuorten ja nuorten aikuisten työelämä ja sen ulkopuolisuus*, Helsinki, Ministry of Economic Affairs and Employment, TEM-analyyseja, 76.

Antikainen, A. (1993) *Kasvatus, koulutus ja yhteiskunta*, Helsinki, WSOY.

Atkinson, W. (2010) *Class, Individualization, and Late Modernity: In Search of the Reflexive Worker*, New York, Palgrave Macmillan.

Beck, U. (1992) *Risk Society: Towards a New Society*, London, Sage Publications.

Bergholm, T. (2016) *A History of the SAK (the Central Organisation of Finnish Trade Unions)*, Helsinki, SAK, The Finnish Federation of Trade Unions [Online]. Available at www.sak.fi/materials/publications/other-material/a-history-of-the-sak-2016-08-02 (Accessed 11 October 2017).

Bjørnåvold, J. and Pevec Grm, S. (2013) *Analysis and Overview of NQF Developments in European Countries: Annual Report 2012*, Working Paper 17, Luxembourg, Publications Office of the European Union.

Borgman, M. and Henriksson, L. (2000) 'Laaja-alaista vai eriytyvää ammattikasvatusta? Sosiaali- ja terveysalan ammatillisia kohtaamisia', in Rajaniemi, A. (ed.) *Suomalaisen ammattikasvatuksen historia*, Helsinki, Opetus-, kasvatus- ja koulutusalojen säätiö, pp. 140–145.

Busemeyer, M. R. (2015) *Skills and Inequality: Partisan Politics and the Political Economy of Education Reforms in Western Welfare States*, Cambridge, Cambridge University Press.

Cedefop (2008) *The Shift to Learning Outcomes: Conceptual, Political and Practical Developments in Europe*, Luxembourg, Publications Office of the European Union.

Cedefop (2017) *On the Way to 2020: Data for Vocational Education and Training Policies: Country Statistical Overviews – 2016 Update* [Online]. Available at www.cedefop.europa.eu/en/publications-and-resources/publications/5561 (Accessed 5 March 2017).

Cedefop ReferNet Finland (2011) *Finland: VET in Europe – Country Report 2011* [Online]. Available at http://libserver.cedefop.europa.eu/vetelib/2011/2011_CR_FI.pdf (Accessed 20 November 2016).

Christiansen, N. F., Petersen, K., Edling, N. and Haave, P. (eds.) (2006) *The Nordic Model of Welfare: A Historical Reappraisal*, Copenhagen, Museum Tusculanum.

Dobbins, M. and Busemeyer, M. R. (2015) 'Socio-economic institutions, organized interests and partisan politics: The development of vocational education in Denmark and Sweden', *Socio-Economic Review*, vol. 13, no. 2, pp. 259–284.

Ekola, J. (1991) 'Miten onnistui ammatillisen keskiasteen koulunuudistuksen toimeenpano?', in Ekola, J., Vuorinen, P. and Kämäräinen P. (eds.) *Ammatillisen koulutuksen uudistaminen 1980-luvulla: Selvitys uudistuksen toteutumisesta ja toteutusympäristöstä*, Helsinki, VAPK-kustannus, 30, pp. 7–64.

Finland. *Ammattitutkintolaki 306/1994* (1994) [Online]. Available at www.finlex.fi/fi/laki/alkup/1994/19940306 (Accessed 20 November 2016).

Finland. *Laki ammatillisesta peruskoulutuksesta. 630/1998* (1998) [Online]. Available at www.finlex.fi/fi/laki/ajantasa/1998/19980630 (Accessed 20 November 2016).

Finland. *Laki ammatillisista oppilaitoksista 487/1987* (1987) [Online]. Available at www.finlex.fi/fi/laki/alkup/1987/19870487 (Accessed 20 November 2016).

Finland. *Laki ammattioppilaitoksista 184/1958* (1958) [Online]. Available at www.finlex.fi/fi/laki/smur/1958/19580184 (Accessed 20 November 2016).

Finland. *Asetus opistoasteen tutkintojen niveltämisestä korkeakouluopintoihin 275/1984* (1984) [Online]. Available at www.edilex.fi/smur/19840275 (Accessed 20 November 2016).

Finland. *Laki oppisopimuskoulutuksesta 1605/1992* (1992) [Online]. Available at www.finlex.fi/fi/laki/alkup/1992/19921605 (Accessed 20 November 2016).

Finnish National Board of Education (2010) *Vocational Education and Training in Finland: Vocational Competence, Knowledge and Skills for Working Life and Further Studies*, Helsinki, Finnish National Board of Education [Online]. Available at www.oph.fi/download/131431_vocational_education_and_training_in_finland.pdf (Accessed 20 November 2016).

Giddens, A. (1990) *The Consequences of Modernity*, Cambridge, Polity Press.

Haapala, P. (2006) 'Suomalainen rakennemuutos', in Saari J. (ed.) *Historiallinen käänne: Johdatus pitkän aikavälin historian tutkimukseen*, Helsinki, Gaudeamus, pp. 91–124.

Heikkinen, A. (1995) *Lähtökohtia ammattikasvatuksen kulttuuriseen tarkasteluun: Esimerkkinä suomalaisen ammattikasvatuksen muotoutuminen käsityön ja teollisuuden alalla 1840–1940*, PhD thesis, Tampere, University of Tampere.

Heikkinen, A. (2001) 'The transforming peripheries of vocational education: Reflections from the case of Finland', *Journal of Education and Work*, vol. 14, no. 2, pp. 227–250.

Heikkinen, A. and Henriksson, L. (2001) 'Ammatillisen kasvun ajat ja paikat', in Anttila, A.-H. and Suoranta, A. (eds.) *Ammattia oppimassa*, Tampere, Työväen historian ja perinteen tutkimuksen seura, pp. 206–263.

Henriksson, L., Wrede, S. and Burau, V. (2006) 'Understanding professional projects in welfare service work: Revival of old professionalism?' *Gender, Work & Organization*, vol. 13, no. 2, pp. 174–192.

Hintsanen, V., Juntunen, K., Kukkonen, A., Lamppu, V.-M., Lempinen, P., Niinistö-Sivuranta, S., Nordlund-Spiby, R., Paloniemi, J., Rode, J.-P., Goman, J., Hietala, R., Pirinen, T. and Seppälä, H. (2016) *Liikettä niveliin: Ammatillisesta koulutuksesta ammattikorkeakouluun johtavien opintopolkujen ja koulutusasteiden yhteistyön toimivuus*, Helsinki, Kansallinen koulutuksen arviointikeskus, 2.

Itälä, J. (2000) 'Ammatillisen koulutuksen rooli Suomen rakentamisessa', in Rajaniemi, A. (ed.) *Suomalaisen ammattikasvatuksen historia*, Helsinki, Opetus-, kasvatus- ja koulutusalojen säätiö, pp. 41–69.

Järvelä, M. (1991) *Palkkatyö ja koulutustarve*, Tampere, Tutkijaliitto.

Kaarninen, M. (2011) 'Oppikoulu yhteiskunnan rakentajana', in Heikkinen, A. and Leino-Kaukiainen, P. (eds.) *Valistus ja koulunpenkki. Kasvatus ja koulutus Suomessa 1860-luvulta 1960-luvulle*, Helsinki, Suomen kirjallisuuden seura, pp. 405–429.

Kaarninen, M. (2013) '"Pitäisi olla puoleksi runoilija voidakseen kirjoittaa historiaa...": Kirjoittavat naiset ja isänmaan historia nuorisolle', in Jalava, M., Kinnunen, T. and Sulkunen, I. (eds.) *Kirjoitettu kansakunta: Sukupuoli, uskonto ja kansallinen historia 1900-luvun alkupuolen suomalaisessa tietokirjallisuudessa*, Helsinki, Suomalaisen Kirjallisuuden Seura, 136, pp. 149–188.

Kärki, S.-L. (2014) 'Lähtökohdat, kansallinen tahtotila ja osaamisperusteisuuden tuomat muutokset', in *Osaamisperusteisuus todeksi – askelmerkkejä koulutuksen järjestäjille*, Helsinki, National Board of Education, 8, pp. 6–8.

Kettunen, P. (2001) 'The Nordic welfare state in Finland', *Scandinavian Journal of History*, vol. 26, no. 3, pp. 225–247.
Kettunen, P. (2013) 'Vocational education and the tensions of modernity in a modern Nordic periphery', in Buchhardt, M., Markkola, P. and Valtonen, H. (eds.) *Education, State and Citizenship*, Helsinki, Nordic Centre of Excellence NordWel, 4, pp. 31–55.
Kilpi-Jakonen, E., Erola, J. and Karhula, A. (2016) 'Inequalities in the haven of equality? Upper secondary education and entry into tertiary education in Finland', in Blossfeld, H.-P., Buchholz, S., Skopek, J. and Triventi, M. (eds.) *Models of Secondary Education and Social Inequality: An International Comparison*, Coltenham, Edward Elgar Publishing, pp. 181–196.
Kivinen, O. and Peltomäki, M. (1999) 'On the job or in the classroom? The apprenticeship in Finland from the 17th century to the 1990s', *Journal of Education and Work*, vol. 12, no. 1, pp. 75–93.
Klemelä, K. (1999) *Ammattikunnista ammatillisiin oppilaitoksiin: Ammatillisen koulutuksen muotoutuminen Suomessa 1800-luvun alusta 1990-luvulle*, PhD thesis, Turku, University of Turku.
Koskela, H. (2003) *Opiskelijoiden haasteellisuudesta ammattiopintoihin sitoutumisen substanssiteoriaan. Grounded theory – menetelmän soveltaminen ammattioppilaitoksen opettajien kuvauksiin opetettavistaan*, PhD thesis, Joensuu, University of Joensuu.
Kuronen, I. (2010) *Peruskoulusta elämänkouluun: Ammatillisesta koulutuksesta syrjäytymisvaarassa olevien nuorten aikuisten tarinoita peruskoulusuhteesta ja elämänkulusta peruskoulun jälkeen*, PhD thesis, Jyväskylä, University of Jyväskylä.
Kuusi, H., Jakku-Sihvonen, R. and Koramo, M. (2009) *Koulutus ja sukupuolten tasa-arvo*, Helsinki, Sosiaali- ja terveysministeriö.
Lasonen, J. and Young, M. (eds.) (1998) *Strategies for Achieving Parity of Esteem in European Upper Secondary Education*, Jyväskylä, University of Jyväskylä, Institute for Educational Research.
Laukia, J. (2013a) 'Education of skilled workers and citizens: Vocational education in Finland', in Aaltonen, K., Isacsson, A., Laukia, J. and Vanhanen-Nuutinen, L. (eds.) *Practical Skills, Education and Development: Vocational Education and Training in Finland*, Helsinki, HAAGA-HELIA University of Applied Sciences, pp. 9–19.
Laukia, J. (2013b) *Tavoitteena sivistynyt kansalainen ja työntekijä: Ammattikoulu Suomessa 1899–1987*, PhD thesis, Helsinki, University of Helsinki.
Meriläinen, R. and Varjo, J. (2008) 'Integroidun nuorisoasteen historiallinen rakentuminen osana suomalaista koulutusjärjestelmää ja -politiikkaa', *Ammattikasvatuksen aikakauskirja*, vol. 10, no. 3, pp. 13–25.
Ministry of Education and Culture (2017) *The Youth Guarantee in Finland Provides Employment, Training and a Customised Service* [Online]. Available at http://minedu.fi/documents/1410845/4150027/The%20Youth%20Guarantee%20in%20Finland/9efd3ac2-0a68-464b-b152-62a8ce2008bb. (Accessed 26 November 2017).
Nieminen, A. (2000) 'Finnish employer confederations – Streamlining inner organization and regulating national capitalism', in Jensen, C. S. (ed.) *Arbejdsgivere i Norden: En sosiologisk analyse af arbejdsgiverorganisering i Norge, Sverige, Finland og Danmark*, København, Nordisk Ministerråd, pp. 287–371.
Numminen, U. (2000) 'Strategies for improving vocational education: The Finnish case', in Stenström, M.-L. and Lasonen, L. (eds.) *Strategies for Reforming Initial Vocational Education and Training in Europe*, Jyväskylä, University of Jyväskylä, Institute for Educational Research, pp. 74–91.
OECD (2007) *Qualifications Systems: Bridges to Lifelong Learning* [Online]. Available at www.oecd.org/edu/skills-beyond-school/38465471.pdf (Accessed 27 September 2017).

Olofsson, J. and Wadensjö, E. (2006) *Lärlingsutbildning – ett återkommande bekymmer eller en oprövad möjlighet?* Rapport till ESS no. 4, Stockholm, Finansdepartementet.

Opetus- ja kulttuuriministeriö (2016) *Luonnos hallituksen esitykseksi eduskunnalle laiksi ammatillisesta koulutuksesta ja eräiksi siihen liittyviksi laeiksi*, Helsinki, Ministry of Education and Culture.

Poutanen, M. (2008) 'Joustavuutta, mahdollisuuksia ja rajoituksia 1990-luvulla', in Lankinen, S. and Viinisalo, K. (eds.) *Ajatuksia oppisopimuskoulutuksesta: Koulutuspolitiikkaa eilen ja tänään*, Helsinki, Helsingin kaupunki, Opetusvirasto, pp. 71–91.

Purhonen, K. (2000) 'Teollisuuden ja työnantajain keskusliitto koulutuspoliittisen vaikuttajana', in Rajaniemi, A. (ed.) *Suomalaisen ammattikasvatuksen historia*, Helsinki, Opetus-, kasvatus- ja koulutusalojen säätiö, pp. 260–265.

Räkköläinen, M. (2011) *Mitä näytöt näyttävät? Luotettavuus ja luottamus ammatillisten perustutkintojen näyttöperusteisessa arviointiprosessissa*, PhD thesis, Tampere, University of Tampere.

Rauhala, P. (2013) 'Kohteleeko julkinen rahoitus tasavertaisesti eri koulutusmuotoja?' *Ammattikasvatuksen aikakauskirja*, vol. 15, no. 2, pp. 9–19.

Ruohotie, P., Nokelainen, P. and Korpelainen, K. (2008) 'Ammatillisen huippuosaamisen mallintaminen: Teoreettiset lähtökohdat ja mittausmalli', *Ammattikasvatuksen aikakauskirja*, vol. 10, no. 1, pp. 4–16.

Sakslind, R. (1998) *Danning og yrkesutdanning: Utdanningssystem of nasjonale moderniseringsprosjekter 103*, Oslo, Norges forskningsråd.

Salminen, H. (1999) 'Ammattikorkeakoulu-uudistuksen ja keskiasteen tutkinnonuudistuksen yhteneväisyyksiä ja eroja', *Kasvatus*, vol. 30, no. 5, pp. 472–490.

Statistics Finland (2016a) *Discontinuation of Education Decreased* [Online]. Available at www.tilastokeskus.fi/til/kkesk/2014/kkesk_2014_2016-03-17_tie_001_en.html (Accessed 20 November 2016).

Statistics Finland (2016b) *Vocational Training 2015* [Online]. Available at www.stat.fi/til/aop/2015/aop_2015_2016-09-27_en.pdf (Accessed 20 November 2016).

Statistics Finland (2017) *Entrance to education* (Online). Avalaible at www.stat.fi/til/khak/2016/khak_2016_2017-12-13_tie_001_en.html [Accessed 15 December 2017].

Stenström, M.-L. (1997) *Educational and Gender Equality in Vocational Education: The Case of Commercial Education in Finland*, PhD thesis, Jyväskylä, University of Jyväskylä.

Stenström, M.-L., Laine, K. and Kurvonen, L. (2006) 'Practice-oriented assessment in Finnish VET – Towards quality assurance through vocational skills demonstrations', in Stenström, M.-L. and Laine, K. (eds.) *Quality and Practice in Assessment: New Approaches in Work-Related Learning*, Jyväskylä, University of Jyväskylä, Finnish Institute for Educational Research, pp. 89–120.

Stenström, M.-L. and Valkonen, S. (2012) 'Ammatillisen koulutuksen opintourat', in Stenström, M.-L., Virolainen, M., Vuorinen-Lampila, P. and Valkonen, S. *Ammatillisen koulutuksen ja korkeakoulutuksen opintourat*, Jyväskylä, University of Jyväskylä, Finnish Institute for Educational Research, pp. 23–108.

Stenström, M.-L. and Virolainen, M. (2014a) *The Current State and Challenges of Vocational Education and Training in Finland: The Finnish Country Report 1B* [Online]. Available at http://nord-vet.dk/indhold/uploads/Finnish-country-report-1B_0912_2014.pdf (Accessed 20 November 2016).

Stenström, M.-L. and Virolainen, M. (2014b) *The History of Finnish Vocational Education and Training: The Finnish Country Report 1A* [Online]. Available at http://nord-vet.dk/indhold/uploads/report1b_fi.pdf (Accessed 20 November 2016).

Stenström, M.-L. and Virolainen, M. (2016) 'Towards the enhancement of school-based VET in Finland', in Berner, E. and Gonon, P. (eds.) *History of Vocational Education and Training in Europe: Cases, Concepts and Challenges, 14*, Bern, Peter Lang, pp. 327–347.

Suursalmi, P. (2003) *Kolmikantaperiaatteen toteutuminen ammatillisen peruskoulutuksen näytöissä*, Helsinki, Opetushallitus.

Tuomisto, J. (1986) *Teollisuuden koulutustehtävien kehittyminen: Tutkimus teollisuustyönantajien koulutustoiminnan ja kvalifikaatiointressien historiallisesta kehityksestä Suomessa*, PhD thesis, Tampere, University of Tampere.

Virolainen, M. and Stenström, M.-L. (2014) 'Finnish vocational education and training in comparison: Strengths and weaknesses', *International Journal for Research in Vocational Education and Training*, vol. 1, no. 2, pp. 81–106 [Online]. Available at www.ijrvet.net/index.php/IJRVET/article/view/32/15 (Accessed 20 November 2016).

Virolainen, M. and Stenström, M.-L. (2015) *Recent Finnish VET Reforms and Innovations: Tackling the Current Challenges: The Finnish Country Report 1C* [Online]. Available at http://nord-vet.dk/indhold/uploads/report1c_fin.pdf (Accessed 20 November 2016).

Virolainen, M. and Persson Thunqvist, D. (2017) 'Varieties of universalism: Post-1990s developments in the initial school-based model of VET in Finland and Sweden and implications for transitions to the world of work and higher education', *Journal of Vocational Education and Training*, vol. 69, no. 1, pp. 47–63.

Väärälä, R. (1995) *Ammattikoulutus ja kvalifikaatiot*, PhD thesis, Rovaniemi, Lapin yliopisto.

Wolf, A. (2011) *Review of Vocational Education – the Wolf Report*. Gov. UK, London, Department of Business, Innovation & Skills, Department of Education [Online]. Available at www.gov.uk/government/uploads/system/uploads/attachment_data/file/180504/DFE-00031-2011.pdf (Accessed 24 November 2017).

Young, M., and Allais, S. (2009) 'Conceptualizing the role of qualifications in education reform', in Allais, S., Raffe, D. and Young, M. (eds.) *Researching NQFs: Some Conceptual Issues*, Employment Sector, Employment Working Paper no. 44, Geneva, Skills and Employability Department, ILO, pp. 5–22. Available at http://www.ilo.org/wcmsp5/groups/public/---ed_emp/---ifp_skills/documents/publication/wcms_119307.pdf (Accessed 20 November 2017).

7 The modern evolution of VET in Sweden (1945–2015)

Jonas Olofsson and Daniel Persson Thunqvist

Introduction

This chapter covers the post-war development of the Swedish vocational education and training (VET) system (1945–2015); departing from the gradual shift from a differentiated system partly based on collective agreements among the labour market partners, toward a state-governed school-based system. Furthermore, the chapter examines dynamic tensions, challenges and turning points (e.g. Streeck and Thelen, 2005) relating to overriding changes in Sweden in recent decades in terms of globalisation and neo-liberal trends in education policy.

Put in an international context, the modern history of vocational education and training in Sweden is perhaps mostly associated with pioneering the 'school-based model' of VET as an integral part of the 'Nordic Welfare Model' (e.g. Antikainen, 2006). This model is often seen as congruent with the long record of social democratic political dominance and equalizing goals in education policy (Busemeyer, 2015). Even in a Nordic context, Sweden stands out as the country that took the lead in promoting parity of esteem between general and vocational education by creating a unified upper secondary school (Young and Raffe, 1998). Compared to the other Nordic countries with similar universal welfare systems, especially Denmark and Norway, Swedish VET programmes have offered much less work-based learning. Working-life contacts, for obvious reasons, are more developed in countries with extensive apprenticeship training. The dominant perspective on Swedish VET has largely been that the school-based model is rather homogeneous given the characteristics of VET as part of a state-governed, non-selective, comprehensive school system with relatively low differentiation between general and vocational education.

However, the picture becomes more complex and varied when one 'zooms in' on the specific VET trajectories and incremental changes that have in part taken place as backstage activity in the large reforms of the rest of the education system: i.e. the construction of a unified comprehensive school (*grundskola*), followed by an integrated upper secondary school (*gymnasium*, in the early 1970s) and a new unified higher education institution (*högskola*, in 1976). To put it somewhat incisively, while research on the reformation and construction of a comprehensive education system in Sweden comprises a well-ploughed furrow (e.g. Wiborg, 2004; Rickardsson, 1999), research on the development of upper secondary VET that combines analysis of education reforms with a welfare perspective is relatively rare (but see e.g. Lundahl et al., 2010; Olofsson, 2005).

Particularly, the chapter provides novel knowledge about the reforms, decision-making processes, and emergent challenges that played a formative role in establishing the school-based VET system. The processes of reform and development in VET were in many ways an extension of the Swedish tradition of negotiation (being a 'negotiation society') between the state and working life, as well as the dual political commitment to economic modernisation vs. egalitarian social policies. At the same time, multiple stakeholders in the field of VET contribute to dynamic tensions and unpredicted outcomes of reforms. Even if the labour market partners have lost some ground in the field of VET, since the 1940s the leading organisations of trade unions (*Landsorganisationen*, LO) and employers' associations (*Svenska Arbetsgivarföreningen*, SAF) have responded to reform proposals from the state, participated in various expert committees that have prepared major vocational training reforms (see as follows) and, more generally, attached great importance to modernising VET by promoting industrial rationalisation, economic growth and international competitiveness (Lundahl and Olofsson, 2014).

Points of departure

The chapter focuses on how the VET trajectories have been shaped by reforms and institutional dynamics in the interplay between the state and the labour market partners involved in VET. In so doing, the chapter further aims to demonstrate path dependencies and turning points in the VET system (Streeck and Thelen, 2005). Three distinguished phases can be traced, and these phases structure the empirical part of the chapter. Firstly, from the end of the 1940s to the establishment of the integrated upper secondary schools in the 1970s, municipal vocational schools underwent a strong expansion. Vocational education became an important part of the Swedish education system at the secondary level. The second phase began with the establishment of coherent upper secondary schools through a reform in 1971. Vocational education became part of an integrated education system at a higher level. VET programmes were given broader content and a more preparatory character. This pattern was further strengthened through a reform at the beginning of the 1990s. VET programmes were extended from 2 to 3 years, and for the first time led to eligibility for higher studies. The third phase can in many ways be interpreted as a reorientation of the Swedish VET system. With the latest reform of upper secondary schools in 2011, the vocational content of VET programmes has been strengthened. Eligibility for higher studies is no longer the main goal of VET programmes; a rich variety of industry-driven training has emerged, and apprenticeships have become a regular feature of Swedish upper secondary school. The old, homogeneous Swedish VET system tends to be more differentiated and controlled by the industries' requirements.

Expanded analysis of the first two phases reveals a remarkable continuity over time: The fundamental structures of the school-based VET system have largely remained intact since 1970, even though the various reforms have pointed in different directions. Once implemented, the big organisations on the labour market have gradually adopted their strategies for skills provision to the school-based VET, and most left-wing and centre-right political parties support the system. The dominance of large export-oriented industries and strong labour movements, including central unions, has played a decisive role in the stabilisation of school-based VET. Hence, in terms of theory, this historical trajectory illustrates a strong path dependency.

However, a significant change has taken place as well. The beginning of the 1990s coincided with deep economic crises, and marks a shift in educational policy in a more liberal direction. The analysis highlights some implications of a more academic-oriented and decentralised VET system from a welfare regime perspective. We argue that although this change did not alter the school-based VET system *per se*, it had significant consequences concerning the governance of VET and the relations between VET and the labour market.

Changes in VET can also be attributed to dynamic tensions in VET policy. Analysis of major reforms in the field of VET reveals how policy priorities have shifted more than once in relation to the main challenges in the field of VET: i.e. promoting skill formation and supporting young people's access to both employment and further education. Since the 1990s a notorious policy dilemma has been the issue of promoting equal access to higher education for practically all young people, while simultaneously promoting socially inclusive goals and battling youth unemployment and social marginalisation. Moreover, policy priorities have been driven by concerns over the need to handle unintended consequences of prior reforms. One major challenge for the school-based system in the past decade has been to counteract weak institutional links between the school world and the labour market, which affect school-to-work transitions. In the context of an increasingly globalised economy and working life, the existing structure of school-based VET is put under pressure. The third trend that is examined in the chapter actualises questions about different possible trajectories for the future of VET, given a turn in VET policy to the world of work and a reintroduction of apprenticeship.

From a differentiated VET system to a school-based VET system: initial steps (c. 1945–1960)

A differentiated system until 1950

The re-organisation of the Swedish education system from 1945 to the early 1970s was part of the construction of the modern 'social democratic welfare state' (Lundahl and Olofsson, 2014; Esping Andersen, 1996). The 'golden age' of the Swedish welfare state following the Second World War also improved the bargaining position of the trade unions vis-à-vis employers. This development was further reinforced by active labour market politics and the associated Rehn-Meidner model (e.g. Olofsson, 2006) of economic policy, which was rather successful in generating economic growth and full employment. Equal education opportunities were regarded as paramount in creating an equal society based on universal rights. However, the Swedish education system was still segregated, as were most other European education systems at the time (Busemeyer, 2015, p. 79). Upper secondary education and higher education were reserved for a minority of children from wealthier families. A 9-year secondary education was not fully introduced until 1962, but since the 1950s comprehensive schools had been quite widespread as a result of the 1950 Act that instructed schools to experiment with the 9-year comprehensive school model (Wiborg, 2004).

Vocational education and training were characterised as a differentiated system, partly based on an apprenticeship system that was not legally regulated but in which collective agreements between the social partners were important (Olofsson, 2005). In 1938 the LO and SAF entered the Basic Agreement ('Saltsjöbaden'), implementing a historical class compromise that was ground breaking for the Swedish tradition of collective agreements in labour-market relations (see Chapter 3). In relation to the Saltsjöbaden negotiations, the labour market partners agreed that vocational training and apprenticeship should be regulated by voluntary collective agreements within each trade (Lundahl, 1997a). From about 1940, the labour market partners also became more committed to gaining influence over the apprenticeship.

However, the view that business should assume responsibility for the essential elements of vocational education drew critical reactions in various contexts, e.g. discussions within the 1946 National School Commission, which was responsible for proposing a 9-year compulsory primary school (Olofsson, 2005). The point of the criticism of apprenticeship training was, firstly, that it was solely practically oriented, and that it offered neither the vocational-theoretical knowledge nor the broad overview of working life that were regarded as crucial aspects of professional competence. Secondly, the training often concentrated on the needs of the individual company rather than those of the occupation. Thirdly, the training was vulnerable to the extent that training places were rapidly withdrawn during times of economic downturn.

Little by little, the employer and labour organisations' views on the relation between company-based and school-based education also began to change. This did not come about immediately, however, but rather gradually; in addition, there remained clear differences of opinion within and between these stakeholders. This change of opinions was also related to the comprehensive primary school and the opportunities for vocational training that were proposed within the framework of prolonged compulsory school attendance. The difficulties of the companies – especially the smaller industrial ones – in investing in a broader form of education constituted a barrier to apprenticeship training that was difficult to surmount. This was very well known within the labour market trade councils. The idea was, of course, that the Swedish Trade Council would improve educational opportunities by offering pedagogical support and encouraging companies to collaborate more to, among other things, redistribute the costs of education within and across trades. The labour market trade councils would form part of the support structure for apprenticeship training in the various trades. As indicated, however, this failed.

There was a trend in which the employer and labour organisations' and companies' direct influence over vocational training diminished. Increasingly, their influence came to be mediated through corporative bodies for decision-making and consultation, while the straightforward administration and educational organisation were taken over by the government and municipalities (Andersson et al., 2015; Olofsson, 2005).

Expansion of the school-based public vocational education system

Next, we will look at important stages in the reform work underlying the vocational education model that emerged during the 1950s and 1960s, and that was completed through the establishment of the programme-based upper secondary school in 1971. The model is characterised by instruction in school-based forms, gradually broadened educational content, and relatively minor elements of apprenticeship and company-based training. It was a matter of a preparatory vocational education (Berner, 1989). In addition to prior research on the reform work, document analysis based on Committee Reports is used as primary data in this section since they played a vital role in the reform processes (Olofsson and Panican, 2017; Andersson et al., 2015; Olofsson, 2005; Ball and Larsson, 1989). Committee reports are proposals and reports, submitted by a commission of enquiry that was appointed by the Government. These reports are then published in the Swedish Government Official Reports Series (SOU) and proposals for new policies and legislation are presented in documents known as Government bills (Andersson et al., 2015).

The work of the 1946 National School Commission resulted in the *Report of the 1946 National School Commission, including guidelines for development of the Swedish school system* (Swedish Government Official Reports, SOU, 1948:27). The report was not only important to the work being done to reform compulsory school education; it was also of fundamental importance to post-compulsory education, particularly vocational training. According to the main proposal by the Commission, the first 6 years of elementary school should be common to all students. It was not until the senior level that some differentiation should be allowed. From the ninth grade, the education should be divided into different study programmes. According to the proposal, there should be two theoretically oriented study programmes and one vocational programme. The two theoretical programmes should prepare students for further studies at the post-compulsory level. On the other hand, the vocational study programme, referred to as 9y, was meant as preparation for entrance into working life or advanced vocational training (Olofsson, 2005).

The National School Commission expected that the ninth-year vocational study programme would comprise a majority of students attending the comprehensive primary school, say between 60 and 70 per cent of an age cohort. The Commission noted the limited extent of school-based vocational education, such as that offered by vocational and workshop schools or conducted in the form of apprenticeship training in trade and industry (SOU, 1948:27, p. 221). Only 10 per cent of an age cohort received any organised, shorter or longer, vocational training. Through the proposal to establish 9y, the proportion of trained workers would increase dramatically.

However, precisely how vocational training during the ninth school year would be organised was left rather unclear in the Commission's main report. It would function as a self-contained programme and as an introductory year prior to vocational school or apprenticeship. It was thought that the vocational programme could be specialised in a particular trade, whereas the Commission, at the same time, repeatedly emphasised the importance of its more general nature.

The ninth school year was meant to offer students certain insight into the conditions of working life. This was a matter of practical work experience, in combination with some general-knowledge subjects as well as elementary vocational theory. It was said, among other things, that "productive work should stand out as the most important subject during the final 9y year of the comprehensive primary school, because during this year the young students should be initiated into industrial life" (SOU, 1948:27, p. 226). The term 'productive work' specifically referred to practical work experience. Proper vocational education was not discussed in any great detail. The Commission also did not submit any proposals concerning vocational or workshop schools. On the contrary, it was thought that the existing educational organisation could remain unaltered except that, in future, the programmes should be based on the 9-year comprehensive primary school rather than on the 7-year elementary school. The courses could thus begin at a more advanced level. In addition, more general theoretical subjects could be left out in favour of earlier specialisation. Moreover, the Commission did not mention anything in particular about the potentials of apprenticeship. Instead, it referred to the position taken by the leading organisations of trade unions (LO) and employers' associations (SAF) on apprenticeship regulation by collective agreement. The Commission apparently believed the responsibility for the final, qualified education should lie outside the school system; the school system could offer general education and preparatory vocational training only.

A more advanced vocational education programme

The comprehensive primary school reform had been dragging on, as noted previously. At stake was also the ability to reach politically acceptable compromises for combining comprehensiveness (allowing for upward mobility) with greater differentiation in terms of more optional choices to meet different interests and needs among pupils (Ball and Larsson, 1989). The baby boom after the Second World War, which resulted in a considerable number of young people in general education, also raised concerns about how to make vocational education a more attractive option for pupils with a working-class background (Ball and Larsson, 1989). The comprehensive primary school reform had one important outcome: vocational education was now placed on par with upper secondary school education (Olofsson, 2005). Vocational school programmes were to be run in parallel with upper secondary school education rather than, as before, corresponding to the secondary school level. This placed greater demands on the standard of education, both qualitatively and quantitatively. According to most concerned parties, if school-based vocational training was to admit students who had opted for vocational courses in the ninth school year, the entire organisation would have to be extended.

In practice, the experimental work with 9y was ultimately not particularly successful, at least not from the point of view of recruitment. Quite contrary to the legislators' intentions, over 80 per cent of students opted for general and academic courses in the ninth school year. This, in turn, generated renewed criticism of the whole 9y project. Vocational elements within the framework of the compulsory primary school were gradually phased out. When Parliament adopted a new curriculum for primary schools (short name: Lgr 69) in 1968, the ninth-year study programme division was finally and completely dismantled.

Discontent with the continued weak and uncertain status of vocational training led to the appointment of a new public enquiry, *Experts on vocational education*, in the early 1950s (SOU, 1954:11). The Committee's task was to review the conditions for vocational education and adapt its structure to the reforms that had been implemented or planned for compulsory education. The Committee proposed increased state subsidies and an expansion of vocational and workshop schools. Business schools and apprenticeship training would also receive more generous funding; although, according to experts, their educational elements were limited in scope. Apprenticeship was perceived primarily as a concern for the traditional handcrafts. Experts on vocational training contributed to increased centralisation and government control of the Swedish model of vocational education.

After the Committee's proposal for increased state funding had been carried through, there was a sharp growth in vocational schools. The number of students who graduated from vocational training almost tripled in the 1950s, amounting to over 40,000 in 1960. During the following 10-year period, there was an additional doubling (Olofsson, 2005). This strong expansion in the number of students reflected the increased state subsidies and the steady spread of vocational schools throughout the country.

The establishment of the upper secondary VET system (c. 1960–1980)

The sharp growth of full-time municipal vocational schools constitutes an important condition on the subsequent integration of VET in the upper secondary school system, since VET had already become an important part of the education system at secondary level. The first steps were taken in the early 1960s, when several initiatives were taken for further co-ordination of upper secondary school level education. In 1960, a special upper secondary school investigation committee was appointed (SOU, 1963:42). Its proposal was presented in a report in 1963, resulting in a 1964 parliamentary decision in principle to establish a new upper secondary school that would comprise the former general upper secondary school as well as the commercial and technical upper secondary schools.

Taking a point of departure in welfare concerns, the reform cycle of the 1960s and 1970s can largely be seen as responses to social and structural shifts toward a post-industrial welfare society (Lundahl, 1997b). The reforms were propelled by increasing social and political demands in society to provide equal access to post-compulsory education (Ball and Larsson, 1989). In addition, there was also a call to bridge perceived gaps between the existing education system and the requirements for entering working life. It was argued that the unified upper secondary school not only served egalitarian ends but was also the best preparation for technological development and changes in economic structure (Lundahl et al., 2010). An urgent need to find new sources of recruitment among young people as the public sector was rapidly expanding also fuelled the demands for more vocational education at the upper secondary level (Persson Thunqvist, 2015). Since 1968, several new vocational tracks also came to be geared to service occupations, including female-dominated healthcare occupations in the welfare state (Lauglo, 1993).

The organisation of the new upper secondary school was to be co-ordinated with the study programmes offered at the two-year continuation and vocational schools. It was hoped that vocational education would gain more status if different programmes, including vocational education, were parts of one and the same system. The Royal High Council of Vocational Education was dissolved, and responsibility for elementary vocational training would henceforth lie with the National Board of Education.

The rapid changes in structure and number of students, as well as the efforts to increase integration resulting from establishment of the compulsory primary school, formed the basis of the appointment of the 1963 Commission on Vocational Education. The Committee's report came to be of crucial importance to the continued fate of upper secondary school, particularly that of vocational education.

The Commission on Vocational Education and the new vocational study programmes

The primary task of the Commission on Vocational Education was to define the significance and role of vocational education and training within the framework of an integrated upper secondary school system. The directives to the Commission emphasised that it should examine how vocational education and training had adapted to the compulsory primary school reform of 1962, as well as to the plans for an undifferentiated upper secondary school. In addition, the Commission was instructed to propose forms for connecting vocational training to working life. The student influx into vocational education programmes was expected to increase from less than 15 per cent of an age cohort in the early 1960s to 25 or even 30 per cent in 1970. This considerable increase in number of students, combined with the build-up of the new upper secondary school, required organisational overview and adjustments to the study programmes. The main principle was that the various study programmes should be as co-ordinated as possible. Also, with regards to instructional content, the vocational programmes should be broadened to allow for some general theoretical instruction.

The Commission proposed extensive changes for the entire vocational education system. In brief, the aim of the proposals was that vocational training would be transformed into fewer and broader 2-year study programmes. To be sure, most vocational and workshop schools already offered programmes of precisely this duration; i.e. 2 years. The major changes concerned regulation of the education as well as its content and timetabling. The vocational study programmes should be co-ordinated with upper secondary school and 2-year continuation school programmes to create a new, integrated upper secondary school. Vocational education was to be streamlined. The management and control of the programmes' educational content should be stricter. Despite the ambitions, resulting from the reforms of the 1950s, to create more co-ordination and uniformity, in the early 1960s vocational schools were still highly dependent on the local initiatives of individual schools or local businesses (Gårdstedt, 1967). Schools were established based on local initiatives, and even within a specific vocational programme the content of the schools' syllabuses varied considerably. Beginning in 1964, in connection with the establishment of the new National Board of Education, a gradual transition to centrally determined syllabuses took place.

The public reforms that paved the way for the upper secondary VET system demonstrate the consensual nature of the VET policy. The political consensus was partly due to the coalition between the leading social democrats and the centre-right party, supported by the centralised unions in educational matters (Lundahl, 1997b). The school-based option, i.e. greater curricular integration between general and vocational education, also played into the notion of workplace 'democratisation' which was actively promoted by the centre party and the unions. Conservatives (*Högerpartiet*, after 1969 *Moderata Samlingspartiet*), by contrast, were in favour of upholding a more demarcated differentiation between vocational and general education. However, as the conservatives were far more engaged in political struggles concerning taxes and reducing public expenditures, they did not actively strive to stop the social democratic-driven education reforms (Lundahl et al., 2010).

The public reforms illustrate a radical policy to reduce inequalities in the education system. Longitudinal research (Härnqvist, 1989; Härnqvist and Svensson, 1980) on the equalising effects of the integrated upper secondary school reveals that the reforms had different effects at different levels in the education system. The studies compared the transition to upper secondary education and higher education between the cohorts born in 1948, 1953, 1958 and 1963 and between different socio-economic groups. One conclusion based on these studies is that the major 1971 reform of upper secondary school has meant little for the equalisation within the university system. The majority (more than 90 per cent) of the university students (mostly from academic homes) among the cohorts born in 1948, 1953 and 1958 had taken the route from the higher education preparatory upper secondary school programmes of 3–4 years duration (Härnqvist, 1989; Härnqvist and Svensson, 1980). However, the transition to higher education increased significantly in the 1963 cohort also among young people from working-class backgrounds. For example, the percentage of students from working class in the 1963 cohort who in 1985 had started higher education was 11 per cent for females and 4 per cent for men (Härnqvist, 1989, pp. 28–29). The increase is related to the establishment of a new higher education system in 1976, where all post-secondary education was integrated in one system (högskola). New vocational programmes in higher education came to be geared toward healthcare (e.g. nursing) and resulted in a greater recruitment of female students from upper secondary VET. In addition, the expansion of upper secondary school means that the proportion of comprehensive school graduates which continued in the gymnasium increased (see Appendix Table A7.1.). The major increase took place between the 1953 and 1958 birth cohort as an effect of establishing the vocational programmes as part of upper secondary education (Härnqvist, 1989). In the mid-1980s, over 75 per cent of new students opted for vocational programmes (SOU, 1986:2). Those vocational students that left upper secondary school in the mid-1980s with a vocational preparation also had obtained so much more general education that they, in addition, had access to higher education in one form or another. This double competence seems to have been particularly attractive for female students from working-class backgrounds (Härnqvist, 1989, p. 28). This is still true today; public statistics on transitions from upper secondary VET to higher education recurrently reveal differences between various VET programmes and related to gender (see Appendix, Table A7.2).

At the same time, the integration of VET in upper secondary school also affected the connections between the school world and working life. The element of workplace-based training was highly limited. An investigation by the *Task force for reviewing upper secondary vocational education* (ÖGY) showed that, on average during the 1983/84 school year, only 6 per cent of the study period was workplace-based.

Changes in the school-based VET 1990–2011: a liberal turn

The 1990s saw several fundamental changes in the Swedish upper secondary school system that can partly be seen in relation to a neo-liberal wave in international educational policy. These changes can be analysed as a turning point in Swedish educational policy, as market forces were allowed to influence schooling (Olofsson, 2006). A long tradition of centralised state regulation was abandoned. The dissolution of the Central School Board (*Skolöverstyrelsen*) and the Regional School Boards (*Länsskolenämnderna*), as well as the liquidation of the earmarked state payment to the municipalities in favour of increasing local economic and political independence, were other signs of loosening state control.

In 1991, Parliament decided to radically change upper secondary school. The reform was anchored in liberal values: management by objectives rather than details, and an individualised school with diversified content rather than a philosophy of equality and integration. One purpose of this reform was to decentralise the responsibility, shifting it away from the government and the county boards of education to the local level (Lundahl and Olofsson, 2014).

Decentralisation was followed by the 1992 private school reform, which resulted in a greater freedom of establishment of schools that did not fall under municipal authority. The reform made it possible for parents and pupils to freely choose between schools, and at the same time forced municipalities to support independent private schools. The private school reform involved a decision to redistribute resources. Thus, a system was introduced in which each individual student was awarded a school capitation allowance; that is, money that followed the student to his/her chosen school. Independent or private schools have expanded sharply; during the past 10 years, for example, the number of such schools at the upper secondary school level has tripled. During the 2014/15 school year, 26 per cent of upper secondary school students attended a school with a private principal (National Agency for Education, 2016).

The 1991 school reform comprised the introduction of 17 3-year national educational programmes, 14 of which were vocational in nature. After the 1991 reform, the vocational programmes were transformed into broader programmes with less pronounced working-life connection. At the same time, the study period was prolonged from 2 to 3 years. The intention here was to broaden the general theoretical elements of the vocational programmes so as to offer all students the opportunity to continue to higher education. This can be seen as a continuation of social democratic-driven educational policy for equal access (Olofsson and Panican, 2017). However, the new educational programmes were also meant to allow more local adaptation as well as individual educational choice, compared to the situation in the former programme-based upper secondary school. Academic and vocational programmes were to pursue the same general theoretical subjects. Basic eligibility for higher education thus became the explicit objective of all upper secondary school programmes. The decision to change vocational streams into broader and longer programmes was motivated by concerns regarding the new economy and its demand on qualifications and flexibility. Longer education and access to higher education should make it possible to reduce the negative social effects of fast technological change and globalisation.

However, almost immediately after the implementation of the more academic-oriented upper secondary VET programmes, the government recognised a growing number of dropouts (Olofsson, 2005). For example, according to the statistics from the National Agency for Education (regarding 2015), 30 per cent of students did not meet the requirements for a final certificate after 4 years of study (National Agency for Education, 2016). The principle of free school choice also reinforced the mismatch between school and working life to some extent. The schools offered the education programmes demanded by students, and therefore vocational education did not necessarily provide the training that leads to jobs (Lundahl and Olofsson, 2014).

Put in a broader context, the school reforms of the 1990s coincided with a deep economic crisis characterised by negative economic growth and a rising public debt. A weaker demand in the private sector as well as cuts in the public sector affected the number of vacancies, and young people were faced with increasing difficulties entering the labour market. Before 1990, youth unemployment had been relatively low and school-to-work transitions rather smooth (Olofsson, 2006). In the years 1994–1995, an average of 7 per cent of young adults aged 20 to 24 were unemployed and almost as many went into different labour market policy programmes. The number of long-time unemployed young people also rose markedly during the 1990s (Lundahl and Olofsson, 2014).

The growing difficulties young adults encountered in finding employment have been one of the most decisive factors behind subsequent changes in upper secondary school and VET. After the reforms in upper secondary school followed an expansion of higher education, as can be seen in Figure 7.1.

The great expansion of the post-secondary education system, in combination with a labour market characterised by increased segmentation, slack demand and excess supply, also meant that those with a higher formal education had to accept jobs demanding lower qualifications (Olofsson, 2006). Consequently, the lower educated – especially those with only education below upper secondary level – find it even harder to gain entrance to the labour market. Given comparatively limited pay gaps – both connected to age and education – there is not much space for low-wage jobs. Instead of being employed in low-paying jobs,

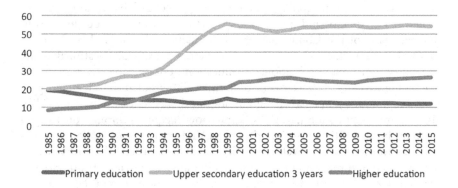

Figure 7.1 Level of highest educational attainment 20–24-year-olds, 1985–2015 (Statistics Sweden, 2016)

as in e.g. the U.S., those without secondary education have been increasingly dependent on social welfare and active labour market policy measures (Olofsson, 2006). The difficulties the young and lower educated faced in gaining entrance to the labour market during the 1990s, affected the general orientations of VET policy with a stronger focus on social inclusive goals of preparing especially vulnerable groups for future jobs.

A third trend toward increased differentiation: 2011–

In the new millennium, several changes have been introduced in Sweden. They have contributed to increased differentiation in vocational education and training, implicating a potential break with the school-based tradition of VET. The main drivers behind these changes can be said to be public reforms, as well as external transactions whereby groups outside education impose new demands on schools (Persson Thunqvist, 2015). While the return of apprenticeship in upper secondary VET has been widely discussed in a policy context in recent decades, the section also illuminates a trend whereby employers and social partners have established influence over vocational education and training in other ways (than through school-organised apprenticeship) that perhaps more naturally tie into the Swedish tradition of voluntary agreements on the labour market.

Furthermore, recent trends toward increased differentiation are analysed in relation to the double challenge in the field of VET toward strengthening school-work ties, while at the same time securing young people's pathways to further studies and higher education. Related challenges involve the simultaneous tasks of improving the esteem of vocational education in relation to general education and promoting socially inclusive goals.

The new trend toward increased differentiation is also driven by structural transformations in terms of globalisation, digitalisation, and new work organisations (Lauder et al., 2006). Although the Swedish economy has managed to cope rather well with the economic and financial crises in Europe in recent years, vocational education and training are challenged by various changes related to the quality and qualification structure of work and occupations in different parts of the labour market. As production systems and processes in industrial and technical sectors become more specialised, vocational training must foster broader vocational qualifications. For example, learning CNC machining involves abstract calculation, three-dimensional thinking, and programming, competencies that require advanced theoretical knowledge. They also require specific industrial skills, 'know-how', acquired through on-the-job training (Berner, 2010). On the other hand, VET also has to function as insurance for further career development in the case of structural transformation (e.g. geographical redistribution of work, closing of industries). Another structural challenge for initial VET is related to the risk of increased segmentation on the labour market (e.g. Thelen and Busemeyer, 2013; Standing, 2011), with a widening polarisation between unskilled work (e.g. as the large service sector) and skilled work in Sweden (Olofsson, 2015). Migration influences VET policy as well. Sweden has been one of the largest recipients of refugees among the EU countries, and immigrants' access to education and work has been placed at the centre of education policy. The introduction of several shorter preparatory education tracks ('introduction programmes') for gaining access to upper secondary education, and vocational tracks tailored for direct access to working life, are examples of recent measures taken for social inclusion (National Agency for Education, 2016). However, urgent questions today also involve how the broader public support system (e.g. liberal folk high schools, active labour market policy) can best be used to support immigrants through their studies and transition to work.

The 2011 reform and a movement to the world of work

Recent changes in Swedish VET are part of a broader policy trend and political movement toward the world of work. Looking at the national education system since early 2000, a common characteristic of VET programmes from different parts of the education system is the effort to bridge the existing gaps between the worlds of education and work (Persson Thunqvist, 2015). For example, regular VET programmes in advanced vocational education (AVE; adult education) and higher vocational education (HVE) provide tailored education in close cooperation with working life.

In 2011, several changes to upper secondary school were introduced to bring initial VET closer to working life as well (Olofsson and Persson Thunqvist, 2014). These reforms have been collectively referred to as the Gy11 reform. The most significant change concerned the content of vocational training, whereby the goal was greater emphasis on the specifically vocational subjects (SOU, 2008:27; Government Bill, 2008/09:199). Since autumn 2011, the new upper secondary school comprises 18 national programmes, 12 of which are vocational. All programmes lead to a diploma. Vocational programme students have the option to choose an apprenticeship track. Already in 2008, a pilot upper secondary apprenticeship project was introduced, and from 2011 apprenticeship is a regular feature of vocational training. The condition for being classified as an apprentice is that at least half of the training period is workplace-based. Apart from the regular capitation allowance, the school and workplace receive a special allowance for each apprentice as compensation for arranging the apprenticeship. The influence of trade and industry over upper secondary vocational programmes was meant to increase. Thus, the schools are now obliged to set up local programme councils for each programme. The councils are to include representatives of businesses and trade union organisations. At the national level, there must also be vocational councils organised through the National Agency for Education. The idea is that representatives of trade and industry will gain increased influence over the programmes via the national councils.

The stronger working-life orientation in VET policy means that equal access to higher education has become a less prioritised goal. One change entailed in

Gy11 is that vocational training no longer automatically leads to basic eligibility for higher education. Many critics believe that the stricter differentiation between higher education preparatory programmes and vocational programmes has a negative effect on students' interest in vocational programmes. Recently, in fact, both the number and proportion of students who apply to vocational education programmes have decreased considerably (see also Figure 7.2 and Table A7.3).

At the same time, companies are experiencing a great need to recruit people with professional qualifications acquired in upper secondary school. However, from autumn 2013, it is possible to acquire basic eligibility for higher education within the framework of all upper secondary vocational programmes without having to choose an extended curriculum. During 2018 a government bill will be presented with a proposal to reintroduce basic eligibility as a standard for the VET programmes (Government Bill, 2017/18:1).

Recent attempts and challenges to improve skill provision and social inclusion

Finally, we will point out recent attempts in upper secondary VET to tackle the challenge to improve skill provision and battle youth unemployment and social marginalisation. These initiatives, from both the government and various sectors in working life (representing multiple stakeholders in VET), also illustrate tendencies toward greater differentiation in VET. Youth unemployment is high, but businesses still have difficulty finding applicants with the right qualifications (Olofsson, 2015). This is the background of the national sectorial collective agreements between employers and unions, on so-called occupational introduction (Sw. *Yrkesintroduktionsavtal*) in certain trades (industry, commerce, nursing and healthcare) whereby young people without relevant occupational experience are offered opportunities to take on time-limited positions that include organised instruction. As we can see, there is a problem of mismatching

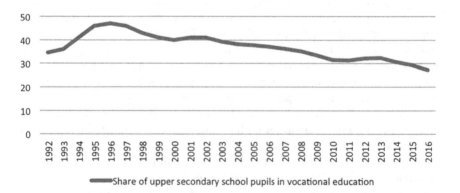

Figure 7.2 Share of upper secondary school pupils in vocational education, 1992–2016 (The Swedish National Agency for Education, 2017)

on the Swedish labour market; that is, too many young people lack the qualifications that are in demand in working life.

Apprenticeship has also become a possible solution to the challenges to improve skill provision and at the same time promote social inclusion aims (e.g. counteract dropping out and non-completion). The reintroduction of apprenticeship was not so much rooted in the Swedish tradition of collective agreements but rather constituted a policy-driven attempt to revitalise the school-work ties.

One vision for vocational training on the political level can be described as a partial implementation of a 'German-style' apprenticeship model in Sweden (e.g. Busemeyer, 2015). Inspired by an ongoing educational debate on whether the dual systems of, e.g. Denmark, Germany and Austria are better at dealing with youth unemployment and fostering skills for modern economies, the former centre-right government (after returning to power in 2006) pushed for an expansion of apprenticeship.

However, for many reasons, the scenario of implementing this German-style apprenticeship model has proven difficult to accomplish in practice. As an apprentice in Sweden, you are not employed (as you would be in, e.g. Germany) but rather a student in formal education. The Swedish tradition of voluntary agreements, combined with the absence of laws regulating apprenticeship as in the dual system governed jointly by the social partners, also places constraints on a genuine apprenticeship. Since the launch of Gy11, the apprenticeship track has not expanded like the initiators of the reform expected. In total it comprises a small share, approximately 5–6 per cent of the pupils in the upper secondary school VET (National Agency for Education, 2016). Before GY11, apprenticeship was also recurrently presented in the education debate as a suitable form of education for the academically unmotivated and people at risk of social exclusion (Olofsson, 2015). Meanwhile, companies want vocational educational programmes to attract ambitious and committed students. Employers and large firms in the industry sector have adjusted their recruitment strategies to school-based VET over time, and were reluctant to initiate apprenticeship presented as a social-political measure (Persson Thunqvist, 2015). It has been pointed out that workplace-based learning within the upper secondary vocational programmes also falls short in several respects. The Swedish School Inspectorate, a national examining authority, has concluded that workplace-based learning does not fulfil the state learning requirements. It does not keep up with the syllabuses used, and workplaces often lack competent supervisors. In addition, schools find it difficult to offer students workplace-based learning to the extent (a minimum of 15 weeks) prescribed by the regulations (Swedish School Inspectorate, 2011). While the new apprenticeship track has largely been driven by the government, there has been an opposite trend in the past decade whereby employers and social partners take a stronger responsibility for vocational education and training in different labour market sectors (Olofsson, 2015). An alternative to genuine apprenticeship is the so-called *vocational college model*. This model is based on cooperation and voluntary agreements between employer organisations, unions and schools, and these cross-alliances, when established, function as intermediary institutions promoting collaboration in the field of VET. For example, technical college and healthcare college (SW: *Teknikcollege, Vård- och omsorgscollege*) are cases in point whereby working-life representatives have initiated far-reaching cooperation with each other and with local schools (Olofsson, 2015). Importantly, the partnership model points to a rather different view on VET compared to top-down approaches (e.g. state-governed VET) as well as a market rationale that submits VET to the short-term requirements of the individual business or student. Education and training are viewed in terms of partnership, implicating a broader network thinking and learning that involves workplaces, educational institutions, individuals and a variety of private enterprises and community organisations (Persson Thunqvist and Hallqvist, 2014).

Quite different to school-organised apprenticeship, the emergence of these new intermediary institutions between education and work is more anchored in the Swedish tradition of voluntary agreements. So far, these three-party constellations and non-profit organisations have played a vital role in improving the connectivity between school and work in certain branches and regions. Although the improvements, in terms of attracting students and increasing the quality of vocational education and training, have been mostly visible in certain regional and local settings, one possible scenario for the future is that these organisational forms will expand to also cover more vocational areas and branches (Olofsson, 2015).

A long-term view of the Swedish model of VET

The changes in the Swedish model of vocational education and training that have taken place during the 20th century can be seen as a movement from unregulated apprenticeship to state-regulated, school-based vocational education at the post-compulsory level (see Chapter 3). There have been ambitions to complement the initial, school-based vocational training with final, qualified workplace training that is regulated by collective agreements. These ambitions, however, have been only partially fulfilled. The establishment of the university-oriented upper secondary school in the 1990s can likely be seen as the final point in the development of the Swedish model of vocational education in an increasingly 'academic' direction.

Since the 1990s, a series of educational reforms have been carried out, in some ways loosening up the educational model established from the 1940s onward. This involves, for example, greater possibilities to establish private schools and students' freedom to choose between schools. After several small-scale experiments with apprenticeship beginning in the 1970s, the latest upper secondary school reform (Gy11) marked a clear shift in views on the status of apprenticeship in upper secondary school. Although the influx of students is not large, it is evident that the interest in developing workplace-based learning is greater than before. There is currently a consensus that workplace-based learning is a necessary component of vocational education.

Moreover, there is an increasingly strong feeling that representatives of working life should be able to influence and guarantee the quality of vocational training to a greater extent. When the Swedish Trade Council was established in the mid-1940s, it was stressed that the aim of vocational education was to make individuals employable and productive. The value of vocational training was ultimately determined in the workplace, and influenced how the labour force was divided into different skill levels in the collective agreements. Because the labour force's training was jointly evaluated by the employer and labour organisations, it was thought that these stakeholders should have a decisive influence over the content and organisation of vocational education (see Chapter 3). This was the primary argument for giving the Swedish Trade Union Confederation and the Swedish Employers' Confederation, via the current Trade Council, exclusive influence over the vocational education that, beginning in the 1950s, was mainly publicly managed. This idea remained even after companies' practical involvement in education and training had begun to appear to be of decreasing importance.

Today, the interest on the part of trade and industry in being involved in defining employability in relation to education and competence requirements has increased once again. The latest upper secondary school reform has improved these actors' opportunities to exert an influence, for example via the local and national programme councils. However, this is not only a matter of changes in upper secondary vocational education and training; it is also a matter of taking advantage of professional boards and other educational organisations to create opportunities for advanced vocational learning outside upper secondary school and the regular education system. Agreements on vocational introduction in certain trades constitute one tangible expression of the creation of opportunity.

Recent changes in the Swedish VET system have been influenced by experiences from other countries. The Danish and Norwegian apprentice systems have attracted great political interest. VET programmes in upper secondary schools generally put more emphasis on work-based learning. However, it is not likely we will see an apprenticeship system in Sweden in the future that is comparable to those in Denmark and Norway.

References

Andersson, I., Wärnvik, G.-B. and Thång, P.-O. (2015) 'Formation of apprenticeships in the Swedish education system: Different stakeholder perspectives', *International Journal for Research in Vocational Education and Training*, vol. 2, no. 1, pp. 1–24.

Antikainen, A. (2006) 'In search for the Nordic model in education', *Scandinavian Journal of Educational Research*, vol. 50, no 3, pp. 229–243.

Ball S. and Larsson, S. (1989) *The Struggle for Democratic Participation: Equality and Participation in Sweden*, Sussex, The Falmer Press.

Berner, B. (1989) *Kunskapens vägar. Teknik och lärande i skola och arbetsliv*, Stockholm, Arkiv förlag.

Berner, B. (2010) 'Crossing boundaries and maintaining differences between school and industry: Forms of boundary-work in Swedish vocational education', *Journal of Education and Work*, vol. 23, no. 1, pp. 27–42.

Busemeyer, M. (2015) *Skills and Inequality: Partisan Politics and the Political Economy of Education Reforms in Western Welfare States*, Cambridge, Cambridge University Press.

Esping-Andersen, G. (1996) *The Three Worlds of Welfare Capitalism*, Cambridge, Polity Press.

Gårdstedt, B. (1967) 'Yrkesutbildning – mer än någonsin', *Tidskrift för praktiska ungdomsskolor*, vol. 9, no. 1, pp. 22–44, Borlänge, Svenska yrkesskoleföreningen.

Government Bill (2008/09:199) *Högre krav och kvalitet i den nya gymnasieskolan*, Stockholm, Utbildningsdepartementet.

Government Bill (2017/18:1) *Budgetpropositionen för 2018*, Stockholm, Finansdepartementet.

Härnqvist, K. (1989) 'Comprehensiveness and social equality', in Ball S. and Larsson, S. (eds.) *The Struggle for Democratic Participation. Equality and Participation in Sweden*, Sussex, The Falmer Press.

Härnqvist, K. and Svensson, A. (1980) *Den sociala selektionen till gymnasiet*, Stockholm, Statens offentliga utredningar, 30.

Lauder, H., Brown, P., Dillabough, J. A. and Halsey, A. H. (2006) *Education, Globalization, and Social Change*, Oxford, Oxford University Press.

Lauglo, J. (1993) *Vocational Training: Analysis of Policy and Modes. Case Studies of Sweden, Germany and Japan*, Paris, International Institute for Educational Planning.

Lundahl, L. (1997a) *Efter Svensk Modell: LO, SAF och Utbildningspolitiken 1944–90*, Umeå, Borås Bokförlag.

Lundahl, L. (1997b) 'A common denominator? Swedish employers, trade unions and vocational education', *International Journal of Training and Development*, vol. 1, no. 2, pp. 91–103.

Lundahl, L., Erixsson Arreman, I., Lundström, U. and Rönnberg, L. (2010) 'Setting things right? Swedish secondary school reform in a 40-year perspective', *European Journal of Education*, vol. 45, no. 1, pp. 46–59.

Lundahl, L. and Olofsson, J. (2014) 'Guarded transitions? Youth trajectories and school-to-work transitions policies in Sweden', *International Journal of Adolescence and Youth*, vol. 19, no. 1, pp. 19–34.

National Agency for Education (Skolverket) (2013) 'Utvecklingen av lärlingsutbildningen', Rapport 397, Stockholm, Skolverket.

National Agency for Education (Skolverket) (2016) *Uppföljning av Gymnasieskolan*. Regeringsuppdrag, Stockholm, Skolverket.

Olofsson, J. (2005) *Svensk yrkesutbildning. Vägval i internationell belysning*, Stockholm, SNS Förlag.

Olofsson, J. (2006) 'Stability of change in the Swedish labour market regime', *Working-paper serien 3*, Lund, Socialhögskolan Lunds universitet.

Olofsson, J. (2015) *Yrkesutbildning i förändring: från lärlingsutbildning till yrkescollege*, Rapport, Stockholm, Ratio, 18.

Olofsson, J. and Panican, A. (2017) 'An education policy paradigm that fails upper secondary school pupils', *Journal of Vocational Education & Training*, vol. 69, no. 4, pp. 495–516.

Olofsson, J. and Persson Thunqvist, D. (2014) *The Swedish Model of Vocational Education and Training: Recent Changes and Future Challenges*, Roskilde University [Online]. Available at http://nord-vet.dk/country-reports (Accessed 11 October 2017).

Persson Thunqvist, D. (2015) *Bridging the Gaps: Recent Reforms and Innovations in Swedish VET to Handle the Current Challenges*, Roskilde University [Online]. Available at http://nord-vet.dk/country-reports (Accessed 08 January 2018).

Persson Thunqvist, D. and Hallqvist, A. (2014) *The Current State for the Challenges for VET in Sweden*, Roskilde University [Online]. Available at http//nord-vet.dk/country-reports (Accessed 11 October 2017).

Rickardsson, G. (1999) *Svensk utbildningshistoria. Skola och samhälle förr och nu*, Lund, Studentlitteratur.

SOU (1948: 27) *1946 års skolkommissions betänkande med förslag till riktlinjer för det svenska skolväsendets utveckling*, Stockholm, SOU.

SOU (1954:11) *Yrkesutbildningen. Betänkande från 1952 års yrkesutbildningssakkunniga*. Stockholm, SOU.

SOU (1963:42) *Ett nytt gymnasium. 1960 års gymnasieutredning IV*, Stockholm, SOU.

SOU (1986:2) *En treårig yrkesutbildning. Del 1. Riktlinjer för fortsatt arbete. Betänkande från arbetsgruppen för översyn av den gymnasiala yrkesutbildningen*, Stockholm, SOU.

SOU (2008:27) *Framtidsvägen – en reformerad gymnasieskola*, Stockholm, SOU.

Standing, G. (2011) *The Precariat: The New Dangerous Class*, London, Bloomsbury Publishing.

Statistics Sweden (2014) *Utbildningsstatistisk årsbok 2014. Gymnasieskolan och kompletterande utbildningar*, Örebro, SCB.

Statistics Sweden. (2016) *Educational Attainment of the Population*, Örebro, SCB.

Streeck, W. and Thelen, K. (2005) *Beyond Institutional Change in Advanced Political Economies*, Oxford, Oxford University Press.

Swedish School Inspectorate (Skolinspektionen) (2011) *Arbetsplatsförlagd utbildning i praktiken – en kvalitetsgranskning av gymnasieskolans yrkesförberedande utbildningar*. Stockholm, Skolinspektionen.

Thelen, K. and Busemeyer, M. (2013) 'From Collectivism Towards Segmentalism. Institutional Change in German Vocational Training', *MPIfG Discussion Paper 08*. Max Planck Institute for The Study of Societies.

Wiborg, S. (2004) 'Education and social integration: A comparative study of the comprehensive school system in Scandinavia', *London Review of Education*, vol. 2, no. 2, pp. 84–93.

Young, M. and Raffe, D. (1998) 'The four strategies for promoting parity of esteem', in Lasonen, J. and Young, M. (eds.) *Strategies for Achieving Parity of Esteem in European Upper Secondary Education*, Jyväskylä, University of Jyväskylä, Institute for Educational Research, pp. 35–46.

Appendix

Table A7.1 The percentage attending upper secondary school at age 17–18 in different birth cohorts and related to sex and socio-economic group

Socio-economic group*	Male students 1948	1953	1958	1963	Female students 1948	1953	1958	1963
Upper class	67	76	88	90	66	72	86	91
Middle class	43	59	79	82	41	54	74	82
Working class	26	48	66	71	25	42	65	75
All	36	56	75	74	34	50	72	79

Source: Modified after Härnqvist, 1989, pp. 26, Table 5.

* In Table A7.1, the aggregation of socio-economic groups made by Härnqvist (1989) is used. Upper class includes academics and the higher level of salaried employees. Middle class includes salaried employees at lower levels. Working class includes workers.

Table A7.2 Transition rate to higher education for upper secondary school graduates within three years 1999/2000–2008/2009

Shares in percentage of number of graduates, by programme and three selected vocational fields and final year

Vocational programmes in upper secondary school	1999/2000	2002/03	2005/06	2007/08	2008/09
Art and Media:					
Art	34	39	42	46	49
Media	24	32	31	36	37
Service:					
Business and Administration	11	14	14	20	19
Hotel and Restaurant	6	7	9	11	11
Care:					
Child and Recreation	6	7	9	11	11
Health Care	18	21	25	29	31
Technology/industry:					
Industrial Technology	3	4	4	6	6
Building and Construction	1	1	2	4	5
Electricity	10	11	9	12	13
Vehicle	1	1	1	2	3

Source: Statistics Sweden (2014) Utbildningsstatistisk årsbok 2014: Gymnasieskolan och utbildningar, Örebro, SCB.

Table A7.3 Distribution of upper secondary school students (year 1) by programme (general, vocational and individual programmes)

Educational programmes	1999/2000	2007/2008	2009/2010	2012/2013
General	51.2%	46.7%	53.3%	58.7%
Vocational	48.8%	39.4%	33.6%	27.5%
Individual		13.8%	13.2%	13.7%

Sources: National Agency of Education, 2013, p. 21.

8 Norwegian VET and the ascent and decline of social democracy 1945–2015

Svein Michelsen and Håkon Høst

Introduction

The year 1945 marked the ascent of the social democratic regime in Norwegian VET. Education evolved into a strategic policy arena for the Labour Party as an integral part of the welfare state, based on universalism and notions of virtuous circles between the economy and welfare. The state intervened in VET in unprecedented ways, and new regulations were passed for both vocational schools and apprenticeship. However, the two VET training institutions went through widely different trajectories. While VET schools continuously expanded, apprenticeship was contested, and became politically marginalized. It survived, which provided the basis for its expansion from prior strongholds in crafts and industry to comprise all sectors of working life in 1994, as an integral part of the comprehensive upper secondary school. Despite the formidable growth in upper secondary general education and the lack of formal access from VET tracks to higher education, VET still represents an attractive option for Norwegian youth, and the number of apprentices now comprises almost one third of a youth cohort. New and more encompassing actor coalitions have been formed around apprenticeship, the space for apprentice training in the firm has been consolidated and the social partners have pledged their support for making VET tracks a trustworthy and stable option for youth, based on a sequentially organized combination of schooling and apprenticeship training in the firm. This particular trajectory poses an interesting puzzle for comparative VET theories, as it combines elements from statist comprehensive school systems and apprenticeship systems, which are assumed to gravitate towards different system logics and different interest coalitions.

Firstly, inspired by historical-institutionalist and political-economy approaches (Thelen, 2004, 2014, Busemeyer, 2014; Busemeyer and Trampusch, 2012; Ansell, 2010), we investigate the formation of the Norwegian post-war VET trajectory at the intersection of state-led, political dynamics on the one hand and employer/employee-involvement on the other. We chart the evolution of state VET policies and state-employer relations during the peak of social democracy, and investigate how they changed under the neo-liberalist turn and new state administrative modernization policies. Secondly, we scrutinize the evolution of school-based VET and firm-based apprenticeship as competing or supplementary institutions in skill formation. Thirdly, inspired by the literatures on the social democratic welfare state and the comprehensive school (Antikainen, 2006; Esping-Andersen, 1991), we focus on the significance of policies for the inclusion of youth in VET.

A more interventionist state

With the Labour Party firmly in power, VET reform proposals that had piled up before the Second World War were re-activated. A new law on vocational schools for industry and crafts, accepted by Parliament in 1940, was implemented in 1945. Vocational schooling for industry and crafts were constructed as an independent policy area protected by law, and an institutional divide was drawn between the vocational schools and general education. Its nationwide character represented a clear departure from prior practices in the area of educational law, where towns and rural areas had been constituted as separate legal entities (Aubert, 1989). The needs of rural youth also had to be taken into account in VET, and new VET schools had to be built. The social policy orientation of the law on vocational schools was clear. The total amount of working hours for education and work should not exceed 8 hours a day. Reactions from the employers in industry and crafts as well as the conservatives were strongly negative to this part of the law, but the Labour Party enjoyed a clear majority in Parliament, the conservatives were weak, and rural interests had little reason to oppose the law.

The workshop schools for industry and craft were in the centre of policy attention in VET. The primary purpose of these schools was the production of qualified workers for crafts and industry. The day-time workshop schools were the preferred choice in industry, compared to the older evening schools, which for the most part were based on a 2-hours teaching a day template, five days a week. Tired and bored students did not provide efficient conditions for teaching and learning. In political circles, the increasing demand for theoretical and general education was regarded as deeply worrying. 'Over-production' of academics was contrasted with the protracted lack of skilled workers. Government policies and fresh resources for capacity building in VET provided the basis for considerable growth, which in total exceed the expansion of the gymnasium up to the 1960s, see Figure 8.1.

The growth in numbers comprised the whole VET sector, where schools for industry and crafts represented a minor part. In 1960, approximately 25 percent of all VET students attended schools for crafts and industry. Commerce, maritime work, agriculture, handicraft, home economics and health care comprised the substantial part of the total number of VET schools.

The Labour Party regime was no longer willing to leave firm-based training and apprenticeship to the discretion of the employers, and an apprentice law was passed by Parliament in 1950. The reform abolished older limitations on the number of apprentices that a master artisan could take on in relation

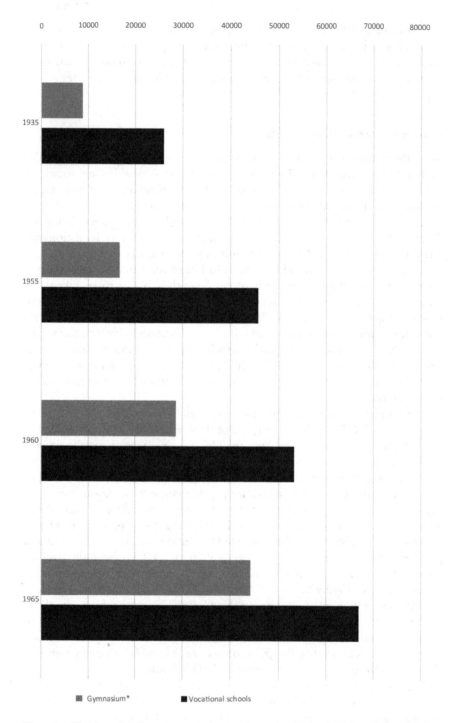

Figure 8.1 Number of students in gymnasiums and vocational schools 1935, 1955, 1960, 1965

Source: Kirke- og undervisningsdepartementet (1967) "Innstilling 1 om det videregående skoleverket", Oslo, Skolekomiteen av, 1965.

to the number of journeymen workers employed. The scope of the apprentice act was restricted to the towns. All the involved employer associations agreed that an apprentice law was urgently required, but when the prospect of a common law for industry, crafts and commerce emerged, all business and employer associations protested. They wanted separate regulations, tailor-made for the different branches and sectors. The protests were to no avail (Jahnsen, 1978). However, the law actually provided the employers and the different trades with a strong formal position. Each trade was regulated by a separate national council, consisting of representatives from the employers and the workers' associations, which organized this specific area of working life. Each of these councils wielded veto powers. The National Apprentice Council, a tripartite arrangement between the state, the employers and the workers' associations, was one of the innovations in the law, but its capacity for coordination across trades was low. Implementation was slow as the trades were integrated under the scope of the new act one by one. In 1958 a total of 45 trades had become formally institutionalized. In some regions, conflicts proliferated at the local level, especially in the artisan trades, where boycott actions were rampant (Jahnsen, 1978). The administration of apprenticeship at the local level was allocated to local labour market offices in the towns. In 1960, a state labour market authority for implementation of labour market policies was formed, and provided with a monopoly on labour market services. Gradually it evolved in the direction of providing training courses for unemployed and unskilled through local labour market centres, strengthening linkages between vocational training and labour market institutions and policies.

Also, education and training for commerce was drawn into the jurisdiction of apprentice law. Commerce education had traditionally been dominated by private interests and norms (Rasmussen, 1958). The labour regime wanted to forge a broader alliance between the white- and the blue-collar workers within the Norwegian Federation of Labour (Messel, 1997). Consequently, the organization of commerce education had to change in the direction of public shop-floor schools and an apprentice system for white-collar workers, and apprentice regulations for commerce trades were drawn up. After a short period of explosive growth, youth demand for apprenticeships dried up completely, and in 1972 apprentice regulations in this part of working life were revoked. Also, vocational education and training for girls was gradually transformed from its prior exclusive focus on the education of the housewife in domestic science into a broader spectre of educations related to female employment.

Educational expansion, welfare and the rise of the comprehensive school model

At the beginning of the 1960s, the educational system in Norway consisted of the comprehensive elementary school, non-obligatory lower secondary schools, upper secondary schools, the post-gymnasium schools and the universities. The boundaries between secondary and post-gymnasium schools were blurred or unclear, and some school types, like engineering and teacher training, recruited from both lower secondary and upper secondary schools. Capacity planning in VET schools and trades was based on static forecasting models for the reproduction of the labour force in the various areas of working life and trades. These 'manpower planning' models were broken down into very detailed plans for capacity building in the various regions until the middle of the 1960s (St. meld. nr. 97 (1964–65)), when the post-war baby boomer's growing demand for education made capacity precarious, and such an approach was considered less adequate. If training capacity was not increased, the numerical development in the future labour force would imply an increasing percentage of unskilled workers and the prospect of a growing, unskilled youth proletariat. The prospective life chances of acquiring training as a skilled worker should not be reduced by demographic processes, it was argued. Youth demand for education and training evolved as the most important parameter for capacity building in skill formation, rather than the present needs in working life. This allowed for more dynamic forecasting models, aiming at flexibility, life-long learning and a flexible mix of skills based on the production of broad and more general skill profiles (St. meld. nr. 45 (1980–81)).

The growing number of students must also be seen as an integral part of larger and more complex social processes, where different social groups developed inclinations for more and better education as a well as new notions of how this could be achieved. Through such processes the percentage of the youth population involved in education increased substantially, see Figure 8.2.

The figure illustrates the emerging universalization of education and training in all youth cohorts. The Social Democrats pursued welfare policies that would promote universalism and equality. The ambition was to fit all social policy elements into an encompassing and coherent framework, that of the welfare state. School reorganization and comprehensivization became strategic elements in this policy formation. The old parallel school structure with separate school types for the different areas like crafts and industry, handicrafts, house economics and commerce, were tightly related to their respective sectors, actors and educational traditions. It was gradually transformed and moved into the purview of the Ministry of Education, creating new and stronger administrative conditions for coordination. New conditions for the transformation of the gendered division of labour were also created, as the Universalist ideal of social rights to education based on citizenship was linked to the normalcy of wage work for both sexes. The early entry of women into the labour market (compared to the rest of OECD) created demand for public services to support participation, which in turn fuelled growing demands for the construction of educations and occupations for these services. The restructuring of the educational system also took on a new meaning in relation to the economy by the discovery of education as the 'third factor' in the production of growth (Aukrust, 1964). The future labour market would present new demands to the educational system. An organizational framework that provided new potential

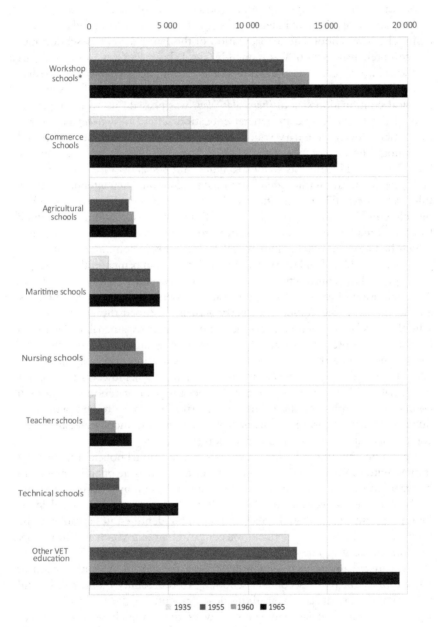

Figure 8.2 Number of students in different types of vocational schools 1935, 1955, 1960, 1965

Source: Kirke- og undervisningsdepartementet (1967) 'Innstilling 1 om det videregående skoleverket', Oslo, Skolekomiteen av, 1965.

for flexible combinations between vocational and general subjects would have a potentially strategic importance for economic development.

After an initial period of indecisiveness, the Labour Party launched the 9-year comprehensive school. The incorporation of the lower secondary schools into the comprehensive school was framed by the Labour Party as an integral part of the democratic tradition in Norwegian schooling (Telhaug and Mediås, 2003), based on equal opportunities for youth. The tradition of the exam-free practical continuation school (*framhaldskolen*) was phased out, while the tradition of the lower secondary general education school (*realskolen*) persevered in a unitary lower secondary youth school, based on mixed ability classes and streaming. The next step was the construction of a unitary upper secondary level. The Social Democrats wanted to reduce the social distance between VET and general education through institutional integration. They intended to build fully elaborated VET specialization tracks of equal status and prestige, as well as flexible combinations of general and vocational subjects, but they also wanted to create broad access to the gymnasium for their own constituency, a policy which had a strong potential for mobilizing a strategic combination of urban, rural as well as liberal and social democratic interests. In principle, the conservatives opposed the construction of one school for the entire 7–19 youth cohorts. The realization of each student's potential was essential in conservative policies, and segments in the conservative party actually regarded the comprehensive school as a relatively neutral instrument, not particularly amenable to partisan conflict. The conservatives wanted to preserve the gymnasium as an elite institution, and argued that the pressure for more education preferably should be alleviated by building more capacity in VET (Seip, 1990). However, there is not much data which support suggestions of persistent polarization and partisan conflict in educational polices. The conservatives' resistance to comprehensive upper secondary reform in Parliament was hesitant and incoherent, and there was no clear alternative reform conception (Sass, 2015).

Apprenticeship was one of the few areas in educational policies that became infused with some measure of ideological conflict. The issue of parity of esteem between education and training for the hand and the mind had beend a core element in the ideology of the Labour Party, but not even here, fixed ideological oppositions in central policy issues can be identified in Parliament. The unprecedented rise in the demand for education among youth had to be met in a pragmatic way. The build-up of capacity in general tracks was considerably cheaper than in the more costly VET tracks, and the decentralization of responsibility for upper secondary schooling to the county municipalities and tight municipal budgets enhanced this development.

While a radical social democratic view of the comprehensive upper secondary school was a system based on modularized tracks, allowing flexible combinations between the older school types, the actual result of the stream of reform decisions proved to be a more pragmatic and watered-down version (Sæther, 1981). During the 1970s a variety of school types were formally integrated into the new comprehensive upper secondary umbrella as separate specialized tracks, but with their own regulatory institutions intact (Briseid, 1984). The various actor groups involved, all defended their older school traditions and practices against coordination and outside interference (Grove and Michelsen, 2005). VET for industry and crafts remained the same (Kokkersvold and Mjelde, 1982). Standardization remained low, based on a fine-grained practically oriented course structure, organized according to the principle of a one-to-one relation between trades/vocations and school courses. The vocational schools kept the old tradition for recruiting pupils somewhat below average, measured by marks previously achieved (Vassnes, 1978). A novelty was the 2-year combined foundation course, providing a combination of general and vocational subjects, but it did not attract much enthusiasm (Berge, 1977). Physical integration processes followed formal organizational integration. In 1989, the majority of upper secondary schools offered education in both VET and general tracks (NOU, 1991:4, p. 47). The temporal organization of teaching also became standardized. While VET schools for industry and craft previously followed the time rhythms of working life, the new tracks for VET in the comprehensive school were formed in accordance with standards set by general education. This actually meant a considerable *reduction* of teaching hours in both general and practical subjects in all VET tracks (Haga, 1990).

VET and the formation of mass higher education

At the outset, the social democratic regime was not particularly interested in the university. It did not matter much for their constituency, and the number of applications and students actually decreased during the 1950s. However, soon the educational expansion process accelerated. From 1955 to 1965, the number of students in the gymnasium tripled. In the 1960s, the number of university students more than quadrupled, from 10.000 to 40.000, which roughly amounted to approx. two thirds of an age cohort (Bleiklie et al., 2000). Of equal significance was the formation and expansion of regional colleges and university colleges, where the number of students tripled from 14.000 in 1965 to 42.000 students in 1981. By 2015, more than 280.000 students were registered in higher education, see Figure 8.3.

An integral part of this transformation was the reclassification of upper secondary VET programmes and occupations like nursing, teaching and engineering into post-gymnasia education during the 1970s and 1980s. This transformation process evolved gradually, where a number of vocational school types were elevated to the new higher education space one-by-one, and thereafter subjected to comprehensive mergers into regional university colleges in 1993. Furthermore, a variety of new higher vocational educations was formed in the new university colleges, based on the skill requirements and demands of the welfare state. The university degree structure was subsequently extended to include the university colleges, providing the basis for an institutionally diversified but coordinated higher education space, where student degrees could be built on transfers and various combinations of programmes from several institutional

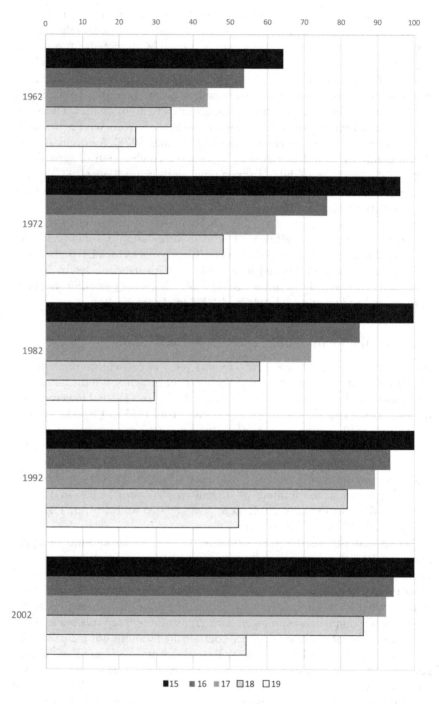

Figure 8.3 Percentage of youth cohorts 15–19 years old in education 1962, 1972, 1982, 1992 and 2002. From 1989 apprentices are included.

types (Vabø and Hovdhaugen, 2014). The general aim was, and still is, that higher education should be flexible and open to all qualified applicants.

A central question which can be raised is if or to what extent new pathways between upper secondary education VET and higher education were constructed. VET tracks did not formally qualify for mobility into higher education, and the expansion of higher education was exclusively fuelled by the gymnasiums. This also remained the case after the construction of the upper secondary comprehensive school, where the gymnasiums were rebranded as upper secondary general education. Efforts at transcending the old institutional 'schism' between VET and higher education did not make an impact. Admittedly, new regulations opened up for 'individual' considerations, based on at least 5 years of experience from working life, but 'individual' qualifications were devised as a general arrangement, irrespective of vocational training and formal, skilled worker certificates. In practice, access to higher education from upper secondary VET tracks remained blocked, and investigations demonstrate that mobility from upper secondary VET to higher education have been very low (Vassnes, 1978; Lesjø, 1986). Alternatives to higher education remained in the form of various post-upper secondary technical institutions, which offered practice-oriented short cycle education and training. In general, these programmes were valued by industry, but numbers were low, and standards varied.

The decline and revival of apprentice training

While the gymnasiums and school-based VET types were growing, the apprentice system was withering. The old social democratic rhetoric around apprentice training education sharpened as post-1968 political radicalization gained ground. Viewed from a radical leftist political perspective, the apprentice system had several important flaws. Economic conditions for apprentices were generally bad, and wages were low. Furthermore, the clear, unambiguous commitment made by the young apprentice to the firm and the trade was considered unfortunate, premature and untimely. A reorganization of VET in the direction of a school-based system could therefore be framed by the Social Democrats as a question of reducing social inequality.

The apprenticeship law of 1950 had been modelled on the Danish dual system, requiring apprentices to combine workplace training with theoretical education and certification. Nevertheless, practices gravitated towards the reproduction of older and more liberal traditions. Whether apprentices attended school or not had no consequences (Michelsen, 1991). The 1966 revision of apprentice law formally enforced the duty to attend school during apprenticeship, but experienced unskilled workers also acquired the right to go through a test qualifying for a skilled workers certificate and status. This was originally a rule meant for workers migrating from rural areas, which were not covered by apprentice law. The experience required was a period 25 percent longer than ordinary apprenticeships, but this could also be dispensed with, if necessary. In principle, these regulations created two pathways to skilled worker status and wages: through apprenticeship contract or through prolonged practical experience in the trade, without any theoretical schooling. In neither case was a skilled workers' test actually obligatory. Case studies from a large number of firms in the shipbuilding industry, a major technological powerhouse, suggest that skilled worker status and skilled workers' wages could be obtained without any formal certification whatsoever (Korsnes, 1996). In spite of increasing legal regulation, apprentice training and skilled worker certification was overflowing with the continuation of practices from the old liberal regime. Even though the number of registered apprentice contracts increased incrementally during the 1950s, this development stagnated in the 1960s (NOU, 1978:30). In Parliament, disappointment with the apprentice system was rampant, and included all political parties. However, apprenticeship regulations were not revoked, but slowly faded from the light of political attention. Instead, it became a recurring object for social policy rhetoric and compensatory symbol policies for the improvement of conditions for problem youth.

In addition, the employers had their eyes turned elsewhere. Since the social democratic turn, employment structures had changed towards industrial production and export (Berge, 1984). Industrial restructuring and increasing foreign competition imposed new rationalization pressures in industrial branches exposed to such competition. The position of the Norwegian Association of Industry (NI) was that the role of the state should be enabling and 'positive', based on positive incentives. 'Negative interference' through the stick (regulation) would not be beneficial (Hald, 1969). In this period, educational policy was not a hot topic for the employer's organizations. Systematic studies of preference formation among employers at the time is lacking, but there is much to suggest a rapprochement between the industrialists, the economists and the social democratic school reformers, which converged in the direction of the new comprehensive upper secondary school. The political salience of the comprehensive school issue made active contestation difficult, and the benefits of structural elaboration and capacity building in the specialized and practically oriented school-based VET structure were appreciated as useful contributions. A large part of the youth population still entered the labour market with no or negligible formal vocational qualifications, and in 1975 as many as one third of youth aged 17–19 had employment as their main activity.

In practice, employers in industry enjoyed considerable autonomy in skill formation. Through the combination of local and central wage negotiations, the employers could control qualification processes and access to the skilled worker category and a skilled worker wage, relatively independent from formal qualifications in the educational system. These practices allowed branch- and firm-specific valuations of practical worker skills and wage drift across the unskilled-skilled worker divide. A variety of firm-specific and branch-specific practices and solutions to recruitment and skill formation problems at the local level were constantly being reproduced (Korsnes, 1996). Local training communities were fragmented and relations between training firms structured by chronic shortage of qualified labour and fear of poaching. Also in the crafts, a journeyman's certificate was far from common. The net result was high employer autonomy and low collective capacity for organizing high quality training in most branches of industry. This situation was sustained by the old institutional distinction in employer organization between the liberally oriented Norwegian Association of Industry (NI), which handled skill formation and structural policies, and wage policies, organized through the Norwegian Federation of Employers (NAF). In the welfare sector, the situation was quite different, where formal certification structured the way to a permanent position in public services. The welfare service educational programmes were dominated by school-based structures and norms, and apprenticeship was not regarded a feasible alternative at the time (Høst, 2006).

Apprenticeship revitalization and conversion

Still, preferences for apprenticeship continued to structure recruitment and training practices in important segments of industry, like the National Association of Mechanical Enterprises (MVL). MVL was one of few branch organizations that argued strongly against the new comprehensive school. MVL saw no possible reason how such a reform could contribute to more adequate vocational training and the needs of the employers for skilling the work force (Bjertnes Tangen, 1984). The continuation of apprentice-based recruitment and training practices in these segments of industry contributed to the revitalization of apprentice training (Olsen, 2008). From the mid-1970s, there was a significant increase in the number of apprenticeships in crafts and industrial trades. This provided the basis for long-term growth in the number of apprenticeships, see Figure 8.4.

The numbers demonstrate the expansion in the number apprenticeships and trades registered, as well as the exposure of apprenticeship to business cycles, as unemployment numbers and the number of apprenticeship contracts have evolved in counter phase around the growing trend (Høst et al., 2008). The expansion could build on older local practices and institutional configurations, where the highly specialized and practically oriented VET tracks in the new comprehensive upper secondary school provided possibilities for flexible combinations of full-time vocational training in school followed by apprentice training or on-the-job-training in the firm, as the duration of school attendance could be deducted from the normal duration of apprenticeship. In 1980, apprentice law was transformed into VET law, and the jurisdiction of the apprentice law was extended from urban areas to the whole country. Arrangements allowing skilled worker certification on the basis of prolonged practical experience in the trade lost its original justification related to flexibility in geographical space, but took on a new one instead, related to the new adult education law of 1976 (Michelsen and Høst, 2002). This pathway to the skilled worker's certification kept its significance by producing around 40 percent of the skilled workers' certificates. A considerable part of the growth in skilled worker certification during the 1980s could probably be attributed

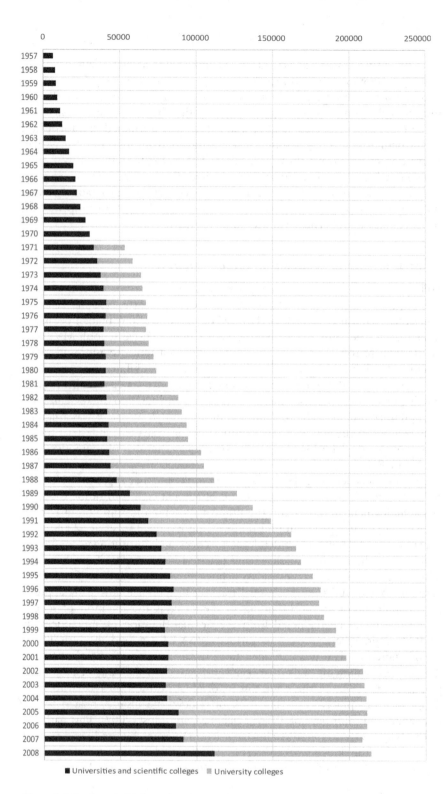

Figure 8.4 Students in higher education in Norway 1957–2008

Source: Norwegian Bureau of statistics, historical statistics.

to the reclassification of rural traditional handicrafts, which previously were not included. Since then, a levelling out of the number of apprenticeships has taken place across counties, as apprenticeships became available for the whole country (Høst et. al., 2008). However, the growth in apprenticeships cannot be reduced to mere reclassification as the growth in apprentice numbers preceded the 1980 reform.

In addition, governance arrangements changed, as a new reorganized VET Council replaced the former Apprentice Council. Formally, an advisory body for the Ministry of Education, it was also provided with a dedicated secretariat, supervising trade regulations and practices. Council capacity for coordination and standardization across different trades was strengthened, as the individual trades lost their old veto position. At the local/regional level, the administration of apprenticeship was decoupled from the State Labour Market Authorities, and became integrated into to the upper secondary school sector in the new county municipalities in 1970. Autonomous councils in apprentice training were formed in each county municipality, protected by juridical fortifications, with a dedicated administrative apparatus and earmarked budgets. These arrangements furnished the social partners and their administrative apparatus with considerable self-government. These bodies were responsible for the certification of apprentice training companies, approval of new apprenticeship contracts and the supervision of the quality of training. Recruitment to the regional apprentice training administration was based on union-related as well as work-related expertise. It was a form of recruitment pattern, which departed sharply from the classical Weberian bureaucracy of civil servants. Supervision and control of firms was implemented by site visits and informal talks based on common norms, which provided the appropriate leniency in the enforcement of training regulations.

However, complaints about the structure and organization of VET had started to escalate. The youth labour market contracted from 25 percent of the 16–19 cohorts in 1975 to 7–8 percent in the mid-1990s. Policy makers interpreted this development as an inevitable process, induced by structural changes in the economy and deindustrialization (Grøgaard, 2006). In the future, it would no longer be possible to enter working life without completing upper secondary education. More systematic investment in youth was required. The educational system had to cater for the whole 16–19 youth cohort, it was argued. The huge economic downturn and increasing long-term unemployment in the late 1980s added to the problem. For elder youth inclined towards work, the upper secondary educational system became a temporary refuge and a substitute for unemployment, and they returned to VET tracks in increasing numbers (NOU, 1991:4). Entrance criteria for upper secondary education rewarding factors like age and experience propelled these processes. For years 20-year-olds or older youth occupied more than 40 percent of the total capacity in upper secondary education.

As the youth problem escalated in combination with its growing political salience, new policies and instruments for youth inclusion had to be developed.

In 1980, a youth guarantee to education or work was set up by the social democratic government in office. It was not a guarantee in a legal sense, but it signalled a strong state commitment to the problem of youth inclusion. However, queues of youngsters without a school place in search of work created capacity problems and huge costs for the labour market authorities each autumn, when schools started up. In order to meet demand for training for those unable to find work in the dwindling youth labour market, VET schools and employers had to be enlisted as suppliers of short-term training courses for unemployed youth on a large scale. Furthermore, the guarantee had the unwelcome effect that it created unrealistic expectations and disappointment among youth in search of work or education. As the distance between political goals for inclusion and performance increased, radical reform became imminent and urgent.

Path shift and compound formation 1990–2010

The social democratic state had secured political stability, consensual policy making and bargaining for more than three decades. What followed was the ascent of a new political wave towards the right, somewhat similar to most countries in Europe, where policies reoriented towards the market, public sector modernization, decentralization and privatization (Hansen, 2011; Pollitt and Bouckaert, 2004). The path shift cannot be precisely identified by specific significant events in Norway; opinions vary among historians (Sejersted, 2011), and policies in this direction were developed by right as well as leftist governments. The economic background for the path shift was deindustrialization, increasing economic problems, recessions and prolonged youth unemployment.

For the most part, these policies were grafted onto older social democratic layers. The Reform 94 represented a specific amalgamation of welfare policies, juridification of individual rights to education and New Public Management (NPM) oriented policies for administrative modernization. A minority labour government proposed the reform, but it received substantial support from the social partners and was carried through Parliament by a consensus drive. A new encompassing and comprehensive space for upper secondary education was formed. Apprenticeship and the skilled worker certificate were defined as the main templates and outlets for upper secondary VET learning and certification. However, the provision of an individual right to 3 years of upper secondary education for 16–19-year-olds was the key component in the new policy. The universalization of the right to upper secondary education for these age cohorts implied a massive redistribution of educational resources between age groups. The labour market authorities were relived from the burdensome responsibility for the inclusion of work-oriented youth under 19 years in labour market activation schemes. The right to employment for this group was no longer a political issue, and the considerable active labour market policy (ALMP) budgets were reallocated to education (Michelsen et al., 1999). Upper secondary school capacity could now be shaped by the size of the target group wielding individual rights to 3 years of upper secondary education, and older patterns of horizontal mobility to other upper secondary education programmes were restricted or prohibited. Actually, total capacity in upper secondary school was significantly reduced compared to the situation before Reform 94. Instead, the reorganization and strong expansion of capacity in higher education during the 1990s provided new educational horizons for the post 19-year cohorts which in practice were ousted from the upper secondary school.

The new Reform 94 programme architecture recombined school-based and firm-based training in a fixed, statutory sequence consisting of 2 years of education in school followed by 2 years of training in the firm as an apprentice, often called the 2+2 model. The reform checked the further upwards expansion of school-based VET, and provided space for firm-based apprentice training in all VET tracks. This policy fuelled a heavy rationalization of the old course structure, slimming down the number of foundation courses from 101 to 12 broader and more theoretically oriented initial courses, structuring the choice of trades in each of the vocational tracks. Further structural rationalization processes reduced the number of available continuation courses from around 100 to 56. A whole repertoire of instruments and policy measures were set up in order to combat the anticipated shortages in the supply of apprenticeships. These included the development of new and more favourable financing systems for firms that took on apprentices with 2 years of upper secondary school education, and heavy public subsidies invested in local training agencies supporting training firms and monitoring workplace training quality (Høst et al., 2014b; Michelsen et al., 1999). Auxiliary solutions to work-based training were also provided in the form of a third year of practical training in school. In theory, work-placed and school-based tracks would lead to the same vocational qualification. In practice, the school-based VET track was generally regarded as inferior by youth, and consequently diminished (Michelsen et al., 1999).

A safety valve was constructed at the intersection between general and vocational education. The increased theoretical content in all VET tracks now allowed students to transfer to general education tracks as an alternative to entering an apprenticeship without loss of time. Such an arrangement made the choice of a VET track less risky. On the other hand, it allowed a systematic drain in the supply of potential apprentices. Although diachronic comparisons of VET status are inherently complicated, the popularity of choosing VET tracks seems to be relatively constant in aggregate terms since Reform 94. Statistics from the Directorate of Education show that around half of each cohort has applied for a study programme defined as vocational. This has been quite stable since the Reform 94. The number of transfers from VET tracks to general education has grown considerably, transforming the safety valve into a major pipeline. The total share of a Norwegian youth cohort who goes through apprenticeship has for the past 20 years varied between 25 and 30 percent, very much influenced by the up- and downturns of the labour market. In the same period, the youth cohorts have increased by approximately 20 percent. This development provided the basis for a significant growth in apprenticeships, see Figure 8.5.

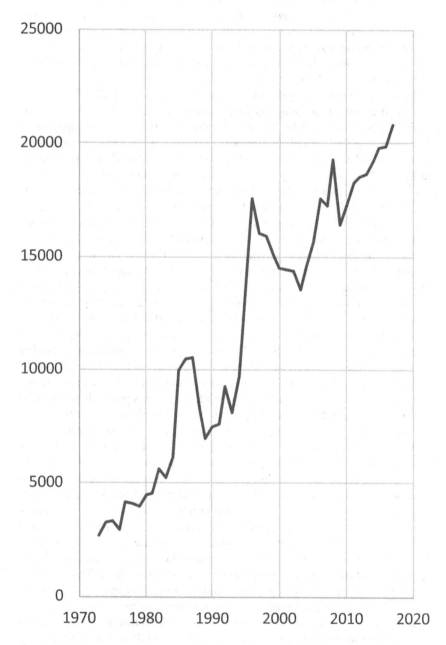

Figure 8.5 The number of new apprenticeship contracts 1973–2017
Source: Høst et al. (2008), updated with data from the Directorate of Education 2008–2017.

The main bulk of the growth has taken place in new trades or vocations in tertiary industries, which includes welfare state services as well as primary industries, fishing and fish farming, while traditional areas have remained stable. The expansion of apprenticeship into the service sector and the public sector has been a partial success. In the public welfare sector, skilled workers are situated at the lower end of the skill hierarchy, where the jurisdictions of the welfare professions structure work organization and work status hierarchies (Høst et al., 2014b). Apprenticeship in the public sector is often regarded as a publicly financed education scheme, with loose couplings between training and employment (Høst and Reegård, 2015). In retailing, recruitment of apprentices has grown incrementally, but still remains insignificant in numbers, compared to widespread informal on-the job training of youth and adults. The Norwegian youth labour market was revitalized and expanded significantly in the period 1994–2008 (Michelsen and Høst, 2012). In effect, the youth labour market has until now been able to absorb a considerable part of the consistently high drop-out during the first two school-based years and at the intersection between school-based upper secondary VET tracks and apprenticeship.

State commitment and employer/employee involvement

The new VET reform required considerable state commitment as well as state funding. It also rested heavily on the collaboration of the employers and the unions. A central element in Reform 94 was a declaration of intent on behalf of the social partners, committing themselves to the extension and stabilization of the apprentice system as a trustworthy educational track. In spite of the declared preference for apprenticeship, no compulsory solutions in the spirit of German-style apprentice corporatism were fashioned, where training firm membership in 'Kammern' is obligatory. The tradition of voluntarism persevered. In fact, the reform amplified formal employer autonomy in some respects. In the older apprentice regulations, hiring youth less than 20 years of age in work areas structured by apprentice law was explicitly forbidden. After Reform 94, a company that wanted to train could do so, either by the apprentice system – if such a profile was available – or through the employment contract, where the training could be tailor-made to specific company requirements. As opposing principles were recombined, the reform forged increased state subsidies with employer commitment to apprentice training, contractual freedom with welfare state universalism and individual rights to education.

This present arrangement has been exposed to the combined critiques of lack of efficiency as well as lack of inclusion, where the enterprises are allegedly creaming the crop. The main bottleneck in the system is located at the juncture from school to firms-based training as apprentices. Around one third of the applicants do not end up with an apprenticeship contract. From a public welfare point of view, it has been argued that state control over upper secondary education is still restricted and incomplete, and that further reforms are long overdue. The solution advocated by political leftists as well as the National Union of

Norwegian Pupils is a further juridification process, securing youth a statutory right to apprenticeship, which would mean the prospect of an unprecedented intervention in internal enterprise processes. The major political stakeholders have meticulously avoided this road. The other side of the individual expansion of rights to education has been a gradual but significant strengthening of discourses on youth obligations to participate actively in skill formation schemes. An increasing percentage of youth remains more or less permanently outside the labour market, and passive income protection of these groups is regarded as problematic. The balance between rights and obligations to activation is a contentious issue, and the willingness of the state to apply sanctions in the case of non-compliance is still restricted. Re-linking active labour market policies to vocational training has been one of the options explored, and apprenticeship in a modularized form is to an increasing extent seen as a tool, which can be applied in active labour market policies in order to facilitate inclusion of vulnerable groups like youth and adult immigrants in the labour market (Meld. St.16 (2015–2016)).

In addition, governance arrangements in VET have been re-formed. New and clear boundaries between the state and society, between policy-making and implementation were at the core of new state administrative policies. One of the consequences was the demolition of the old educational councils, and the formation of a new Directorate of Education in charge of implementing educational policies devised by the Ministry of Education. The National VET Council, where the social partners were in charge, was among the few councils which survived, mainly due to perceived International Labour Organization (ILO) obligations. The VET Council had its mandate redefined and aligned to the new administrative policies. The autonomy to supervise the quality of vocational education and training, was withdrawn, and its dedicated secretariat replaced by the Directorate of Education. The old internal structure, consisting of numerous trade-specific councils was simplified and aligned to the new, rationalized VET track structure. The social partners also lost control over the regional apprentice councils to the county municipal executive, and the traditional hands-on VET administration, peer control and close informal contacts with training firms substituted by increasing formalization, audits and quality control frameworks, working at a distance (Michelsen and Høst, 2015). Tasks previously performed by the regional apprentice training councils and their administrative apparatus have been taken over by new, intermediary Local Training Agencies (Høst et al., 2014a). These agencies, which for the most part are owned and governed by the employers, control more than 80 percent of apprentice recruitment. Norwegian training firms are quite small, the median training company has 12 employees, and there is a lack of local obligatory arenas for employer participation in apprentice training (Høst et al., 2012). In this context, the training agencies have become increasingly important in the formation of employer preferences and practices in skill formation at the local level.

The social coalitions backing skill formation in VET have also changed. The old institutional cleavage in employer organization between skill formation/

structural policies and wage policies became increasingly blurred, and was eventually bridged by mergers into one new peak employer organization: the Confederation of Norwegian Enterprises (NHO) in 1983. The new organization became dominated by the employer policy tradition. Older liberal practices in skill formation have been shored up, and the skilled worker category in industry has been homogenized in terms of formal qualifications. However, NHO and the Norwegian Confederation of Trade Unions (LO), have lost their former monopoly as governors of the system of apprentice training, and other employer and employee organizations from adjacent sectors of working life, e.g. from services and the public sector, have been awarded rights of representation in VET councils. In the new administrative architecture, the employer and employee organizations seem to operate more as external pressure groups lobbying for resources, than deeply integrated participants, sharing space with the state in the administration of VET (Michelsen and Høst, 2015).

Furthermore, the influence of LO has been steadily declining in relation to other employee organizations. In the 1970s, about 75 percent of the organized labour population were members of the LO. In 2014, the LO share has dropped to less than 50 percent of all unionized employees (Nergaard, 2014). The gender composition of the labour market has also changed significantly. Norway has supported a dual-earner family policy conducive to labour market participation for both men and women with children/care responsibilities, and 'housewives' more or less disappeared as a social category between the mid-1970s and the 1990s. The growing welfare sector became heavily dominated by female labour, leading to a strongly occupationally segregated labour market. The increasing female labour force participation was initiated by the expansion of public employment, which in turn created the basis for demands for new and modernized VET programmes in these areas, and the reconstruction of older school-based programmes into apprenticeships. This transformation was defined in terms of equalization of life chances between the sexes, social justice and welfare. It seems reasonable to suggest that the political salience of such issues in skill formation correlated with the massive inclusion of women in politics, in public administration and in the labour market organizations. Even within the LO, the old stronghold for industrial workers, power relations between the male- and the female-dominated sectors have changed as the percentage of women members increased from 24 percent in the 1970s to 51 percent in 2010.

A similar development can be identified in VET governance institutions, where the numerically strong welfare occupations and their training traditions and perceptions have assumed increasing importance. Through its embeddedness in the comprehensive school, the apprentice institution has been converted to comprise all sectors of working life, incorporating new and broader ideas about the appropriate character of apprenticeship, more aligned to the school-based training traditions and practices prevalent in welfare education. While building heavily on the artisan apprentice rhetoric, the new policies have marginalized these preferences to a considerable extent, and arts and craft interests have remained loudly discontent with the track structure and the growing lack of trade specific training in school.

Discussion

During the age of social democracy, education evolved into a strategic policy arena, based on universalism and notions of virtuous circles between the economy and welfare. The Labour Party invested heavily in the financing and regulation of VET. This was a strategic choice in the production of a new egalitarian society, where vocational and general education would enjoy equal status. Initially these policies produced a segmented structure where VET schools, apprenticeship and general education were organized under separate institutional arrangements. In Parliament, there was considerable consensus on the build-up of vocational schooling. This paved the way for the expansion and structural elaboration of VET tracks in a broad array of fields, where schools for industry and crafts were among many. The expansion was increasingly driven by youth demand rather than manpower needs.

The formation of the comprehensive school provided the prime vehicle for the massification and universalization of upper secondary schooling. The construction of the lower comprehensive secondary school in 1969 formed a unitary baseline for recruitment to upper secondary education. The forming of the comprehensive upper secondary school in 1976 integrated VET and general education tracks. The political salience of the comprehensive school made it difficult for the employers to resist. Parliamentary consensualist dynamics and actor-driven implementation processes contributed to a watered-down version of the comprehensive school, where the older school-types and their governance structures were reproduced as programmes within the new comprehensive umbrella.

While the expansion of VET schooling can be characterized as a stable and consensual process, the apprentice path has been more volatile. Apprenticeship had historically been an institution for the crafts. The 1950 apprentice law provided the basis for the extension and institutionalization of apprenticeship into industry and commerce. The state intervened with new regulations, protecting the skilled worker, but boycott and local resistance inhibited growth, and schooling-, certification- and wage-practices continued to adhere to older liberal traditions, blurring the qualification boundaries between the skilled worker and the unskilled worker. This illustrates the limits of state power in collective skill formation. It also reveals weaknesses in the corporatist arrangements in VET, with a comparatively strong level of collective peak organization of the social partners at the national level, not being able to impose constraints on skill formation. VET schooling was generally regarded by the Social Democrats as preferable, and apprenticeship scarcely survived in core branches of industry and in the crafts. Apprenticeship started to regain ground in the mid-1970s, and in 1980, it was converted from its old base in the towns to include rural areas as well. Certification regulations for unskilled workers in rural areas were converted into an instrument for lifelong learning, sustaining older mechanisms for mobility from unskilled to the skilled worker category.

Through Reform 94, the state took advantage of the potential for increased central coordination and rationalization, and restructured the school programmes in a general and less skill specific direction. Apprenticeship and school-based VET were recombined in a fixed sequence, eradicating the flexibility of the older structure. The provision of individual rights to education for 16–19-year-olds provided new conditions for social inclusion processes and made upper secondary VET into a far more age homogenous institution. Older constituencies were directed elsewhere, as new institutions and increased capacity were being built in the higher education space. Apprenticeship was extended to all areas of working life gradually converted and generalized as a template for skill formation. In the new comprehensive structure, VET has been stabilized as an attractive educational option, which approximately 50 percent of the applicants prefer.

The main tensions in the system run between the Universalist and inclusive school sequence, and the more selective, firm-based, apprentice training sequence. Instead of applying for apprenticeships, a significant share of the VET students prefers to switch to general education after the 2 years of schooling in order to gain formal access to higher education. Still, the number of apprenticeships is growing and now comprises around one third of the youth cohort. Governance structures have changed significantly. The National VET Council has had its mandate redefined and aligned to the new administrative policies. The power to supervise the quality of vocational education and training has been taken over by the state. Important elements of the traditional voluntarism have been sustained as employers have retained considerable autonomy in skill formation. They also achieve substantial subsidies in return for their continued support of apprenticeship.

In view of the accumulated empirical material, a number of questions could be asked to the comparative literature on VET systems. The Norwegian case does not conform well either to established notions of statist or collectivist skill formation systems. In general, the comprehensive school has been conceptualized as a prime example of a statist system in the political economy of skill formation literature. When the state advanced, the employers retreated, and firm-based apprentice training was lost (Dobbins and Busemeyer, 2014). The Norwegian case suggests that the rise of the comprehensive school institution does not necessarily imply the fall of firm-based training and the decline of social partner involvement in training, as these arrangements seem to be able to coexist in various forms. Perhaps Kathleen Thelen's notion of state-led collective skill formation systems could be useful here (Thelen, 2014). The Norwegian VET system is definitively collectivist, and based on the involvement of strong collective actors in working life, but the state is in the driver seat. Furthermore, one of the advantages normally attributed to statist school-based VET systems is the ability to construct new pathways from upper secondary to higher education. The Norwegian system does not display such features, but has still been able to retain its attractiveness to Norwegian youth. Last but not least, it combines apprenticeship with voluntarism and autonomy in skill formation processes, where employer involvement in apprenticeship is based on positive incentives and subsidies rather than binding institutions. Norwegian VET looks like an amalgamation, which combines statism, collective skill formation and liberal firm autonomy in a unique constellation.

References

Ansell, B. (2010) *From the Ballot to the Blackboard*, Cambridge, Cambridge University Press.
Antikainen, A. (2006) 'In search of the Nordic model in education', *Scandinavian Journal of Educational Research*, vol. 50, no. 3, pp. 229–243.
Aubert, V. (1989) *Continuity and Development in Law and Society*, Oslo, Universitetsforlaget.
Aukrust, O. (1964) 'Factors of economic development: A Review of recent research', *Weltwirtschaftliches Archiv, (1964) Heft 1*, pp. 23–43.
Berge, Å. (1977) *Teknologiutvikling og kunnskapsorganisering. Ei analyse av yrkesutdanning og samfunnsutvikling, og av forsøka med 2-årig kombinerte grunnkurs i den vidaregåande skolen*, Oslo, Magisteravhandling, Institutt for sosiologi, Universitetet i Oslo.
Berge, D. M. (1984) *Industristrategi og industriinteresser. Om forholdet mellom industripolitikk og industristruktur i Norge på 70-tallet*, Bergen, Institutt for administrasjon og organisasjonsvitenskap, Universitetet i Bergen.
Bjertnes-Tangen, H. (1984) 'En felles videregående skole, skadelig for yrkesopplæringen?', in Bjørndal, B. (ed.) *Videregående skole for alle*, Oslo, Universitetsforlaget, pp. 82–89.
Bleiklie, I., Høstaker, R. and Vabø, A. (2000) *Policy and Practice in Higher Education*, London, Jessica Kingsley.
Briseid, O. (1984) 'Kombinerte skoler og de mange muligheter', in Bjørndal, B. (ed.) *Videregående skole for alle*, Oslo, Universitetsforlaget, pp. 65–73.
Busemeyer, M. R. (2014) *Skills and Inequality: Partisan Politics and the Political Economy of Education reforms in Western Welfare States*, Cambridge, Cambridge University Press.
Busemeyer, M. R. and Trampusch, C. (2012) 'The comparative political economy of collective skill formation.', in Busemeyer, M. R. and Trampusch, C. (eds.) *The Political Economy of Skill Formation*, Oxford, Oxford University Press, pp. 3–40.
Dobbins, M. and Busemeyer, M. L. (2014) 'Socioeconomic institutions, organized interests and partisan politics: The development of vocational education in Denmark and Sweden', *Socio-Economic Review*, vol. 13, no. 2, pp. 259–284.
Esping-Andersen, G. (1991) *The Three Worlds of Welfare Capitalism*, Princeton, NJ, Princeton University Press.
Grøgaard, J. B., Markussen, E. and Sandberg, N. (2006) *Seks år etter. Om kompetanseoppnåelse fra videregående opplæring og overgang til arbeid og høyere utdanning for det første Reform 94-kulle*, Oslo, NIFU.
Grove, K. and Michelsen, S. (2005) *Lærarforbundets historie*, Bergen, Vigmostad og Bjørke.
Haga T. (1990) *Mekaniske Verksteders Landsforening og yrkesopplæringen i perioden 1960–1990*, AHS, Bergen, Universitetet i Bergen.
Hald, K. (1969) *Norges Industriforbund 1919–21 januar 1969*, Oslo, Norges Industriforbund.
Hansen, H. F. (2011) 'NPM in Scandinavia', in Christensen, T. and Lægreid, P. (eds.) *Ashgate Research Companion to New Public Management*, Aldershot, Ashgate, pp. 113–129.
Heiret, J. (2003) 'Samarbeid og statlig styring 1945–1977', in Heiret, J., Korsnes, O., Venneslan, K. and Bjørnson, Ø. (eds.) *Arbeidsliv, historie samfunn. Norske arbeidslivsrelasjoner i historisk, sosiologisk og arbeidsrettslig perspektiv*, Bergen, Fagbokforlaget, pp. 109–176.

Høst, H. (2006) *Utdanningsreformer som moderniseringsoffensiv. En studie av hjelpepleieryrkets rekruttering og dannelseshistorie, 1960–2006*, Bergen, Institutt for administrasjons og organisasjonsvitenskap, Universitetet i Bergen.

Høst, H., Gitlesen, J. P. and Michelsen, S. (2008) 'How the number of apprentices is influenced by policy and economic cycles,' In Høst, H. (ed.) *Continuity and Change in Norwegian VET*, Oslo, NIFU STEP, pp. 17–28.

Høst, H. and. Reegård, K. (2015) Fagopplæring eller statlig utdanning i arbeidslivet? Oslo, NIFU.

Høst, H., Skålholt, A. and Nyen, T. (2012) *Om potensialet for å få bedriftene til å ta inn lærlinger*, Oslo, NIFU.

Høst, H., Skålholt, A., Reiling, R. and Gjerustad, C. (2014a) *Hvorfor blir lærlingordningen i kommunal sektor annerledes enn i privat sektor?* Oslo, NIFU.

Høst, H., Skålholt, A., Reiling, R. and Gjerustad, og C. (2014b) *Opplæringskontorene i fag- og yrkesopplæringen – avgjørende bindeledd eller institusjon ute av kontroll?* Oslo, NIFU.

Jahnsen, B. R. (1978) *Fra faglig tilsyn til statlig kontroll. Lærlingelovens organer 1950–1970*, Bergen, Sosiologisk Institutt, Universitetet i Bergen.

Kokkersvold, E. and Mjelde, L. (1982) *Yrkesskolen som forsvant*, Oslo, Gyldendal.

Korsnes, O. (1996) *Industri og samfunn. Framlegg til et program for studiet av norsk arbeidsliv*, Bergen, Sosiologisk Institutt/AHS – Gruppe for flerfaglig arbeidslivsforskning, Universitetet i Bergen.

Lesjø, J. H. (1986) *Yrkesopplæring, kvalifikasjon og arbeidsmarkedstilpasninger*, Lillehammer, Østlandsforskning.

Meld. St. 15 (2015–2016) 'Fra utenforskap til ny sjanse – Samordnet innsats for voksnes læring'.

Messel, J. (1997) *Samling og strid. Norsk Tjenestemannslag 1947–1997*, Oslo, NTL/Tiden Norsk Forlag.

Michelsen, S. (1991) 'Yrkesopplæringspolitikkens forvaltning. Institusjonaliseringen av det norske styringssystemet for yrkesutdanning 1937–58', in Halvorsen, T. and Olsen, O. J. (eds.) *Det kvalifiserte samfunn?* Oslo, Ad Notam Forlag, pp. 256–274.

Michelsen, S. and Høst, H. (2002) 'Some remarks on Norwegian education and training policies and lifelong learning,' in Harney, K., Heikkinen, A., Rahn, S. and Schemmann, M. (eds.) *Lifelong Learning: One Focus, Different Systems*, Frankfurt am Main, Peter Lang, pp. 87–98.

Michelsen, S. and Høst, H. (2012) 'Apprenticeship, youth and labour market outcomes: A diachronic investigation into the Norwegian case', in Stolz, S. and Gonon, P. (eds.) *Challenges and Reforms in Vocational Education*, Bern, Peter Lang, pp. 215–234.

Michelsen, S. and Høst, H. (2015) 'Om arbeidet med kvalitet i fag- og yrkesopplæringen', in Høst, H. (ed.) *Kvalitet i fag- og yrkesopplæringen: Sluttrapport*, Oslo, NIFU.

Michelsen, S., Høst, H. and Gitlesen, J. P. (1999) 'Mot en ny fagopplæringsordning?' in Kvalsund, R., Deichmann-Sørensen, T. and Aamodt, P. O. (eds.) *Videregående opplæring – ved en skillevei? Forskning fra den nasjonale evalueringen av Reform 94*, Oslo, Tano Aschehoug, pp. 19–47.

Nergaard, K. (2014) *Organisasjonsgrader, tariffdekning og arbeidskonflikter*, Oslo, Fafo.

NOU (1978:30) 'Om lærlinglov'.

NOU (1991:4) 'Veien videre til yrkes- og studiekompetanse til alle'.

Olsen, O. J. (2008) *Institusjonelle endringsprosesser i norsk fag- og yrkesopplæring. Fornyelse eller gradvis omdannelse? Notat 5–2008*, Rokkansenteret, Universitetet i Bergen.

Pollitt, C. and Bouckaert, G. (2004) *Public Management Reform: A Comparative Analysis*, 2nd ed., Oxford, Oxford University Press.

Rasmussen, S. (1958) *Fra underordnet handelsstand til moderne fagforbund*, Oslo, Norges handels- og kontorfunksjonærers forbund.

Sæther, E. O. (1981) *Høyre og enhetsskolen 1954–1974*, Oslo, Historisk Institutt, Universitetet i Oslo.

Sass, K. (2015) 'Understanding comprehensive school reforms: Insights from comparative-historical sociology and power resources theory.' *European Educational Research Journal*, vol. 14, no. 3–4, pp. 240–256.

Seip, Å. A. (1990) *Lektorene. Profesjon, organisasjon og politikk 1890–1980*, Oslo, Fafo.

Sejersted, F. (2011) *The Age of Social Democracy: Norway, Sweden in the Twentieth Century*, Princeton and Oxford, Oxford University Press.

St. meld. nr. 45 (1980–81) 'Utdanning og arbeid.'

St. meld. nr. 97 (1964–65) 'Om landsplan for den videre utbygging av yrkesskolene for håndverk, industri, handel og kontorarbeid m. m. for perioden 1965–1970/71.'

Telhaug, A. O and Mediås, O. A. (2003) *Grunnskolen som nasjonsbygger: fra statspietisme til nyliberalisme*, Oslo, Abstrakt forlag.

Thelen, K. (2004) *How Institutions Evolve: The Political Economy of Skills in Comparative-Historical Perspective*, New York, Cambridge University Press.

Thelen, K. (2014) *Varieties of Liberalization and the New Politics of Social Solidarity*, Cambridge, Cambridge University Press.

Vabø, A. and Hovdhaugen, E. (2014) 'Norway', in Ahola, S., Hedmo, T., Thomsen, J.-P. and Vabø, A. (eds.) *Organizational Features of Higher Education: Denmark, Finland, Norway and Sweden*, Oslo, NIFU Working Paper 2014–14, pp. 61–105.

Vassnes, F. (1978) *Et glimt inn i yrkesskolen*, Oslo, Pedagogisk seminar for yrkeslærere, Statens yrkespedagogiske høgskole.

9 The modernisation of the apprenticeship system in Denmark 1945–2015

Christian Helms Jørgensen

The aim of this chapter is to explore the development of the Danish VET system from 1945 until 2015. The Danish VET system is based on the apprenticeship model, and it is organised separately from general education (the gymnasiums). The system is closely linked to the employment system, but has weak links to general and higher education (Jørgensen, 2017). Since the 1970s, reforms in the other Nordic countries have taken steps to establish a unified upper secondary school in accordance with the idea of the Nordic model of education. In contrast to this, Denmark has maintained a strong form of tracking between general and vocational at this level of education. The chapter explores why the Danish VET system developed along a special trajectory, and what this implies for the current situation for VET. It takes a problem-based approach that examines how the main stakeholders defined the challenges for VET, and how their responses to these challenges have changed the institutional architecture of the VET system. Challenges are defined as internal or external conditions that question the existing organisation and functioning of the VET system. The shifting challenges for VET are marked by major crises and changes in policies that delineate three periods in the development of VET, from 1945 until today. In the first period from 1945 until 1970, the main challenges were to expand the capacity of the VET system in order to absorb the large youth cohorts and to adapt VET to new requirements of industry. The next period started with a reform to manage a major crisis for apprenticeships in the early 1970s, when enrolment dropped and the dropout rate increased. The main challenges now were to raise the esteem of VET and reduce social inequality in education by integrating vocational and general education. The third period started in the early 1990s, when reforms defined social inclusion of disadvantaged youth and early school leavers to be the key challenge for VET. These reforms also entailed the decentralisation of the VET system marked by neo-liberal inspiration. The period ended in 2014 when a reform defined the reversion of the declining esteem and declining enrolments as the main challenges for VET.

Before 1945, a solid institutional architecture around apprenticeships had been established through a strong alliance between the craft unions and the employers, backed by financial and legal support from the state. The Apprenticeship Act of 1937 had consolidated a system of occupational self-governance at the local and national level. The act was passed by a government led by the Social Democratic Party, which dominated governments from 1932 until 1968. The act gave the labour market organisations the legal authority to supervise the quality and to define the content of the apprentices' training. In agreement with the craft unions that dominated the trade union confederation (LO), the Social Democratic Party accepted the apprenticeship system, despite earlier demands for a state-led upper secondary school.

After the Second World War, the Danish production regime was dominated by small, craft-based companies (Pettersson, 2006). Occupational labour markets and craft workers had a dominant position in the employment structure. In 1935, half of the employees in craft and industry were skilled workers, one-third were unskilled workers and 18% were semi-skilled (Christensen, 1985, p. 40). A journeyman's certificate was required for membership in the craft unions that had a high union density. The employers agreed to hire only union members for any kind of tasks classified as skilled work, and accepted the union membership book as proof of a completed apprenticeship (Galenson, 1955). A boundary committee in the LO decided on disputes between skilled and unskilled unions over the demarcations of work. For most young people, the apprenticeship system was the only opportunity for post-compulsory education. Only around 5% of every youth group, mainly from the social elite, enrolled in the gymnasiums in the early post-war period. In contrast to the other Nordic countries, initiatives in the interwar years to establish municipal, school-based vocational training parallel to apprenticeships had no success in Denmark.

The large youth cohorts and industrialisation 1945–1970

After the war, vocational education acquired a central position in the state's attempt to manage the post-war challenges. Levels of production recovered only slowly, and the apprenticeship system had a limited capacity. With the expected large youth cohorts leaving compulsory school, the threat of youth unemployment became a central challenge for policy makers. During the war, the established political elite and the authorities suffered a loss of authority in the eyes of the younger generation. The government addressed this challenge by setting up a Youth Commission, which found that less than 20% of a youth group completed education beyond the 7-year elementary school (Ungdomskommissionen, 1952a). To increase the supply of apprenticeships, the commission highlighted the opportunities for dividing up skilled areas of work to make room for more semi-skilled workers, performing specialised tasks with shorter training than traditional apprenticeships. The proposal was not only meant as a way to provide more training placement. It was also driven by industrial employers' demand for more specialised labour and less stringent occupational demarcations (Bøndergaard, 2014). The skilled workers unions strongly opposed this proposal, because they feared an erosion of the quality and esteem of the occupations, and a reduction in wage levels. Employers in many craft occupations supported the skilled workers' attempts to maintain the broad skill profiles of apprenticeships (Christensen, 1985). The position on this issue differed between the tradition-bound crafts and the industrial occupations within the iron and metal industry. The reform proposal divided both the employees' and the employers' organisations internally. To tackle youth unemployment, the commission also proposed the establishment of full-time, school-based vocational programmes for young people who could not get access to an apprenticeship and who had not qualified for the gymnasium (Ungdomskommissionen, 1952b).

A Labour Market Commission was set up in 1949 and it followed up by proposing an increase of the intake of apprentices by 40%, which was accepted by two thirds of the trade committees. The commission also proposed to ease the requirements for authorising companies to train apprentices, and recommended the introduction of vocational pre-schools. The contested nature of these proposals meant that in 1952, they were handed over to a new Apprenticeship Commission. The Commission discussed the idea of a full-time school-based vocational programme parallel to apprenticeships, but this was clearly rejected by the labour market organisations (Bøndergaard, 2014). They argued that an introduction of a full-time, school-based vocational education would be a costly and inadequate solution (Betænkning 145, 1956). In this respect, the development of the vocational schools in Denmark differed from the other Nordic countries, where full-time, school-based vocational training was introduced before the war and then expanded after the war, which contributed to the reduction of apprenticeships in the post-war period.

Introducing full-time day schools and labour market training

The challenge for the VET system of expanding the capacity was resolved by a major reform in 1956. In accordance with the recommendations of the Apprenticeship Commission, most occupational programmes were divided and specialised. The number of approved training occupations increased from 91 occupations in 1954 to 166 in 1966. While the iron and metal industry increased the number of occupational programmes from 12 to 32 in order to meet the industry's need for qualified labour, the construction industry resisted specialisation (Ellersgaard et al., 1981). The reform eased some of the quality requirements in order to increase the supply of training placements. It also abolished the restrictions on the number of apprentices that a master could take on in relation to the number of journeymen employed. Generally, though, the apprenticeship programmes retained their qualities of broad occupational training, supplemented with expanded theoretical school-based teaching. The most significant change introduced by the reform in 1956 was the introduction of the mandatory periods of full-time day school attendance in all occupations, most often by adding six weeks of full-time, school-based compulsory training for every year of the apprenticeships ('block release'). The introduction of the day school required more specialised training and a strong centralisation of the vocational schools. By the end of the 1960s, the number of schools was reduced from 350 to 52 schools (Rasmussen, 1987). While the role of the vocational schools in the VET system was strengthened, they retained their strong vocational profiles, and general subjects had low priority. School-based training was mainly intended to supplement the work-based learning in a company. This modernisation contributed to a significant increase in the number of apprentices (Figure 9.1), in contrast to the trend in the other Nordic countries, where apprenticeships declined. The reform of 1956 made school-based training mandatory in all apprenticeships, and the schools were taken over by the state. This could have been a step towards the integration of all upper secondary education in Denmark, similar to what happened in the other Nordic countries. However, in Denmark, path dependencies emanating from the prewar period were manifest, and the state took no measures to improve the connections of VET with general and higher education. The reason was primarily that a strong coalition of employers and craft unions wanted to maintain the close connections of apprenticeships to the employment system (Bøndergaard, 2014; Christensen, 1985). The continuing separation of vocational and general education was one of the reasons for the crisis for apprenticeships in the late 1960s (Betænkning 453, 1967).

Another challenge for the VET system was to meet the growing requirements for specialised technical skills for the growing industrial mass production (Sørensen et al., 1984). While the shift from craft-based to industrial forms of production in other countries was decisive for the decline of apprenticeships, this was generally not the case in Denmark. One reason was that the pressure on apprenticeships was alleviated by the establishment of a new labour market training system (*ArbejdsMarkedsUddannelser*, AMU) in 1960, aimed at the unskilled workers. The AMU system was organised separately from the apprenticeship system with regard to governance, stakeholders and target groups. This initiative created a two-tier training system that sustained the demarcations between skilled and unskilled jobs, and between skilled, unskilled and semi-skilled workers in the trade union federation. During the 1950s and 1960s, the unemployment rate was 5 to 10 times higher for unskilled workers than for skilled workers, and some former skilled areas of work (food industry, shipyards) were taken over by semi-skilled workers (Christensen, 1985). But generally, the share of skilled workers in the industrial workforce only decreased slightly in this period. From the 1970s on, this trend was reversed, as the unskilled jobs were heavily hit by automation and outsourcing. In the 1980s, the unskilled and semi-skilled workers unions developed a strategy to upgrade all unskilled jobs and to offer vocational skills to all their members. As a consequence of this policy, a range of new vocational programmes were established to cover former unskilled fields of work, and the AMU and VET system were merged in 2001. Partly as a response to this challenge, the main skilled workers union (Dansk Metal) launched a strategy to enhance and extend some of the apprenticeship programmes and take over some of the more complex tasks from the technicians and middle managers (Rasmussen, 1987). Therefore, some apprenticeships take 5½ years and equal the short-cycle, higher education programmes.

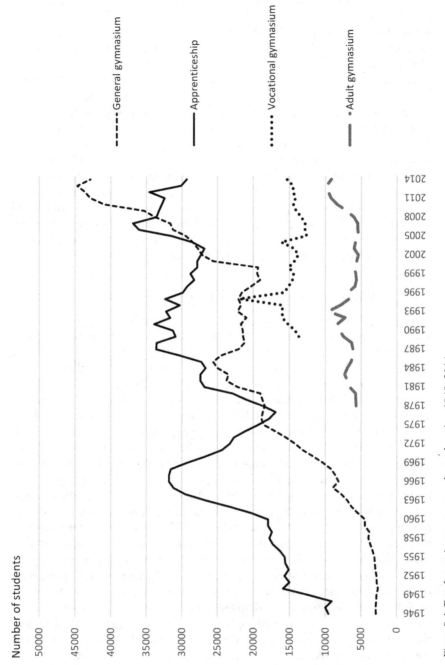

Figure 9.1 Enrolment in upper secondary education 1948–2014

In addition, on the initiative of the labour market organisations, an extensive system of state-funded further training (CVET) was developed to support the skilled workers' work-based careers. For skilled workers, CVET and post-secondary training is an attractive alternative to vocational higher education, and explains some of the low rates of progression from apprenticeships to higher education in Denmark.

To sum up this first period after the war, the main challenges to the existing VET system came from the proposals to establish school-based VET programmes and from the narrow specialisation associated with industrial mass production. The concerted response of the main stakeholders was to modernise the apprenticeship system by extending full-time, school-based training as part of apprenticeships, and to increase specialisation in some areas. This response preserved the apprenticeship model and succeeded in increasing the enrolment levels significantly. However, the response also preserved some of the weaknesses of the apprenticeship model. The continued significance of work-based learning in the VET programmes made it difficult to offer students eligibility for higher education. This emerged as a major challenge when the expansion of higher education gained momentum from the early 1960s.

From crisis to revival of apprenticeships 1970–1991

During the 1950s and until the mid-1960s, the number of apprentices rose steadily, partly as a response to the growing demand from the large cohorts entering the labour market and partly due to the high levels of economic growth. More than half of the boys and more than one third of the girls aged 18 years in 1966 were apprentices (Betænkning 504, 1968, p. 29). However, this changed in the following years. In only 10 years, from 1965 to 1975, the rate of enrolment in apprenticeships was halved (Albæk, 2004). In addition, the dropout rate rose to 25% of those who started an apprenticeship (Betænkning 612, 1971). At the same time, the number of students entering the academic track (the gymnasiums) increased strongly (Figure 9.1). Young people voted with their feet: They turned their back on apprenticeships, and increasingly opted for the gymnasiums and higher education. Alternatively, they went directly into the labour market, where they could easily find well-paid employment due to the rapid growth of industry. The resulting crisis for apprenticeships was part of a general crisis for the post-war political settlement that was manifested in the erosion of traditional authority, student revolts and waves of strikes and a general swing to the left in politics (Jørgensen, 2002). One of the key demands of the social movements was to reduce social inequalities and to widen access to all levels of education. These demands contrasted with the division of upper secondary education into two strongly separated tracks, which implied a selection of young people according to their social origin. The Social Democratic Party saw the expansion of the education system as a way to promote social equality and justice. The party required that general subjects and schooling for democratic participation should be given higher priority in the vocational programmes. In addition, it required that the VET programmes should qualify participants for access to higher education, so that the programmes did not become dead ends in the education system (Socialdemokratiet, 1973).

Apprenticeships were criticised for offering too little qualified training and too much exploitation of the apprentices' cheap labour under paternalist conditions (Sørensen et al., 1984). This critique was raised in 1966–1967 by the national apprentices' association, which organised in opposition to the union leadership for the abolition of apprenticeships. Hesitatingly, the unions supported some of this critique, while at the same time trying to suppress the opposition of the apprentices (Nielsen, 2013). Moreover, the large employers criticised apprenticeships for being too specialised and too narrowly based on specific occupational skills. This structure was seen as limiting the flexibility and mobility of the skilled work-force at a time of rapid changes in the labour market. The technological shifts in the export-driven industrial production required other competencies than the traditional crafts.

A commission was set up to prepare a reform of apprenticeships. It criticised the VET system for its early vocational specialisation, which took place when young people were unable to make a qualified choice. The work-based training was criticised for giving priority to the companies' financial interests rather the education of the apprentices. Moreover, it was seen as a problem that many companies had become so specialised that they were unable to offer the apprentice the required broad qualification profile of the occupation (Betænkning 1112, 1987). The sharp drop in the number of new apprentices, the rise in the dropout rate and the increasing popularity of the gymnasiums resulted in a series of reform proposals in the early 1970s.

From radical to moderate reform

The first reform proposal had the radical aim of integrating all programmes of upper secondary education, the gymnasium and apprenticeships. The proposal was similar to the reforms in Norway, Finland and Sweden, where Social Democratic governments introduced reforms to establish unified upper secondary schooling in the early 1970s (Wiborg, 2009). In Denmark, a political agreement was reached in 1958 to introduce comprehensive schooling at the lower secondary level. In 1975, the unified compulsory school was extended from 7 to 9 years. A key argument for this reform was to reduce the 'social class division' in education. The aim of the first proposal was to form a unified upper secondary school, which would make it easier to switch between the tracks and continue from upper secondary VET to the tertiary level of education. The proposal was thus directly addressing the challenge of linking VET closer to higher education in order to reduce social inequality in higher education and, at the same time, to raise the esteem of VET.

The vision of a unified upper secondary school met strong opposition from the right wing in Parliament and from the influential labour market organisations, and it was replaced by a more moderate reform, which maintained two separate tracks. Various reasons can explain why the crisis for the VET system in Denmark in the early 1970s ended with a different outcome than in the other Nordic countries, which were faced with many of the same challenges. The parliamentary position of the Social Democratic Party in Denmark was weaker than in the neighbouring Nordic countries. In contrast to Sweden, Denmark was dominated by a craft-based form of small-scale production that relied heavily on skilled labour (Pettersson, 2006; Kristensen, 1996). The trade union movement and the Social Democratic Party were strongly influenced by the skilled workers unions, who opposed the merging of VET into a unified school (Christensen, 1985). Moreover, in contrast to the other Nordic countries, no school-based VET system had been established parallel to the apprenticeship system in the post-war period. Therefore, there were no obvious alternatives to a reformed apprenticeship system in Denmark.

The outcome of this critical juncture for VET was not determined by these specific circumstances alone, but also by a shift in the parliamentary situation and the timing of the policy process (Dobbins and Busemeyer, 2014; Haue, 2009). The Social Democratic Party suffered a significant defeat in the election in the early 1970s, which saw the arrival of a number of new centre-right parties that opposed the social democratic vision of state planning and non-selective education (Wiborg, 2009). They wanted to preserve apprenticeships under the control of the labour market organisations, a position that was backed by the main craft unions. In the mid-1970s, a liberalist critique of 'egalitarian' policies in education, and an anti-academic critique of the expansion of higher education (Haue, 2009), was combined with requirements for cuts in public spending.

In 1976, a moderate reform introduced a new VET system, Initial Vocational Education, ('*Erhvervsfaglig Grunduddannelse, EFG*'), which was meant to replace apprenticeships. All the EFG students started with a broad, 1-year, school-based 'basic course' that included 40% general subjects, which was intended to improve their opportunities for later progression to the tertiary level of education. During the basic course, the students were introduced to a broad vocational field, before choosing a specific occupation. After completing the basic course in EFG, the students had to obtain a 2–3 year training contract with a company, similar to apprenticeships. Extended periods of work-based training in a company alternated with shorter periods of block release for school-based training. The reform process revealed significant disagreements on both sides in the labour market organisations. A coalition of the craft associations, backed by conservative and liberal parties, opposed the agreement of the large industrial organisations to abolish traditional apprenticeships. Apprenticeships were preserved as a parallel programme to the EFG programme until 1991 (Haue, 2009). The VET system retained its close connection to the labour market, and young people who succeeded in obtaining a training placement had easy access to employment. The EFG reform was implemented during a period of economic crisis and high youth unemployment, due to the large youth cohorts leaving compulsory school and a shortage of training placements (Sørensen et al., 1984). Young people could start a school-based EFG basic course without a training contract. However, after completing the 1-year basic course, more than half of the students dropped out due to a shortage of training placements. This seriously reduced the esteem of the EFG programme and made the parallel apprenticeship programme appear more attractive. However, apprenticeships were only an option for a limited number of young people due to the lack of training placements during the 1980s. Therefore, the challenge of high youth unemployment and the growing number of young people not in education, training or employment came high on the political agenda for the next reform of VET in 1991.

VET – a 'dead end' or a pathway to higher education?

The reforms of VET had failed to broaden the progression routes from VET to higher education. Neither apprenticeships nor the EFG offered direct access to higher education, except for a limited number of shorter, post-secondary programmes. Enrolment in higher education tripled in the 20 years after 1960 (Börjesson et al., 2014). The number of students choosing the gymnasiums followed a similar pattern, and in the mid-1970s it exceeded the enrolment in VET (Figure 9.1). The shift from elite to mass higher education made the VET system appear as a 'dead end', due to its weak links to higher education. A central aim of the reform of VET in 1976 was to improve the permeability from VET to higher education, in order to reduce social inequality in participation in education. The reform did not succeed in offering students in VET general eligibility for higher education.

Higher education in Denmark had developed a binary structure, with a division between universities offering master and doctoral degrees, and university colleges offering bachelor degrees. Earlier, a journeyman's certificate gave access to a variety of post-secondary educations (1–2 years duration) and some 3-year higher vocational programmes. However, during the last decades, the gap between upper secondary VET and vocational education at the tertiary level has been widening. One cause of the widening gap is the academisation of vocational higher education. An example of this is the Teknikum engineer, an applied engineering education that was organised by the technical schools from 1905 and which required a journeyman's certificate for admission. This changed during the 1960s, however, when admission required formal eligibility for higher education. The Teknika were separated from the vocational schools, merged with the 'Academic Engineering' programme and included in the universities (Jørgensen, 2017). This 'academic drift' of the Teknika gradually shifted the recruitment from journeymen to students from the gymnasiums and reduced the opportunities for upwards social mobility among skilled workers (Christensen and Erno-Kjolhede, 2011). This is an example of the growing gap between the VET system and the emerging system of higher education that integrated the post-secondary professional educations from the 1960s (Kyvik, 2009).

With the defeat of the unification strategy for upper secondary education, the political strategy of the main stakeholders in the following decades was to *build bridges* from VET to higher education (Lasonen and Manning, 2000). One of these bridges was the vocational gymnasiums. The technical and business gymnasiums were reformed in the early 1980s with the aim of connecting the vocational track and the general track of upper secondary education. In the 1980s, students could start in a vocational programme (EFG basic course) and then decide after six months whether they would opt for higher education, or whether they would continue in a training placement and get a journeyman's certificate (Rasmussen, 1987). The intention was to create more bridges between the tracks and reduce the number of dead-ends. However, the vocational gymnasiums gradually cut the links to the VET system and became more closely connected to the classic gymnasium. Through a reform in 2005, they were granted equal status with the classical gymnasium.

The vocational gymnasiums succeeded in recruiting from wider social groups that are unfamiliar with academic education. Since the 1980s, the programmes have become a remarkable success and they recruit more than 15% of a youth cohort today. However, the vocational gymnasiums did not become a bridge between the VET system and higher education. The vocational gymnasiums are not part of the VET system, but are full-time, school-based programmes that do not offer a journeyman's certificate. The effect of the introduction of the vocational gymnasiums was, in some respects, the opposite of the political intentions behind these new programmes (Sørensen, 1987). Some of the most academically oriented students were diverted away from the ordinary VET programmes and into the vocational gymnasiums. Consequently, they did not contribute to increasing the number of ordinary apprentices who progress to the tertiary level of education, but have more likely reduced it instead (Jørgensen, 2013).

In the mid-1980s, the Government established a commission to examine the higher technician and engineering programmes. The commission found that the introduction of the EFG programme had not fulfilled the goal of increasing the progression from VET to higher education (Betænkning 1074, 1986). It pointed out that the opportunities for higher education were relatively unknown and invisible for VET-students, and that economic barriers prevented skilled workers from taking up higher education. The commission recommended that the vocational students should have better opportunities to achieve eligibility for higher education in the VET programmes, and should be encouraged to use them. This was a basis for the subsequent reform of the VET system in 1991, which was repeated with the reform in 2000. However, even though the students formally have the right to choose additional qualifications in VET programmes, this opportunity has rarely been used. The main reason is the strong vocational orientation of the students. They are mostly aiming at a position as a skilled worker, and few students are acquainted with higher education from their social background (Frederiksen et al., 2012). Though the promise of access to higher education in the reform of 1976 had not been fulfilled, this was no longer considered the main challenge during the 1980s, when youth unemployment rates continued to remain at a high level.

Social inclusion and education for all 1991–2014

With the high dropout rates from VET and the high rates of youth unemployment, the situation for the VET system had become critical in the late 1980s. In addition, a liberal-conservative government had taken office in 1982 and proclaimed a break with the social democratic policy in education. A commission was appointed in 1986 to prepare the new reform of the VET system. It emphasised some crucial weaknesses in the existing VET system: high dropout rates, lack of training placement, programmes that were too narrowly specialised, the weak connection between general and vocational subjects, the weak links between VET and higher education and the rivalry between the EFG and the apprenticeship programmes (Betænkning 1112, 1987). The reform in 1991 merged the EFG and apprenticeships and combined elements from both. The new standard pathway was to start with 6 or 12 months in school-based training to qualify the students' choice of a specific occupation and prepare them for apprenticeship training in a company. The remaining part was similar to the apprenticeship programme, but interrupted by shorter periods of school-based training (typically 10 weeks per year). However, the lack of training placements was still acute, and no solution was provided for the demand for direct access from VET to higher education. The enrolment levels in the gymnasiums continued to increase (Figure 9.1), and this situation exposed a critical weakness of the Danish VET system.

Historically, the dual system of VET in Denmark has been efficient at integrating young people from the working class and from disadvantaged social backgrounds into the labour market and into society. This has contributed to low youth unemployment and a low level of social inequality in Denmark (Busemeyer, 2015). VET has provided an attractive pathway for young people who do not opt for higher education. Today still, the VET programmes offer work-based learning, a vocational identity and an alternative learning environment compared to school-based training. However, while the apprenticeship model promotes easy access to employment for those who complete the programme, it is quite selective. In periods of economic recession, the scarcity of apprenticeships blocks access to vocational education for many young people, especially for gender and ethnic minorities. The Danish VET system is highly gendered, as half of all the 109 programmes are dominated (> 80%) by either men or women (Jørgensen, 2015). Gender and ethnic minorities have special difficulties gaining access to a training placement. A considerable proportion of training placements are allocated through informal social networks. Boys from ethnic minorities have significantly higher dropout rates than ethnic Danish boys, and they are over-represented in the group of young people who do not complete any post-compulsory education (Jensen and Larsen, 2011).

From the late 1980s, the governments have been increasingly alarmed over the growing proportion of young people not in education, employment or training (the NEET group), and have set goals for universalisation of upper secondary education for youth. The new Social Democratic-led government in 1993 formulated the target that 95% of a youth cohort should complete an upper secondary education. Another response was to introduce the active labour market policy from 1993, with a specific focus on youth (Jørgensen and Schulze, 2011). This policy has contributed to making almost all young people continue in upper secondary education, but has also increased the number of students dropping out of VET. As a result of the activation policy, an increasing proportion of the students in VET have low grades from basic school, and they often struggle with other disadvantages (family, drug and housing problems etc.). This shift in the recruitment pattern has contributed to the rising dropout rate in VET since the mid-1990s. It is also one of the reasons why the proportion of graduates from VET who continue to higher education, has declined.

Since the turn of the century, only half of the students who take up a VET programme complete the programme. The lowest retention rates are found in the initial school-based basic course of 6 to 12 months duration, which precedes the 3-year main course in a work-based training placement. Over the decades, the conceptualisations of the dropout problem and the solutions to reduce dropout rates have changed many times (Jørgensen, 2016). A reform of VET in 2007 gave high priority to social inclusion and retention in VET, but this has had serious unintended consequences.

The high share of disadvantaged students in VET and the high dropout rates have reduced the social esteem of the VET system. The enrolment of young people coming directly from compulsory school has dropped, which is an indication of the declining esteem of VET. Young people rate the VET programmes as the lowest rung of the status hierarchy of upper secondary programmes, especially the male-dominated technical programmes. Four times as many students in the gymnasiums have parents who have graduated from higher education compared to students in the vocational schools (Holm et al, 2013; Jensen and Larsen, 2011).

While the number of young people in VET has declined, the number of adults has increased. The average age at completion of a VET programme is now 28 years. This is partly a result of young people's increasingly non-linear transitions from school to work. It is also the result of government initiatives to upgrade and retrain adults in the VET system. New VET programmes and an adult apprenticeship scheme have been established to provide VET-certification in sectors with many unskilled and semi-skilled workers (service, transportation). In addition, sectors with many adults, like Health and Agriculture, have been integrated into the overall VET system, and the systems for initial VET and continuing VET have been merged. The VET system, based on the apprenticeship model, has thus been extended to cover almost all sectors and age groups. The decline in the number of young people in VET has been offset by a growing number of adults, so that the total enrolment in the VET system has remained unchanged since the 1980s – though with fluctuations (Figure 9.1).

The declining enrolment rate for young people in VET and a future shortage of skilled workers was seen as a major challenge by the government and the labour market organisations. Consequently, a new reform in 2014 gave priority to reducing the number of disadvantaged students in VET by introducing admission requirements based on the students' grades in basic school. The reform aimed to raise the esteem of VET and redirect students from the gymnasiums to VET. Moreover, the reform introduced new talent streams and high-level courses with the aim of attracting more high-performing students and raising the esteem of VET. This initiative, as well as the earlier reforms, demonstrates the trade-off between social inclusion in VET and high esteem of VET.

Training placements – the weak link

A critical weakness of the apprenticeship system is the shortage of training placements, especially during recessions. The availability of apprenticeships depends on the booms and slumps in the market, while the demand depends on the size of the youth cohorts and young people's choices of vocational programmes. The result has been recurrent mismatches between supply and demand for training placements, especially in times of economic stagnation. Various measures have been taken to overcome this weakness, either through financial stimulation of the supply of training placements, or by giving the vocational schools a greater responsibility for the training of apprentices.

In 1993, a provisional, full-time, school-based training programme (in Danish: 'skolepraktik' or 'SKP') was established for students who were unable to obtain a regular training placement. This school-based training was only intended as a temporary, compensatory measure in times of shortage of training placements (Juul and Jørgensen, 2011). Over the years, the volume of students on the SKP programme has been adjusted upwards and downwards depending on the situation within the training market. After the financial crisis in 2008, the SKP programme has expanded considerably, and the students on this full-time programme accounted for 15% of all VET students in 2016. Thus, the programme constituted a significant alternative pathway to the work-based programmes, and could be seen as a competitor to the dual system. However, most of the students who start in the SKP programme acquire an ordinary apprenticeship placement before completing the programme. Students completing this SKP programme acquire a journeyman's certificate similar to an ordinary apprentice. In 2013, the SKP was changed into a new and permanent institution, the 'training centre' ('praktikcentre'), which offers work-based training and takes responsibility for coordinating the students' shorter placements in multiple companies. The position of the 50 Danish training centres in the institutional architecture resembles that of the Norwegian training offices. A significant difference is that the Danish training centres are managed by the state under the auspices of the vocational schools, while the Norwegian training agencies are controlled by the employers.

As a measure to address the shortage of training placements for the large cohorts of young people leaving compulsory school, a training levy for collective funding of training was established in 1977 (the Employers' Reimbursement Scheme, AUB). As early as the 1950s, some occupations had established local schemes to distribute the cost of training apprentices between all companies by establishing funds to which the entire industry contributed. With the AUB, this collective funding scheme was extended in the form of a general training levy on all companies to share the cost of the apprentices' training.

Access to the labour market

The Danish VET system and the apprenticeship model is generally associated with low levels of youth unemployment and a rapid and direct transition to the labour market (Wolbers, 2007). A number of qualities of the apprenticeship system can explain the smooth transition to employment. One explanation for the high rates of employment for newly graduated apprentices is the institutional complementarity between vocational programmes and occupational labour markets. Both are organised according to the occupational principle (Deissinger, 1998). The trade committee for each VET programme defines a curriculum that corresponds to occupations that are standardised at a national level. The regulatory mandate of the committees is quite wide-ranging and is defined in the legal framework for vocational education. It includes the specification of the curriculum for the individual programmes, the continuous upgrading of the qualifications profiles, the approval of training companies and the supervision of the quality of training placements, conflict resolution, examination etc. This close involvement of the labour market partners in Denmark is a guarantee for the relevance of the programmes for the labour market (Clematide and Wittig, 2009). In addition, the occupational profiles imply a high degree of transparency for young people in the transition from education to employment. A significant share of the young people, who start a vocational programme, do so because they are attracted by an occupation, a specific kind of work, more than they are attracted by the vocational school. The occupation has the role of a 'sign post' guiding young people's transition to the labour market (Heinz, 2002).

Another explanation for the smooth transition is that it takes place as an integral part of the work-based training in apprenticeships (Heinz, 2002). An apprentice who completes a programme already has several years of real work experience. More than half of the apprentices continue as ordinary employees in the training company after acquiring their journeyman's certificate. In addition, the workplace training provides specific occupational skills that are applicable not just in the training company, but also across companies in an occupational labour market. The skills provided in the Danish VET system are highly standardised, and this contributes a high level of mobility and flexibility in the occupational labour markets. The average job tenure in Denmark is among the lowest in Europe and job mobility is the highest (Jørgensen and Schulze, 2011). This can be explained by the Danish flexicurity model and the welfare model that provides universal social security. Due to liberalisations and a shift away from a welfare system towards a new workfare regime, this security has been reduced significantly during the last three decades (Antikainen, 2010).

The liberal-conservative governments during the 10 years from 1982 questioned the strong involvement of the labour market organisations and the national standardisation in the VET system. A large number of reforms were passed to decentralise and deregulate the labour market institutions and the VET system. The VET-reform in 1991 was designed with neo-liberal inspiration and signalled that the corporatist system of governance would be replaced by decentralised and market-based forms of regulation. This posed a new challenge to the occupational self-governance and the common national standards in VET (Juul and Jørgensen, 2011). The VET-reform, though, did not change the key role of the trade committees and the occupational self-governance in the VET system. Even though the reform extended the opportunities for local adaptation of the programmes, this option has only been sparingly utilised. The aim of the reform was mainly to introduce performance-based funding and not to change the content of the programmes (Juul and Jørgensen, 2011; Cort, 2010). The survival of the corporatist form of collective skill formation in times of neo-liberal deregulation can be explained by the benefits of this system for all stakeholders. The Danish version of 'flexicurity' offers companies flexibility regarding the provision of skills, a key asset for smaller companies under conditions of globalisation and unstable markets (Emmenegger, 2010). The companies have access to a pool of skilled workers with standardised and certified skills, and the skilled workers acquire widely recognised specific vocational qualifications (Marsden, 1999; Deissinger, 1998). This system would be endangered by a thorough deregulation and decentralisation of the VET system. Moreover, the benefit of the corporatist institutions is that they promote a high degree of trust and consensus on other issues like flexible employment and the constant reorganisation of production (Thelen, 2014; Streeck, 1992). This can explain the continuation of the strong alliance of skilled workers' unions and the employers' associations in the field of VET. Accordingly, three decades of neo-liberal reforms have had a limited effect on collective skill formation in the Danish context (Thelen, 2014).

Higher esteem and hybrid qualifications

Despite numerous political initiatives to increase the retention of students in VET, the drop-out rate has remained at a high level. In addition, direct enrolment in VET from compulsory school has continued to decline, and forecasts predict a serious shortage of skilled workers. To address these challenges, a new government committee in 2013 focussed on initiatives to increase enrolment rates by raising the esteem of VET. One measure to achieve this was a new hybrid programme, EUX, which offers a journeyman's certificate in combination with general eligibility for higher education. As the two types of qualifications are provided in an integrated form in a single programme of around 4-year's duration, it represents a real innovation (Jørgensen, 2013). The programme has been well received, but due to the highly compressed curriculum of the programme, it is only an option for the most high-performing students.

Another initiative was a reform of short-cycle, higher vocational educations, which in 2009 were merged into a new independent institution, the Vocational Academies (EA). The aim of these institutions is to make the opportunities for higher education more visible and accessible for students in apprenticeships. However, a report from 2012 found that only 13% of the entrants to the Vocational Academies had a background in the apprenticeship system (Rambøll, 2013). Another study has examined the rate of progression to higher education of four cohorts of VET-students from 1991 until 2006 (Frederiksen et al., 2012). It found that in most occupations, the progression rate had dropped significantly over the last two decades, especially in the traditional crafts. Two reasons can be identified for the lack of success for a variety of political initiatives over three decades intended to increase the permeability from VET to higher education. One is the favourable situation in the labour market and the smooth transition to employment for newly educated journeymen. Another reason is the active labour market policy and the emphasis on social inclusion in VET, which since the mid-1990s has increased the share of low performing students in VET.

Managing the trade-offs in VET

The development of the Danish VET system since 1945 can be explained by the shifting challenges for VET and the responses of the key stakeholders to these challenges. The two key challenges in the initial period after 1945 was first, to include the 'baby-boom' generations of young people, and secondly to meet the new skill requirements from the booming industrial production. In order to manage these challenges, periods of full-time, school-based training became mandatory in all apprenticeships, many programmes were specialised and shortened, and the level was reduced. However, the political coalition behind the VET system maintained the key qualities of the apprenticeship system. Moreover, from the 1970s, a de-specialisation and an upgrading of the programmes took place as a response to the threat of automation and out-sourcing of low-skilled jobs.

Before the war, the state had left the management of VET to the labour market organisations, and had secured a universal legal framework for their self-governance of VET. From the late 1960s, however, the state adopted a more active role in VET, first with reforms to improve the linkages of VET with general and higher education, and secondly with reforms to improve social inclusion of disadvantaged youth in VET. The simple task for VET of delivering vocational skills for the labour market was supplemented by a range of other political aims, especially education for citizenship, preparation for higher education and social inclusion. Moreover, VET had to compete with the gymnasiums, which became the preferred choice for young people. In the 1970s, proposals to extend comprehensive schooling to the upper secondary level were rejected in Denmark, in contrast to what happened in the other Nordic countries in the same period. One explanation for the strong path dependency in the development of the Danish apprenticeship system is the durable cross-class alliance of employers and craft unions that dominated the LO. Moreover, the Social Democratic Party abandoned the demand for a unified state-led system of upper secondary education and accepted apprenticeships as a separate track. However, this political settlement did not address the challenge of improving the links between VET and higher education. As higher education turned into mass education (Kyvik, 2009), it became clear that the strength of the Danish VET system also constitutes a serious weakness (Jørgensen, 2013). The Danish VET system performs well in providing direct access to employment for one third of a youth cohort, including a large group of disadvantaged youth. However, as 60% of the 2015 youth cohort is expected to complete a higher education programme, the VET system increasingly appears to be a dead-end in the education system. The dual system of VET supports the transition of the students to the labour market, but at the same time diverts them from progression to the tertiary level of education (Shavit and Müller, 2000). Despite persistent political reforms intended to improve the permeability from VET to higher education, the rate of progression from VET to higher education has been decreasing over the last two decades. After the unification strategy for upper secondary education failed in the 1970s, the main stakeholders have pursued a strategy for enhancement of VET (Lasonen and Manning, 2000). This strategy seeks to improve VET as a separate track and emphasizes the distinct qualities of vocational education. However, this strategy tends to strengthen the academic-vocational divide, which leaves VET in an inferior position in the so-called knowledge society.

From the early 1990s, the political priorities shifted away from providing access to higher education. Instead, governments have increasingly seen the VET system as a solution to the challenge of a shrinking youth labour market and growing youth unemployment. The apprenticeship system has historically offered an attractive pathway to skilled employment for low-attaining youth. However, two decades of policies for social inclusion in VET have demonstrated the limits of this policy. The active labour market policy and the inclusion policy have overburdened the VET system. The dropout rates have soared and the esteem of VET has dropped. The employers' supply of training placements has declined and the enrolment of young people has also dropped. As a response to this critical situation for VET, the reform in 2014 marks a sharp turn in policy by giving priority to the 'talent tracks', elite programmes and hybrid programmes that offer direct access to higher education. This and earlier shifts in policy indicate that there is a basic trade-off for the Danish VET system between providing social inclusion and social equality. Giving priority to social inclusion by offering 'practical' skills, vocational qualifications and work-based learning is difficult to reconcile with offering academic qualifications and eligibility for higher education. Policymaking in Denmark has mainly been addressing the challenges separately, without paying attention to the basic trade-offs and dilemmas for the VET system. Therefore, policies have tended to solve one problem at a time, while letting the other problems grow. The historical examination in this chapter has demonstrated some of the main trade-offs and dilemmas in the Danish VET system. The question for the future is whether the apprenticeship model can be reformed to attain the goal of the Nordic Model of Education to combine social inclusion and social equality.

References

Albæk, K. (2004) *Om lærepladsspørgsmålet*, Memo no. 212, Blå Memoserie, Copenhagen, University of Copenhagen.
Antikainen, A. (2010) 'The capitalist state and education: The case of restructuring the Nordic model', *Current Sociology*, vol. 58, no. 4, pp. 530–550.
Betænkning 1074 (1986) *Ingeniør- og teknikeruddannelsernes fremtid*, Copenhagen, Undervisningsministeriet.
Betænkning 1112 (1987) *Betænkning om grundlæggende erhvervsuddannelse*, Copenhagen, Statens Informationtjeneste.
Betænkning 145 (1956) *Lærlingekommissionen*, Copenhagen, Statens Trykningskontor.
Betænkning 453 (1967) *Undervisning og uddannelse*, Aarhus, Aarhus Stiftsbogstrykkeri.
Betænkning 504 (1968) *Betænkning vedrørende kvinders uddannelsesproblemer*, Copenhagen, S. L. Møllers Bogtrykkeri.
Betænkning 612 (1971) *Betænkning om erhvervsfaglige grunduddannelser*, Copenhagen, Statens Trykningskontor.
Bøndergaard, G. (2014) *The Historical Emergence of the Key Challenges for the Future of VET in Denmark*, Nord-VET, Roskilde University.
Börjesson, M., Ahola, S., Helland, H. and Thomsen, J. P. (2014) *Enrolment Patterns in Nordic Higher Education, ca 1945 to 2010*, Working Paper no. 15, 2014, Oslo, NIFU.
Busemeyer, M. R. (2015) *Skills and Inequality, the Political Economy of Education and Training Reforms in Western Welfare States*, Cambridge, Cambridge University Press.
Christensen, E. (1985) *Konflikter mellem faglærte og ufaglærte arbejdere*, Aalborg, Aalborg Universitetsforlag.
Christensen, S. H. and Erno-Kjolhede, E. (2011) 'Academic drift in Danish professional engineering education. Myth or reality? Opportunity or threat?', *European Journal of Engineering Education*, vol. 36, no. 3, pp. 285–299.
Clematide, B. and Wittig, W. (2009) 'Dänemark', in Bertelsmann Stiftung (ed.) *Steuerung der beruflichen Bildung im internationalen Vergleich*, Gütersloh, Bertelsmann, pp. 113–153.
Cort, P. (2010) 'Europeanisation and policy change in the Danish vocational education and training system', *Research in Comparative and International Education*, vol. 5, no. 3, pp. 331–343.
Deissinger, T. (1998) *Beruflichkeit als "organisierendes Prinzip" der deutschen Berufsausbildung*, Markt Schwaben, Eusl Verlag.
Dobbins, M. and Busemeyer, M. R. (2014) 'Socio-economic institutions, organized interests and partisan politics: The development of vocational education in Denmark and Sweden', *Socio-Economic Review*, vol. 13, no. 2, pp. 1–32.

Ellersgaard, B., Jensen, S. H. and Nielsen, O. Z. (1981) *Efg på vej – hvorhen?* Aalborg, Aalborg Universitetsforlag.
Emmenegger, P. (2010) 'The long road to flexicurity', *Scandinavian Political Studies*, vol. 33, no. 3, pp. 271–294.
Frederiksen, J., Hersom, H. and Jørgensen, C. H. (2012) *Muligheder og barrierer på erhvervsuddannede unges vej til videregående uddannelse*, Roskilde, Roskilde University and Undervisningsministeriet.
Galenson, W. (1955) *Arbejder og arbejdsgiver i Danmark*, Copenhagen, Danske Forlag.
Haue, H. (2009) 'En socialdemokratisk fiasko. Skole-og uddannelsespolitikken i 1970erne', *Arbejderhistorie*, no. 2, pp. 35–50.
Heinz, W. R. (2002) 'Transition discontinuities and the biographical shaping of early work careers', *Journal of Vocational Behavior*, vol. 60, no. 2, pp. 220–240.
Holm, A., Jæger, M. M., Karlson, K. B. and Reimer, D. (2013) 'Incomplete equalization: The effect of tracking in secondary education on educational inequality', *Social Science Research*, vol. 42, no. 6, pp. 1431–1442.
Jensen, T. P. and Larsen, B. Ø. (2011) *Unge i erhvervsuddannelserne og på arbejdsmarkedet, Værdier, interesser og holdninger*, Copenhagen, AKF.
Jørgensen, C. H. (2013) 'Linking the dual system with higher education in Denmark', in Deissinger, J., Aff, A. Fuller, and Helms Jørgensen, C. (eds.) *Hybrid Qualifications*, Bern, Peter Lang, pp. 53–78.
Jørgensen, C. H. (2015) 'Some boys' problems in education – what is the role of VET?', *Journal of Vocational Education & Training*, vol. 67, no. 1, pp. 62–77.
Jørgensen, C. H. (2016) 'Shifting problems and shifting policies to reduce students' drop-out, – the case of vocational education policy in Denmark', in Bohlinger, S., Dang, K. A. and Klatt, G. (eds.) *Education Policy*, Bern, Peter Lang, pp. 325–353.
Jørgensen, C. H. (2017) 'From apprenticeships to higher vocational education in Denmark – building bridges while the gap is widening', *Journal of Vocational Education & Training*, vol. 69, no. 1, pp. 64–80.
Jørgensen, H. (2002) *Consensus, Cooperation and Conflict: The Policy Making Process in Denmark*, Cheltenham, Edward Elgar.
Jørgensen, H. and Schulze, M. (2011) 'Leaving the Nordic path? The changing role of Danish trade unions in the welfare reform process', *Social Policy & Administration*, vol. 45, no. 2, pp. 206–219.
Juul, I. and Jørgensen, C. H. (2011) 'Challenges for the dual system and occupational self-governance in Denmark', *Journal of Vocational Education & Training*, vol. 63, no. 3, pp. 289–303.
Kristensen, P. H. (1996) 'On the constitution of economic actors in Denmark', in Whitley, R. and Kristensen, P. H. (eds.) *The Changing European Firm: Limits to Convergence*, London, Routledge, pp. 118–58.
Kyvik, S. (2009) *The Dynamics of Change in Higher Education*, Dordrecht, Springer.
Lasonen, J. and Manning, S. (2000) 'Improving the standing of vocational as against general education in Europe: A conceptual framework', in Lasonen, J. and Stenström, M. L. (eds.) *Strategies for Reforming Initial Vocational Education and Training in Europe*, Jyväskylä, University of Jyväskylä, pp. 316–325.
Marsden, D. (1999) *A Theory of Employment Systems: Micro-Foundations of Societal Diversity*, New York, Oxford University Press.
Nielsen, K. H. (2013) 'Lærlingeoprør i fagbevægelsen: LLO og Faglig Ungdom 1966–1979', *Arbejderhistorie*, vol. 22, no. 3, pp. 22–43.
Pettersson, L. (2006) *Är Danmark bättre än Sverige? Om dansk och svensk yrkesutbildning sedan industrialisering*, Malmö, Øresundsinstituttet.

Rambøll (2013) *Evaluering af erhvervsakademistrukturen*, Copenhagen, Rambøll.

Rasmussen, W. (1987) *Erhvervsuddannelsessystemet i Danmark*, Berlin, CEDEFOP, European Centre for the Development of Vocational Training.

Shavit, Y. and Müller, W. (2000) 'Vocational secondary education: Where diversion and where safety net?', *European Societies*, vol. 2, no. 1, pp. 29–50.

Socialdemokratiet (1973) *Socialdemokraterne former Fremtiden*, Working Programme adopted at the congress in September 1973.

Sørensen, J. H. (1987) *Arbejdsmarkedets parters rolle i ungdoms- og voksenerhvervsuddannelserne*, Berlin, Cedefop.

Sørensen, J. H., Rasmussen, P. H., Nielsen, O. Z., and Lassen, M. (1984) *Lærlingeuddannelse og udbytning [apprenticeships and exploitation]*, vol. 1, Aalborg, Aalborg Universitetsforlag.

Streeck, W. (1992) *Social Institutions and Economic Performance: Studies of Industrial Relations in Advanced Capitalist Economies*, London, Sage Publications.

Thelen, K. (2014) *Varieties of Liberalization and the New Politics of Social Solidarity*, New York, Cambridge University Press.

Ungdomskommissionen (1952a) *Samfundet og ungdommen: afsluttende udtalelse*, Copenhagen, Schultz.

Ungdomskommissionen (1952b) *Ungdommen og arbejdslivet*, Copenhagen, Schultz.

Wiborg, S. (2009) *Education and Social Integration: Comprehensive Schooling in Europe*, New York, Palgrave Macmillan.

Wolbers, M. H. J. (2007) 'Patterns of labour market entry: A comparative perspective on school-to-work transitions in 11 European countries', *Acta Sociologica*, vol. 50, no. 3, pp. 189–210.

10 Conclusions

Svein Michelsen

Introduction

The agenda of this book is broad and ambitious, the reconstructing of the evolution of vocational education and training in Finland, Norway, Sweden and Denmark over an extended period of time (1850–2015). It draws in an eclectic way on a number of different theoretical perspectives and questions raised by empirical observations. The concluding chapter follows an inductive logic, where the four Nordic trajectories are compared. The four stories about the development of VET each country could be narrated separately, but they are also entangled in different ways in different periods in time. The chapter summarizes the main findings, both along the cross-national and the longitudinal dimensions. It goes somewhat beyond the scope of the individual country chapter and explores continuities and coalitions in the formation of national VET systems. The analysis provides insights in the differences between the country specific trajectories but also explores similarities. The results speak to the comparative literature on vocational training/skill formation systems as well as debates on issues of institutional change.

The chapter is organized in two parts. The first part analyzes the reform paths taken by the four countries. The second part explores reform paths and the coalitions which have produced them. Strongly simplified, we have identified three periods in this long-term trajectory of Nordic VET. Processes of political and economic liberalization dominated the first period, up to 1945. Central elements in this trajectory were the demise of the guilds, and the formation of new school-like institutions of vocational or practical character. The postwar period marked a juncture where VET policies became re-embedded into a broader set of social democratic welfare policies aiming at the reduction of social inequality, the provision of more equal education for all, as well as policies for educational expansion and universalization. Towards the end of the millennium, new processes of political and economic liberalization challenged these policies and practices, where the Nordic states had to cope with reconstruction problems, deindustrialization, recessions and youth unemployment problems, to which new VET policies were devised.

192 Svein Michelsen

I have condensed available information in a series of three tables which provide information on significant reform events in the formation of VET policies in the four Nordic countries. VET policies can generically be regarded as the totality of deliberate or intentional state interventions into the field of vocational education and training. As policy areas like VET have the ability to contract and expand over time, the criteria for selection have to be associated with some measure of discretion. The focus on reform and law-making obviously has its shortcomings, especially as far as the identification of slow burning processes over time, but this kind of representation nonetheless provides a useful shorthand for the identification of reform trajectories in time as well as comparisons between the four countries.

The liberalization of VET (1850–1945)

The country chapters amply illustrates that national governments in the Nordic countries liberalized VET from the constraints of the old guild order and introduced new regulations and VET institutions (Table 10.1).

The point of departure is illustrated through the statutes and Ordinances in the regulation of the guilds in the Nordic countries. A key element in these regulations was their rigid and compulsory character, a feature that faded under

Table 10.1 Nordic VET trajectories in the liberal period (1850–1945)

Denmark	Norway	Sweden	Finland
1682: Regulations for journeymen and apprentices	1682: Regulations for journeymen and apprentices	1720: General guild order	1739: Ordinance on halls
1857: Free Trade Act	1816: Guild monopoly on trade		1868: Guilds abolished
	1839: Guild regulations softened		
	1849: First state financing for a selection of VET schools		1879: Freedom of Trade Act
1862: Guilds abolished	1870: Guilds abolished	1864: Free Trade Act, guild regulation ceased	1885: Decree on craft schools
1889: Law reinstating the apprentice contract	1894: Law for the crafts reinstating the apprentice contract		1900: New regulations on craft schools
1921: Apprentice act		1918: Law on practical vocational schools	1920: General vocational schools act
1937/38: Law on apprenticeship	1940: Law on vocational schools	1921: Law on the formation of municipal training schools	1923: Apprenticeship Act issued

the impact of economic development and new liberal ideas. During this phase, freedom of trade was instituted as well as contractual liberty. Older restrictions on the right to exercise a trade were abolished one by one. A common denominator for the demise of the guilds in the Nordic countries was that liberalization came from above, not from below as in Britain, where it was pursued by traders and manufacturers. State reason collided with guild reason (Stratman, 1993, p. 39). The movement was instigated through the French revolution but also found resonance in Prussia through the Stein-Hardenberg laws as well as in the Nordic countries. These processes of liberalization and their particular realizations are charted in all four empirical chapters.

The reactions were demands for a return to an order, which provided the crafts organizations with a more important role. The lack of quality in training, the loss of mutual obligations between master-artisans and journeymen/ apprentices, and youth socialization issues were among the reasons. Here the first branching point can be identified. In Denmark, Norway and later in Finland, legislation to protect the interests of artisans were passed, granting master-artisans control over the training of apprentices which they previously had been denied. Through these processes, law and new formal structures replaced the old tradition of apprenticeship.

The Danish 1889 law was the first crucial step in the re-institutionalization of apprenticeship. It was the first modern regulation of apprenticeship in the world. The 1921 and 1937 reforms underscore the gradual modernization of apprentice training in Denmark. These reforms reinstated apprentice contracts and formalized the role of the artisanal associations in the formation and administration of training in the firm. It was also possible to extend and consolidate regulations of apprenticeship across crafts and industry. In Norway, a new law on crafts was passed in 1894, but industry was not included. Compared to Denmark, the result was a bifurcated institutional structure, between craft training regulated by law and 'unregulated' industrial training.

The Swedish and Finnish trajectories illustrate a somewhat different pattern. Here the contours of a system for school-based vocational education evolved, separate from craft traditions. In Sweden, the development of school-based VET received a push through plans for an organic reorganization of the school system and the practical/vocational school reform in 1918, while firm-based apprentice training remained legally unregulated. In Finland, the regulation of VET schooling was developed through a series of acts, first initiated in 1885, then followed by regulations on craft schools in 1900 and a general act on vocational schools in 1920, also providing government funding to private vocational schools. Parallel to the 1920 act, a law on apprentice training was passed.

As illustrated by the Swedish reform path, vocational schooling was affected by reforms in the elementary school. Of particular importance was the formation of new practical, non-obligatory school forms. In an age of ongoing industrialization, adolescence was increasingly perceived as a societal problem of integration and discipline by contemporary observers. The target group for the practical continuation schools was youth who otherwise would have entered the labour market after completion of the obligatory school. As the growth of vocational schools coincided with the emergence of the 'practical' continuation schools for working-class youth and plans for increased obligatory schooling, this paved the way for political modernization projects of systemic integration in two directions; towards general education or towards VET 'proper'. These dilemmas were 'solved' differently in the different Nordic countries. In Norway and Finland, separate practical continuation schools were constructed that competed with ordinary VET schools. In Sweden, it provided the basis for the 1918 school reform integrating VET schools and the continuation school. In Norway, similar reform attempts failed, and in Denmark municipal VET schools failed to make much of an impression.

Post-1945 developments – VET and the social democratic regime

The post-war period marked a change in the repertoire of VET reform, intensified state intervention, increased spending, and a stream of reforms aimed at the expansion and reorganization of VET (Table 10.2).

Table 10.2 Nordic VET trajectories in the social democratic period (1945–1990)

Denmark	Norway	Sweden	Finland
1956: New apprentice law and mandatory day school attendance	1945: Vocational school law (1940)	1940: National Labour Market Commission formed	1958: Law for the provision of VET schools
1960: Labour Market Training Institution (AMU) established	1950: Apprentice law for crafts, industry and commerce	1955: VET school law	1968: School Systems Act
1976: Basic vocational training introduced parallel to apprenticeship	1960: State Labour Market Authority formed 1973: commerce apprenticeship terminated	1964: Principles for a comprehensive upper secondary school established	1968: Apprentice law
	1976: Upper secondary comprehensive school formed 1976: Adult education law	1971: Integration of VET into a new programme-based upper secondary comprehensive school	1974: Upper secondary reform initiated
1978: Mandatory employer levy on apprentice training	1980: New apprentice law for state subsidies of apprentice training introduced		1978: Upper secondary schools proposal
1980: Youth guarantee 1980: Vocational gymnasiums formed	1981: Youth guarantee		1982: Youth guarantee 1990: Youth guarantee abandoned

The table displays considerable parallels in VET policy repertoires and chronologies across countries in this period. A common aim was parity of esteem between VET and general education and the expansion of VET provision. Through long-term growth, the capacity in secondary education was expanded in order to cater for the whole of the relevant youth cohorts. In that process, youth demand for education and training and youth unemployment evolved as increasingly important parameters for Nordic, welfare-oriented educational policies. As the universalization of access to upper secondary education for youth evolved into a general norm, new policy instruments like the youth guarantee were formed in order to enhance inclusion and combat youth unemployment. Policy-makers in Denmark, Norway and Sweden developed such guarantees at the beginning of the 1980s, followed by Finland. The primary focus of these guarantees was the inclusion of younger youth in vocational education and training, but such policy measures also came to comprise older age target groups in periods of transitions in individual life.

Furthermore, the focus on vocational training for youth was broadened to include extended systems of upskilling and retraining of the labour force. Early on, the unions had started labour exchange services as one of the tools in the economic struggle on the labour market. Gradually the State took over labour exchange by establishing local labour exchange offices, which subsequently were provided with a monopoly. The formation of the Swedish Labour Market Commission (AMS) in 1940 was path breaking and the formation of separate labour market authorities followed in the three other countries. Gradually these institutions evolved in the direction of providing practical training for the unemployed and unskilled. The combined effect of these reforms was that all four Nordic VET systems expanded significantly in terms of target groups and capacity.

These features might be represented in terms of a striking convergence between the four countries. However, these policy streams have gravitated in different directions in the four countries. In Sweden, Finland and Norway, the passing of acts on VET schooling provided a legal and financial basis for a significant expansion in rise in the number and duration of vocational schools. In Denmark, the 1956 act reorganized the older master apprenticeship, and mandatory periods of full-time day school attendance in all occupations were instigated. As youth demand for apprentice training was growing, pressures for an increase in the number of apprenticeships surfaced. This was attempted to be alleviated by the establishment of 2-year, specialized apprenticeships (Jørgensen, 2018). The Norwegian and Finnish post-war trajectory displays a double orientation, towards reform-making in VET schooling and reforms in apprentice training. In Sweden, apprenticeship remained legally unregulated, in spite of several unsuccessful attempts (Olofsson and Persson Thunquist, 2018b).

In this period the position of VET as a separate type of institution was challenged by the rise of the social democratic comprehensive school. Sweden was the frontrunner in the movement towards secondary school reform. All the four countries passed and implemented comprehensive lower secondary reform. The next step was the new upper secondary comprehensive school, which was debated in all four countries, but which materialized only in Sweden and Norway. The Swedish reform was the more radical. The character of the VET-programmes changed, the highly specialized courses broadened, and programme contents more centralized and standardized, while in Norway the reform trajectory was more gradualist, as VET tracks remained based on the logics and traditions of the older fine-grained school types. In Sweden the new VET programmes provided formal access to higher education, while in Norway, access to higher education from VET tracks remained blocked.

In Denmark and Finland, upper secondary comprehensive reform was not accepted. The position of the gymnasium as the exclusive route to higher education was not changed. In Denmark, the reform trajectory closed in on the apprentice path, towards new financing arrangements, where a mandatory levy on training was imposed on all employers, and the formation of a broader Basic Apprenticeship Programme in 1976, parallel to the old master apprenticeship programme, where young people could start a school-based basic course without an apprentice training contract. In Finland, VET remained separate from the gymnasiums, and the path from VET to the university remained blocked. Apprenticeship was an option deliberated by policy-makers in Norway, Finland and Sweden in the whole post-war period. In Sweden, apprentice regulation did not materialize, in spite of several attempts. However, in Norway and Finland, the pattern where apprenticeship law became updated and reformed in tandem with reforms in VET schooling continued.

1990 and onwards – liberalization

In the last decades of the 20th century, a new policy agenda emerged in Nordic VET. It is difficult to pinpoint the exact timing of these changes, and the change processes evolved differently in the four countries. During that period the Nordic countries (as well as the rest of Europe) adopted a number of neoliberal policies in order to promote business competitiveness and employer autonomy, and induce budgetary rigor (Table 10.3).

In education, NPM policies evolved later than in other comparable sectors (Green-Pedersen, 2002). For the most part, VET policies continued to focus on classical social democratic goals like universalization of inclusion, but these older polices were supplemented with decentralization and administrative modernization processes in educational institutions, closing in on ex ante incentives and ex post performance measures in various combinations with traditional forms of steering. In Sweden, the NPM marketization profile was the most clear-cut, while the Norwegian and Danish policies focused on administrative modernization, mergers and institutional integration.

The recessions during the 1990s induced a constant concern about youth unemployment and 'outsiders'. This situation instigated a second wave of reforms, oriented towards activation and labour market policies for various target groups, circumscribed by a blend of social democratic concerns for social investment in training and neoliberal goals of activation and balancing budgets.

Table 10.3 Nordic VET trajectories of liberalization (1990–2015)

Denmark	Norway	Sweden	Finland
1991; EFG and master apprenticeship merged	1994: Comprehensive upper secondary school act, including apprenticeship, 2+2 model	1991: Upper secondary school reform, decentralization and marketization	1992: New apprentice act launched
1993: Active labour market policy for youth SKP 1993: a provisional full-time school-based training programme	1994: Individual right to 3 years of upper secondary education instituted 1994: Increased state subsidies to apprentice training	1992: Private school reform	1994: Vocational Qualifications Act
1995: AMU reorganized and extended 2001: AMU and VET system merged	2003: Quality assurance system devised	1996: Advanced vocational education act	1996: Youth under 24 years obliged to participate in education/training 1998: Act on Initial Vocational Education
2007: New VET reform on social inclusion and retention	2006: Knowledge promotion reform and decentralization	2008: Pilot apprentice scheme	2013: New youth guarantee
2015: New VET reform to raise the esteem of and enrolment in VET		2011: Reform to introduce apprenticeships and emphasise differences between VET and general upper secondary education	2015: New national curriculum reform

Through these processes, VET training and upskilling was expanded to include almost all sectors and a growing number of target groups, but with a strong focus on youth inclusion, youth unemployment and transitions from school to work. In Finland, Sweden and Norway, VET programmes have been extended, broadened in contents, rationalized and streamlined. While access to higher education from VET has remained restricted and usually required detours of various types in Norway, the Swedish system has taken on a stronger division between VET and academic tracks, and after 2012 VET tracks no longer provided general eligibility to higher education. In Finland, initial vocational education has gradually been developed as a route that leads to eligibility for tertiary education since the 1990s. However, the liberalist turn also shaped a new appreciation of the value of firm-based training, and the integration of production and training. The space for employer discretion in skill formation has increased (Baccaro and Howell, 2017). In all three countries, the broadening of contents and programme profiles have been supplemented by an increased focus on working life and 'apprenticeships', but in different ways. Decentralization processes and new national qualification frameworks have created a new space for local school-employer relations and an increased recognition of experience from training in working life, and possibilities for on-the-job training and firm placements have increasingly been incorporated in ordinary VET study programmes.

Also the organization of relations between VET proper and labour market training diverged. The main rule has been institutional differentiation between the labour market authority and VET. A clear institutional division of labour between labour market (training) services and education has been sustained in Sweden and Finland, while Denmark merged labour market training services and VET tasks into one institution in 2001. This reorganization probably improved conditions for the coordination of training and upskilling for various target groups, including the unemployed. According to Crouch et al. (2001) such a move might create the danger that training might suffer from lack of credibility. In 2015, these policies for inclusion were abandoned as VET was suffering from lack of esteem, and institutional differentiation was restored. In Norway, labour market services have been merged with old age pensions and social policy into one broad welfare sector institution, the NAV, while VET remained locked in the comprehensive school. The Norwegian sectorization structure increased the potential for coordination between the various welfare policy areas into 'one-stop shops', but probably reduced the potential for coordination between VET and social policies.

The four Nordic countries vary in terms of organizational patterns as well as flexibilization trajectories. In spite of differences in formal organization and higher education VET relation, the Swedish and Finnish approaches under liberalization could be described as the modernization of older centralized school-based VET structures combined with active labour market policies, social security and labour market flexibility, producing standardized general vocational skill profiles acquired in school, while flexibilization policies have gravitated towards increased emphasis on decentralization, activation and individualization as well as increased local employer influence.

The Danish reform trajectory from the 1990s and onwards could be interpreted in terms of reorganization and flexibilization of older structures inherited from apprenticeship. The new system combines older occupational profiles structured by occupations/trades with the construction of individualized training paths over the life course; it combines the dismantling of traditional boundaries between initial and continuing VET, between youth and adults, as well as between the employed and the unemployed (Thelen, 2014). Still, the flexibilization trajectory is not that clear cut, but comprises adjustments in several directions (Jørgensen, 2018), where the esteem of VET have been pitted against inclusion. A stricter division between labour market services and VET has been restored, and divisions between youth and adult (>25 years) programmes have been re-introduced. Additional tensions in the Danish system have emerged at the nexus between the universal school-based part and the more selective firm-based apprenticeship parts.

The Norwegian trajectory has produced new conditions for qualification profiles structured by occupations/trades and the skilled workers certificate. However, not much trace of proactive dismantling of older boundaries between the vocational and academic parts of the upper secondary school can be identified, in spite of formal organizational integration of apprenticeship into the comprehensive school. As in Denmark, the main tensions have run along the divide between the school-based part and the more selective apprentice part of the VET programmes, providing conditions for considerable drop-out rates as well as a flow of transfers from VET to general education. The volume of active labour market policies for youth as well as CVET has been small compared to the other countries, as the youth labour market has been able to absorb much of the dropout surplus, and VET and social policies have gravitated towards different institutional constellations.

Explaining institutional change in Nordic VET trajectories

Comparing contents of reform charts and interpretations of the direction of reform in the three periods invites questions on the historical continuities in VET. On the one hand VET policies have changed considerably. The reform charts illustrate that VET reform is a diverse phenomenon, consists of many interrelated elements, and that the understanding of VET is historically contingent and fluid. They also illustrate considerable parallels between the trajectories in the four countries based on the specificities of the periods pointed out. In classical versions of historical institutionalist theory, the stability of paths has been a central issue. Paths are stable, subjected to radical change in critical periods of transition, because of external shocks, often called critical junctures. In this type of reasoning, longer periods of equilibrium are subjected to shorter periods of radical change. Diachronic analysis of the three reform periods could be interpreted around a common theme of 'comparative statics', producing four different Nordic routes in VET, routes that are specific for each of the four Nordic countries. They could also be read in terms of two different routes: that of the genesis and reproduction of the apprenticeship route and the school-based VET route, leading up to two different types of systems – that of the statist school-based system and an apprentice-based system. Based on reform trajectories listed, a case could be made for the formation and stabilization of the various paths, and the significance of the shadow of the past in Nordic skill formation.

Alternatives emphasize the significance of endogenous factors rather than external shocks (Mahoney and Thelen, 2010), where institutional change is seen as a process of coalitional politics and compliance (Mahoney and Thelen, 2010). The implication of this perspective is that institutional reform originates in political conflict or compromise among actors. In this view institutions are constantly perishable rather than stable and self-sustaining. In Chapter 1, I indicated several theoretical lenses along which the origins and development of VET systems could be scrutinized and political coalitions identified. Primary sources of inspiration were a combination of historical institutionalism, the primacy of politics literature, where the evolution of VET systems can be explained in terms of political systems and political dynamics, and the varieties of capitalism literature (VoC). In the following section, I attempt a further investigation of the four Nordic paths in VET along these lines, synthesizing and extending material from the country chapter with additional material.

Cross-national comparison and analysis: the origins and evolution of the four Nordic VET systems

The early phase of democratization and industrialization contribute significantly to the analysis of variation in the evolution of VET in the Nordic countries. This was a period of enfranchisement, where political parties emerged and new political systems formed. All the Nordic countries evolved from majoritarian two-party systems (M) into Proportional Representation (PR) multiparty system systems. Following democratization, the locus of power shifted from the elite to the middle classes, and then to the mobilization of the farmers and the workers. These waves of class mobilization paved the way for the rise of the Nordic social democratic parties to power, but in different ways. The role of the employers and their ability to act collectively represent another important dimension explaining the formation of VET policies and practices. Following processes of economic liberalization and the abolition of the guilds, the formation of employer preferences, their articulation through peak organizations and relations to workers unions in the form of collective agreements have been important in all the Nordic countries. The Nordic countries moved towards a new type of coordinated capitalism. The Nordic states reacted by providing vocational training through the channels which were available to them. However, the specific paths of the four countries and the coalitions developed around VET varied significantly. In the following I have compiled short and rather stylized presentations of the three periods in VET in the four countries in order to illustrate differences in policy paths in VET and the coalitions that produced them.

Coalitions and policy paths in the liberal period

Sweden

The Swedish path towards a statist system could be traced in a specific sequence of events in time. In political terms, Sweden was one of the least democratic counties in Western Europe in the 19th century (Berman, 2006), and the liberal epoch between the earlier conservative elite-based regimes and the later social democratic dominance was much shorter in Sweden than in Norway and Denmark. For a long time, social democratic and liberal attempts at reform through parliament did not yield much when confronted with a strong system of veto players entrenched in a bicameral structure. The 1918 school reform can fruitfully be interpreted as the foundation for the Swedish school-based VET system (Olofsson and Persson Thunquist, 2018a). Timing was important, as the reform benefitted from the ongoing democratization processes (Lindell, 1992). Universal suffrage for men and women was granted relatively late in Sweden (1909 and 1918), and parliamentary rule was formally established in 1918. The school law was based on a coalition between the liberal and the social democrats, united in the fight for democratization. The fundamental aspect of the law was intentions of socialization and civic integration, where vocational schools for industry played a minor part in the political discussions. The result was the formation of a form of vocational training that remained separate from employment and apprenticeship.

A freedom of trade act had been passed in 1864, and guild regulations were revoked, producing conditions for laissez faire in the labour market. In a situation of late democratization and strong veto powers in parliament, the labour market became an important political arena for reform, and action was deliberately taken out of the parliamentary arena by social democratic and liberal reformers. The conservatives, on the other hand, attempted to curtail and regulate labour market dynamics, but were also consistently voted down by the liberals and the social democrats. Anti-union labour regulations (as in Germany) were not imposed by the state in labour law (Hasselblanc, 1993). In so far as the Swedish labour movement was created 'en bloc' through swift and late industrialization, the labour movement became heavily connected to the Social Democratic Party (Korpi, 1978), and unions became organized along industrial lines rather than crafts, as in Denmark. Not only was the Swedish craft sector weaker than its Danish counterpart, but smaller Swedish firms were also increasingly overshadowed by larger export-oriented enterprises and their preferences and orientations. The issue of legal regulation in apprenticeship was continuously debated among the employers and the unions, and with considerable ambivalence on both sides (Olofsson and Persson Thunquist, 2018b). The avenue of labour market 'laissez faire' regulation was subsequently solidified though the Saltsjøbaden agreement, where the labour market partners agreed that school-based, publicly organized vocational education should be strengthened and that apprenticeship should function as a complement to, rather than a main road for, vocational learning. Further, firm-based training and apprenticeship should be regulated by voluntary collective agreements within each trade (Olofsson and Persson Thunquist, 2018a). The doctrine of freedom of the labour market from state intervention came to dominate in Sweden for a long time (Elvander, 2002). The employer and the workers' organizations contributed to block all initiatives for legislation of apprenticeship. Businesses' willingness to recruit and train apprentices was low, as individual employers' feared that their investments in apprenticeship would finally favour competing firms, and apprentice wages were considered as too high compared to unskilled workers. Apprenticeship was primarily seen as a concern for individual businesses and employer and labour organizations.

Finland

In Finland, vocational training policies emerged as a product of a similar but still somewhat different type of constellation, where the interest of the Finnish export industries merged with the development of the agricultural sector in the interest of socializing a labour force from rural areas. Like Sweden, Finland could be described in terms of an eastern Nordic path based on large-scale export manufacturers and cartels, and the guilds were weak (Fellman, 2008). The Finnish economy evolved as a liberal market economy, but with elements of cooperation and coordination, as well as some measure of state intervention, coined as 'qualified liberalism' by Fellman (2008). The result was the formation of generally oriented, preparatory vocational schools as a consistent focus. Finnish VET was at its origin shaped by a combination of older mercantilist institutions from Swedish rule and Russian bureaucracy, which in turn created considerable inertia in the legal system. Eventually, liberalization made an impact in the form of freedom of trade and the abolition of the guilds. Most mercantilist restrictions were abolished in the period 1859–1868. At the time Finland was one of the most markedly agrarian countries in Europe (Senghaas, 1985, p. 72).

Swift political democratization preceded industrialization. The unprecedented landslide 1906 election placed the new Labour Party in an absolute majority in Parliament. However, the civil war which fired up after the new state formation in 1917 and the defeat of the 'reds' created a very difficult political situation. The Finnish state was weak but active (Fellman, 2008), and the 1920s were marked by weak centre coalition governments and the need for political compromises. The civil war had served to erode what was left of trust in laws and decrees, and it is reasonable to assume that the Finnish state did not have the resources to impose training regulations on the employers.

Compared to the other Nordic states, institutionalization of labour agreements happened relatively late. Employer coordination was weak, and for the most part took the form of cartelization and state enterprises (Fellman, 2008). As in Sweden, Finnish employers started to organize mainly as a reaction to organization of a workers' movement (Fellman, 2008). The goals were to influence authorities in order to pursue the interest of Finnish industrial life as well as fighting the unions. Factory-owners had little interest in instructing apprentices, as skills requirements in general were low. Also the trade unions considered it a better solution to increase the number of vocational schools. They had little interest in vocational training, as other priorities came first. The employers did not respond positively to the law on apprenticeships in 1923. It meant more state regulation, and trust between the labour market parties was low. A broad 'Scandinavian' class compromise like the Saltsjöbaden agreement was strikingly absent in Finland until the 1940s (Kettunen, 2001). Relations between the worker's unions and the employer's organizations were adversarial or outright hostile. The Finnish labour movement mobilized first politically and the parliamentary channel of participation was opened before the corporatist. This feature left considerable space for the radical fraction of the unions and radical activism at the local level.

The Finnish path illustrates the significance of contingency. In fact, employers anticipated that Finnish industrial relations would develop in the same direction as in the Scandinavian countries with branch-level collective agreements, and prepared for such a scenario (Rainio-Niemi, 2004). However, this kind of development was not to materialize because the 1917 October Revolution in Russia, and tense class relations led to a bloody civil war in the spring of 1918. The employers held the unions responsible for the civil war, and thereafter refused negotiations on collective bargaining. The main aim for the employers was to keep the relationship between the employer and the workers on a firm bilateral basis (Rainio-Niemi, 2004). The Finnish trade union movement had to rely on the tight and strong local workers' communities, rather than on the strength of a centralized trade union movement in collective bargaining and participation in apprenticeship training was resisted for several reasons, but mainly because of low salaries. The result was an institutional configuration which made skills and wage formation a matter between the individual employer and the workers, rather than an issue of collective bargaining. In this adversarial context, the 1923 apprentice act floundered (Stenström and Virolainen, 2018a). There was no other viable option than organizing VET around vocational preparatory schools which developed into the largest and most significant form of VET for crafts and industry from the 1920s onwards. Training remained the domain of the individual, industrial firm, while the state took care of preparatory VET schools.

Denmark

The genesis of the Danish apprentice path could be related to the reproduction of the crafts and the rise of new apprentice legislations. Central elements in this trajectory were the role of smaller entrepreneurs, the development of agricultural capitalism, the strong position of the crafts and the productive tensions between the employers' and the workers' organizations in skill formation. The result was the contours of a state-supported, firm-based and employer-dominated VET system. However, the interest coalitions which produced this path were far from stable. The abolition of absolutist rule, the institutionalization of parliament and a new constitution in 1848–1849 had set the scene for a liberalist turn and the development of agrarian capitalism (Trampusch and Spies, 2014). But it was the repercussions after the loss of Schleswig and Holstein and the conservative reaction that provided the context for the apprentice act of 1889, which was passed by a deeply conservative government, in the midst of the struggle against the extension of franchise and parliamentary rule.

The apprentice law ensured the position of the state as a regulator in VET, the imposition of the apprentice contract ensured the masters' rights to control and oversee apprentice labour, and regulations of apprenticeship across crafts and industry were imposed. The 1921 and 1937 apprentice reforms were based on quite different political reform coalitions. In 1901, the old regime was finally overthrown, and a political system change carried out. In the new parliamentarian political structure, the liberal parties came to wield substantial political influence. The Danish 1921 apprentice reform was a product of a liberal minority government. Its primary stipulation was the re-establishment of journeyman's exams. Opening up for representation from the labour movement in the bodies regulating exams was a thorny issue, as the Liberal Party was against any intervention in the managerial rights of the employers (Juul, 2009). Liberal minority rule was followed by a left wing radical and social democratic coalition. These very diverse political constellations opened up for collectivist-liberal regulations of apprentice training in 1937. The liberals adjusted their position in terms of employer prerogatives, and the social democrats, on the other hand, adjusted their preferences towards liberal apprenticeship regulation. The law also contained legislative improvements on apprentices' working conditions, and provided the labour market parties with considerable powers of self-regulation.

This move presupposed a number of crucial institutional conditions. Danish liberalism was strong, but assumed a cooperative form (Iversen and Andersen, 2008). The formation of collective actors in working life took place early in Denmark, and associational structures bridging crafts and industry emerged. The formation of a national employers association gave the impetuous for the first national confederation of workers in 1898. A basic agreement on the rules of the game was concluded between the Danish Trade Union Confederation and the Danish Employers' Confederation in 1896, where the interest structure was characterized by persistent small-industry guild traditions, a mixture of many small craft unions and a small number of more general unions for unskilled workers. The famous September Agreement in 1899 paved the way for constructive relations between the state and the labour market parties. Labour market policy-making was deliberately taken out of the parliamentary arena and lifted into the labour market, not by the left, as in Sweden, but by the conservatives, in anticipation of the imminent system change coming up in 1901 (Nelson, 2012). At first, the institutionalized cooperation of the social partners concentrated on regulating wages and working conditions, but with the 1937 reform it evolved into an integral part of the legal regulation of the apprenticeship system (Juul and Jørgensen, 2011). The employers' organization, for its part, was in favour of collective regulation in order to secure the quality of training, but resented that the labour movement and the employers' organizations were represented on an equal footing in the bodies regulating the Danish VET system. The employers preferred a German solution, which provided the employers with a more dominating position, but also here compromises were fashioned, producing conditions for self-regulation in apprentice training for the labour market parties.

Norway

The Norwegian route was less clear-cut and the interaction between industrialization and democratization considerably different from that of Sweden and Denmark. Norway was dominated by a civil servant state with a strong laissez faire orientation. Principles of freedom of enterprise were not only a doctrine enshrined in the constitution, but also a political practice, which led up to the abolition of the guild system. The Norwegian parliament was not bicameral, like in Denmark and Sweden, and there were no institutional checks (Sejersted, 2011, p. 51). The rise of parliamentary rule after 1884 made the Norwegian parliament *the* dominant venue for policy formation, and the employers in industry and crafts had no other choice than working through Parliament.

When confronted with the consequences of the withering of guild regulations, the crafts mobilized and reorganized. A new central level association was formed in 1886 based on a Danish solution, bridging craft and industrial interests. In 1894, a new law for the crafts was passed by Parliament, but an extension of legal regulations to include industry did not succeed, and a common approach to training and remuneration based on the strong position of the skilled worker did not materialize in industry, as in Denmark. Differences reflected local-, firm- and industry-specific training practices and traditions, as well as an industrial interest structure based on small firms and low capacity for coordination. After the initial confrontations between the employers and the unions, a pattern gradually emerged, where union formation and collective agreements were viewed as producers of stability, conducive to both employer and worker interests (Bjørnson, 2001). This development culminated in the Basic Agreement in 1935, where the rights to unionization, worker representation, wage negotiations and principles for layoffs became institutionalized. However, industrialists felt that industrial training was a matter for industry and not the state to decide.

Also the role of the labour party differed from the Danish and Swedish situation. When the great liberal coalition, that lead to parliamentary rule, deteriorated, the contours of a multiparty system evolved, where the Norwegian labour party (DNA) grew in strength. But after its radicalization, the labour party refrained from taking an active part in the central parliamentary arena. This paved the way for liberalist re- consolidation and attempts at new liberal reform policies in VET. A number of policy options were investigated. One of the options was a 'Swedish solution', modelled on the 1918 school law. Unlike in Sweden, connections between the practical continuation school reform and democracy could not easily be established. The timing was different, and democracy was primarily associated with the old, liberal comprehensive school project (Michelsen and Høst, 2018a). Another competing option was apprenticeship based on a 'Danish solution', but also this option was not able to muster the necessary support in parliament or among industrialists. The result was a subsequent regulatory demise of law-making in vocational training in industry, and the continuation of older 'voluntarist' practices based on the collective bargaining system. The political situation was characterized by unrest and shifting party constellations until 1935, when the labour party had turned revisionist and achieved a majority in the parliament. Legal VET regulations did not materialize until 1945.

Social democratic VET (1945–1990)

The second period provided different constellations of actors in the formation of VET polices and structures. During the first half of the 20th century, the Nordic countries had moved towards multiparty systems structured by PR where the Social Democrats had a strong position (Svåsand and Demker, 2005). The 1950s and 1960s was the high point of electoral success, when the social democratic parties evolved as genuine mass parties. VET institutions had been highly skewed towards the working class and the crafts, and the labour parties found increased public investments in vocational secondary education beneficial. During the 1960s this strategy was broadened to include the expansion of general education as well. This trajectory rested on the strong position of the Social Democrats, the Scandinavian class compromise, high growth rates and the rise of the universal Nordic welfare state (Esping-Andersen, 1991), but also on the employers and their strategies. The development of welfare state did not only provide conditions for decommodification, universalization of services and income protection. The same processes also increased new conditions for commodification (Kettunen, 2006). The swift entry of women into the labour market fuelled demand for services, in order to supportparticipation, which in turn fuelled a growing public welfare sector. A large, well-organized public sector evolved into an important factor in Nordic politics as well as in the union and employer structure. To a considerable extent, these developments offset the effects of the decline in older manufacturing industries and the tendency towards disorganization in other types of services, and paved the way for new and broader reform coalitions in Nordic welfare (Pierson, 2004). These constellations provided conditions for expansive educational policies, where the esteem of VET was an important priority. In spite of these general tendencies, systematic differences between the Nordic countries were sustained.

Sweden

The actor constellations and the policies that had been formed during the liberal period set the scene for post-war developments. When democratization was 'completed', the Swedish social democrats broke off the collaboration with the liberals, and a major split emerged between the socialists, who assumed a dominant position in parliament, and the non-socialists. This constellation led up to the formation of a state-governed, school-based VET system, which up to the 1970s was characterized by a gradually broadened, civic-oriented educational content, supplemented with minor elements of apprenticeship and company-based training. It was preparatory education rather than skilled worker education and training. The preferences of the business community gravitated towards VET in school, supplemented with firm-specific on-the-job training in a tight labour market. The formation of the Swedish Labour Market Commission (AMS) in 1940 was at the core. Under conditions of labour market shortages, the AMS provided a mechanism for re-training and upskilling of the labour force. Egalitarian pressures induced by centralized wage bargaining were compensated by investing in active labour market policies. As 'unproductive' firms were pushed out of the market, redundant workers were retrained for expanding, high productivity industries. The unions, as well as the employer's organizations (Swenson, 2002) supported these policies. Training in the firm remained regulated though the bargaining system rather than through law and the importance of apprenticeship diminished into rare exceptions. The employers adjusted their preferences to the situation (Huber and Stephens, 2001). The employers' and labour organizations' influence over vocational training was transformed in the process, and mediated through a variety of corporative bodies for decision-making and consultation (Olofsson and Persson Thunquist, 2018b). The labour market organizations also took an active part in shaping VET policies by participating in important public committees that prepared the major vocational training reforms (Lundahl, 1997).

The rise of the comprehensive school constituted the second phase in the Swedish post-war VET trajectory. The stream of reforms included upper secondary level in 1971. It was the first structural reform in VET since 1918. The decision on comprehensive upper secondary reform was sustained by the persistent and strong position of the Labour Party, which continuously held office up to the end of the 1970s, supported by strong party–union links (Korpi, 1978). Still, considerable elements of consensus and compromise in the formation of VET policies could be noted in the form of huge majorities in Parliament in VET reform.

The comprehensive upper secondary education reform has been interpreted by some researchers in terms of the hegemony of the Swedish social democracy and the trade union movement (cf. Lundahl, 1998). In this perspective, the comprehensive school reform was the final product of the old struggle of organized labour for equal opportunities in education, providing new pathways to higher education. Greater curricular integration and egalitarian participation in education were seen to go hand in hand with democratization of the work place advocated in the new labour laws (Hickox and Lyon, 1998). The reform also depended heavily on the employers and their orientations. Firms had earlier on adjusted their personnel strategies in order to build on the public provision of VET in vocational schools with broad, flexible skills. But important conditions for the old Saltsjøbaden agreement was faltering, as a deluge of new labour market legislation was instigated by a compact majority in Parliament and supported by the labour unions (LO). Interpretation of the dynamics vary, from power resource compatible perspectives, where parliament came under increasing pressure from a radicalized LO (Kjellberg, 2002), or partisan politics interpretations, that emphasize the leading role of the radicalized social democratic parties and the initial reluctance of the LO (Nycander, 2002). Furthermore, the dominant position of the LO and SAF was challenged through structural changes associated with the emerging welfare state, the growth of the service industries and the white-collar workers, academics and professionals. Several of these sector groups were organized equally well or even better than the diminished manufacturing sector and the reduced LO. The characteristic Swedish split between the blue-collar and the white-collar academic unions pitted these interests against each other, while SAF emerged into a more encompassing employer organization, incorporating an increasingly heterogeneous interest structure. In spite of these strong tensions, where marked and consistent differences between the SAF's and LO's ideologies on education and training as well as a host of other issues were clearly visible, Lundahl holds that actors' constellations, consensus and co-operation in matters of VET schooling remained fundamentally unchanged (Lundahl, 1997). This suggests that increasing conflict in the collective bargaining area did not necessarily translate into VET corporatist arenas. On the other hand, SAF was sceptical to far-reaching integration of vocational and general education within the upper secondary school, while LO supported such a course of action. Even so, SAF remained more pragmatic to educational reform than the conservatives (Lundahl, 1997).

Finland

Also the Finnish post-war reform trajectory could be interpreted as a long-term project of the formation of school-based VET system. The significant event was the formation of a new law on Vocational schooling in 1958, which consolidated school-based VET as the dominant model of the VET, and set the scene for strong growth in capacity. The end of the Second World War changed the political situation in Finland. The Communist Party was legalized, and the Social Democrats strengthened their position. However, compared to the other Nordic countries, the Social Democratic Party was consistently smaller, the agrarians larger and the liberals smaller. The Finnish political system remained one of the most fragmented in Western Europe, and no single party has since come close to winning a majority, which in turn necessitated coalition government, cooperation and compromise between the parties in the cabinet as well as in the parliament (Arter, 2008). While the Centre Party constituted the core party of governing coalitions up to the 1970s, the Social Democrats emerged as the biggest core party for the period up to 1991. The 'red-green' coalition was a key factor in the continuity of Finnish education policy until 1987, closing in on policies of expansion and the equalization of possibilities for education in rural and central areas.

However, Finnish Social Democrats contemplated a rapidly changing institutional landscape, where the close connection to the labour market parties constituted an increasingly important element. The Finnish Employer's Confederation and the Central Organization of Finnish Trade Unions (SAK) acknowledged each other and promised to negotiate on labour market issues.

The principal opposition to collective agreements was abandoned among the employers and SAK recognized the employers' right to manage (Rainio-Niemi, 2004). Union numbers expanded, and collective agreements spread quickly. Together with post-war political changes, this class compromise between capital and labour paved the way for new constellations and new dynamics, where the unions and the employers' organization rate improved in tandem with Finland's unprecedented economic 'catch-up' process (Kangas and Palme, 2005). In that process Finland developed similar patterns of union organization as Sweden.

But the employers had no common interest in developing firm-based apprentice training in the direction of a collective skill formation system, and the major responsibility for youth training was left to the state. Both employers and worker organizations saw apprenticeships as a minor route to school-based forms of vocational education, and not as a main option. Actually, it could be asked whether trade unions had an independent view on vocational education in the 1950s (Stenström and Virolainen, 2018b). However, as in the other Nordic countries, the unions and the employers participated in corporatist arenas and VET councils, in order to influence government planning and decision-making.

Also in Finland, the development of the comprehensive school was a central element in social democratic policies during the 1970s. The left-wing governments, now led by the Social Democratic Party, made educational reform one of their primary goals. This period was characterized by the creation of institutions and frameworks for a welfare-based, more egalitarian educational system. A comprehensive lower secondary level reform was passed and implemented, but at the upper secondary level, the comprehensive school was contested. Employers regarded the suggestion of a comprehensive upper secondary school as a threat to the quality of vocational studies. Upper-secondary schoolteachers also fought to block the changes. The teachers union, which was the strongest single actor in the 'umbrella organization' for all the academic professions, held a firm grip on school policy (Sahlberg, 2010). In 1974, the Cabinet decided that vocational education should be developed into a competitive alternative to the upper secondary general school. The gymnasiums and the vocational schools remained institutionally separated, and very modest steps towards greater integration of academic and vocational education were taken (Young, 1993), and linkages from VET to higher education were weak (Stenström and Virolainen, 2018b). The employers' and employees' attitudes to VET differed. For the most part the (big) employers emphasized occupational skills as a central task of VET, whereas the workers' and employees' organizations stressed the importance of the more general components. Also at this point, employers were not obliged to take greater responsibility for the training of newcomers to their industrial field (Stenström and Virolainen, 2018b). Rather, along with the employee representatives, they retained their preferences for leaving initial VET to the state. The power of white-collar and academically educated labour unions also increased in the 1970s (Nieminen, 2000). When the focus of reform shifted to upper level education and higher education, these organizations became all the more tightly integrated into the planning system as well as the political process, increasing the number of stakeholders and veto players. In this environment, the expansion of VET was considered important for a number of different reasons, from parity of esteem to relieving the pressure on upper secondary general education and the university.

Denmark

In Denmark, previous reforms in apprenticeship had created significant preconditions for post-war developments. Up to the mid-1960s, the main challenges were to expand the capacity of the VET system in order to absorb the large youth cohorts and to adapt VET to new requirements in working life. The idea of a full-time school-based vocational programme parallel to apprenticeship was rejected. The 1956 apprentice law increased the number of approved training occupations significantly, and expanded the school-based component of VET to complement firm-based training. The apprentice system was now adjusting to industry's growing demand for skilled labour. The act was passed by a government led by the Social Democratic Party, which dominated governments until 1968. In agreement with the craft unions and the Danish trade union confederation (LO), the Social Democratic Party re-confirmed its prior acceptance of the apprenticeship system. The skill demands which emanated from the strong industrialization were also alleviated by the establishment of a new labour market training system (AMU) in 1960, aimed at skilling of unskilled workers. This initiative created a two-tier training system that sustained the demarcations between skilled and unskilled jobs, and between skilled, unskilled and semi-skilled workers in the trade union federation. However, the move towards a more centralized bargaining structure gradually strengthened the power of the unskilled workers' unions vis-a-vis that of the skilled workers, creating conditions for a dynamic mix of qualifications and competing upskilling agendas.

The 1970s brought a major economic crisis. While the number of apprentices had risen significantly in the 1950s and 1960s, the rate of enrolment halved from 1965–1975 and the dropout rate increased. It was a time of continued political search for path change in the direction of the comprehensive school model, as such a model was considered more beneficial for the reduction of social inequality, equity and economic growth than the parallel school model. The Social Democratic Party required that general subjects and schooling for democratic participation should be given higher priority in the vocational programmes. In addition, it required that VET programmes should qualify participants for access to higher education. A political agreement had been reached in 1958 between the Social Democrats, the Radical-Liberal Party and the liberals on the formation of the 10-year 'folkeskole'. But the political conditions for path change in VET were less beneficial. The earthquake of the 1973 election reduced the electoral base of the Social Democrats significantly. In spite of consistently being the strongest party, their ability to pass transformative legislation was restricted by their participation in minority coalitions, short tenure as well as internal differences and disagreements. The new vision of a unified upper secondary school met strong opposition in the parliament and from the labour market parties. The radical liberals insisted on maintaining the state-funded technical and commercial schools and the apprenticeship system. The new Progress Party advocated that firms maintained responsibility for VET and opposed state funding, while the Conservative-Liberal Party was traditionally also in favour of upholding apprenticeship. There was no real political basis for radical VET system transformation. Instead, the Social Democrats launched the Initial Vocational Education act, (*EFG*). The scheme expanded the schooling component and reduced the firm-based training component. This particular feature received strong support from the unskilled unions, but was challenged by a coalition of the craft associations, the conservative and liberal parties and the skilled workers' unions, who opposed the abolition of traditional apprenticeships. The scheme denied the employers a year of productive apprentice time, an important feature for small firms. The scepticism of the employers towards school-based training was not based on the idea that the qualifications obtained were not comparable to the ones obtained at the workplace, but rather on issues of apprentice socialization to the world of work (Juul, 2009). The opponents were not able to squash the reform bill, but they did manage to avoid the obliteration of the old master apprenticeship structure. The result was a compromise, where the EFG programme layered into the old master apprenticeships scheme, which was preserved as a parallel programme to the EFG programme until 1991, when the two programmes merged and mutated into a hybrid, combining elements from both. In 1977, the Social Democrats were able to bring a collective levy-grant proposal through the parliament with the consent of the social partners and the opposition. This reconfirmed the party's pledge to apprenticeship, improving the apprentice's situation and the economic basis of the employers, establishing a new compromise around the logic of firm-based VET. In the 1980s, the unskilled workers' unions developed a strategy to upgrade all unskilled jobs and to offer vocational skills to all their members and a range of new vocational programmes were established in order to cover former unskilled fields of work. On the one hand, state-induced youth educational logics gained momentum and the concept that young students needed an introductory year before entering apprenticeship level was accepted. On the other hand, the reforms underlined the social superiority of the apprentice option (Jørgensen, 2018).

Norway

Education was also a strategic policy arena for the Norwegian labour party. In the new egalitarian society, vocational and general education would enjoy equal status, the party maintained, but how this was to be accomplished was unclear. Unlike Sweden and Denmark, Norwegian Labour Party policies followed two different pathways in VET, that of strengthening a system of practically oriented vocational schools and that of regulating apprenticeship training in the firm.

Vocational schooling was an important political project for the Labour Party, which catered for its primary political constituency. This paved the way for the expansion and structural elaboration of VET programmes in a broad array of fields, covering both rural and urban areas. The regulation and expansion of apprenticeship into industry and commerce proved to be a far more conflictual story. In commerce, it failed, and in industry the number of apprentice contracts remained small. Boycott and local resistance in the crafts inhibited growth, and schooling, certification and wage practices continued to adhere to older liberal traditions, blurring the qualification boundaries between the skilled and the unskilled worker (Michelsen and Høst, 2018b).

The 1970s marked a change. After almost three decades of strong Labour Party rule, the Social Democrats were temporarily turned out of office. The 1970s was a period of ideological tensions, minority government and cabinet alterations. Apprenticeship was now considered a major disappointment among all parties in Parliament and subjected to harsh ideological critique from the radical socialists, but it survived and regulations were updated in order to serve a variety of new purposes related to social policy. But in general, educational polices were circumscribed by consensus and compromise in the parliament even during the 1970s (Telhaug and Mediås, 2003). The bill on comprehensive upper secondary schooling was prepared by a Labour government, but carried through Parliament by a centre-right government with small alterations. The growing comprehensive school project was changing the educational structure towards a system based on ladders rather than parallel school types, producing conditions for an alignment between VET and general education in a comprehensive upper secondary school. By now, the Social Democrats had adjusted their educational policies towards a widening of youth choice and towards expansion in general education as well as higher education. The conservatives wanted to preserve the gymnasium as an elite institution, but their resistance to the comprehensive upper secondary reform in parliament was hesitant, and they had no alternative reform conception. The formation of the comprehensive school provided the prime vehicle for the massification and universalization of upper secondary schooling. The political salience of the comprehensive school made the issue difficult for the employers, who also were divided on the issue. However, most actors involved in the implementation process, including the teachers, resisted attempts at strong, central coordination of programmes in the upper secondary comprehensive school. Within that structure, the employers managed to retain space for various firm-specific adaptive practices and strategies in the formation of training practices, and apprenticeship numbers unexpectedly expanded.

The new liberalization (1990–2015)

The turn towards liberalization was preceded by the general weakening of social democratic hegemony, and the strengthening of the right in Nordic politics. The combination of economic shocks, increased globalization and increased rigidities in the institutional set-ups put new pressure on governments to devise new policies. The social democratic parties in the north tried to cope with the electoral decline as best they could. The result was a new direction which broadly speaking might be called (neo)-liberalization. This term incorporated a diverse set of trajectories ranging from New Public Management (NPM) in the form of marketization and deregulation policies, pushing back the boundaries of the state, to modernization policies, providing the state with new instruments and capabilities (Hansen, 2011; Pollitt and Bouchaert 2004). It also comprises issues relating to employer/union coordination ranging from attempts at active dismantling of coordination capabilities to the reconstruction of such capacities and the introduction of new flexibility, decentralization and increased employer discretion (Baccaro and Howell, 2017). These developments came to complement older and more conventional social democratic notions of quality and equity in VET. Yet, the profile of the new liberalization varied considerably across the four countries.

Sweden

In Sweden, the antecedents of new liberalization reform in VET could perhaps be dated to 1982, when the SAP came back into power after a brief spell of non-socialist governance. The background was the fierce attack of the non-socialists on the Swedish Nanny state (Green-Pedersen, 2002). The new SAP government, therefore, put public sector reforms on top of its agenda. In 1991, SAP suffered a historic defeat in the election, which paved the way for new, nonsocialist centre-right governments in 2006 and 2010 in a period when the Swedish economy experienced a meltdown and youth unemployment exploded. The market type of educational reforms implemented by the non-socialist government during the 1990s actually followed the path laid out by the Social Democrats and strengthened it. Sweden seems to be one of the countries where NPM ideas have had a strong impact in education, stronger than in Norway and Denmark. Nevertheless, the 1991 upper secondary education reform was also motivated by quality issues (Lundahl, 1997). It was an important task for VET to provide the labour market with a well-educated and flexible workforce. In practice, this meant a broad basic vocational training with increased weight on core subjects. LO and SAF as well as the white-collar workers and the academic professionals subscribed to such a view. An overwhelming consensus has emerged among political parties and the labour market organizations on the importance of meeting rapid changes at places of work, in society and in the economy, by means of a flexible and well-educated workforce. Higher education expanded significantly in order to cope with youth unemployment. The possibilities for firms to participate in vocational training increased, but the LO has been restrictive or hostile towards apprenticeship training, other than as a marginal complement to the rest of upper secondary education. The policy of the Social Democratic Party, on the other hand, appears to be more ambivalent.

From the 1980s, the Saltsjøbaden model appeared close to collapse, as Swedish employers withdrew from the main corporatist institutions (Rothstein, 2010). Still, conditions for macro-coordination have been recreated. This process started in 1997, when the trade unions and employer associations in the manufacturing sector signed a path-breaking *Industry Agreement*, followed by a stream of similar agreements. The discretion of the employers has increased and contents have changed, but it is still balanced by a strong labour movement. Employers, unions and state actors have reconstructed a system that looks very familiar compared to the old, but which has been significantly reinterpreted and converted to include new purposes (Baccaro and Howell, 2017). Although somewhat reduced, levels of organization remain high, and collective agreements cover almost the entire labour market. There has been a revitalization of school-enterprise ties at the local level as well as attempts at creating apprenticeship experiments. But new apprenticeships are not governed by the social partners. There are no branch-specific agreements on skill formation, and school-based training is still the fundamental component. Thus, Sweden remains far from a Danish-style model of trade self-management, and instead has attempted to create a mixed model in which school-based education and training is complemented with small-scale (school-organized) apprenticeships and active labour market policies.

Finland

Like Sweden, Finland's economy drifted into deep crisis in the 1990s, forcing policy-makers to impose heavy budget cuts. As a consequence, the education system was exposed to the double task of reducing escalating costs as well as meeting the rising demand for upper-secondary and higher education. The result was a turn in policies, where the education system was intended to support the transition of Finnish society into a more competitive market economy. The expansion of the public welfare sector came to an end. Political power constellations changed as the right was set to dominate state educational policy formation for more than a decade. After 1995, Finland became governed by the five-party 'Rainbow Coalition', where the coalition partners have tended to be compromise oriented and accommodating in educational policies. Thus, the Finnish case combines a strong political shift to the right with strong elements of consensus and compromise. Finland was slow to implement market-oriented education reforms, and the development of educational policies have been grounded in a mix of older notions of equal opportunities for all, equitable distribution of resources, decentralization and flexibility rather than competition. The unexpected Finnish PISA miracle had the effect that further market-driven reform plans in schooling were effectively shelved.

The creation of the universities of applied science (UAS) was the key innovation in educational policies during the 1990s. The situation prior to 1990, characterized by weak linkages to higher education and working life in VET, changed significantly, as 3-year VET programmes were developed in 1998, and new pathways from VET to HE formed. Higher education cohort participation rate in Finland skyrocketed to 49 per cent in 2010 after the formation of the UAS institutions in 1990 (Välimaa and Neuvonen-Rauhala, 2008).

In contrast to Denmark and Sweden, Finland tried to overcome the labour market crisis during liberalization by restoring centralized collective bargaining, combining active state policies towards industrial development and skill formation. In contrast to Denmark and Sweden, Finland tried to overcome the labour-market crisis during liberalization by restoring centralized collective bargaining within a tripartite framework, combining active state policies towards industrial development and skill formation. Tripartite relations between the government, the employers and the labour federations continued, but the position of the employers was significantly strengthened. The system of collective agreement was retained, but in a new and more decentralized form, and the decision-making power of local authorities was increased.

There is much to suggest that the deep economic crisis produced a basis for a broad compromise and consensus between government, the private sector, labour unions and educators in a number of important VET issues, where the most important single item on the political agenda was the high unemployment among young people. In this context, policies for inclusion became extremely important, where VET has evolved into an important pathway for Finnish youth. There are some clear parallels between the Finnish and the Swedish case. In both countries a revitalization of school-enterprise ties at the local level can be observed, but school-based education and training is still the fundamental component. Also in Finland attempts have been made in order to create a mixed model in which school-based education and training is complemented with (school-organized) practical training in the firms supplemented by apprenticeship and active labour market policies (ALMP) as arrangements for adult learning and training. But unlike in Sweden, where VET is thinning out and access to HE has been restricted, Finnish VET is growing in quantitative terms, and new pathways to the UAS have been developed.

Denmark

Since the preceding phase, the Danish VET system has largely remained intact. In general this has been a period where Denmark had right-wing governments from 1982 to 1993, and again from 2001 to 2009 – a total of 19 years. Thus, the Right in Denmark has held power for a much longer period than in the other Nordic countries. The Danish rightist government in office wanted to abort social democratic central planning and to introduce NPM methods and structures. The new regime also questioned the strong involvement of the labour market organizations and the national standardization in the VET system (Jørgensen, 2018). The VET-reform in 1991 signalled the replacement of the corporatist system of governance by decentralized and market-based forms of regulation. But the labour market parties would have none of it. Unlike in Sweden, the Social Democrats opposed policies for marketization. The corporatist system in VET survived, as the employers' organizations, in conjunction with the unions, defended occupational self-governance within the legal boundaries set by the state, even when the employers had the opportunity to side with the conservative-liberal government in furthering more radical deregulation policies.

When the Social Democrats returned to power, they built on the new modified structure in order to enhance participation in VET as well as in higher education. In this period, preferences in VET among political parties seemed to converge in the direction of policies that promoted access and transparency. Through these policies, the inclusion of disadvantaged or marginal groups also became a focal point. In 2012, all major parties supported the effort led by Social Democrats to optimize the VET system in improving the accessibility and output of training. The liberalization of the vocational education market, by making all vocational educational institutions self-governed, and the introduction of performance-based funding in both upper secondary and higher education, have enhanced formal institutional autonomy and added considerable financial weight to policies for inclusion. The comprehensive Danish VET arrangements have been very effective in supporting skilled worker's careers as well as providing possibilities for upskilling of unemployed (Thelen, 2014).

But strategies for building bridges between apprenticeship and higher education have not paid off, and none of the bridging initiatives from apprenticeship to higher education have been successful so far (Jørgensen, 2018). Facing declining esteem, high dropout rates, lack of training placements, programmes that were too narrowly specialized and increasing tensions and discrepancies between the school market and the apprentice market, older inclusion policies suffered a backlash in 2015, where new policies gravitated towards quality rather than inclusion. The 2015 reform can be interpreted as a call for a new realignment in vocational education. The aim is to reduce the number of 'academically challenged' students in the system combined with attracting 'academically strong' students. This development has played in tandem with the decentralization of the bargaining system, towards diluting the power of the unskilled workers unions and restoring the weight and position of the skilled workers and their unions. In turn, the LO has turned training into a centrepiece of its new strategy. These policies have gravitated in different directions, but within the same general frame. Also in higher education, the expansion has been curtailed, and the viability of academic programmes is increasingly subjected to state scrutiny based on output criteria and the absorption of candidates in the labour market.

Norway

The Norwegian Reform 94 represented a specific amalgamation of older social democratic welfare policies, juridification of individual rights to education and New Public Management (NPM)-oriented administrative policies. The reform was proposed by a minority Labour government, but it received substantial support from the social partners and was carried through the Parliament by a consensually oriented process. The reform restructured the programmes in a general and less skill specific direction. It also recombined the apprenticeship and school-based, general VET in a fixed sequence. The provision of individual rights to education for 16–19-year-olds made upper secondary VET into a far more age homogenous institution, and older constituencies were directed else, many towards higher education, where capacity was being built.

The new VET reform required considerable state commitment and as well as state funding. It also rested heavily on the collaboration of the employers and the unions. A central element in Reform 94 was a declaration of intent on behalf of the social partners, committing themselves to the extension and stabilization of the apprentice system. In spite of the declaration of preference for apprenticeship, no compulsory solutions in the spirit of German-style apprentice corporatism were fashioned. The tradition of voluntarism persevered. In fact, the reform amplified formal employer autonomy in some respects. The employers have achieved substantial subsidies in return for their support of apprenticeship. As in Finland, decentralization of the bargaining system has been limited, and the peak level actors (LO and NHO) have retained a stronger position than their Danish and Swedish counterparts. The old institutional cleavage in employer organization between skill formation/structural policies and wage policies has been bridged by comprehensive mergers into one new peak employer organization. Older liberal practices in skill formation have been shored up in industry, and the skilled worker category in industry has been homogenized in terms of formal qualifications and skill profiles. However, NHO and LO have lost their former monopoly as governors of the system of apprentice training, and other employer and employee organizations from adjacent sectors of working life, e.g. from services and the public sector, have gained participation rights and influence. As a consequence, new and broader coalitions have been formed around apprentice training.

The main bottleneck in the system is located at the juncture from school to firm-based training as apprentices. The tensions between these subsystems and the lack of youth inclusion in the firm-based sequence predictably fuel political tensions in Parliament. From a public welfare point of view, the political left argues that state control over apprentice training is still restricted and incomplete, and that youth should acquire a legal right to an apprentice place. On the other hand, the Norwegian Parliament has consistently defended the autonomy of the employers against 'unnecessary' interventions. Through its embeddedness in the comprehensive school, the apprentice institution has been converted to comprise all sectors of working life. The result has been continued growth in apprentice numbers, but also the incorporation of new and broader ideas about the appropriate character of apprenticeship, more aligned to the school-based training traditions prevalent in welfare education and welfare service practices. While building heavily on the artisan apprentice rhetoric, the new policies have marginalized these interests to a considerable extent.

Social democracy, the educational system and the collective organization of skill formation

In view of the accumulated empirical material presented here, a number of questions could be asked to the comparative literature on the evolution of VET systems in social democracies, the role of the employers/unions and relations between VET and the educational system. The first two set of issues addresses the relation between VET and the comprehensive school in the evolution of Nordic social democracies, and relations between the state and the employers. The third set of issues addresses relations between VET and higher education.

As previously mentioned, it has been argued that a specific Nordic or social democratic school model has evolved, the publicly funded comprehensive school system (Lundahl, 2016; Wiborg, 2009; Antikainen, 2006; Arnesen and Lundahl, 2006; Telhaug, Mediås and Aasen, 2006). All four Nordic countries developed comprehensive lower secondary schools, but they diverged as far as the issue of upper secondary comprehensive school was concerned. The primacy of the political explanation would focus on the position of the social democratic parties. The Swedish Social Democratic Party was the strongest with an average of 47 percent of the voters for the period 1940–1971, followed by Norway (45 percent), while the Danish and Finnish parties were weaker (Arter, 2008). The Danish Labour Party was in a less powerful position than its Swedish and Norwegian counterparts, and the party was increasingly dependent on compromises with the Centre-Right and Liberal parties. A comprehensive course of action was abandoned, and a binary upper secondary system was kept. Also in Finland, a binary upper secondary level was sustained. These constellations suggest a lovely picture of symmetry between Social Democratic Party strength and the realization of the upper secondary comprehensive school. Where the social democrats were the stronger (Norway and Sweden), the institutional integration of VET and general education was accomplished, while it failed where the social democrats were weaker (Finland and Denmark).

However, this picture might be a bit too simplistic, for several reasons. The social democratic parties developed different strategies from early on. This makes strategic orientations into an important mediating 'variable' (Kitschelt, 1994). These orientations can be called ideological, pragmatist as well as lobbyist, and relations between the three might vary over time. In a specific sense the term social democracy denotes a pragmatist element, where the main orientation was, contrary to revolutionary socialism (Berman, 2006), to regulate capitalism by a mixture of corporatist trade unionism, collective employer organization and state intervention. At the core of social democratic influence was their ability to build broad alliances behind policy reform, often together with agrarian or liberal interests. Central parliamentary agreements were struck in Denmark in 1933 (*the Kanslergade forlig*), in Sweden in 1934 (*Kohandlen*) and in Norway in 1935 (*kriseforliket*). In effect, all the four Nordic social democratic parties developed what Kitschelt has called 'essentially pragmatic, doctrineless, and populist redistributive programmes' (Kitschelt, 1994, p. 268). In Sweden and Denmark, the labour parties turned revisionist quite early. In the first decades of the 19th century the social democrats in these countries engaged in coalitions with the liberals but in different ways. In Denmark, these strategies paved the way for compromises on collective liberalist regulations in VET, and the modernization of apprenticeship. In Sweden, it produced an orientation towards the school as part of emerging democratization processes. The Norwegian labour party was radicalized and turned revisionist later than the others. This constellation left more political space for the liberals and several failed attempts at regulating VET schooling as well as apprenticeship. In Finland, temporalities were quite different, where the sudden majority of the social democrats quickly waned.

Also during the high point of social democratic rule, significant elements of the type of pragmatism can be identified, where the social democratic parties deliberated and implemented changes in the choice of means in VET policies. The ancestry of the comprehensive school in the four countries illustrates this type of pragmatism. Even though the Danish labour party had confirmed its preferences to apprenticeship in the mid-1950s, the crisis in apprenticeship during the 1960s challenged older orientations in the party, and new Nordic policy horizons pointed towards the adoption of the statist comprehensive school model in school policies. A path change towards a strong state-oriented unitary school confronted considerable resistance which could be attributed to core features of Danish state-society relations and the liberal tradition of Grundtvig. In partisan political terms, its ancestry could be dated back to the conservatives, whose reform proposals towards a unitary state-based school were strongly opposed by the Danish leftist-liberal movement (Froestad and Ravneberg, 2006). The construction of the comprehensive lower secondary school succeeded, providing a new basis for upper secondary level reform. But when political conditions deteriorated, the Social Democratic Party had to fall back to other forms of less radical VET reform, which closed in on social improvements based on the apprentice template.

In Norway, the comprehensive school project was originally a liberal project aiming at nation-building (Telhaug and Mediås, 2003). It reflected the subordinate role of Norway in relation to Denmark in the twin kingdom. The comprehensive school had been a major policy agenda for the great liberal coalition that lead up to democratization in the 1880s, and unlike in Denmark, it carried considerable legitimacy and support. The Labour Party had been divided on the issue of school policies, and strong radical segments in the party considered school integration as erroneous in principle. They wanted a parallel structure, a separate and more practical school for labour-class youth and a separately organized VET system. Until the end of the 1950s, this was the official party line. While the Norwegian social democrats in some sense 'stole' old robes from the liberals in school policies, the Swedish comprehensive school had a different ancestry. In Sweden, the conservatives and the farmer had been sceptical towards such a school (Richardsson, 1963), and the comprehensive school was a political programme that became identified with the social democrat reform during the 1960s. In Finland the comprehensive school was inspired by the

Swedish social democrats, and the social democrats were able to garner support from the agrarians. The development of the comprehensive school has followed different long-term paths in the Nordic countries, circumscribed by different actor constellations and traditions, where the social democrats have assumed different positions in time and in the different countries.

The expansive redistributive agenda of public funding in education and welfare and the massification of upper secondary education and training for youth represented another vital element in the social democratic toolbox. Also this agenda has been widely accepted in the Nordic countries. The explanation usually offered is that expenditure in education has evolved into a non-contested policy issue among most parties in the Nordic countries. As suggested by Ansell (2013), under conditions of mass education, even the conservatives have been willing to support increased spending on education. The increasing demand and changing aspirations in the population in education created challenges with which both the right and the left had deal. Also policies for the build-up of capacity in VET were supported by huge majorities in Parliament, but for different reasons. The right wanted to protect the gymnasiums as an elite institution, and advocated investments in VET as a mechanism of alleviation. Among labour party voters there was also an increased demand for general and higher education and support for a widening of choice. Even during the ideologically oriented 1970s, the political dynamics displayed considerable pragmatism and consensus on investments in education in general as well as in VET rather than strong and persistent conflicts along major party cleavages. All the country chapters display indications that support for the main direction in national VET policy has been and still is widespread in the four Parliaments. In general, the social democrats have pursued a pragmatic course of redistribution in VET based on various forms of modernization policies, also during liberalization, perhaps with Sweden as a marketization outlier. This finding conforms reasonably well with more general conclusions from broader comparative studies of administrative reform policies (Hansen, 2011; Pollitt and Bouckaert, 2004), as well as quantitatively oriented studies of relations between the social democratic government and policy reform in welfare (Merkel and Petring, 2007)

The second set of issues focuses on relations between the political dynamics and the preferences of collectively organized employers and unions in the formation of VET. Patterns of employer organization developed relatively parallel in Norway, Denmark and Sweden, Finland somewhat later. In Denmark, the formation of a national employers association gave the impetuous for the formation of the first national confederation of workers union. In Norway, the situation was the reverse.

As early as in the 1930, Sweden, Denmark and Norway were among the top countries measured by international statistics on union density, while Finland was one of the countries at the bottom. After the initial confrontations between the employers and the unions, a pattern gradually emerged, where central agreements and tariff building gradually emerged as conducive to both employer and worker interests. During the second period of the 20th century, the Nordic industrial relations landscape changed. Older structures were consolidated and rationalized, collective bargaining was centralized and organized around solidaristic wage policies, and wage dispersion remained low. As labour markets were liberalized and the service economy developed, the general European picture is characterized by a weakening of employer coordination (Hassel, 2015). But the Nordic countries do no display much sign of employer disintegration. Actually employer organization density has increased in the Nordic countries (Hassel, 2015). The fast decline of manufacturing and transition to services did not produce a significant decline in unionization rates either. While unionization in industries may have been weakened somewhat, the female-dominated welfare services have gained strength, and unionization rates have for some time been stronger in these areas of working life than in industry. The situation in Germany, where union density is highly skewed towards manufacturing and male blue-collar workers, is a strong contrast. Measured by employer organization and union density, the four Nordic countries have developed and sustained important conditions for coordination. As such, the Nordic countries should have a considerable capacity for coordination and collective action in VET, but still VET systems and employer preferences vary considerably.

Here the literature on skill formation systems provides some important insights. The political economy of skill formation literature treats the formation of VET as a product of the tensions between the state and parliamentary democracy on the one hand and the employers on the other, and how these tensions gravitated in different directions at particular historical moments. This type of explanation emphasizes the structuring of historically shaped configurations of actors and institutions (Dobbins and Busemeyer, 2014; Busemeyer and Trampusch, 2012b). A central distinction in this literature is statist versus collective skill formation systems (Busemeyer and Trampusch, 2012a). In general, the comprehensive school has been conceptualized as a prime example of a statist system in the political economy of skill formation literature, and as a proxy for measuring power relations between the state and the employers. Strongly simplified, when the state-based comprehensive school advanced, as in Sweden, the employers retreated (Dobbins and Busemeyer, 2014). When the employers were sufficiently strong, as in Denmark, firm-based apprentice training was retained, and the comprehensive school was shelved. Adding the Norwegian and Finnish cases to the comparison might provide new insights as well as new puzzles. The Norwegian case suggests that the rise of the comprehensive school institution does not necessarily imply the fall of firm-based apprentice training and the decline of employer involvement in training, as these arrangements seem to be able to coexist in various forms. Actually apprenticeship training in the firm has been growing in numbers since the formation of the upper secondary comprehensive school, and expanded to all areas of working life, heavily supported by state subsidies. The Finnish case presents a different complexion of actor constellations and trajectories. The Finnish industrial VET systems have many similarities to the Swedish, and unions/employers are organized along similar lines. Finnish employers have consistently followed a path where VET is the responsibility of the state, not the employers. The Finnish state has intervened more forcefully into labour market relations than the other Nordic countries, and there is nothing like the Swedish Saltsjøbaden tradition. Skill formation in the firm has remained the business of the individual employer. However, like the other Nordic countries, Finnish employers have been integrated in the state through corporatist arrangements and integrated participation in commissions of various types. Employers and unions have been able to develop influence on standardized curricula, training procedures and examination practices as well as definitions of proper implementation of state regulations in education and training and related activities. Arguably, the Nordic states seem to share a specific and persistent participatory modernization trajectory in VET, which should be explored further. Neither of the Nordic systems can fruitfully be described as 'pure' statist systems, like the French Napoleonic system, where the role that societal actors legitimately can play is small or almost illegitimate (Peters, 2008). As we have tried to unpack the puzzle of Nordic skill formation systems, the analytical value of statist systems as a counter model to collective skill formation systems or dual systems might be questioned. It could be asked whether autonomy and self-regulation in collectivist VET systems could be achieved through the state and the comprehensive school, and not from the state, which seems to be the normal asumption in the political economy of skill formation literature.

The third set of issues focuses on relations between VET and higher education and their embeddedness in the educational system. The historical formation of relations between higher education and VET in the Nordic countries has unfortunately not been much researched, and we will have to make do with bits and pieces. At the beginning of the First World War the percentage of students at the university comprised 0.8 percent in Norway, 0.9 percent in Sweden and 0.4 percent in Denmark, against the European average of 1.2 percent (Anderson, 2004). When such a very small percentage of the population progressed from primary education to the university, the term 'higher education' was often used to refer to secondary education (Schriewer et al., 2000). Higher education as a specific level in the educational structure evolved in the 1960s as part of the development of long-term planning in education. The general policy ideal was the construction of a new educational system capable of handling the new educational expansion: a system characterized by positive relations between educational level and tracks, a system which did not produce dead ends, a system that could accommodate the new spiralling demand for more and more equal education. The prevailing view of the universities changed, from institutions of culture to instruments for the democratization of society. Another central element in the common reform trajectory was the construction of new non-university higher education institutions. These institutions were in general formed through upgrading and mergers of vocational educations from the secondary level.

All the Nordic countries have developed Mass Public Models, characterized by high enrolment rates, by being almost entirely public and supported by high funding levels in higher education, and all four have reached a stage that can be described in terms of the universalization of access (Børjesson, Ahola,, Helland and Thomsen, 2014). However, the organization of their HE systems varies significantly. Denmark and Finland have developed towards a dual or binary higher education system: that is, a structure where higher education was taught in universities alongside more vocationally oriented college institutions, while Norway and Sweden have developed comprehensive HE systems. 'Comprehensive' does not mean lack of institutional diversity, but points towards standardization and the construction of comprehensive frameworks regulating relations between the university and the college sector. A crude description of structural characteristics might look like this, see Table 10.4.

Strongly simplified, the Norwegian and Swedish system combines comprehensive HE with comprehensive secondary systems, while Finland and Denmark combine binary systems at both levels. These processes did not produce 'disparate ladders' (Heidenheimer, 1997). Unlike other systems, as in Germany, early branching systems have been abolished in favor of the comprehensive school. The move towards the comprehensive organization of the educational system provided the basis for uniformly organized transitions across levels in time.

Up to the 1970s, different types of regulations and institutions structured VET and general education. During the 1970s, Sweden and Norway developed comprehensive systems where VET and general education potentially could be flexibly combined. In the binary form of organization, similar processes would take place within separate institutions designed for different purposes and target groups. The binary systems re-produced loose couplings between the gymnasiums and VET institutions, while comprehensive systems opened up space for institutional unification and even prospects of flexible combinations. Implementation processes did not confirm to these expectations, though, and early attempts at designing tracks crosscutting the old general education-VET divide have for the most part failed in both binary and comprehensively organized systems (Høst and Michelsen, 2018b; Jørgensen, 2018), even if individuals can combine modules from both types of tracks.

Also strategies for the promotion of VET and VET-HE relations vary. In Denmark, we can observe strategies which could be characterized as 'enhancement

Table 10.4 Structural characteristics of educational systems in four Nordic countries

Level/country	Denmark	Norway	Sweden	Finland
Higher education	Binary	Comprehensive	Comprehensive	Binary
Upper secondary	Binary Apprentice-based	Comprehensive Mixed	Comprehensive School-based	Binary School-based
Lower secondary	Comprehensive	Comprehensive	Comprehensive	Comprehensive

of VET' (Lasonen and Manning, 2000). This strategy seeks to improve VET as a separate track and emphasizes the distinct qualities of vocational education as well as the construction of bridges to the vocational part of higher education. Also Finland could be placed in this category, but with some elements of mutual enrichment between VET and general education. In Finland, this pattern has recently set the scene for the development of positive relations between Finnish higher education and upper secondary VET, as the number of applicants to the VET tracks is increasing and new pathways to the vocational part of HE are presently emerging. In Denmark, similar strategies can be identified, which also comprises attempts at 'softening' of levels at the intersection between upper secondary VET and the vocational part of higher education, and the development of 'open education', where 'normal' admission criteria do not apply. However, attempts at increasing permeability between VET and HE has not been particularly successful, measured by enrolments, which have remained small or negligible.

Within the two comprehensive systems, there are tendencies that could be interpreted in terms of 'structural harmonization' or perhaps even 'mutual enrichment' rather than 'different but equal' strategies. In Sweden and Norway, the formation of VET programmes has increasingly been measured by the standards provided by general education tracks, and VET programmes have been extended, broadened in contents, rationalized and streamlined. The idea of transcending the divide between general education and the development of flexible combinations between VET and general education during the 1970s made it difficult to rely on a 'different but equal' strategy. The integration and growth of apprentice training in the VET part of the comprehensive school in the 1990s have provided Norwegian VET programmes with a clear vocational profile. Even the Swedish system has recently taken on a stronger division between VET and academic tracks. Also in the two comprehensive systems, it has been difficult to develop increased permeability between VET and HE, as issues of academic drift, quality assurance policies, standardization, horizontal coordination across the vocational colleges and the universities in an encompassing HE field have made flexible adjustments on the vertical dimension towards VET difficult.

Reform patterns vary. As in secondary education, Sweden took the lead in reorganizing and reforming higher education. In 1977, all post-secondary education were upgraded in one comprehensive reform leap, and subjected to a common regulatory framework (Bauer et al., 1999). The university was now seen by social democratic policy-makers as a tool for the democratic reconstruction of Swedish society rather than an autonomous cultural institution in the old 'Humboldtian' sense. More than any other country in Europe, Sweden was in front in establishing a unified higher education system (Kim, 2002). The student population eligible for higher education was extended significantly to include vocational tracks. However, expanding formal criteria for access into higher education did not translate directly into higher education expansion and the construction of new pathways from VET. The 1977 reform was a strange combination of the expansion of access towards mass education with the introduction of *numerus clausus* policies restricting access (Bauer et al., 1999). In Norway, Finland and Denmark reform processes in HE had a more incremental character. But also in these countries, access was restricted by similar mechanisms setting limits to higher education intake. As a result, the growth in student number was slowed down or in some cases even reversed, in spite of a growing number of applications. In practice, mobility from VET to HE remained limited in all four countries. Since the 1990s Sweden and Finland have moved in different directions. In Finland new pathways have been constructed from VET to the vocational part of HE, while Sweden has reintroduced restrictions on access to HE in 2012.

A crude analysis of patterns of expansion in HE shows similar patterns for all four countries since the 1960s (Børjesson, Ahola, Helland and Thomsen, 2014). Two great waves of expansion can be identified for the four countries: one in the 1960s, the other in the 1990s. Very different conditions were at hand for each of the two phases. The first expansion of the 1960s was driven by stable economic growth, an increasing demand for a more skilled labour force and demographic growth. The expansion in the 1990s occurred in a time of economic stagnation, and with a declining youth population. Different reform trajectories and reclassifications of institutions migrating from secondary to HE in this period makes diachronic comparisons across educational levels difficult, but available data from 2010 show that Finland had the highest participation rate measured by age cohort data, followed by Norway, Denmark and Sweden (Børjesson, Ahola, Helland and Thomsen, 2014). Finland has had the strongest growth in HE admissions since the 1990s, and in 2010 the HE system could accommodate over 70 percent of the 19-year cohort (Ahola and Hedman, 2014). Norway has probably developed the most welfarist type of HE, where practically anyone that is formally qualified can obtain a study place. In the other countries access have been more restricted, circumscribed by matriculation requirements and/or capacity restrictions. Available data suggest that Denmark and Sweden combine high growth in HE with a marked reduction in youth enrolments in VET since the 1990s, while Norway and Finland combine high growth in HE enrolments with steady or slowly growing youth enrolments in VET upper secondary tracks. These data make it difficult to support conclusions on the distinct character of VET-HE relations, measured by expectations according to conventional distinctions between statist systems and apprentice-based/collective skill formation systems.

A possible Nordic model of skill formation

As discussed in the introduction, earlier studies of human capital formation or skill formation systems have identified different types of skill formation systems related to different types of political and capitalist environments, producing different dynamics and trajectories. Liberal (Anglo-Saxon) countries have developed educational systems with a bias towards academic HE with the USA as the undisputed leader in this development. The US system is highly stratified with world-class universities on top (Paradeise and Thoenig, 2013). However, the VET system is generally considered a choice for disadvantaged low-skilled youth who did not succeed in entering HE (Thelen, 2014). HE expansion has been seen as an important condition for US innovation capacity. Nevertheless, open-admission policies have had considerable costs. Continental countries like Germany make a clear contrast. Here the apprenticeship system has remained a popular alternative with prospects of getting into stable and well-paid jobs, and the scale and scope of HE remains below average for OECD countries in terms of enrolment and funding (Powell and Solga, 2011).

These profiles seem to suggest a possible trade-off between VET and HE, as strong systems of vocational training may inhibit the overexpansion of HE and 'master disease' (Busemeyer, 2014). The Nordic social democratic skill formation system may be seem as the expression of a type of skill formation system, characterized by strong state involvement, strong state financing and low individual funding. Nordic upper secondary and HE reforms might be seen as integral element of a similar social democratic reform programme, that of changing the educational system into a more efficient, egalitarian and democratic system, providing universal access and a flexible mix of skills. An alternative view, which might be suggested, is that the supply of skills is a product of two vast, publicly funded policy fields or organizational fields that have been weakly, if at all, coordinated. Major interest groups and the political parties representing them have provided broad interest coalitions that have favoured expansion. In all four countries VET and HE policies have been strongly oriented towards inclusion. However, as HE has reached conditions of saturation, this might be changing. There are now clear signs of a turn towards labour market relevance. In Finland the policy has been not to expand the system any more since the millennium, and to accommodate excess demand by rationalization processes (Ahola and Hedman, 2014). Also in Denmark, the growth rate in HE has been formidable the last 10 years, propelled by taximeter arrangements, leading to critical questions being asked about the need for an increasingly higher educated work force in the future (Thomsen, 2014). The Danish Productivity Commission considers the match between the production of new HE candidates and future labour market needs to be poor, and measures have been taken to reduce further expansion and increase labour market relevance in HE. Even though growth has continued in Norway and Sweden, there is an increasing focus on 'master disease' in Norway, and new actor constellations articulate the need for a shift in educational expansion towards new combinations of academic and more practical skills. Like VET, universities and university colleges have also become tools for the new social investment state (Morel et al., 2015) in all four countries. New mechanisms for employer influence in skill formation at the central and local levels have been constructed in order to secure labour market relevance and legitimacy in VET as well as in HE. This has challenged the institutional, organizational and cultural divide between VET and HE. These developments open up a number of intriguing research questions about the formation of HE and VET as educational and organizational fields in the Nordic countries, how these fields and their inter-relations have evolved remains to be answered in a more systematic way.

Some empirical and theoretical implications

In this book the various contributions have investigated various forms of change taking place in VET, in each of the periods identified. They have investigated state-induced reform and the resilience of institutions and practices in the formation of specific national paths. The paths taken by the four VET systems display a number of telling examples of institutional continuities, where intended radical reform plans that go against the grain have been blocked and relocked into national paths. The reform trajectories presented in the first part of the chapter and the examination of the coalitions that produced them emphasize a number of such processes. But the empirical chapters also focus on investigations of more slow-burning processes. Through conversion political actors are able to redirect VET institutions towards purposes beyond their original intent (Hacker, Pierson and Thelen, 2015). This can happen in a number of ways, through redirection or reinterpretation of rules. Conversion requires active reinterpretation of institutions and formal rules in order to serve new ends. A different mechanism is drift. Drift refers to the failure of decision-makers to update formal rules when the effects of these rules change due to changing contexts.

The Norwegian case of apprentice training and the skilled worker provide an interesting example of such gradual processes. The 1950 apprentice training reform was the first major regulation of apprentice training in industry. At first, the reform was 'eaten up' by the environment it was supposed to reform rather than transforming it, as practices in industry continued to adhere to older practices developed through the collective bargaining system, where the individual firm decided on the placement of the individual worker in the collective wage grid. The status and wages of the skilled worker could be obtained without any certification whatsoever over 20 years later in core areas of industry. As apprenticeship and skilled worker certification was evolving as the main road to the skilled worker category, these regulations were reinterpreted and tighter relations between the skilled worker wage category and certification gradually emerged. As older regulations specifying the possibility for workers from rural areas to take a skilled workers test when migrating to areas covered by apprentice regulations were reinterpreted, this option was subsequently converted into a general mechanism for the certification of all adult workers. As a result, two roads to the skilled worker category emerged, one through apprenticeship practice and schooling and the other through the prolonged practice in the firm supplemented with a skilled workers test. When the apprentice act was generalized to include the whole country, regulations on adult worker certification and mobility in space were reinterpreted and updated and apprentice law was transformed to VET law, suited to and incorporating adult learning in

1980. The two roads are now firmly entrenched in Norwegian regulations, and even if strong actors have wanted to erase the adult way to the skilled worker-category, it has so far been impossible to dismantle. This example illustrates the continuous tensions between formal regulations and practices in apprenticeship and certification in important areas of Norwegian industry. It also demonstrates the need to focus relations between different arenas, between skill formation regulations and the workings of the wage bargaining system over time.

Mixed or hybrid VET systems provide yet another interesting environment for the study of mechanisms of gradual change. Multiple interests might reproduce such patterns over time type where successful coalitions that produce reforms might generate reactions from other actors, where competing interests are mobilized and alternative policy solutions advocated in other parts in loosely coupled or mixed systems. At some points they might also evolve into new compounds, producing a new path or even a new delta of converging paths. Finland and Norway provide reform paths where reforms in VET schooling have been accompanied in apprentice training. At several points in time these reforms have come in pairs, during the period of liberalization as well as in the social democratic period. As such they represent relatively durable elements of the evolution of VET in both countries, and there is considerable overlap in the political justifications that have been made for their survival as instruments for social policy and adult learning. As far as the Norwegian development is concerned, we might even speak of a double institutionalization of two paths: the apprentice path and the VET schooling path as two competing or intertwined paths with different dynamics, before they were merged and amalgamated in the upper secondary comprehensive school, producing a new compound of general education, VET schooling and apprenticeship in 1994. In Finland, apprenticeship looks more like an auxiliary safety valve rather than a main road in skill formation, but policy-makers have found its survival sufficiently important to secure updating and modernization. The contrast to Sweden is interesting, where the formation of 'productive constraints' in the form of collectively organized apprenticeship arrangements for a long time has been a continually failing political project due to blocking activities among the employers and the unions. The Nordic experience illustrates that apprenticeship can be used for a number of political purposes and that it has been politically contested among political actors. In one country it emerged as the mainstay of VET, while in others it has been blocked, redirected and/or exposed to conversion.

The reform trajectories could be interpreted around a common theme of 'comparative statics', that is, that institutional differences explain cross-national divergence. The focus on coalitions has provided a more nuanced view. The contributions in this book have attempted to provide a new light on the formation of Nordic VET. We have also attempted a broad outlook where VET has been related to welfare capitalism and the comprehensive school system. The contributions point in various directions. The broad approach which has informed this book has provided a rich outlook on Nordic VET systems, and the suggestions provided should fuel further research on the history of Nordic VET systems and a possible Nordic skill formation system. There is yet much work to be done before we can make solid claims on the causes of VET change over such a long period. But this book will hopefully point out some promising directions for further research.

References

Ahola, S. and Hedman, J. (2014) 'Finland,' in Børjesson M., Ahola, S., Helland H. and Thomsen, J.-P. (eds.) *Enrolment Patterns in Nordic Higher Education ca. 1945–2010*, Oslo, NIFU Working Paper 15/2014.

Anderson, R. (2004) *European Universities From the Enlightenment to 1914*, Oxford, Oxford University Press.

Ansell, B. W. (2013) *From the Ballot to the Blackboard: The Redistributive Political Economy of Education*, Cambridge, Cambridge University Press.

Antikainen, A. (2006) 'In search of the Nordic model in education', *Scandinavian Journal of Educational Research*, vol. 50, no. 3, pp. 229–243.

Arnesen, A. L. and Lundahl, L. (2006) 'Still social and democratic? Inclusive education policies in the Nordic welfare states', *Scandinavian Journal of Educational Research*, vol. 50, no. 3, pp. 285–300.

Arter, D. (2008) *Scandinavian Politics Today*, Manchester, Manchester University Press.

Baccaro, L. and Howell, C. (2017) *Unhinged: Industrial Relations Liberalization and Capitalist Instability*, MPIfG Discussion Paper 17/19, Cologne, Max Planck Institute for the Study of Societies.

Bauer, M., Askling, B., Marton, S.G. and Marton, F. (1999) *Transforming Universities: Changing Patterns of Governance, Structure and Learning in Swedish Higher Education*. Philadelphia, Taylor and Francis.

Benavot, A. (1983) 'The rise and decline of vocational education', *Sociology of Education*, vol. 56, no. 2, pp. 63–76.

Berman, S. (2006) *The Primacy of Politics: Social Democracy and the Making of Europe's Twentieth Century*, New York, Cambridge University Press.

Bjørnson, Ø. (2001) 'The social democrats and the Norwegian welfare state: Some perspectives', *Scandinavian Journal of History*, vol. 26, no. 3, pp. 197–223.

Bleiklie, I., Høstaker, R. and Vabø, A. (2000). *Policy and Practice in Higher Education: Reforming Norwegian Universities*, London and Philadelphia, Jessica Kingsley Publishers.

Børjesson M., Ahola, S., Helland H. and Thomsen, J.-P. (eds.) (2014) *Enrolment Patterns in Nordic Higher Education ca. 1945–2010*, Oslo, NIFU Working Paper 15/2014.

Börjesson, M., Bertilsson, E. and Dalberg, T. (2014) 'Sweden', in Børjesson M., Ahola, S., Helland H. and Thomsen, J.-P. (eds.) *Enrolment Patterns in Nordic Higher Education ca. 1945–2010*, Oslo, NIFU Working Paper 15/2014, pp. 93–125.

Busemeyer, M. R. (2014) *Skills and Inequality: Partisan Politics and the Political Economy of Education reforms in Western Welfare States,* Cambridge, Cambridge University Press.

Busemeyer, M. R. and Trampusch, C. (2012a) 'The comparative of political economy of collective skill formation', in Busemeyer, M. R. and Trampusch, C. (eds.) *The Political Economy of Collective Skill Formation*, Oxford, Oxford University Press, pp. 3–40.

Busemeyer, M. R. and Trampusch, C. (eds.) (2012b) *The Political Economy of Collective Skill Formation*, Oxford, Oxford University Press.

Campbell, J. L. (2004) *Institutional Change and Globalization*, Princeton, Princeton University Press.

Christiansen, F. C. and Markkola, P. (2006) 'Introduction', in Christiansen, N. F., Petersen, K., Edling, N. and Haave, P. (eds.) *The Nordic Model of Welfare, a Historical Reappraisal*, Copenhagen, Museum Tuscalanum Press, University of Copenhagen, pp. 17–59.

Christiansen, N. F. and Petersen, K. (2001) 'The dynamics of social solidarity: The Danish welfare state, 1900–2000', *Scandinavian Journal of History*, vol. 26, no. 3, pp. 177–196.

Crouch, C., Sako, M. and Finegold, D. (2001) *Are Skills the Answer? The Political Economy of Skill Creation in Advanced Industrial Countries*, Oxford, Oxford University Press.

Demker, M. and Svåsand, L. (2005) 'Den nordiska fempartimodellen: En tilfällighet eller et fundament?', in Demker, M. and Svåsand, L. (eds.) *Partiernas århundre. Fempartimodellens uppgång och fall i Norge och Sverige*, Stockholm, Santerus Forlag, pp. 9–38.

Dobbins, M. and Busemeyer, M. L. (2014) 'Socioeconomic institutions, organized interests and partisan politics: The development of vocational education in Denmark and Sweden', *Socio-Economic Review*, vol. 13, no. 2, pp. 259–284.

Dølvik, J. E. (2008) 'The Negotiated Nordic Labour Markets. From Bust to Boom,' Center for European Studies, Working Paper Series 162, Harvard University.

Elvander, N. (2002) 'The labour market regimes in the Nordic countries: A comparative analysis', *Scandinavian Political Studies*, vol. 25, no. 2, pp. 117–137.

Esping-Andersen, G. (1991) *The Three Worlds of Welfare Capitalism*, Princeton, NJ, Princeton University Press.

Esping-Andersen G. (2005) 'Education and equal life chances: Investing in children', in Kangas, O. and Palme, J. (eds.) *Social Policy and Economic Development in the Nordic Countries*, Basingstoke, Palgrave Macmillan, pp. 147–162.

Fellman, S. (2008) 'Growth and investment: Finnish capitalism, 1850–2005', in Fellman, S., Iversen, M. J., Sjøgren, H. and Thue, L. (eds.) *Creating Nordic Capitalism: The Business History of a Competitive Periphery*, Basingstoke, Palgrave Macmillan, pp. 139–218.

Froestad, J. and Ravneberg, B. (2006) 'Educational policy, the Norwegian unitary school and the social construction of disability', *Scandinavian Journal of History*, vol. 31 no. 2, pp. 119–143.

Gingrich, J. and Ansell, B. (2015) 'The dynamics of social investment: Human capital, activation and care', in Beramendi, P., Haüsermann, S., Kitschelt, H. and Kriesi, H. J. (eds.) *The Politics of Advanced Capitalism*, Cambridge, Cambridge University Press, pp. 282–304.

Graf, L. (2013) *The Hybridization of Vocational Training and Higher Education in Austria, Germany and Switzerland*, Berlin and Toronto, Budrich UniPress Ltd.

Green-Pedersen, C. (2002) 'New public management reforms of the Danish and Swedish welfare states: The role of different social democratic responses', *Governance*, vol. 15, no. 2, pp. 271–294.

Hacker, J., Pierson, P. and Thelen, K. (2015) 'Drift and conversion: Hidden faces of institutional change', in Mahoney, J. and Thelen, K. (eds.) *Advances in Comparative-Historical Analysis*, Cambridge, Cambridge University Press, pp. 180–210.

Hall, P. H. and Soskice, D. (2001) *Varieties of Capitalism: The Institutional Foundations of Comparative Advantage*, Oxford, Oxford University Press.

Hansen, H. F. (2011) 'NPM in Scandinavia', in Christensen, T. and Lægreid, P. (eds.) *Ashgate Research Companion to New Public Management*, Aldershot, Ashgate, pp. 113–129.

Hassel, A. (2015) 'Trade unions and the future of democratic capitalism', in Beramendi, P., Haüsermann, S., Kitschelt, H. and Kriesi, H. (eds.) *The Politics of Advanced Capitalism*, Cambridge, Cambridge University Press, pp. 231–258.

Hasselblanch, O. (2003) *The Roots – the History of Nordic Labour Law*, Stockholm, Stockholm Institute for Scandinavian Law.

Heidenheimer, A. (1997) *Disparate Ladders: Why School and University Policies Differ in Germany, Japan, and Switzerland*, New Brunswick, Transaction Publishers.

Heikkinen, A. (2004) 'Models, paradigms or cultures of vocational education', *European Journal of Vocational Training*, vol. 32, no. 2, pp. 32–44.
Hickox, M. and Lyon, E. S. (1998) 'Vocationalism and schooling: The British and Swedish experiences compared', *British Journal of Sociology of Education*, vol. 19, no. 1, pp. 25–37.
Huber, E. and Stephens, J. D. (2001) *Development and Crisis of the Welfare State. Parties and Policies in Global Markets,* Chicago, University of Chicago Press.
Iversen, M. J. and Andersen, S. (2008) 'Co-operative liberalism: Denmark from 1857 to 2007', in Fellman, S., Iversen, M. J., Sjøgren, H. and Thue, L. (eds.) *Creating Nordic Capitalism: The Business History of a Competitive Periphery*, Basingstoke, Palgrave Macmillan, pp. 265–335.
Iversen, M. J. and Thue, L. (2008) 'Creating Nordic capitalism – the business history of a competitive periphery', in Fellman, S., Iversen, M. J., Sjøgren, H. and Thue, L. (eds.) *Creating Nordic Capitalism: The Business History of a Competitive Periphery*, Basingstoke, Palgrave Macmillan, pp. 1–19.
Iversen, T. and Soskice, D. (2006) 'Electoral institutions and the politics of coalitions: Why some democracies redistribute more than others', *American Political Science*, vol. 100, no. 2, pp. 165–181.
Iversen, T. and Stephens, J. D. (2008) 'Partisan politics, the welfare state and the three worlds of human capital formation', *Comparative Political Studies*, vol. 41, no. 4–5, pp. 600–637.
Jørgensen, C. H. (2018) 'The modernisation of the apprenticeship system in Denmark 1945–2015', in Michelsen, S. and Stenström, M.-L. (eds.) *Vocational Education in the Nordic Countries: The Historical Evolution*, London, Routledge, pp. 171–189.
Jørgensen, C. H. and Bøndergaard, G. (2018) 'Historical evolution of vocational education in Denmark until 1945', in Michelsen, S. and Stenström, M.-L. (eds.) *Vocational Education in the Nordic Countries: The Historical Evolution*, London, Routledge, pp. 84–101.
Juul, I. (2009) 'Fra lavsvæsen til fagligt selvstyre. Arbejdsgivernes indflydelse på erhvervsuddannelserne i perioden 1857–1937', *Økonomi/Politik*, vol. 82, no. 3, pp. 3–14.
Juul, I. and Jørgensen, C. F. (2011) 'Challenges for the dual system and occupational self-governance in Denmark', *Journal of Vocational Education & Training*, vol. 63, no. 3, pp. 289–303.
Kangas, O. and Palme, J. (2005) 'Coming late – catching up: The formation of a "Nordic model", in Kangas O. and Palme, J, (eds.) *Social Policy and Economic Development in the Nordic Countries,* Basingstoke, Palgrave Macmillan, pp. 17–53.
Kettunen, P. (2001) 'The Nordic welfare state in Finland', *Scandinavian Journal of History*, vol. 26, no. 3, pp. 225–247.
Kettunen, P. (2006) 'The power of international comparison – A perspective on the making and challenging of the Nordic welfare state', in Christiansen, N. F., Petersen, K., Edling, N. and Haave, P. (eds.) *The Nordic Model of Welfare. Copenhagen: A Historical Reappraisal,* Copenhagen, Museum Tuscalanum Press, pp. 31–67.
Kim, L. (2002) *Lika olika. En jamförande studie av høgre utbildning och forskning i de nordiske länderna*, Stockholm, Høgskoleverket.
Kitschelt, H. (1994) *The Transformation of European Social Democracy*, Cambridge, Cambridge University Press.
Kjellberg, A. (2002) 'Ett nytt fackligt landskap – i Sverige och utomlands', *Arkiv för studier i arbetarrörelsens historia*, vol. 86–87, pp. 44–96.
Korpi, W. (1978) *The Working Class in Welfare Capitalism*. London, Routledge and Keegan Paul.
Lasonen, J. and Manning, S. (2000) 'Improving the standing of vocational as against general education in Europe: A conceptual framework', in Stenström, M.-L. and Lasonen, J. (eds.) *Strategies for Reforming Initial Vocational Education and Training in Europe*, Jyväskylä, University of Jyvaskylä, pp. 316–325.
Lindell, I. (1992) *Disiciplinering og yrkesutbildning. Reformarbeidet bakom 1918 års praktiska ungdomsskolereform*, Forening for svensk Undervisningshistorie.

Lundahl, L. (1997) 'A common denominator? Swedish employers, trade unions and vocational training', *International Journal of Training and Development*, vol. 1, no. 2, pp. 91–103.

Lundahl, L. (2016) 'Equality, inclusion and marketization of Nordic education: Introductory notes', *Comparative & International Education*, vol. 11, no. 1, pp. 1–10.

Lundahl, L., Erixon Arreman, I., Lundström, U. and Rönnberg, L. (2010) 'Setting things right? Swedish upper secondary school reform in a 40 year perspective', *European Journal of Education*, vol. 45, no. 1, pp. 46–59.

Lundahl, L. and Sander, T. (1998) 'Introduction: Germany and Sweden – two different systems of vocational education?', in Lundahl, L. and Sander, T. (eds.) *Vocational Education and Training in Germany and Sweden: Strategies of Control and Movements of Resistance and Opposition. Report From a Symposium*, Thematic Network of Teacher Education in Europe (TNTEE) Publications, Umeå, vol. 1, no. 1, pp. 7–24.

Mahoney, J. and Thelen, K. (2010) 'A theory of gradual institutional change', in Mahoney, J. and Thelen, K. (eds.) *Explaining Institutional Change: Ambiguity, Agency and Power*, Cambridge, Cambridge University Press, pp. 1–37.

Martin, C. J. (2012) 'Political institutions and the origins of collective skill formation systems', in Busemeyer, M. R. and Trampusch, C. *The Political Economy of Skill Formation*, Oxford, Oxford University Press, pp. 41–68.

Martin, C. J and Swank, D. (2012) *The Political Construction of Business Interests. Coordination, Growth and Equality*, Cambridge, Cambridge University Press.

Merkel, W. and Petring, A. (2007) 'Social democracy in power: Explaining the capacity to reform', *Zeitschrift für Vergleichende Politikwissenschaft*, vol. 1, no. 1, pp. 125–145.

Michelsen, S. and Høst, H. (2018a) 'The case of Norwegian VET- origins and early development 1850–1945', in Michelsen, S. and Stenström, M.-L. (eds.) *Vocational Education in the Nordic Countries: The Historical Evolution*, London, Routledge, pp. 66–83.

Michelsen, S. and Høst, H. (2018b) 'Norwegian VET and the ascent and demise of social democracy 1945–2015', in Michelsen, S. and Stenström, M.-L. (eds.) *Vocational Education in the Nordic Countries: The Historical Evolution*, London, Routledge, pp. 146–170.

Morel, N., Palier, B., Palme, J. (eds.) (2015) *Towards a Social Investment Welfare State? Ideas, Policies and Challenges*, Bristol, Policy Press.

Nelson, M. (2012) 'Continued collectivism: The role of trade self-management and the social-democratic party in Danish vocational education and training', in Busemeyer, M. R. and Trampusch, C. *The Political Economy of Skill Formation*, Oxford, Oxford University Press, pp. 179–205.

Nielsen, S. P. and Cort, P. (1998) *Vocational Education and Training in Denmark*, 2nd ed., Thessaloniki, European Centre for the Development of Vocational Training.

Nieminen, A. (2000) 'Finnish employer confederations, streamlining in organization and regulating national capitalism', in Jensen, C. S. (ed.) *Arbeidsgivere i Norden. En sociologisk analyse av arbeidsgiverorganiseringen i Norge, Sverige, Finland og Danmark*, NORD 200:25, København, Nordisk Ministerråd, pp. 287–365.

Nilsson, A. (2007) 'Current national strategies in vocational education and training: Convergence or divergence?', *European Journal of Vocational Training*, no. 41, pp. 150–162.

Nycander, S. (2002) *Makten över arbetsmarknaden. Ett perspektiv på Sveriges 1900-tal*, Stockholm, SNS Förlag.

Olofsson, J. and Persson Thunquist, D. P. (2018a) 'Sweden: The formative period for VET (1850–1945)', in Michelsen, S. and Stenström, M.-L. (eds.) *Vocational Education in the Nordic Countries: The Historical Evolution*, London, Routledge, pp. 46–65.

Olofsson, J. and Persson Thunquist, D. P. (2018b) 'The modern evolution of VET in Sweden (1945–2015)', in Michelsen, S. and Stenström, M.-L. (eds.) *Vocational Education in the Nordic Countries: The Historical Evolution*, London, Routledge, pp. 124–145.

Paradeise, C. and Thoenig, J.-C. (2013) 'Academic institutions in search of quality: Local orders and global standards', *Organization Studies*, vol. 34, no. 2, pp. 189–218.

Peters, J. B. (2008) 'The Napoleonic tradition', *International Journal of Public Sector Management*, vol. 21, no. 2, pp. 118–132.

Pierson, P. (2004) *Politics in Time: History, Institutions, and Social Analysis*, Princeton and Oxford, Princeton University Press.

Pollitt, C. and Bouckaert, G. (2004) *Public Management Reform: A Comparative Analysis*, 2nd ed., Oxford, Oxford University Press.

Pontusson, J. (2005) *Inequality and Prosperity: Social Europe Versus Liberal America*, Ithaca and London, Cornell University Press.

Powell, J. J. W. and Solga, H. (2011) 'Why are higher education participation rates in Germany so low? Institutional barriers to higher education expansion', *Journal of Education and Work*, vol. 24, no. 1–2, pp. 49–68.

Rainio-Niemi, J. (2004). *Path in Austrian and Finnish History: Finland*, Helsinki, University of Helsinki.

Richardson, G. (1963) *Kulturkamp och Klasskamp. Ideologiska och sociala motsättningar i svensk skol- och kulturpolitikk under 1800-talet*, Gøteborg, Akademiforlaget.

Rothstein, B. (2010) *The Social Democratic State: Swedish Model and the Bureaucratic Problem*, Pittsburgh, University of Pittsburgh Press.

Sahlberg P. (2010) 'Educational change in Finland', in Hargreaves A., Lieberman A., Fullan M. and Hopkins D. (eds.) *Second International Handbook of Educational Change*, Springer International Handbooks of Education, vol. 23, Dordrecht, Springer, pp. 323–349.

Sejersted, F. (2011) *The Age of Social Democracy: Norway and Sweden in the Twentieth Century*, Princeton and Oxford, Princeton University Press.

Senghaas, D. (1985) *The European Experience: A Historical Critique of Development Theory*. New Hampshire, Berg Publishers.

Stenström, M.-L. and Virolainen, M. (2018a) 'The development of Finnish vocational education and training from 1880 to 1945', in Michelsen, S. and Stenström, M.-L. (eds.) *Vocational Education in the Nordic Countries: The Historical Evolution*, London, Routledge, pp. 24–45.

Stenström, M.-L. and Virolainen, M. (2018b) 'The modern evolution of vocational education and training in Finland (1945–2015)', in Michelsen, S. and Stenström, M.-L. (eds.) *Vocational Education in the Nordic Countries: The Historical Evolution*, London, Routledge, pp. 102–123.

Stratmann, Karlwilhelm (1993) *Die gewerbliche Lehrling Erziehung in Deutschland. Modernisierungsgeschichte der betrieblichen Berufsbildung*, Band 1. Frankfurt am Main, Verlag zur Förderung arbeitsorientierter Forschung und Bildung.

Streeck, W. and Thelen. K. (2004) *Beyond Continuity: Institutional Change in Advanced Political Economies*, Oxford, Oxford University Press.

Streeck, W. and Thelen, K. (2005) *Beyond Continuity: Institutional Change in Advanced Political Economies*, Oxford, Oxford University Press.

Swenson, P. A. (2002) *Capitalists Against Markets: The Making of Labour Markets and Welfare States in the United States and Sweden*, New York, Oxford University Press.

Telhaug, A. O and Mediås, O. A. (2003) *Grunnskolen som nasjonsbygger: fra statspietisme til nyliberalisme*, Oslo, Abstrakt forlag.

Telhaug, A. O., Mediås, O. A. and Aasen, P. (2006) 'The Nordic model in education: Education as part of the political system in the past 50 years', *Scandinavian Journal of Educational Research*, vol. 50, no. 3, pp. 245–283.

Thelen, K. (2004) *How Institutions Evolve: The Political Economy of Skills in Germany, Britain, The United States, and Japan*, Cambridge, Cambridge University Press.

Thelen, K. (2014) *Varieties of Liberalization and the New Politics of Social Solidarity*, Cambridge, Cambridge University Press.

Thelen, K. (2015) 'Drift and conversion: Hidden faces of institutional change', in Mahoney, J. and Thelen, K. (eds.) *Advances in Comparative-Historical Research*, Cambridge, Cambridge, University Press, pp. 180–208.

Thelen, K. and Busemeyer, M. L. (2012) 'Institutional change in German vocational training: From collectivism toward segmentalism', in Busemeyer, M. R. and Trampusch, C. (eds.) *The Political Economy of Skill Formation*, Oxford, Oxford University Press, pp. 68–101.

Thomsen, J.P. (2014) 'Denmark', in Børjesson M., Ahola, S., Helland H. and Thomsen, J.-P. (eds.) *Enrolment Patterns in Nordic Higher Education ca. 1945–2010*, Oslo, NIFU Working Paper 15/2014, pp. 17–34.

Thue, L. (2008) 'Norway: A resource based and democratic capitalism', in Fellman, S., Iversen, M. J., Sjøgren, H. and Thue, L. (eds.) *Creating Nordic Capitalism: The Business History of a Competitive Periphery*, Basingstoke, Palgrave Macmillan, pp. 394–494.

Trampusch, C. and Spies, D. C. (2014) 'Agricultural interests and the origins of capitalism: A parallel comparative history of Germany, Denmark, New Zealand, and the USA', *New Political Economy*, vol. 19, no. 6, pp. 918–942.

Välimaa, J. and Neuvonen-Rauhala, M.-L. (2008) 'Polytechnics in Finnish higher education', in Taylor, J. S., Brites Ferreira, J., de Lourdes Machado, M. and Santiago, R. (eds.) *Non-University Higher Education in Europe*, Higher Education Dynamics, vol. 23, Netherlands, Springer, pp. 77–98.

Wiborg, S. (2009) *Education and Social Integration: Comprehensive Schooling in Europe. Secondary Education in a Changing World*, New York, Palgrave Macmillan.

Young, M. (1993) 'Bridging the acdemic/vocational devide: Two nordic case studies', *European Journal of Education*, vol. 28, no. 2, pp. 209–214.

Index

Note: Page numbers in **bold** indicate a table on the corresponding page, and page numbers in *italic* indicate a figure on the corresponding page.

access to higher education 108–109, 126, 133, 137, 155, 167, 177, 179, 187, 196
access to labour market/employment 126, 137, 178, 181, 184–185, 187
active labour market policies (ALMPs) 16, 160, 164, 198–199, 207, 214, 215
adult education *see* advanced vocational education (AVE)
advanced vocational education (AVE) 137
agriculture: in Denmark 88–89; in Finland **30**, 30–31, 37, 103–104, 116; in Norway 68, 147
ammattikorkeakoulu (AMK) 110
ammattikoulut see vocational schools
apprenticeship *see under specific countries*
Apprenticeship Commission 173
Arbeiderpartiet (Labour Party) 71
ArbejdsMarkedsUddannelser (AMU) 174
Arbetsmarknadens yrkesråd (labour market trade council) 50
area studies 8–9
Association of Finnish Trade Unions (*Suomen Ammattijärjestö*) 36

Basic Agreement (Saltsjöbaden) 53, 54–56, 74, 127, 205

capitalism: agricultural 88, 203; coordinated 200; and liberalization of guild forms 7; and social democracy 218; and VET research 4–5; and welfare 3; and the West Nordic model 10–11; *see also* variety of capitalism (VoC); welfare capitalism
Central Organisation of Finnish Trade Unions (SAK) 36, 38, 106, 208–209
Central School Board (*Skolöverstyrelsen*) 134

collective skill formation systems 12–14, 222
commodification 15–16, 206; *see also* decommodification
comprehensive school/schooling 3, 4, 7, 12, 13, 14, 19, 47, 48, 49, 78, 79, 81, 84, 95, 106, 107, 112, 113, 118, 124, 127, 133, 146, 147, 149, 152, 153, 155, 156, 157, 165, 166, 167, 177, 179, 187, 194, 195, 198, 199, 205, 207, 209, 210, 212, 217, 218, 219, 220, 221, 222, 223, 224, 228, 240
comprehensive systems 224
Confederation of Danish Employers (DA) 89
Confederation of Norwegian Enterprises (NHO) 165, 217
continuation schools 29, 31–32, 41, 79, 152, 194
coordinated market economies (CMEs) 9, 18
Council of Vocational Training 77
craft associations 71–72, 178, 211
crafts and industry **10**, 28–32, 66, 71–75, 77, 147

Danish Confederation of Trade Unions (LO) 89, 96, 172, 187, 210, 216
decommodification 3, 14–16, 206
deindustrialization 159–160, 191
democratization 66, 80, 200–202, 205–207, 219, 222
Denmark: apprenticeship and VET in 171–172, 176–181; coalitions and policy paths in 203–204; decline and revival of apprenticeships in 90–91; development of

VET since 1945 in 186–188; enrolment in upper secondary education in *175*; guilds and apprenticeship regulation in 85–88; guilds and the Free Trade Act in 88–90; historical evolution of VET in 84–85, 97–98; hybrid qualifications 185–186; industrialisation and youth cohorts in 172–176; liberalization and VET in 215–216; the Social Democratic Party and VET in 95–97; social democratic VET in 210–211; social inclusion and education for all in 181–186; social inclusion and VET in 181–186; the state and VET in 91–95; *see also* Nordic countries

diachronic analysis 4, 6, 161, 199, 225
drawing schools 67
drivers 9–12

elementary education *see* unified comprehensive school
elementary school 28, 47–48, 128
Employers' Reimbursement Scheme (AUB) 184
employment 16, 34, 52, 90, 93, 115, 126, 135, 156, 163, 171, 184, 187
European Credit System for VET (ECVET) 112
Europeanisation 109–116, *113*
European Qualification Framework (EQF) 112
European Union 109
evening schools 27, 51, 67–68, 75, 80, 94

farmers 32, 68, 71, 88, 91, 98, 200; *see also* agriculture
Fennoman nationalist movement 24–25, 29, 40–41
Finland: apprenticeship training in 37–40, **39**, 105; coalitions and policy paths in 202–203; employer and employee organisations in 35–37; folk schools and VET in 28–30; foundation phase of institutionalized VET in 30–33; globalisation and VET in 109–116, *113*; guild systems and VET in 25–26; historical background to VET in 24–25, 40–41, **45**; liberalization and VET in 214–215; links between VET and working life in 110–112; modern evolution of VET in 102–103, 116–119; reform of vocational upper secondary education in 107–108; social democratic VET in 208–210; social inclusion and VET in 33–35, **34**; strengthening school-based VET in 107–108; Sunday schools and VET in 26–28; transition from VET to labour market and higher education in 115–116; the welfare state and VET in 103–109, **105**; *see also* Nordic countries
Finnish Employers' Confederation (EK) 38
Finnish Employers' Confederation (STK) 35–36, 106
Finnish National Board of Education (FNBE) 105
First World War 49, 88, 222
folk school 27–31
framhaldskolen see continuation schools
Free Trades Act of 1857 84

gender 133; and Danish VET system 181; and division of labour 150; and Finnish VET system 34–35, 104, 114; the folk school and 28; Norwegian labour market and 165; and UAS system 116
General Confederation of Employers (*Suomen Yleinen Työnantajaliitto*) 35
general education: folk school in Sweden 27–30; and modern evolution of VET in Finland 107–108; *see also* gymnasiums
globalisation 109–116, *113*, 117, 124, 134, 136, 185
Grundtvigianism 91
guilds 8–9, 191, **192**, 192–193, 200; in Denmark 84–92, 94, 97; in Finland 25–26, 29, 37, 105, 118, 202; in Norway 8, 69–71, 81; in Sweden 46
gymnasiums: binary systems and 223; in Denmark 92, 95, 96, 171, 173, 176–177, 179–183; as elite institutions 212, 220; in Finland 209; and higher education 196; in Norway 147–149, *148*, 152–155; in social democratic period 194; in Sweden 124, 133

higher education (HE)/higher education systems 2, 4, 8, 11–12, 17–18, 108–110, 114, 115–116, 117, 133, 134, 138, **144**, 153–155, *158*, 167, 176–181, 186–188, 196–197, 216, 222–225
higher vocational education (HVE) 110, 118, 137, 153, 186
historical institutionalism 4–8, 9, 19, 85, 200
Høire (conservatives) 71, 76

industrialization: and democratic welfare 15; in Denmark 88, 91, 172, 210; in Finland 25, **30**, 30–33, 39, 41, 102–104, 202; in Norway 66, 68, 69, 73, 80; in Sweden 46, 63; and VET formation 8, 200; *see also* deindustrialization

initial vocational education and training 41, 102, 105, 111, 114, 115, 118
Institute for Occupational Advancement (*Ammattienedistämislaitos*) 33
International Labour Organisation (ILO) 62, 164

joint representations **10**, 72, 89

kansakoulu see folk school

labour market **10**, 15–16, 37–40, 50, 92–93, 98, 115–116, 136–137, 173–176, 184–185
Labour Market Commission 173, **194**, 195
Labour Party: in Denmark 218; in Finland 202; in Norway 71–72, 146–149, 152, 166, 205–206, 211–212, 219; in Sweden 207
laissez faire 70–72, 74, 77, 80, 201, 205
Laki ammattioppilaitoksista see 'Vocational Institutions Act'
Latin School *see* Learned School
Learned School 93
liberal market economies (LMEs) 9

market economies *see* coordinated market economies (CMEs); liberal market economies (LMEs)
Mass Public Model(s) 18, 223
mercantilism 69–70
migration 30, 32, 104, 137

National Association of Mechanical Enterprises (MVL) 157
National Society of Women 78
National Union of Norwegian Pupils 163–164
New Public Management (NPM) 160, 196, 213, 215, 216
Nordic countries: approaches to research on VET in 4–5; comparative study of VET in 191–192, 200, 206, 212–213, 218–225, **223**; incorporation of VET into policy agendas of 16; institutional change in VET trajectories in 199–200; liberalization and VET in 196–199, **197**; the liberalization of VET in **192**, 192–194; and origins of VET 1–4, 18–19; similarities between x, 1–2; social democracy and VET in **194**, 194–196; theoretical perspectives on VET in 5–9; trajectories and drivers of VET in 9–12, **10**
Nord-VET x–xi, 85, 115

Norway: apprenticeship in 155–160, *158, 162*; ascent of the liberal state in 71–72; coalitions and policy paths in 205–206; collective institutions in 72–74; the comprehensive school model in 149–153, *151*; crafts and industry in 74–75; democratic and bureaucratic origins of VET in 68–69; formation of VET in 66–68, 80–81; guilds in 69–71; higher education and VET in 153–155, *154*; the interventionist state and VET in 147–149, *148*; liberalization and VET in 216–217; policy shifts in 160–163; school modernization concepts in 78–80; social democracy and VET in 146–147, 166–168, 211–212; state commitment and employer interest in VET in 75–78, 163–166; *see also* Nordic countries
Norwegian Association of Crafts (NHF) 75, 77
Norwegian Association of Industry (NI) 75, 77, 156–157
Norwegian Confederation of Trade Unions (LO) 165, 217
Norwegian Federation of Employers (NAF) 73, 80, 157
Norwegian Federation of Labour (AFL) 73, 80
Norwegian Handicraft Association 78

partisan politics 4–5, 11–12, 80, 207–208
peruskoulu see unified comprehensive school
polytechnics 109–110, 116, 214–215
poverty 34, 104
private industrial schools (*Yksityisteollisuuden ammattikoulut*) 33

Regional School Boards (*Länsskolenämnderna*) 134
Royal Norwegian Society for Development 78
rural communities 26, 32; *see also* agriculture; farmers

Saltsjöbaden *see* Basic Agreement
school-based education and learning 46, 55–56, 94, 118, 214–215
school-based model/system 46, 112, 117, 118, 124, 155, 199
school-based training 85, 91, 95, 97, 98, 174, 176, 178, 181, 183, 186, 211, 214, 217
school-based VET 14, 28, 31, 38, 39, 41, 46, 50, 53, 54, 56, 84, 103, 104, 106,

107–108, 117, 125, 126–130, 133–136, 155, 156, 161, 167, 176, 178, 193, 198, 201, 206, 208
Second World War: and baby boom in Sweden 130; and collective agreements in Finland 35; and coordinated labour market system in Finland 36; and employment structure in Denmark 172; and trade unions in Sweden 127; and VET in Finland 32–33, 103–106, **105**, 109, 112–114, 116–118, 208; and VET in Norway 147; and VET in Sweden 56
September Agreement 89–90, 92, 204
skill formation 1–4, 17–18, 198–199, 221–222, 228–229; in Denmark 85–88; in Finland 215; Nordic model of 225–227; in Norway 68, 74, 77, 80–81, 156–157, 164–168, 217; and social investment 2–3; *see also* collective skill formation systems
skolepraktik (SKP) 183, **197**
social democracy 1, 7–8, 15, 166, 218–225
social democratic parties 11–12, 15, 95–97, 200, 206, 213, 218–219
Sunday schools 26–28, 31, 38, 51, 67, 94, 104
Sweden: apprenticeship system in 50–51, 53–56; coalitions and policy paths in 200–202; compulsory education and VET in 47–50; differentiated VET system in 126–128, 136–140, *138*; formative period for VET in 46–47, 63; interwar period and VET in 51–53; liberalization and VET in 213–214; long-term view of VET in 140–141; modern evolution of VET in 124–126, **144, 145**; school-based VET system in 128–130, 133–136, *135*; social democratic VET in 206–208; upper secondary VET system in 130–133; voluntary initiatives and VET in 56–63; workshop schools in 53–56; *see also* Nordic countries
Swedish Association of Industry 75
Swedish Employers' Confederation (SAF) 53–55, 57–58, 125, 127, 129, 208, 213
Swedish Government Official Reports Series (SOU) 128
Swedish School Inspectorate 139
Swedish Trade Union Confederation (LO) 53, 57–58, 125, 127, 129, 213

Technical Society (*Det Tekniske Selskab*) 94
training centre (praktikcentre) 183
trajectory/trajectories 4–7, 9–12, 191–192, **192, 194, 197**, 199–200
transition(s) 79, 84–85, 115–116, **144**

unemployment 52, 53, 60, 110, 135, 159, 181
unified comprehensive school 84, 107, 124
unified upper secondary school 108, 110, 124, 131, 171, 177, 211
universalism 8, 15, 146, 150, 163, 166
universities of applied sciences (UAS) *see* polytechnics
USA 225–226

variety of capitalism (VoC) 9, 12, 17, 200
Venstre (liberal party) 71
VET programme 109, 125, 137, 176, 180, 182, 224
virtuous circle 15, 146, 166
Vocational Academies (EA) 186
vocational education and training (VET): defined 5; empirical and theoretical implications for 227–229; and private industries 32–33; *see also* initial vocational education and training; vocational schools; *see also under* Denmark; Finland; Nordic countries; Norway; Sweden
'Vocational Institutions Act' 32, 40, 104
vocational schools: in the Nordic countries **192**, 193–194, 195, 201; in post-war Denmark 173–174, 179, 182–184; in post-war Finland 105, 108, 118, 209; in post-war Norway 147, *148, 151*, 211; in post-war Sweden 125, 130–132, 207; in pre-war Denmark 85, 93–96; in pre-war Finland 24–25, 27–28, 31–34, 38–40, **45**, 193, 202; in pre-war Norway 66, 75, 77–78, 80; in pre-war Sweden 48–53, 56–60
Vocational Training Council (Ammattikasvatusneuvosto) 37, 107

welfare 3–5, 124–126, 191, 206, 220–221; and apprenticeship system in Denmark 97; and skill formation 17–18; and VET in Denmark 91, 185; and VET in Finland 102–109, 116, 118; and VET in Norway 146–147, 149–150, 157, 160, 163, 165,

198; and VET in Sweden 127, 131, 136; *see also* welfare capitalism
welfare capitalism 3–5, 14–16, 17, 228
women 33–35, 62, 114, 165; entry into labour market 16, 150, 206; the women's movement 30; *see also* gender
work-based learning 93, 102, 118, 124, 176, 181

work-based training 161, 177, 178, 182, 183, 184
workshop schools 51–56, 67, 129–130, 132, 147

Youth Commission 172
youth education pilot project 105, 109–110
youth guarantee 115, 160, 195